HISTORICAL DICTIONARIES OF RELIGIONS, PHILOSOPHIES, AND MOVEMENTS
Jon Woronoff, Series Editor

1. *Buddhism*, by Charles S. Prebish, 1993.
2. *Mormonism*, by Davis Bitton, 1994. *Out of print. See no. 32.*
3. *Ecumenical Christianity*, by Ans Joachim van der Bent, 1994.
4. *Terrorism*, by Sean Anderson and Stephen Sloan, 1995. *Out of print. See no. 41.*
5. *Sikhism*, by W. H. McLeod, 1995. *Out of print. See no. 59.*
6. *Feminism*, by Janet K. Boles and Diane Long Hoeveler, 1995. *Out of print. See no. 52.*
7. *Olympic Movement*, by Ian Buchanan and Bill Mallon, 1995. *Out of print. See no. 39.*
8. *Methodism*, by Charles Yrigoyen Jr. and Susan E. Warrick, 1996. *Out of print. See no. 57.*
9. *Orthodox Church*, by Michael Prokurat, Alexander Golitzin, and Michael D. Peterson, 1996.
10. *Organized Labor*, by James C. Docherty, 1996. *Out of print. See no. 50.*
11. *Civil Rights Movement*, by Ralph E. Luker, 1997.
12. *Catholicism*, by William J. Collinge, 1997.
13. *Hinduism*, by Bruce M. Sullivan, 1997.
14. *North American Environmentalism*, by Edward R. Wells and Alan M. Schwartz, 1997.
15. *Welfare State*, by Bent Greve, 1998. *Out of print. See no. 63.*
16. *Socialism*, by James C. Docherty, 1997. *Out of print. See no. 73.*
17. *Bahá'í Faith*, by Hugh C. Adamson and Philip Hainsworth, 1998. *Out of print. See no. 71.*
18. *Taoism*, by Julian F. Pas in cooperation with Man Kam Leung, 1998.
19. *Judaism*, by Norman Solomon, 1998. *Out of print. See no. 69.*
20. *Green Movement*, by Elim Papadakis, 1998.
21. *Nietzscheanism*, by Carol Diethe, 1999. *Out of print. See No. 75.*
22. *Gay Liberation Movement*, by Ronald J. Hunt, 1999.
23. *Islamic Fundamentalist Movements in the Arab World, Iran, and Turkey*, by Ahmad S. Moussalli, 1999.
24. *Reformed Churches*, by Robert Benedetto, Darrell L. Guder, and Donald K. McKim, 1999.

25. *Baptists*, by William H. Brackney, 1999.
26. *Cooperative Movement*, by Jack Shaffer, 1999.
27. *Reformation and Counter-Reformation*, by Hans J. Hillerbrand, 2000.
28. *Shakers*, by Holley Gene Duffield, 2000.
29. *United States Political Parties*, by Harold F. Bass Jr., 2000.
30. *Heidegger's Philosophy*, by Alfred Denker, 2000.
31. *Zionism*, by Rafael Medoff and Chaim I. Waxman, 2000.
32. *Mormonism*, 2nd ed., by Davis Bitton, 2000.
33. *Kierkegaard's Philosophy*, by Julia Watkin, 2001.
34. *Hegelian Philosophy*, by John W. Burbidge, 2001.
35. *Lutheranism*, by Günther Gassmann in cooperation with Duane H. Larson and Mark W. Oldenburg, 2001.
36. *Holiness Movement*, by William Kostlevy, 2001.
37. *Islam*, by Ludwig W. Adamec, 2001.
38. *Shinto*, by Stuart D. B. Picken, 2002.
39. *Olympic Movement*, 2nd ed., by Ian Buchanan and Bill Mallon, 2001. *Out of print. See no. 61.*
40. *Slavery and Abolition*, by Martin A. Klein, 2002.
41. *Terrorism*, 2nd ed., by Sean Anderson and Stephen Sloan, 2002.
42. *New Religious Movements*, by George D. Chryssides, 2001.
43. *Prophets in Islam and Judaism*, by Scott B. Noegel and Brannon M. Wheeler, 2002.
44. *The Friends (Quakers)*, by Margery Post Abbott, Mary Ellen Chijioke, Pink Dandelion, and John William Oliver Jr., 2003.
45. *Lesbian Liberation Movement: Still the Rage*, JoAnne Myers, 2003.
46. *Descartes and Cartesian Philosophy*, by Roger Ariew, Dennis Des Chene, Douglas M. Jesseph, Tad M. Schmaltz, and Theo Verbeek, 2003.
47. *Witchcraft*, by Michael D. Bailey, 2003.
48. *Unitarian Universalism*, by Mark W. Harris, 2004.
49. *New Age Movements*, by Michael York, 2004.
50. *Organized Labor*, 2nd ed., by James C. Docherty, 2004.
51. *Utopianism*, by James M. Morris and Andrea L. Kross, 2004.
52. *Feminism*, 2nd ed., by Janet K. Boles and Diane Long Hoeveler, 2004.
53. *Jainism*, by Kristi L. Wiley, 2004.

54. *Wittgenstein's Philosophy*, by Duncan Richter, 2004.
55. *Schopenhauer's Philosophy*, by David E. Cartwright, 2005.
56. *Seventh-Day Adventists*, by Gary Land, 2005.
57. *Methodism*, 2nd ed., by Charles Yrigoyen Jr. and Susan Warrick, 2005.
58. *Sufism*, by John Renard, 2005.
59. *Sikhism*, 2nd ed., by W. H. McLeod, 2005.
60. *Kant and Kantianism*, by Helmut Holzhey and Vilem Mudroch, 2005.
61. *Olympic Movement*, 3rd ed., by Bill Mallon with Ian Buchanan, 2006.
62. *Anglicanism*, by Colin Buchanan, 2006.
63. *Welfare State*, 2nd ed., by Bent Greve, 2006.
64. *Feminist Philosophy*, by Catherine Villanueva Gardner, 2006.
65. *Logic*, by Harry J. Gensler, 2006.
66. *Leibniz's Philosophy*, by Stuart Brown and Nicholas J. Fox, 2006.
67. *Non-Aligned Movement and Third World*, by Guy Arnold, 2006.
68. *Salvation Army*, by Major John G. Merritt, 2006.
69. *Judaism*, 2nd ed., by Norman Solomon, 2006.
70. *Epistemology*, by Ralph Baergen, 2006.
71. *Bahá'í Faith*, by Hugh Adamson, 2006.
72. *Aesthetics*, by Dabney Townsend, 2006.
73. *Socialism*, 2nd ed., by Peter Lamb and James C. Docherty, 2007.
74. *Marxism*, by David M. Walker and Daniel Gray, 2007.
75. *Nietzscheanism*, 2nd ed., by Carol Diethe, 2007.
76. *Medieval Philosophy and Theology*, by Stephen F. Brown and Juan Carlos Flores, 2007.
77. *Shamanism*, by Graham Harvey and Robert Wallis, 2007.
78. *Ancient Greek Philosophy*, by Anthony Preus, 2007.
79. *Puritans*, by Charles Pastoor and Galen K. Johnson, 2007.

Historical Dictionary of Ancient Greek Philosophy

Anthony Preus

Historical Dictionaries of Religions,
Philosophies, and Movements, No. 78

The Scarecrow Press, Inc.
Lanham, Maryland • Toronto • Plymouth, UK
2007

SCARECROW PRESS, INC.

Published in the United States of America
by Scarecrow Press, Inc.
A wholly owned subsidiary of
The Rowman & Littlefield Publishing Group, Inc.
4501 Forbes Boulevard, Suite 200, Lanham, Maryland 20706
www.scarecrowpress.com

Estover Road
Plymouth PL6 7PY
United Kingdom

British Library Cataloguing in Publication Information Available

Library of Congress Cataloging-in-Publication Data
Preus, Anthony.
  Historical dictionary of ancient Greek philosophy / Anthony Preus.
      p. cm. — (Historical dictionaries of religions, philosophies, and
movements ; no. 78)
  Includes bibliographical references.
  ISBN-13: 978-0-8108-5487-1 (hardcover : alk. paper)
  ISBN-10: 0-8108-5487-2 (hardcover : alk. paper)
  1. Philosophy, Ancient–Dictionaries. I. Title.
B111.P74 2007
180.3–dc22   2006039368

∞™ The paper used in this publication meets the minimum requirements of
American National Standard for Information Sciences—Permanence of Paper
for Printed Library Materials, ANSI/NISO Z39.48-1992.
Manufactured in the United States of America.

Contents

Editor's Foreword   *Jon Woronoff*   ix

Citations and Abbreviations   xi

Note on Transliterating Greek Characters to English   xv

Chronology   xix

Introduction   1

THE DICTIONARY   31

Glossary   283

Bibliography   307

About the Author   345

Editor's Foreword

In some ways, this volume is the cornerstone for the many others in the subseries on philosophy, just as the Ancient Greco-Roman world provided a cornerstone not only for medieval and modern Western philosophy but also Islamic philosophy and thinking elsewhere. The period of the "ancients," running from roughly the middle of the first millennium BC to the middle of the first millennium AD, was amazingly fertile, heavily influenced by Plato, Aristotle, and Socrates, as well as dozens of other philosophers. The period saw some of the earliest valid work on what remain major fields of philosophy, particularly epistemology, logic, and ethics, and the trail was blazed the way in others. Obviously, some — perhaps most — of this thought has since been revised, and many supposed "answers" have turned out to be wrong as our interests and emphases have shifted. But most of the questions that exercised the minds of the "ancients" are still important for us, and knowing what they thought is still of considerable use to us today.

This *Historical Dictionary of Ancient Greek Philosophy* summarizes some of the most important aspects, describes the different and often contesting schools of thought, and presents the questions and answers, the approaches and concepts. It also introduces us to most of the important philosophers, not only the greats but those whose contributions were more modest although still significant. The bulk of this information appears in the dictionary, which is extensively cross-referenced. It is also buttressed by a broad introduction that offers an overall framework within which the details make more sense. In another way, the chronology puts things into context so we know which thinkers emerged when and what their legacy was. Admittedly, in this age of the Internet, this is not the biggest nor the broadest source of information, but it is incredibly handy, covering a vast array of topics and, above all, providing an exceptional guide that probably will be referred to time and again by students (and even scholars) while reading the works of the ancient philosophers or more recent secondary literature.

The author of this volume, Anthony Preus, has been studying and working with Ancient Greek Philosophy for over four decades now. First came the learning, at Oxford University and the Johns Hopkins University, where his doctoral thesis (1968) was devoted to Aristotle's biology. This learning has continued to the present day, obviously interspersed increasingly with teaching, as he is a professor of philosophy at Binghamton University. It has assumed a written form in many articles and especially in two books, *Science and Philosophy in Aristotle's Biological Works* and *Aristotle and Michael of Ephesus on the Movement and Progression of Animals*. Dr. Preus has also edited or co-edited a series of collections of essays in Ancient Greek Philosophy. In addition, he has been active in the scholarly community, among other things, serving as secretary of the Society for Ancient Greek Philosophy. He has no doubts as to how important the "ancients" are for us "moderns," and this is one more, very successful attempt to bring the two together.

Jon Woronoff
Series Editor

Citations and Abbreviations

Citations of works by ancient writers follow this adaptation of standard practice:

Homer

Il.   *Iliad*
Od.   *Odyssey*

Sophocles

Oed. Tyr.   *Oedippus the King*

Early Greek Philosophers: Fragments

Fragments of early Greek philosophers are numbered as in Diels-Kranz (see bibliography), abbreviated DK. In that context, the letter "f." stands for "fragment," with the DK number following. Diels-Kranz assign a number to each Presocratic philosopher; and they include "testimonia" or descriptions of the philosopher's position in the "A" section, and quotations that they take to be genuine in the "B" section. Thus, because Anaximenes is number 13, the citation DK 13B2 refers to the second "fragment" of Anaximenes in their collection.

Plato

Citations of works by Plato include the standard (Stephanos) numbers. Abbreviations of titles of works by Plato are as follows:

Apol.   *Apology*
Parm.   *Parmenides*

Rep	*Republic*
Soph.	*Sophist.*
Tht.	*Theaetetus*
Tm.	*Timaeus*

Titles of other dialogues cited in this work are not abbreviated.

Xenophon

Mem.	*Memorabilia*
Symp.	*Symposium*

Aristotle

Citations of works by Aristotle use the standard (Berlin edition) numbers. Abbreviations of titles of works by Aristotle are as follows:

APo	*Posterior Analytics*
Cael.	*De Caelo (On the Heavens)*
Cat.	*Categories*
De An.	*De Anima (On the Soul)*
Div. Somn.	*Divination by Dreams*
EN	*Nicomachean Ethics*
GA	*Generation of Animals*
GC	*On Generation and Corruption*
HA	*History of Animals*
Int.	*On Interpretation*
Metaph.	*Metaphysics*
Meteor.	*Meteorologica*
PA	*Parts of Animals*
Phys.	*Physics*
Pol.	*Politics*
Rhet.	*Rhetoric*
SE	*Sophistical Refutations*
Top.	*Topics*

Titles of other works of Aristotle are not abbreviated in citations.

CAG

Commentaria in Aristotelem Graeca: This is a series of works by ancient and medieval Greek authors.

Theophrastus

Sens.   *De Sensibus*

Stoics

SVF   *Stoicorum Veterum Fragmenta*, ed. von Arnim. Numbers refer to volume number (there are four) and page number

Cicero

de Fin.   *De Finibus (On Ends)*

Diogenes Laertius

DL, Diogenes Laertius, *Lives of Eminent Philosophers*: the first number is the book, the second is the paragraph.

Plutarch

de def. orac.   *On the Failure of the Oracles*

Alexander of Aphrodisias

in Top.   *Commentary on Aristotle's Topics*

Plotinus

Enn.   *Enneads*

Iamblichus

Vit. Pyth.   *On the Pythagorean Life*

Proclus

De mal. Subst.   *de malorum subsistentia (On the Existence of Evils)*
Elem. Theol.   *Elements of Theology*

LSJ   Liddell, Scott, Jones, and McKenzie, *Greek-English Lexicon,* Oxford University Press, 1973

Note on Transliterating Greek Characters to English

The Greek and Roman alphabets are closely related, so transliterating between Greek and English is not all that complicated; however, there are a few hints that will help someone who is looking at a word written in a Greek font and wants to look it up in the present dictionary.

Greek Alphabet	English Equivalent
A, α	A, a
B, β	B, b. At some point it came to be pronounced as "v."
Γ, γ	G, g, but when it occurs before a hard consonant, like "K," it is pronounced "n," and sometimes transliterated "n."
Δ, δ	D, d, but eventually softened to "th" as in "this"
E, ε	E, e, short "e" as in "pet"
Z, ζ	Transliterated Z, z, pronounced "ts" as in the Hebrew tsadik
H, η	Ē, ē, long "e" like the "a" in "pane"
Θ, θ	Th, th: English-speakers usually pronounce this letter like the "th" in "thing," although purists claim that it was closer to a "t" actually followed by an "h."
I, ι	I, I, pronounced most often like the "i" in "pit"
K, κ	K, k
Λ, λ	L, l
M, μ	M, m
N, ν	N, n
Ξ, ξ	X, x: pronounced "ks"
O, o	O, o: short "o," perhaps something like the "o" in "on"
Π, π	P, p

Ρ, ρ	R, r, but see also below on "breathing marks"
Σ, σ, ς	S, s
Τ, τ	T, t
Υ, υ	Y, y or U, u. Scholars do not agree on whether to transliterate this letter as "y" or as "u"; in this volume, it is usually "y" except when it appears in the diphthong "eu." This letter, as an ancient vowel, was probably pronounced something like a German "ü," so English speakers waver between "ī" and "oo."
Φ, φ	Ph in this volume, although some transliterate it as "f," which is the way that English speakers usually pronounced it. Purists claim that it was pronounced as a "p" followed by an "h."
Χ, χ	Transliterated Ch, ch, to distinguish it from Ξ; pronounced something like the "ch" in the German "ach," or like a Hebrew "chai."
Ψ, ψ	Ps, ps, pronounced that way, except that English speakers generally pronounce an initial ψ as an "s," as in psychology.
Ω, ω	Ō, ō, Long "o," as in "tome."

DIPHTHONGS

Classical Greek readily combines two (or more) vowels, and the assumption of scholars is that each vowel was individually pronounced, originally. In the course of time, diphthongs came to be pronounced as single vowels. The classical diphthongs with their English transcriptions are:

αι	ai
αυ	au
ει	ei
ευ	eu
οι	oi
ου	ou
ηυ	ēu
υι	ui

BREATHING MARKS

Breathing marks: vowels that begin a word always have a "breathing mark" in classical Greek: for example, 'α is an alpha with a smooth breathing, 'α is an alpha with a rough breathing. In transliteration, smooth breathings are ignored, rough breathings are transliterated by the letter H, h; thus transliterated Greek words that begin with "h" would begin with the following vowel, when written in Greek, with a rough breathing. "*Harmonia*" would be an example. The letter rho (P, ρ) also gets a breathing mark (sometimes even in the middle of a word), in which case it is written Rh, rh, but actually pronounced in Greek "Hr."

Many Greek proper names and philosophical terms have a history of translation into Latin and subsequently into English, and that transition has some effects on how these words are spelled. For example, the Greek name of "Socrates," if transliterated directly from the Greek by the rules listed above, would be "Sokratēs," and there are people who insist on that, and "Euclid" was originally "Eukleides." The most usual masculine nominative ending in the very common second declension is, in Greek, -os, but in Latin, -us, so the associate of Aristotle "Eudemos" is generally known as "Eudemus."

Chronology

c. 1180 BCE   Trojan War

Hellenic Period

776   First Olympic Games

750–700   Homer's *Iliad* and *Odyssey* written down

700   Hesiod; Midas King of Phrygia (742–696). This is the period when the Ionian Greeks sent out many commercial colonies around the Mediterranean and Black Seas.

687–652   Gyges King of Lydia

664–610   Psammetichus I of Egypt; Delta Egypt opened for Greek trade

650–600   Period of the Greek lawgivers (Lycurgus, Draco)

c. 635–558   Solon of Athens Poet and political reformer

626–547   Croesus of Lydia (king from 560)

c. 620–540   Thales of Miletus

c. 610–546   Anaximander of Miletus

600   Sappho, Alcaeus

585   Thales' eclipse

c. 585–528   Anaximenes of Miletus

c. 576 –529   Cyrus the Great, king of Persia

c. 570–465   Xenophanes of Colophon

c. 570–490   Pythagoras of Samos

c. 570–490   Alcmaeon of Croton

546   Cyrus conquers Lydia and the Ionian Greeks. Pythagoras leaves Samos for Egypt. Xenophanes leaves Colophon.

520   Darius, King of Persia, takes Babylon.

500   fl. Heraclitus

c. 510–450+   Parmenides of Elea

c. 500–428   Anaxagoras of Clazomenae

c. 492–432   Empedocles of Acragas

490   Marathon; Pindar

c. 490–420   Protagoras of Abdera

483–373   Gorgias of Leontini

480   Second Persian invasion, Aeschylus

c. 480–400   Leucippus of Abdera

c. 475   Parmenides writes his poem.

470–399   Socrates

c. 470–442+   Melissus of Samos

c. 470–385   Philolaus of Croton

c. 460–399+   Prodicus of Ceos

c. 460   Zeno of Elea writes his collection of arguments.

460–429   Pericles in power in Athens

c. 460–370   Democritus of Abdera

450   Parmenides and Zeno visit Athens?

c. 450–380   Eucleides of Megara, founder of the Megarian School

447   Parthenon built; Sophocles, Euripides writing plays

c. 440–370   Antisthenes of Athens

c. 435–356 Aristippus of Cyrene, founder of the (hedonistic) Cyrenaic school

431 Peloponnesian War begins

427–347 Plato of Athens

423 Aristophanes *Clouds*; Diogenes of Apollonia active in Athens

415 Athens attacks Syracuse.

c. 412–322 Diogenes of Sinope, leader of the Cynic practice of philosophy

c. 408–339 Speusippos (Plato's nephew); became Scholarch of the Academy after the death of Plato

404 Athens surrenders to Sparta

399 Death of Socrates

c. 396–314 Xenocrates, Scholarch of the Academy after Speusippos

384–322 Aristotle

380 Isocrates *Panegyric*

c. 380–330 Stilpo, of the Megarian school

c. 371–287 Theophrastus of Eresos

367 Aristotle to Academy; Dionysius I of Syracuse dies

356 Birth of Alexander of Macedon, Demosthenes in power in Athens

c. 350–266/5 Polemon, Scholarch of the Academy after Xenocrates

347 Death of Plato; Aristotle gone from Athens

343 Aristotle in Pella as Alexander's tutor

340–270 Epicurus

340 Aristotle leaves Pella.

335 Aristotle founds Lyceum.

c. 334–262 Zeno of Citium

331 Founding of Alexandria in Egypt

331–232 Cleanthes of Assium

c. 325–265? Euclid of Alexandria, mathematician, author of the *Elements*

Hellenistic Period

323 Alexander dies, Diogenes the Cynic dies, Epicurus to Athens.

322 Aristotle dies, Demosthenes dies.

321 Menander's first play

313 Zeno of Citium to Athens

297 Theophrastus rejects Ptolemy I Soter's invitation to come to Alexandria; sends Demetrius of Phaleron instead; Demetrius was the first head of the Museion which included the great Alexandria library.

c. 280–206 Chrysippus of Soli

214–129 Carneades

c. 185–108 Panaetius of Rhodes (in Rome 145–129)

c. 135–51 Posidonius of Apamea

106–43 Cicero

c. 99–55 Lucretius, author of *De Rerum Natura*, presentation of Epicureanism in Latin

98–45 Publius Nigidius Figulus, reviver of Pythagoreanism

88 Mithridates of Pontus takes Athens.

86 Sulla, leading a Roman army, takes Athens from Mithridates: Academy and Lyceum destroyed or seriously damaged

79/78 Cicero studies philosophy in Athens.

Roman Imperial Period

20 BCE–50 CE Philo of Alexandria

c. 4 BCE–65 CE Seneca

c. 46–122 CE   Plutarch of Chaeronea

c. 55–135   Epictetus

121–180   Marcus Aurelius

fl 160–180   Numenius of Apamea

c. 130–c.200   Galen of Pergamum

200 fl.   Alexander of Aphrodisias

d. 215   Clement of Alexandria

d. 242   Ammonius Saccas

d. 254   Origen (Christian)

204–270   Plotinus

233–309   Porphyry

c. 245–c. 325   Iamblichus of Chalkis

c. 275–339   Eusebius of Caesarea

330–379   Basil of Caesarea

329–389   Gregory Nazianzus

c. 335–394   Gregory of Nyssa

347–407   John Chrysostom

347–420   Jerome (translator of the Bible into Latin)

354–430   Augustine of Hippo

d. 432   Plutarch of Athens

d. 437   Syrianus

fl. 410–439   Martianus Capella

411–485   Proclus

415   The martyrdom of Hypatia

393–466   Theodoret of Cyrrhus, Christian apologist

c. 440– after 517   Ammonius son of Hermeias teaching in Alexandria

c. 462–after 538 Damascius (Scholarch in Athens when Justinian closed the Platonic school)

late 5th, early 6th (pseudo) Dionysius the Areopagite

476 Conventional date for the fall of the western Roman Empire (the young boy Romulus Augustulus deposed)

480–524/6 Boethius

490–560 Simplicius

529 Philosophical schools in Athens closed by Justinian

495/505–565 Asclepius, Olympiodorus (teaching in Alexandria)

fl. 541 "Elias" pagan (?) commentator on Aristotle

490–570 John Philoponus: Christian commentator on Aristotle

610–641 Heraclius, regarded as first Byzantine emperor (as distinct from "eastern Roman"); any remaining schools teaching Greek philosophy appear to have been closed during his reign.

622 The Hegira of Mohammed, beginning of the Muslim era

Introduction

"Philosophy" is a word invented by the ancient Greeks, most likely by Pythagoras in the late sixth century BCE. Before the time of Pythagoras, there was a lively tradition, shared with other literate cultures around the Mediterranean, of collections of "wisdom" literature (*"Sophia"*).[1] In Greece, lists were made of outstanding contributors to such collections, that is, of "wise" people, or *sophoi*. The story goes that when Leon of Phlius asked Pythagoras what he was, he replied, "a *philosophos*," a lover of or seeker for wisdom.[2] To the extent that an ancient Greek invented the word "philosophy" is an ancient Greek invention, and we can trace the history of those who called themselves, or were called by others in their culture, *philosophoi*. Certainly the ancient Greeks recognized that many of their ideas and practices came from other neighboring cultures—Egypt, Persia, and Babylon, for example—and we can discern parallels between their ideas and practices and some contemporary with them that they knew nothing about—Taoism and Confucianism for example. Thus, *for us* "ancient Greek philosophy" is a part of a much larger history—a history of human thought about the most fundamental and intractable questions that people attempt to resolve.

The ancient Greeks learned to write, using characters borrowed from the Phoenicians, about 750 BCE. The Homeric epics, passed down orally for centuries, were written down probably before 700 BCE; Hesiod, author of the poems "Birth of the Gods" and "Works and Days," was working shortly after 700. We have fragments or individual short poems of perhaps a dozen poets who wrote over the next 150 years or so—people like Sappho and Alcaeus, who wrote around 600 BCE. In that group, we note especially Solon, who established many legal traditions of Athens.

The "Presocratic" period of ancient Greek philosophy is marked by speculation about the natural world, fueled by dissatisfaction with traditional mythological explanations. These speculations moved very

1

quickly to attempts to understand "being" and "becoming," how anything whatever "is" and how existence and change are related. The continuation of these speculations shapes the entire history of ancient Greek philosophy.

On a different note, the Presocratic or Pre-Platonic period of ancient Greek philosophy is also marked, for us, by the fact that everything we know about the period comes to us through the accounts of later thinkers or through fragments quoted by later writers who of course had their own agendas.[3] We do have a significant percentage of the first part of Parmenides' poem, and a good many fragments of Heraclitus and Empedocles and some others, although it is often difficult to know how those fragments fit together into a coherent whole in the original work of these thinkers. But at the end of the day, all of the reasonably well-attested bits of the Presocratics fit into one not very large book.[4] For Plato and Aristotle, the situation is very different, as we note below.

Diogenes Laertius, author of *Lives of the Philosophers* in the third century CE, attempted to trace the history of Greek philosophy by identifying teacher-student relationships; thus he was interested particularly in groups of people who might have learned from each other. Diogenes finds that the first philosophical teacher-student relationship in Ionia is Thales-Anaximander, and the relationship that begins the philosophical tradition in southern Italy is Pherecydes-Pythagoras.

Thales of Miletus was born about 620 and died about 546 BCE. Anaximander, author of a cosmological and geographical text, was a little younger than Thales but probably died about the same time. A third member of the Milesian group was Anaximenes. Aristotle describes this group as the initiators of a way of thinking that focuses on nature (*physis*); that description implies, reasonably enough, that the Milesians took important steps in the direction of the activity that we call natural science.

Pherecydes of Syros seems to have written a cosmological book around 540; most sources make little of Pythagoras' relationship with him and much more of the stories that Pythagoras spent a good deal of time in Egypt, and possibly also visited Persia, before establishing his religious and philosophical cult in Croton of southern Italy.[5] He seems to have introduced the idea of transmigration of the soul (*psychē*) into the Greek world and to have focused attention on the mathematically discoverable characteristics of the world; the fact that he established an ongoing organization dedicated, at least in part, to intellectual pursuits is also of great importance since it led to the establishment of philosophical institutions and thus a kind of permanence and growth in this endeavor. For some time after Pythagoras, the word "*philosophos*" was used primarily to designate his followers or people influenced by his way of proceeding.

Two other thinkers active around 500 BCE have had a significant impact on the development of philosophy: Xenophanes of Colophon and Heraclitus of Ephesus. Xenophanes was primarily an itinerant poet, but in some of his poems he supports a kind of epistemological skepticism ("If the Gods had not made yellow honey, people would think figs far sweeter than they do") which he applies to traditional anthropomorphic deities: not only does he point out that the Ethiopians have black deities with wide noses and the Thracians deities with red hair and blue eyes, but if horses and cattle had hands they would fashion Gods like themselves— getting in a dig at some of the neighbors of the Greeks who did have animal-shaped deities. Xenophanes believes in one supreme deity, the mind (*nous*) of the universe, an idea that continues to be developed and sharpened throughout the history of ancient philosophy.

Heraclitus, perhaps influenced by Zoroastrian ideas (his native Ephesus was under Persian domination during his lifetime), made fire central, not only as material element but as activating energy, and as deity—"Thunderbolt steers all things"—stripping away the anthropomorphic Zeus and leaving the power. With his emphasis on the *logos*, his eminently quotable lines, his stress on the ambiguity of language and the dynamic tensions of the natural world, Heraclitus was highly influential on ancient thought and continues to capture philosophical imaginations even today.[6]

The poem of Parmenides marks a significant turning point in early Greek thought. An argument is presented that tells us that "being is" and "not-being is not." But if not-being is not, then we cannot use not-being as an explanatory term, either alone or in conjunction with being. So there is no coming into being (no not-being for something to come from) nor destruction (no not-being for something to go to); being must be one and continuous, since there is no not-being to divide it, and changeless, since an account of change would have to involve not-being.[7] His disciple Zeno of Elea added several arguments to defend the idea that being is one, not many, and incidentally to demonstrate that motion is impossible. It is also important to mention that Zeno pioneered a method of argumentation that came to be called "dialectical," in which one starts with the assumptions of one's opponents and demonstrates that they lead to paradoxical or self-contradictory conclusions.

Subsequent philosophers of nature, *physikoi*, like Empedocles, Anaxagoras, and Democritus, had to find a way to deal with the Eleatic arguments. For Empedocles, who had accepted much of the Pythagorean philosophy, particularly the transmigration of the soul, the answer was to posit four elements: earth, water, air, and fire, and then assert that *those* are "being"; they are neither created nor destroyed, and individually they are changeless, so all change is a rearrangement of those materials, under the influence of cosmic principles of Love and Strife. Anaxagoras, who was also advisor to Pericles, posits a much larger list of irreducible material elements, combined and separated ultimately by the power of a cosmic Mind (*nous*).

The Atomists, Leucippus and Democritus of Abdera, turned the Eleatic argument against itself by accepting the changelessness of being but asserting an indefinitely large number of beings moving randomly in not-being, or empty space. Since reason discovers the existence of atoms, it can yield reliable knowledge, whereas the senses are deceptive; all of our sensual judgments are "conventional, *nomoi*," according to Democritus.

At the same time, a number of people set themselves up as teachers of wisdom (*sophia*)—Sophists. Protagoras, a citizen of the same town as Leucippus and Democritus, Gorgias of Leontini, a student of Empedocles, and several others proposed to teach young men the skills they would need to take leadership positions in the Greek states. For Gorgias, who seems to have studied philosophy only to reject the enterprise entirely,[8] the task of a teacher is to provide students with rhetorical skills, the ability to argue any side of any argument as effectively as possible. Protagoras, in contrast, defended a form of relativism—there is a truth, it is a truth that human beings create. His goal was thus to enable his students to maximize their impact on that process.

Other well-known Sophists include Hippias of Elis, Prodicus of Ceos, and Antiphon. We have significant fragments of Antiphon in which he contrasts law (*nomos*) and nature (*physis*), arguing that law is repressive and causes inequality between people, whereas by nature all are free and equal.

SOCRATES AND PLATO

For many people, the phrase "ancient Greek philosophy" immediately brings to mind the figure of Socrates, bearded, snubbed-nosed, pot-bellied, asking annoying questions of everyone he met. Educated people tend to be aware that Socrates was executed in 399 BCE after a trial by an Athenian jury, and if they have read Plato's *Apology of Socrates*, they know that the charges on which he was convicted were "corrupting the young" and "not respecting the Gods, but introducing new and different divinities." The life and death of Socrates, as presented by Plato are dramatic and inspiring; the dialogues continue to be fresh and challenging both as literature and as philosophy.[9] It is also worth remembering that we have a great deal more text from Plato than we do from any Greek philosopher before his time. There are about 30 extant dialogues attributed to Plato; at least 25 of them are really from his hand.[10]

In getting an idea of Socrates (470–399), we also have dialogues by Xenophon, plays by Aristophanes, and reports by Aristotle and others that focus on Socrates, allowing us to triangulate on his activity. Socrates was widely regarded as a Sophist by his contemporaries, but several of Plato's dialogues emphasize the differences. The Sophists claimed to be able to teach something and demanded to be paid for the service; Socrates is represented as claiming that he does not teach anything and is not paid. More importantly, despite his protestations of ignorance, Plato's Socrates clearly rejects both skepticism and relativism, repeatedly demonstrating that he believes that value terms have objective definitions discoverable by the sort of dialectical inquiry that he carries on with his interlocutors. Although we do not get an objective definition of "temperance" in the *Charmides* or of "courage" in the *Laches*, it is clear that Socrates believes that such a definition is in principle available, and that those who teach that there is no such thing are very wrong to do so.

The Socrates of the dialogues has proven to be a model and inspiration for the philosophical life, in a sense an ostensive definition of the word "philosopher." The image is so dominant that we call all of those philosophers who are chronologically "pre-Platonic" rather "Presocratic" even if, like Democritus, they outlived Socrates by decades.

Some scholars have argued that Plato's thought developed over the 50 years or so that he was writing; philological analyses have to some extent contributed to that argument by supporting a rough chronology of composition.[11] But there is also a strong tradition that assumes, as Paul Shorey put it, the "unity" of Plato's thought.[12] Certainly the ancient Neoplatonists believed that Plato always was putting forward the same message.

In the context of the mid-fourth century BCE, Plato's Academy was in competition with the school of Isocrates, which also claimed to be teaching "philosophy," but the Academy was clearly the more successful institution. Attracting leading scholars like Eudoxus of Cnidus (c. 408–355 BCE) and able students like Heraclides of Pontus (c. 388–c. 310 BCE) as members,[13] it was a major source for leading philosophers of the next generation.[14] Aristotle was associated with the Academy for some 20 years; Aristotle's closest associate, Theophrastus (371–c. 287 BCE), was also associated with the Academy. Plato's nephew, Speusippos (c. 410–340 BCE), who took over the directorship of the school on Plato's death, was an active and creative philosopher, as was his successor, Xenocrates (396/5–314/3 BCE). For the subsequent history of Plato's school, *see* Academy.

It is clear that Plato had strong views about a significant range of issues; in some of his dialogues we find him putting those views into the mouth of his character Socrates, a practice that many have thought something of a misrepresentation of the historical Socrates. In the *Phaedo*, Socrates argues for an essentially Pythagorean theory of the immortality of the soul; in the *Republic* he provides a kind of definition of the cardinal virtues (justice, temperance, courage, wisdom) that he had generally avoided defining and paints a picture of an ideal state that many have seen to be repressive, even totalitarian, and also possibly Pythagorean in inspiration.

Plato's leading characters in his dialogues—Socrates, Timaeus, the Eleatic Stranger—argue repeatedly for the existence of permanent, separate, immaterial objects of knowledge. The Forms are not material, so a primary assumption of the *physikoi* is rejected—physical objects are not the ultimate things known. At the same time, because the Forms are objectively real, neither relativism nor agnosticism stand as attractive positions for those who claim to have a definite message to teach; to the extent that the Platonic message is accepted, the Sophists seem to be defending a futile position.

Both of them were to some extent following the example of Pythagoras in that respect, but neither the school of Isocrates nor Plato's Academy presented itself as a religious cult. In both cases, the writings of the founder served as a representation of the sort of education that one might expect to find were one to enroll. The success of dialogues like the *Phaedrus* and the *Theaetetus* can be marked by the fact that students continue to find within themselves the desire to study philosophy as a consequence of reading about the chariot of the soul, or the birdcage of memory.

There continued to be "unaffiliated" philosophers during the fourth century BCE (and later)—it is hard to pin down Antisthenes (440–370 BCE) and the Cynicism of Diogenes of Sinope (410–322 BCE) as a "school."

ARISTOTLE

Aristotle arrived at the Academy in about 367 and remained there for 20 years, until shortly before the death of Plato. For a good part of that time Aristotle taught subjects like rhetoric and logic. Upon the death of Plato in 347, Speusippus took over the Academy. Aristotle visited Hermeias in Assos, where Hermeias had become the local ruler under the Persian Empire. A year or two later he was joined by some of his friends on the island of Lesbos, the home of his closest friend from the Academy, Theophrastus. In 343, Aristotle was invited to become tutor to the young Alexander; three years later, Alexander was appointed regent of the Macedonian Kingdom while his father Philip was away at war. When Philip died and Alexander had consolidated his power, Aristotle returned to Athens in 335 and established his own school at the Lyceum. Xenocrates had been elected Scholarch of the Academy in 339, so for the period from 335 to 323 (shortly before the death of Aristotle), there were two leading philosophical schools in Athens, the school founded by Plato and led by a distinguished follower, and the school founded by a somewhat rebellious former student of Plato.[15] Athens was also the home of Cynics: Diogenes of Sinope was in his old age at this time, and Crates was a younger man—his relationship with Hipparchia should date from shortly after the death of Aristotle.

The Aristotelian Corpus,[16] in something like its present arrangement, must also date from the period of Aristotle's final dozen years in Athens. The treatises are essentially Aristotle's lecture notes, and while he doubtless prepared many of them when he was teaching in the Academy or Lesbos, he seems to have arranged them at least to a certain extent for the benefit of the students in the Lyceum and to have made them available in his library. The Aristotelian Corpus reveals preoccupations that set the Peripatetic School apart from the Academy in several interesting ways. For one thing, the Academy seems not to have had much interest in empirical investigation of nature, at any rate not after Aristotle and Theophrastus left in the middle of the fourth century. Aristotle, in contrast, continued to have great interest in the structure and lives of many different species of animals; he obviously thought that understanding biological facts would be helpful for a wide range of philosophical problems and encouraged people to turn their attention to this area of study. He was perhaps most successful with Theophrastus, who wrote extensively on plants; however, other Peripatetics also pursued this interest, as evidenced not only by the development of the collection known as the *Problemata* but also by the surviving fragments of Eudemus of Rhodes (late fourth century BCE) and in the next generation, Strato of Lampsacus (c. 340–268 BCE).

Aristotle rejected Plato's separate forms, arguing that the form of dog must be present in this dog for it to be a dog, that a separate form adds nothing to what we can empirically discover about the functions and capacities of the living dog. Indeed, the form of the dog is the soul of the dog, and the soul of the dog is not separable from the organs that carry out the life functions of the animal. So Aristotle rejects the thesis presented in the *Phaedo*, *Phaedrus*, and elsewhere, that souls may exist separately from their bodies, and might come to be reborn in other individuals.

Aristotle is a bit puzzled about the capacity of Mind (*nous*), which seems to him not exactly tied to a specific organ of the body (unlike vision or hearing, for example), and seemingly unlimited in its possibilities of conceptualization. Some think that in his theory of the mind he approaches a kind of Platonism. Even his own successor, Theophrastus, was puzzled by this part of his teacher's philosophy.

Both the Academy and the Lyceum functioned as training centers for future political leaders, teaching rhetoric, ethics, and political theory. However, they continued to resemble their Pythagorean roots to the extent that they were communities of scholars to a degree well beyond many modern educational institutions.

HELLENISTIC PHILOSOPHY

Aristotle, Alexander of Macedon, Diogenes of Sinope, and Demosthenes, the leading Athenian politician of the day, all died within about a year of each other, 323/2 BCE. The Macedonian Empire was divided up between Alexander's generals; the last quarter of the fourth century and first few years of the third century BCE proved to be an interesting period for philosophy as well.

Theophrastus succeeded Aristotle as Scholarch of the Lyceum;[17] Eudemus of Rhodes had left the Lyceum before the death of Aristotle and established a school in Rhodes. Aristoxenus (c. 370–300 BCE) was a student of Aristotle's who wrote an extant work on music[18] and some other things that survive in fragments. Dicaearchus of Messene (c. 350–285 BCE) was a student in the Lyceum who went on to establish a significant reputation in several fields and is credited with inventing the system of mapping the terrestrial sphere with lines of latitude and longitude.[19]

Polemon took over from Xenocrates at the Academy in 315. He and his student and colleague Crantor (c. 336–276/5 BCE) continued a certain degree of Platonic orthodoxy, something that would change in the latter years of Polemon's scholarchy (see below).

In the last years of the fourth century BCE, new things were happening in philosophy. Pyrrho of Elis, who had accompanied Alexander all the way to India, where he met Indian philosophers, seems to have established a school in his native Elis upon his return — Pyrrho was to become the inspiration for the skeptical mode of philosophy. While we do not have writings by Pyrrho, his disciple, Timon of Phlius (c. 325–235 BCE) wrote about him, and inspired subsequent skeptical philosophers. In the same general vein, we should note that Crates of Thebes (c. 368–288 BCE) was still very active in Athens in this time period.

Epicurus (c. 341–c. 270 BCE), who may have visited Athens as a young man during the lifetime of Aristotle, returned in 307 to establish his Garden; two of his closest associates in his school were Hermarchus of Mytilene (330s–250s BCE) and Metrodorus of Lampsacus (331–278 BCE). Epicureanism taught[20] that the world is reducible to atoms, that human life is a more or less accidental consequence of the arrangement of atoms, that there is no life after death, and thus no reason to be worried about punishments after death. We are best off living as undisturbed a life as possible in the present.

Zeno of Citium (c. 334–261/2 BCE) began studying in Athens not long after Polemon became Scholarch of the Academy, though his favored teacher seems to have been Crates. He began teaching in an organized way in the Stoa Poikile around 300. Zeno and the other early Stoics[21] synthesized much of early Greek philosophy into a consistent system, with a strong dose of Cynical critique. Like the Cynics, but unlike the Academics, Peripatetics, and Epicureans, the Stoics were very much out in the open, in public areas, preaching and attracting converts. Of the immediate students of Zeno, we must mention especially Cleanthes of Assos (?331/0–230/29 BCE), author of the extant Hymn to Zeus, and Zeno's successor in the Stoa.[22] Chrysippus of Soli (280/76–208/4 BCE) succeeded Cleanthes; his many writings (surviving only in extensive fragments) solidified the Stoic philosophy in the mid to late third century BCE.

It was also around 300 that Demetrius of Phaleron, under Ptolemy I, established the Library of Alexandria. Alexandria quickly became a leading center for mathematical and scientific investigation as well as philosophical discussion. Euclid, the great geometer, was writing his *Elements* right about the time of the founding of the Library; Herophilus of Chalcedon (c. 330–260 BCE) was carrying out serious medical investigations and was joined in that endeavor by Erasistratus of Ceos (c. 315–240 BCE). The Library and Museum of Alexandria continued to flourish, not necessarily as a philosophical center but as a center for "high culture," including science and mathematics. Apollonius of Rhodes (d. 247 BCE), a poet and author of the extant *Argonautica*,[23] was a distinguished head of the Library in Alexandria. Eratosthenes (c. 276–194 BCE), the successor of Apollonius, was educated as a Stoic by Aristo of Chios but is best known as a mathematician and geographer.

By 300 BCE, several of the major philosophical institutions of the ancient world had been established. Although Athens was clearly the leading location for philosophical study, members of the Athenian schools often established themselves elsewhere in the Greek-speaking world, especially Alexandria and Rhodes.[24]

THE ACADEMY BECOMES SKEPTICAL

During the time that Polemon was Scholarch in the Academy, some of his leading colleagues moved in the direction of a Skeptical philosophy. His close friend Crates of Athens (not the same person as Crates the Cynic) succeeded him as Scholarch but was there for only a short time. The successor of Crates as the leading Platonist, Arcesilaus (c. 316–c. 241 BCE), seems to have read Plato's dialogues essentially as refutations of all positive philosophical positions put forward and used the Socratic techniques to combat Stoicism, which he took to be overly dogmatic on too many issues, especially epistemology.[25] The Athenian successors of Plato continued to be primarily skeptical and critical until the middle of the first century BCE, when a more dogmatic form of Platonism reappeared.

The skeptical and critical posture of the Academy seems to have been directed most especially against the Stoics, who often seemed overly confident that they could discover the truth. Some of the Stoics who were objects of Academic critical attention included Zeno of Tarsus (late third, early second BCE), the successor of Chrysippus as Scholarch of the Stoa, Diogenes of Seleucia (or Babylon) (c. 228–140 BCE), and Antipater of Tarsus (c. 200–c. 130 BCE).

Philosophical life in Athens is indicated by looking at the delegation sent by the city of Athens to Rome in 155 BCE. It included three philosophers: Critolaus from the Lyceum, Diogenes of Seleucia from the Stoa, and Carneades the Skeptical Academic. We know little about Critolaus beyond a few comments by Cicero; he seems to have been about as orthodox an Aristotelian as one might find. We know that Diogenes was the teacher of Panaetius (c. 185–109 BCE); in most respects, he is cited for arguments in support of positions put forward by Zeno or Chrysippus, but he is said to have expressed doubts about the theory of the periodic conflagration (*ekpyrosis*). Plutarch tells us, in his "Life of Cato the Elder," that Carneades gave demonstrations of his dialectical skill by arguing forcefully for one side of the argument on one day, then arguing just as forcefully on the other side the next day. Cato the Elder was not favorably impressed.[26] Presumably no Epicurean was included in the delegation because of their choice not to be involved with political affairs.

From 146 on, Greece was under Roman rule, with an exception noted below. Thus, it was readily possible for Greeks to visit Rome on a friendly basis—notably, Panaetius the Stoic was frequently seen in a group organized by Scipio Africanus the Younger; we may be sure that he conveyed a great deal of Greek philosophy to an eager group of Romans. Judging from the reports of his teachings, especially by Cicero, Panaetius readily included Platonic and Aristotelian doctrines in his teachings; it was this revisionist Stoicism that became so popular with the Romans.

In the second to first centuries BCE, many Romans studied philosophy, not only with visitors from Greece but also by traveling to Athens or elsewhere. For much of the philosophy of this period, our most nearly contemporary sources are often in Latin rather than in Greek: the most important examples are Lucretius (c. 90–c. 50 BCE), who gives the fullest account of ancient Epicureanism available, and Cicero (106–43 BCE), who did the most to translate the Greek philosophical vocabulary into Latin.

The years 88 to 86 BCE mark a disastrous period for philosophy in Athens. In 88, the Athenians sided with Mithridates VI, king of Pontus, against the Romans. When Sulla put down the rebellion, he caused great damage in Athens, cutting down the trees in the gardens used by the philosophers and probably destroying or severely damaging buildings belonging to the philosophical schools. This event brought about a reorganization of philosophical instruction in Athens such that we can no longer talk about the Academy or Lyceum as a continuing institution.

Cicero, who studied in Athens in 79–77 BCE, recounts a dispute among the philosophers who regarded themselves as, in some sense, Academics, or followers of Plato. For some time, the Academy had been a center for critical philosophy—what has come to be called "Academic Skepticism," epitomized by Carneades and still pursued by members of the Academy at the beginning of the first century BCE. Philo of Larissa was said to have been Scholarch at the time of Sulla's conquest of Athens; on that occasion, he moved to Rome where Cicero had studied with him before leaving for Athens. We are told that Philo was an Academic Skeptic in the first part of his career and then later recommended returning to the text of Plato in order to develop a more dogmatic position. In Athens, Cicero studied with Antiochus of Ascalon (c. 130–c. 68 BCE), who had become alienated from Philo, and also taught a kind of dogmatic Platonism at the time when Cicero was in Athens. We hear that Aenesidemus, still a Skeptic, was disgusted with both of them, calling them Stoics fighting with Stoics, and appealed to what he understood of the skepticism of Pyrrho to establish a viable alternative philosophical stance to those of the Academy and Stoa.

The Stoa, too, was experiencing some changes in direction—Panaetius of Rhodes had made Stoic ethics rather more Aristotelian than it had been, and Posidonius of Apamea (135–51 BCE) extended the range of Stoic scholarship and philosophy to many scientific areas that had been ignored by his predecessors. Cicero was well acquainted with Posidonius, having met him in Rome, and studied with him in Athens in 77; they continued to be in contact, and we may suppose that the Stoic tendencies in Cicero's thought owe much to his influence.

Another Stoic with significant Roman contacts was Antipater of Tyre (first century BCE); we know that he taught Stoic philosophy to Cato the Younger (the great-grandson of Cato the Elder, who had been so annoyed with Crantor a hundred years earlier).

We have very few intact philosophical texts from the Hellenistic period. Cicero's philosophical works and the poem of Lucretius are easily the most extensive, putting the historian of philosophy in the position of having to reconstruct the progress of thought from fragmentary remains, often derived from much later writers who may not have understood their sources very well or who could have been frankly antagonistic. This circumstance changes significantly in the Roman Imperial period where we do have extensive literary remains.

PHILOSOPHY IN THE ROMAN IMPERIAL PERIOD

The Roman Imperial Period is conventionally taken to begin August 1, 30 BCE, the date Octavian took Egypt, defeating the last of his opponents. Octavian must have seen it that way, since after he had taken the name Augustus he renamed the month previously known as Sextilis after himself. (The month Quintilis had previously been renamed in honor of Julius Caesar.) In Egypt, more precisely in Alexandria, Octavian met Arius Didymus, an Aristotelian, and invited him to come with him to Rome as a kind of court philosopher.

Alexandria had become an intellectual center rivaling and perhaps surpassing Athens during the Ptolemaic period, and that continued under the Roman Emperors—Egypt was regarded as the personal property of the emperor, and that legal status tended to shelter Egypt and Alexandria to some extent from some of the conflicts that impacted other parts of the Empire. Hero of Alexandria (c. 10–70 CE) taught and wrote there, and a little later Claudius Ptolemy (c. 85–165) did the same.

Platonism had a serious foothold in Alexandria: Eudorus of Alexandria, a contemporary of Arius Didymus, wrote a "Concise Survey of Philosophy"[27] and took an interest in Pythagoreanism.[28] In terms of surviving philosophical texts, perhaps the most interesting first-century Alexandrian is Philo (20 BCE—50 CE). Philo, a Jew, attempted to synthesize the Torah with Greek philosophy, for example bringing together the creation story of Plato's *Timaeus* with *Genesis* I and describing Abraham very much as a Stoic sage.

Although Augustus had an Aristotelian court philosopher and Emperor Tiberius had a Platonist (Thrasyllus, a Pythagoreanizing Alexandrian who doubtless was most interesting to Tiberius because he could cast horoscopes), Rome continued to be a center for Stoic philosophy. Seneca (4 BCE–65 CE) was tutor of Nero and wrote many extant works; Musonius Rufus (30–100 CE) and Epictetus (50–135 CE)[29] were active in Rome also, although Epictetus left Rome and set up his school in Epirus in northwest Greece.

We have little information about what was happening philosophically in Athens[30] from the time that Cicero studied there until 66/7 CE, when Plutarch of Chaeronea (c. 45–125 CE) studied Platonism with Ammonius. This Ammonius was an Egyptian and doubtless brought Alexandrian Platonism to Athens. We have a very great many surviving works of Plutarch, so we know quite a lot about him and his activities. He was named to a priesthood in Delphi, traveled to Rome, and led a lively philosophical circle in his native Chaeronea. Plutarch was ready to adopt a good deal of Aristotelian virtue theory in his ethics, but the ultimate goal is "likeness to God." From the perspective of more "orthodox" Platonists, his support of the interpretation of the Timaeus, that said that creation had occurred at a specific moment in time, and his strongly dualistic ontology, asserting the existence of evil *daimones*, made him seem less than reliable.

The second century CE has left us a significant number of texts from a wide range of traditions. Both the Hermetic corpus (ascribed to the mythical "Hermes Trismegistus")[31] and the Chaldean Oracles appeared in the second century. Nicomachus of Gerasa, an avowed Pythagorean, wrote an extant *Introduction to Arithmetic*;[32] Claudius Ptolemy (c. 90–c. 168 CE), working in Alexandria, produced his epoch-making treatise on astronomy, known now universally by its Greco-Arabic name, *Almagest*.[33] Oenomaus of Gadara, a Cynic who critiqued magicians and charlatans, seems to have been on friendly terms with the Jewish rabbis (Gadara is not far from the Sea of Galilee).

We have a remarkable Epicurean text from the second century, the inscription of Diogenes of Oenoanda.[34] Just as remarkable, and much better known, is the work known as the *Meditations* of the Stoic emperor Marcus Aurelius (121–180 CE).[35] The second century is also the time of two authors, almost exact contemporaries, who wrote highly entertaining compositions with a good deal of philosophic bite: Lucian of Samosata (c. 120–180 CE) and Apuleius of Madaura (c. 123–180 CE). It is somewhat difficult to tell where Lucian's philosophical sympathies lie—perhaps with the Epicureans; Apuleius, however, despite his fantastical and highly amusing *Metamorphoses* (*Golden Ass*), is quite clearly a Platonist. There is a treatise "On Plato and His Teachings" ascribed to him, another, "On the God of Socrates," that is clearly his, and a couple of other philosophical works.

The Syrian city of Apamea had been the home town of Posidonius the Stoic; in the second century CE, the leading philosopher of Apamea was Numenius, a Platonist whose extensive fragments[36] tend to focus on ways in which Platonists had strayed from the true meaning of the text of Plato. Numenius was convinced that Plato had combined the philosophy of Pythagoras with the wisdom of several religious traditions in developing his philosophy. The Apamea school of Numenius continued to be a center for Platonic study for hundreds of years after the time of Numenius and may ultimately have played a crucial role in the transfer of Greek philosophy to Islamic thinkers.

More shadowy as an author is Alcinous, the author of the *Didaskalikos*, or *Handbook of Platonism*.[37] The text is, in itself, straightforward enough, and it gives us a good idea of how Plato was understood in the period. We know second-hand quite a lot about another Platonist, Celsus, an anti-Christian polemicist, from the refutation written by Origen.

While one might hesitate to say that "the Academy" was functioning in Athens, there certainly was, during the second century, an active Platonic school. Calvenus Taurus, a native of Beirut, was the acknowledged leader of Athenian Platonism around 150 CE; Aulus Gellius, in his *Attic Nights*, provides some lively descriptions of his teaching.[38]

In 176 CE, the Emperor Marcus Aurelius[39] endowed four chairs of philosophy in Athens, one for each of the four major schools of philosophy: Platonist, Aristotelian, Stoic, and Epicurean. Atticus seems to have been named as the Platonist; at any rate, we have significant fragments of a work of his in which he rakes an unnamed Aristotelian over the coals for claiming that Aristotle's philosophy was the culmination of all previous philosophies, including Plato's.[40]

Lively controversy seems to be part of the philosophic life of Athens. One of the extant works of Alexander of Aphrodisias, dating from 198 CE, is his treatise "On Fate," designed to provide an Aristotelian critique of Stoic determinism (fatalism). Alexander is also well known for his excellent extant commentaries on Aristotle and his treatise on the soul.

The late second to early third centuries is the period in which Galen (129–after 210 CE) wrote his massive corpus.[41] Galen, a native of Pergamum, professes allegiance to Platonism, but in fact he follows whichever philosopher is most convenient for the subject at hand. His anatomical works are more Aristotelian than anything else; his treatise on the "Passions and Errors of the Soul" is rather Stoic in inspiration. However, when he is in a combative mood (often enough), he readily defends the thesis that Plato and Hippocrates were in fundamental agreement, and were right.

Another combative writer of the period is Sextus Empiricus—he was a convinced Skeptic, and delighted in pointing out the idiocies of other philosophical schools. Translations of the titles of some of his extant books tell the tale as well as anything: *Against the Logicians*, *Against the Grammarians*, *Against the Ethicists*, *Against the Astrologers*, and *Against the Musicians*.

Less combative but still engaging is Diogenes Laertius' *Lives of Eminent Philosophers*, a work to which we very frequently refer in this dictionary; it, too, dates from somewhere around the year 200. Another great source for early Greek philosophy is the less well-known work by Hippolytus, Bishop of Rome,[42] the *Refutation of All Heresies*. Hippolytus has the habit of quoting verbatim in order to make his point, and often those quotations are just about all we have of the philosophers whom he cites.

Turning our attention once again to Alexandria, we find two remarkable teachers: Clement of Alexandria (Titus Flavius Clemens, d. 205

CE), and Ammonius Saccas (c. 175–242 CE). Clement taught at and eventually directed the Christian school in Alexandria; of his works, the one most often cited by historians of ancient philosophy is the *Stromateis*, or *Miscellany*, an unfinished collection of bits of classical thought, often with Clement's Christian commentary attached.

We do not have any text from Ammonius Saccas (c. 175–242 CE), but we know that his teaching was of great importance to the subsequent development of philosophy in the ancient world. While the Christian Origen (c. 185–254/5 CE) may have heard Clement, he surely spent a great deal more time in the company of Ammonius. We hear of several other students of Ammonius,[43] but the most important was surely Plotinus (204–270 CE). After attempting to visit India in the entourage of the Emperor Gordian, Plotinus proceeded to Rome and established his school there in 245 CE.

Plotinus was joined by Amelius, who had been studying with Numenius in Apamea (Plotinus may well have visited Apamea during his eastern tour). Amelius remained until the death of Plotinus, when he returned to Apamea to become the teacher of Iamblichus. After Plotinus had been teaching in Rome for several years, he was also joined by Porphyry of Tyre (234–c. 305 CE) who had been studying in Athens. Porphyry is mainly known for putting together the work of Plotinus into the *Enneads*, but he is also a significant author in his own right.[44] It is difficult to convey the philosophical power of Plotinus' arguments in the *Enneads*; although he certainly believed that everything that he taught came straight out of Plato's dialogues, in fact he created a synthesis that responds to the entire history of philosophy in the 600 years since the death of Plato. Porphyry made that synthesis accessible first by editing Plotinus' writings and then through his own writings that are considerably more understandable to the philosophically unsophisticated.

The next great Neoplatonist, Iamblichus of Chalkis (c. 245–325 CE), began his philosophical studies in Apamea with Amelius, and then went on to study with Porphyry, presumably in Rome. He had a number of disagreements with Porphyry: for example, Plotinus and Porphyry agree in being skeptical of the practice of theurgy, or attempting to get deities to do what one wants them to. Porphyry's views are presented in his *Letter to Anebo*. Iamblichus defends theurgy in his treatise often called *On the Egyptian Mysteries*, but in fact it is a direct, point-by-point, critique of Porphyry's arguments and is called *The Reply of Abammon*, who is represented as Anebo's superior.

In about 305, Iamblichus returned to Apamea to direct the school there for the remainder of his life. There, he taught Dexippus, who wrote a commentary on Aristotle's *Categories*, part of which survives, and Aedesius, who went on to teach at Pergamum.

Returning to Rome, for a moment, we should note Marius Victorinus (280–365 CE). A Neoplatonist who converted to Christianity, Victorinus wrote commentaries on Aristotle and on Porphyry, for example. We do not know whether he studied directly with Porphyry, but the philosophical influences are clear. After his conversion, he wrote several commentaries on New Testament books and was an important influence on Augustine. Another Christian writer in the same time period, also with significant influence, was Nemesius of Emesa: his *On the Nature of Man* is full of information about many ancient thinkers' theories of the soul.

It was around 350 that Calcidius did his translation of the first part of Plato's *Timaeus* into Latin—as it turned out, that was the only bit of Plato available to Latin readers throughout most of the Medieval period. In the East, the Emperor Constantine converted the city of Byzantium into a new capital for the Empire; soon, a leading Peripatetic philosopher, Themistius, would pursue both a political and academic career in the city that had become Constantinople.[45]

In this connection, we should mention the three Cappadocian Fathers, two brothers and a good friend, whose philosophical and theological erudition established much of the intellectual foundation for the Orthodox Christian church: Basil of Caesarea (c. 330–379), Gregory of Nyssa (c. 335–394), and Gregory of Nazianzus (329–389), who was Bishop of Constantinople for a time. Another leading Christian writer of the time, John Chrysostom (347–407), was a fiery preacher in Constantinople and was associated with this group.

Eunapius (c. 346–after 414) was a contemporary of Chrysostom but was a pagan, living and teaching in Athens, where he wrote a book of biographies of the (pagan) philosophers of his time and a few generations earlier.[46] In the next generation in Athens, we find Plutarch of Athens (d. 432 CE), who had studied with the successors of Iamblichus in Apamea and returned apparently to reestablish the Platonic school in Athens. Plutarch of Athens was the teacher of Hierocles of Alexandria,[47] Syrianus (d. c. 437) who succeeded Plutarch but only for a few years, and Proclus (412–485), who did much to bring the Athenian Platonic School back to its former glory.

It was not a good time for philosophy in Alexandria. Hierocles, having returned to his native city, was evicted by the authorities; he then went to Constantinople, where he was thrown into prison and flogged. Theon (d. 405), possibly the last director of the Museum of Alexandria, was primarily a mathematician, and according to the historians of mathematics, not a particularly able one at that. His daughter, Hypatia, was clearly a brilliant woman who became head of the Platonic school in Alexandria in about 400. She was murdered in 415 by Christians who felt threatened by her.

In the Roman world, Jerome (Eusebius Sophronius Hieronymus, 347–420) translated the Bible into Latin. His slightly younger contemporary, Augustine (354–430 CE) may be said to have translated Platonic philosophy into Christian. Both have had, of course, immeasurable influence on the subsequent course of western European thought.

Two other Latin writers of the period who have had some influence on Western thought are Martianus Capella, to whom we owe the phrase "liberal arts" and much of the intellectual structure of what counts as "liberal arts,"[48] and Macrobius (Ambrosius Theodosius Macrobius, fl. 395–423), author of a miscellany called *Saturnalia* and a commentary on Cicero's *Dream of Scipio*. Both works indicate Neoplatonist preoccupations.

On the subject of miscellanies, John of Stobi (Stobaeus), writing in Greek in Macedon, produced in this time period a truly massive assemblage of quotations for the edification of his son. This is one of the most important sources of fragments of earlier philosophers—somehow, John of Stobi had a fabulous library available to him and made good use of it. He quotes more than 500 authors, providing us with a great deal of information available nowhere else. Some day a diligent scholar will translate all of this into English.

In Syria, a Christian apologist, Theodoret of Cyrrhus (a town not far from Apamea; 393–466), wrote a work of some interest to historians of ancient philosophy, *Cure of the Greek Maladies*. In attempting to refute philosophical pretensions, Theodoret at least conveys something of the way that non-philosophers perceived the theories of the philosophers, particularly the then dominant Platonists.[49]

In Athens, Proclus constructed what would be the final, most elaborate, pagan Neoplatonic system of antiquity. He had studied in Constantinople and Alexandria before coming to join the school of Plutarch of Athens and Syrianus. Most of his writings are commentaries on dialogues of

Plato: *Alcibiades, Cratylus, Parmenides, Republic, Timaeus*; he also wrote a commentary on Euclid's *Elements*. His *Elements of Theology* and *Platonic Theology* bring together his system.

Marinus (c. 450–500 CE), the successor of Proclus as Scholarch of the Platonic school of Athens, wrote a biography of Proclus that survives, so we know more than usual about this great Neoplatonist. A contemporary of Proclus as student of Syrianus was Hermeias; while Proclus was revitalizing the Athenian school, Hermeias moved to Alexandria; his son Ammonius (c. 440–c. 520 CE) and successor Olympiodorus (before 510–after 565 CE)[50] continued his production of commentaries on classical texts and instructed some influential students, including the Christian Aristotelian, John Philoponus (c. 490–570 CE).[51]

Damascius (c. 462–after 538 CE) was the last leader of the Platonic school of Athens. He had studied with the students of Proclus in Athens, particularly Marinus; among his students was the great commentator on Aristotle, Simplicius (c. 490–560). The Emperor Justinian closed the Athenian school in 529 and drove the people who were there into exile into the Persian Empire, possibly to Harran; however, when a peace treaty was agreed upon between Byzantines and Persians, one of the clauses was that the philosophers would be able to return to the Greek-speaking world and not be molested. It is not clear where they went—possibly to Alexandria, since the industry of writing commentaries on the works of Aristotle (and others) continued for a while, somewhat mysteriously—we have commentaries ascribed to "Elias" and "David" but really no information about who composed them, although Alexandria seems most likely as the location of composition. The commentaries by "Elias" and "David" could plausibly be written by a Christian; very likely Simplicius was the last significant "pagan" philosopher of antiquity. Thus, the date of 529 CE, when the School of Athens was closed by Imperial Decree, is a convenient marker for the "end" of the continuous ancient philosophical tradition.

Two other very interesting people from the same time period give a good picture of where things were going in the philosophical world in the sixth century CE. One is the writer who used the pseudonym "Dionysius the Areopagite." Applying Neoplatonic concepts to Christianity, he developed a frankly mystical theology, a system with enough complexity to keep students (and monks) involved indefinitely.[52] The other individual is Boethius (Anicius Manlius Severinus Boethius, c. 480–524/6 CE).

Boethius was a man of considerable culture and education, and it is something of a puzzle to figure out where he got it, since Rome was by this time under the rule of the Ostrogoths, and education and culture were not a priority. We know that he had an important position in the court of Theodoric, the ruler of the Latin-speaking West. One of his surviving works is a philosophical commentary on Porphyry's *Eisagoge*, or *Introduction to Philosophy*. He proposed for himself the worthy project of translating all of Aristotle's works into Latin. He got as far as sketching out a good bit of the Organon and doing a finished translation of the *Categories* and *On Interpretation*, the first two (short) treatises in the Corpus. At that point, Boethius was arrested, thrown into jail, and separated from his library but not from paper and writing implements. While in jail, he composed the very influential *Consolation of Philosophy*, based on what he could remember and apply of philosophy in that circumstance. He was executed in 524 or 525.

The next significant "Western" man of letters of interest to historians of philosophy was Isidore of Seville (560–636). His *Etymologia* provided encapsulated bits of knowledge about many things classical, including philosophy, always from a Christian perspective. With Isidore of Seville, we cross the threshold into the medieval period of Western philosophy.

THE SURVIVAL AND TRANSMISSION OF GREEK PHILOSOPHY IN THE MEDIEVAL PERIOD

There are three stories to be told of the fate of Greek philosophy from the 7th to approximately the 12th century—a Byzantine, an Islamic, and a Latin story.

The Greek-speaking part of the Roman Empire continued to function as a political entity during the first part of the period known to western Europeans as the "middle ages." A series of mainly effective emperors managed for several hundred years to fend off the destructive invasions experienced in the West and, usually, to resolve the internal disputes that might have threatened the coherence of the state. There was, however, a significant period of social domination by Christian leaders who were unwilling to accept any alternative worldviews; for two or three centuries that tended to submerge all forms of philosophy other than the orthodox philosophical theology.

Sometimes the "Byzantine" period of philosophy is said to have begun in 529 when the school of Athens was closed by order of Justinian. As we note in the dictionary section of this book, philosophical instruction continued a bit longer in Alexandria. Higher education, for the sake of training civil servants, did continue at the Imperial school at the palace of Magnaura, often referred to as the University of Constantinople, although independent speculation must often have been seriously restricted.[53] The Greek world continued to have significant libraries, not only in Constantinople but in other places as well. Doubtless those who wished to read classical texts might well have had them available, and there was no language barrier. Perhaps more freedom of thought persisted in the eastern centers, lost to the expansion of Islam toward the end of the reign of Heraclius (575–641)—and that is part of the next story.

The Orthodox Christian Church did continue to educate its clergy, and for some time people noted by the history of philosophy came primarily from that sort of preparation. For example, Maximos the Confessor (580–662), for a time secretary to the Emperor Heraclius, retired to a monastery and wrote a number of works that provided an acceptably orthodox way of reading (pseudo) Dionysius the Areopagite.[54] The next notable figure is John of Damascus (c. 674–749), also primarily a theologian; his writings attracted the attention of Christian writers in the West, contributing to the development of medieval Latin Neoplatonic theology.

In the ninth century, Leo the Mathematician appears to have acquired his education, beyond elementary, on his own, but in about 855 he was made the head of a Philosophical School at Magnaura ("University of Constantinople") with endowed chairs in Philosophy, Grammar, Geometry, and Astronomy.[55] In the same time frame, Photios (820–893) did a great deal to revive interest in classical literature, preserving the thought of some classical philosophers that we otherwise would not have known much about. Arethas of Patras (also known as Arethas of Caesarea) (c. 862–after 932) commissioned the copying of manuscripts, including manuscripts of Plato and Aristotle; some of those commissioned manuscripts still exist today, as do some of his marginal scholia on these and other classical works. Constantine VII Porphyrogenitus (905–959) as emperor gave a great deal of encouragement to scholarly activities, as well as engaging in literary activities himself.

With the accession of Alexios Komnenos (1048–1118), scholarly, and to some extent philosophical, activity gained a new burst of energy in the Byzantine Empire. Michael Psellos (1018–1096) returned to the classical texts and revived the Neoplatonism of the pagan philosophers, arguing that classical Neoplatonism was a good deal more consistent with Christian faith than had been thought for several centuries. As director of the University of Constantinople, Psellos encouraged a rationalistic and wide-ranging study of classical subjects, a practice followed by his successors in that position, particularly John Italus, who got in trouble with the Emperor for it.[56] Anna Comnena, talented daughter of Alexius, seems to have encouraged attention to Aristotle's works, including commentators like those of Eustratius of Nicaea (c. 1050–1120) and Michael of Ephesus (1018–1096).[57] This group provided much of the inspiration and many of the manuscripts that fueled the scholastic movement in western Europe, including philosophers such as Robert Grosseteste, Albertus Magnus, and Thomas Aquinas.

In 1204, Constantinople was taken by the fourth Crusade; the Hellenes reorganized at Nicaea and eventually retook Constantinople in 1261. A university was organized at Nicaea under the direction of Nikephoros Blemmydes (1197–1272); many active scholars were educated there, and subsequently in the re-founded university at Constantinople. As the remaining Byzantine Empire lost ground to the advancing Turks, many scholars looked to the West, particularly to Italy, where many of the states had become both prosperous and hospitable to Greek scholars. Fortuitously, as the Hellenes and their manuscripts arrived in Italy, especially during the 15th century, around the date of the taking of Constantinople by the Turks (1453), the printing of books with movable type had become possible, and a market for those books was growing throughout the West.

For the Muslim world, the turning point of history is the Hadj, or Pilgrimage, of Muhammad, in 622 CE, at which point the Prophet became both a religious and secular leader of a movement that rapidly expanded from its beginnings in the Arabian peninsula to Syria and Iraq. These lands were home to both Jews and Nestorian Christians; these people were not on good terms with the Byzantine power structure, and they tended to preserve a considerable measure of classical Greek civilization, including some measure of continuity of the educational institutions that had functioned there for hundreds of years.

Within Islam, Christian and Jewish intellectual institutions were in most localities permitted to function and indeed to flourish; the synthesis of the classical traditions with Islamic thought gained considerable impetus during the Caliphate of Al-Mamun (786–833 CE). Establishing the "House of Wisdom," Al-Mamun commissioned translations into Arabic of classical Greek philosophy and science. Many works had already been translated into Syriac; others were translated directly from Greek into Arabic.[58]

One of the earliest, and greatest, of the Islamic thinkers inspired by the Greek texts thus made available was Al Farabi (870–950), who developed an Islamic version of the Neoplatonic philosophy, including the sort of reading of Aristotle's works typical in late antiquity. The next great Islamic philosopher was Ibn Sina (Avicenna) (980–1037), who lived in eastern Persia (now Uzbekistan) and wrote extensively on medicine as well as pursuing the goal of a purified Aristotelianism within the Islamic context.

In the Islamic west (Andalusia, now Spain and Morocco), Ibn Rushd (Averroes) (1126–1198) wrote extensive commentaries on Aristotle's works as well as defending philosophical investigation against the growing attacks on (Hellenophile) philosophy that were developing within Islam, typified by the work of Al Ghazali (1058–1111), *The Incoherence of the Philosophers.* Ibn Rushd's reply, *The Incoherence of the Incoherence*, ultimately failed to sustain the vivacity of the philosophical tradition within Islam, and eventually Islamic fundamentalism marginalized the philosophical tradition in most parts of the Islamic world.

However, some of the works of Al Farabi, Ibn Rushd, Ibn Sina, and other scholars and philosophers of the Arabic and Persian speaking world were being translated into Latin, and those translations inspired much of the late medieval attention to Aristotle, in particular, in western Europe.

Thus we turn to our third story of the Middle Ages, that of western Europe.

In the Latin West during the sixth to eighth centuries, social conditions severely limited the number of people who could gain an education that would enable them to read, let alone read philosophical texts. Charlemagne (747–814), the most powerful ruler in the West for many years in either direction, learned to read only as an adult, and it was clearly regarded at the time as a remarkable accomplishment for a member of the laity. Charlemagne sponsored the copying of a large number of Latin manuscripts—it is certainly due to the renewed activity of monastic scriptoria during and following his reign that we have as many classical Latin works as we do. As education became somewhat more widespread during the next few hundred years, in western Europe it was primarily a Latin education. Alcuin (735–804), a scholar from Britain, spent some time at Charlemagne's court and strongly influenced the organization and content of Western education for a considerable period of time.

Johannes Scotus Eriugena (815–877) is a remarkable and rare individual for this period. Born in Ireland, he knew Greek—apparently a scholarly tradition had continued in Irish monasteries—and took a serious interest in Neoplatonic philosophy. His translation of (pseudo) Dionysius the Areopagite into Latin and his original treatise *Periphyseon*, or "On Nature," were read widely by medieval intellectuals and had a significant influence on the continuity and development of philosophical thought in the Latin west.[59]

The next philosopher of significant stature in the West was Anselm of Canterbury (1033–1109). In a sense, Anselm embodied the turning point for philosophy in western Europe, since from his day onward one can often count simultaneous important Western contributors to philosophy by the dozen or more. Some of the notable thinkers of the generation after Anselm of Canterbury were Anselm of Laon (d. 1117), Roscellinus (1050–1122), William of Champeaux (1070–1121), Gilbert de la Porrée (1070–1154), Bernard of Chartres (d. c. 1130), Hugh of St. Victor (1078–1141), Peter Abelard (1079–1142), and Bernard of Clairvaux (1090–1153).

All of these thinkers, from Anselm to Bernard of Clairvaux, and beyond, were essentially reliant on texts that existed in Latin—of Plato, only part of the *Timaeus*; of Aristotle, only the *Categories* and *Interpretation*, existed in Latin translation. To be sure, Cicero and Seneca, for pagan examples, and Augustine and many other Christian philosophers, were available in various ecclesiastical school settings, but we think of the 11th-century philosophers as seriously restricted in their scope of investigation.

All that was to change rapidly when scholars turned to translating classical texts into Latin. Gerard of Cremona (1114–1187) translated Aristotle's *Posterior Analytics* (with Themistius' commentary), *Physics, De Caelo, Generation and Corruption*, as well as *Ptolemy's Almagest* (and other scientific works) from Arabic to Latin. Robert Grosseteste (1175–1253), with the help of his very able staff, translated Aristotle's

Nicomachean Ethics along with the Greek commentary on that work, directly from the Greek. Albertus Magnus (1193–1280) found a number of Greek manuscripts in the Greek-speaking part of southern Italy and organized their translation into Latin. William of Moerbeke (1215–1286) became a master of the Greek language, spending many years working in Byzantine locations to translate as much as possible of Aristotle directly from Greek into Latin. He also translated Hero of Alexandria, Archimedes, and Proclus' *Elements of Theology*. All of these Aristotle translations contributed powerfully to the largely Aristotelian philosophical renaissance in which Thomas Aquinas was the most famous proponent, but many other thinkers also participated during the 13th and 14th centuries.

Translations of Plato lagged. With very few, and minor, exceptions, most of Plato was unknown in Latin until translated by Marsilio Ficino (1433–1499); Ficino also translated a number of Neoplatonic and Hermetic texts. But that is the "Renaissance."

A major turning point in the history of ancient Greek philosophy occurred in the last years of the 15th and first years of the 16th century. Aldus Manutius, a great Venetian humanist scholar, and printer, with the help of Greek scholars in exile, so to speak, produced printed editions of the works of Aristotle (1495–1498), Plato (1513), and many other important classical texts. Those printed texts, widely disseminated in western Europe, and their descendants assured the survival of the ancient Greek philosophical tradition into the modern era.

In this connection, we should mention that the standard printed edition of Plato's works was published in Geneva in 1578 by Henri Estienne (1528–1598), Latinized "Stephanus." We still use the pagination of that edition to refer to places in Plato's writings; the text was accompanied by a Latin translation (by Jean de Serres).[60]

This summary of the transmission of Greek philosophy to the Renaissance and modern world is provided to give a bit of an idea of how the texts and understanding of ancient Greek (and Roman) philosophers were preserved—to the extent that they were preserved—from the world of Hypatia, Simplicius, and John Philoponus to the world of Francis Bacon, William Harvey, and Rene Descartes. How the ancient texts were, in a sense, rediscovered in the 19th century by G. W. F. Hegel, Friedrich Nietzsche, and a host of other scholars and how the study of ancient philosophy became a specialization within the general discipline of philosophy is a separate story told elsewhere.

NOTES

1. The books of *Proverbs* and *Ecclesiastes* in the Hebrew Bible are good examples; there are some very old examples from Egypt, books of "Wise Instruction." The genre continued throughout antiquity, ultimately serving as our source for fragments of books that have otherwise been lost. It continues today, for example in the books entitled *Chicken Soup for the Soul* and variations.

2. Diogenes Laertius, *Life of Pythagoras*, 6.

3. Borderline exceptions to this generalization: There are two set speeches presumed to be by Gorgias; neither is particularly philosophical in character. If we count the medical Hippocrates of Cos as a kind of Presocratic, we may imagine that some of the treatises in the corpus attributed to him are really by him, and they have some philosophic moments, though they are aimed chiefly at medical speculation.

4. Kathleen Freeman, *Ancilla to the Presocratic Philosophers* (first published in 1948 and still in print at Harvard University Press) is perhaps the best example of a volume that attempts to do just that. It is 174 pages long, including a fair amount of material in addition to the translations.

5. Herodotus Book II.

6. C. Kahn, *The Art and Thought of Heraclitus*, Cambridge, 1979, is a good place to find out more about Heraclitus.

7. P. Curd, *The Legacy of Parmenides*, Princeton, 1998, explains the arguments and their consequences very well.

8. As many have pointed out, an explicit rejection of philosophy is also a philosophical position. Gorgias is reported to have demonstrated the futility of the Eleatic mode of argumentation, an eminently philosophical endeavor.

9. For an outline of the groups of dialogues, see the Plato entry in the dictionary.

10. The Hamilton and Cairns *Plato* (Princeton University Press) runs to 1,743 pages; the Cooper *Plato* (Hackett) is 1,808 pages; it is a little longer because it aims at absolute completeness of all the works attributed to Plato. The "standard" pagination of Plato's works refers to the first complete printed edition, edited by Henricus Stephanus, in 1578. There are three volumes with 542, 992, and 416 pages, respectively: 1,950 pages of rather large hand-set type.

11. Wincenty Lutoslawski, *The Origin and Growth of Plato's Logic*, London, 1897. L. Brandwood, *The Chronology of Plato's Dialogues*, Cambridge University Press, 1990. Gerald R. Ledger, *Re-Counting Plato: A Computer Analysis of Plato's Style*, Oxford University Press, 1989. H. Thesleff, *Studies in Platonic Chronology*, Commentationes Humanarum Litterarum 70. Helsinki: Societas Scientiarum Fennica, 1982. Charles M. Young, "Plato and Computer Dating," *Oxford Studies in Ancient Philosophy* 12 (1994), pp. 227–250.

12. Paul Shorey, *The Unity of Plato's Thought*, Chicago, 1903.

13. Diogenes Laertius (3.46) provides a list of names of the members of the Academy; interestingly, the list includes the names of two women, Lastheneia of Mantinea and Axiothea of Phlius.

14. Other schools established in the same time frame include those at Megara, Elis, and Cyrene, also by individuals associated with Socrates.

15. Some of the schools founded by associates of Socrates continued to function in this time period, notably the Cyrenaic and Megarian; the Elian school had been taken over by the Academic Menedemus and moved to Eretria.

16. The standard edition of Aristotle, done by Augustus Bekker in Berlin in the mid 19th century, runs to 1,462 pages, followed by a number of pages of collected fragments of lost works of Aristotle. Those are very large pages, not very large type, in double columns. The standard English translation, *The Complete Works of Aristotle*, edited by Jonathan Barnes (Princeton University Press) is in two volumes with a total of 2,487 pages. Even allowing that some of the works may not be by Aristotle himself but by members of his school, there is a lot of text to be studied and analyzed.

17. We have a significant amount of text remaining from Theophrastus. He wrote two large works on botany, an influential description of different typical sorts of people called the *Characters*, treatises on stones and other topics, and sufficient fragmentary remains to occupy two largish volumes. W. W. Fortenbaugh, ed., *Theophrastus of Eresus*, Leiden: Brill, 1992.

18. Aristoxenus, *Elementa Harmonica*, R. da Rios, ed., Rome, 1954.

19. There is a collection, in ten volumes, of the literary remains of the early Peripatetic School, F. Wehrli, *Die Schule des Aristoteles*, Basel, 1966–1969.

20. From Epicurus himself, there is a two-page document called the "Principal Doctrines," and two letters, each about the same length; otherwise, there are fragments and reports of his teaching in later authors. The most complete presentation of Epicureanism is Lucretius' long poem, *On the Nature of Things*.

21. H. von Arnim, ed., *Stoicorum Veterum Fragmenta* is in four volumes totaling more than 1,000 pages, but much of that consists of second-hand reports of their views, and there are no "complete" works from the early Stoics. Stoics of the Roman period are another matter—then we have a good deal of text, both in Greek and in Latin.

22. Diogenes Laertius notes (7.36–37) Persaeus, a fellow citizen of Citium; Aristo of Chios; Herillus of Carthage; Dionysius of Heraclea; Sphaerus of Bosporus; Philonides of Thebes, Callippus of Corinth; Posidonius of Alexandria; Athenodorus of Soli; and Zeno of Sidon (or Tarsus).

23. English translation by P. Green, Berkeley, University of California Press, 1997.

24. In 170 BCE, Eumenes II, King of Pergamum, dedicated a library in competition with the Alexandrian institution, perhaps to complement the existing Asclepeion or medical center. We may note that the word "parchment" is de-

rived from the name of the city, and that Galen was a citizen and got his early education there.

25. See Leo Groarke, "Ancient Skepticism," *Stanford Encyclopedia of Philosophy*, 2006: http://plato.stanford.edu/entries/skepticism-ancient/#Ac1

26. The relevant passage (from Plutarch's *Lives*) is available online at http://www.fordham.edu/halsall/ancient/plut_carneades.html

27. J. Dillon, *The Middle Platonists*, p. 116.

28. Renewed interest in Pythagoreanism goes back at least to a contemporary of Cicero, P. Nigidius Figulus, and the religious aspects of Pythagoreanism took off seriously with the influence of Apollonius of Tyana (2 BCE–98 CE) and Moderatus of Gades (c.50–100 CE).

29. We have a short summary of his teaching, the *Handbook*, and a hefty volume of his discourses with students, copied down by one of them, Arrian.

30. A tantalizing hint that philosophers were active in Athens is provided by the story in *Acts* 17 that "some of the Epicurean and Stoic philosophers" brought Paul to the Areopagus in order to hear what he had to say.

31. Tr. B. Copenhaver, *Hermetica,* Cambridge, 1995.

32. Tr. M. L. D'Ooge, New York, 1926, reprint 1972.

33. Tr. G. J. Toomer, Princeton, 1998.

34. See http.//www.anchist.mq.edu.au/272/Diogenes%20of%20Oenoanda .html for pictures of the site.

35. Tr. A. S. L. Farquharson, 2 vols. Oxford, Clarendon Press, 1944.

36. Tr. K. Guthrie, *The Neoplatonic Writings of Numenius*, Lawrence Kan.: Selene, 1987.

37. Tr. J. Dillon, Oxford, 1993.

38. See J. Dillon, *The Middle Platonists*, pp. 237ff.

39. Also the author of the essentially Stoic *Meditations*.

40. See J. Dillon, *The Middle Platonists*, pp. 247ff.

41. C. G. Kuhn, *Galeni Opera Omnia*, Leipzig: 1821–1833, repr. Olms, Hildesheim, 1965, comprises 22 hefty volumes. Not all of these works have been re-edited since the early 19th century, and only a minority are translated into English. Daremberg's 1856 translation into French is the most complete into any modern language.

42. There is a story behind the appellation "Bishop of Rome." Hippolytus was engaged in a theological controversy with Callistus; when Callistus was elected Pope (Bishop of Rome) in 217, the supporters of Hippolytus rallied and elected *him* as Bishop of Rome, or if you like "antipope." In 222, Callistus died and was succeeded by Pontianus, and Hippolytus was reconciled to the Church. Both Hippolytus and Pontianus were exiled to Sardinia by the Emperor Maximinus Thrax, who was less friendly to Christians than his predecessor. They died in exile, and today Hippolytus (Hippolyte), Callistus (Calixte), and Pontian are counted as saints by the Church, the two exiles as Martyrs.

43. We could mention particularly Cassius Longinus (c. 213–273) who went on to teach in Athens, where he taught Porphyry before Porphyry went to Rome to study with Plotinus. Longinus subsequently became counselor to Queen Zenobia of Palmyra in her revolt against the Romans, for which he was executed.

44. For a list of the works of Porphyry translated into English, see the Bibliography.

45. The surviving speeches of Themistius fill three volumes, and his surviving commentaries on Aristotle fill several more.

46. Eunapius is bound with Philostratus in the Loeb series.

47. His commentary on the *Carmen Aureum*, an introduction to philosophy, and some fragments of his work *On Providence* are extant.

48. His *Satyricon*, or *De Nuptiis Philologiae et Mercurii et de septem Artibus liberalibus libri novem*, was much read and admired during the period when western European universities were being organized. It has been mainly forgotten since, and no modern translation is available.

49. *Thérapeutique des maladies helléniques,* 2 vols., ed. & tr. P. Canivet, Paris: Cerf., 2000–2001. Theodoret is also known for his works in church history, commentaries on books of the Bible, and a work on Divine Providence.

50. The commentaries of Olympiodorus on Alcibiades I and Gorgias give a good idea of philosophical instruction in his period.

51. See Christian Wildberg, "Philoponus," in the *Stanford Encyclopedia of Philosophy*, 2003: http://plato.stanford.edu/entries/philoponus/

52. See K. Corrigan and M. Harrington, "Pseudo-Dionysius the Areopagite," *Stanford Encyclopedia of Philosophy*, 2004: http://plato.stanford.edu/entries/pseudo-dionysius-areopagite/

53. We hear of one Stephen of Alexandria who taught philosophy in Constantinople during the reign of Heraclius; Paul Lemerle, *Byzantine Humanism*, p. 88.

54. Basil Tatakis, *Byzantine Philosophy*, p. 65.

55. Lemerle, p. 281.

56. Anna Comnena's *Alexiad* recounts this story, see Tatakis, pp. 169–171.

57. A. Preus, *Aristotle and Michael of Ephesus on the Movement and Progression of Animals,* Olms: Hildesheim, 1981, pp. 2–21.

58. Dmitri Gutas, *Greek Thought, Arab Culture: The Greco-Arabic Translation Movement in Baghdad and Early Abbasid Society*, New York: Routledge, 1998.

59. Dermot Moran, "John Scottus Eriugena," *Stanford Encyclopedia of Philosophy*, 2004: http://plato.stanford.edu/entries/scottus-eriugena/ accessed 8/28/2006.

60. Bernard Suzanne, "Quoting Plato: Stephanus References," 2004: http://plato-dialogues.org/faq/faq007.htm

The Dictionary

– A –

ABSTRACTION. The Greek term is *aphairesis*, an abstract noun built on the verb *aphairein*, to take away, for example to draw blood. **Aristotle** introduced a technical sense of the term to refer to separating out by thought something that is not (for him) ontologically separable. He uses the term in this sense primarily of **mathematical attributes** (e.g., *Metaph.* XI.3, 1061a29ff).

ACADEMIC SKEPTICISM. *See* ACADEMY; *SKEPTIKOS*.

ACADEMY. Plato's school in **Athens**, established some years after the death of **Socrates** (383 BCE?) in a location that had previously been used as a wrestling school. (At *Lysis* 203, Socrates is represented as walking from the wrestling school at the Academy to the wrestling school at the **Lyceum**.) The school was in a sacred grove of olive trees (**Thucydides** II.34), respected by the Spartans when they invaded Attica. The grove was a public space; Plato acquired a small garden in the vicinity, presumably including a building and possibly the gymnasium of the Academy; discussion and instruction occurred in any of these places, collectively called "the Academy."

After the death of Plato, his nephew **Speusippus** seems to have inherited the private property and to have taken over the role of **Scholarch**. In 339, **Xenocrates** was elected Scholarch, and **Polemon** in 314. Polemon was succeeded by **Crates**, then **Arcesilaus**, and Lacydes; then a series of people of whom we know little but their names. With Crates, the Academy became less dogmatic and more skeptical, reading Plato's dialogues as models of avoiding definitive conclusions in philosophical discussions.

The olive grove that had been respected by the Spartans was cut down by Sulla to aid in his siege of Athens (86 BCE); he may have destroyed or severely damaged the gymnasium and other buildings that may have comprised the physical structure of the Academy at that time. We do not know the extent of the physical reconstruction of the Academy that might have occurred in subsequent years or just where Platonic instruction was offered. To a considerable degree, the word "Academy" became metaphorical or an idea of a school, more than a physical place.

Cicero tells, in his *Academica*, how matters stood in his student days. **Philo of Larissa** was formally Scholarch, but was visiting Rome at the time of the Sullan invasion. He remained in Rome, and Cicero studied with him there before going to Athens. Another of Philo's students, **Antiochus of Ascalon**, had philosophical disagreements with Philo (recounted by Cicero), and is said by **Numenius** to have "founded another Academy." Cicero studied with Antiochus in Athens in 79 BCE, but does not say much about the physical location of that instruction.

The next snapshot of Platonic instruction in Athens comes from 66/7 CE, when **Plutarch of Chaeronea** (46–c. 122 CE) studied Platonism with a philosopher named **Ammonius.** Although Plutarch did a great deal to revive interest in Platonism, he seems to have favored his native Chaeronea as the home of his Platonic circle.

Another snapshot comes from 176 CE when the Emperor **Marcus Aurelius** endowed four chairs of philosophy (as we would say) in Athens: Platonism, Aristotelianism, Stoicism, and Epicureanism. A philosopher named **Atticus** seems to have been the first occupant of that chair. Certainly by this time and probably already by the time of Cicero, "Academic" philosophy had come to mean the intellectual tradition stemming from Socrates and Plato, not owing allegiance to **Aristotle, Epicurus,** or **Zeno of Citium.**

In that sense, Academic philosophy seems to have continued, with a notable revival in the fifth century CE, until 529 CE, when the Platonic school of Athens was closed by order of the Emperor Justinian. *For Academic Skeptics, see SKEPTIKOS.*

ACCIDENT, ACCIDENTAL. The philosophical definition of "accident" is a "non-essential **attribute**" of something. Essential attributes are those that are included in the definition of a **species**—the elephant essentially has a long nose—but if a **particular** elephant has a hoodah, that is an accident. This is an **Aristotelian** distinction; he calls accidents *symbebēkota*. "Accident" is derived from the Latin equivalent of "*symbebēkos*." In the context of causal explanations of things, some events or some descriptions of events are described as *kata symbebēkos*, or "accidental."

In *Physics* II, Aristotle distinguishes a class of "accidental" events that he attributes to "luck" (*tychē*) and a larger class that he attributes to *to automaton*, which we may translate as "the automatic" or simply "chance." A lucky event is one that a person would have chosen if he had known—like meeting "accidentally" with someone who owes you money, and the person actually has money along, or buying a lottery ticket "at random" and actually winning a prize. An event attributed to *to automaton* is a random event that according to some description occurs contrary to expected regular processes. If you happen to be washing your face when an eclipse of the moon occurs, neither event is causally connected to the other; they are correlated *kata symbebēkos*.

Epicurus speaks of *symptomata*, characteristics of bodies attributed as a consequence of **particular** perceptual relations to those bodies (*Letter to Herodotus*, 72). These would be "accidental" in approximately the same sense.

ACCOUNT. *See LOGOS.*

ACTUALITY. "*Actualitas*" is a Latin word invented in the medieval period to translate **Aristotle**'s *energeia* and *entelecheia*. Since "*actus*" is the past participle of "*agere*," to do, or impel, originally actuality was not a bad translation. "Actuality" has come to have something of a static connotation, and *energeia* is definitely dynamic, so perhaps "activity" would often be a better translation. Aristotle lays out his theory of *energeia* in **Metaphysics** IX.6–9.

ADĒLON. Unclear, non-evident. **Anaxagoras** says, "Phenomena are a glimpse of the *adēla*" (B21). For the **Epicureans**, *adēla* are those things that exist but cannot be directly perceived, only demonstrated on the basis of observation—for example, the void. Academic skeptics were accused of making *everything* non-evident. *See also PHAINOM-ENON; SKEPTIKOS.*

ADDITIONAL PREMISE. *See PROSLĒPSIS.*

ADIAPHORA. Indifferents. According to orthodox **Stoic** doctrine (**Zeno**), anything that does not directly contribute to virtue (aretē) is "indifferent." Thus, life, health, pleasure, **beauty**, wealth, strength, and so on are "indifferents" since any of them can contribute to vice (*kakia*) as well as to virtue (*aretē*). But then some Stoics distinguish within the class of "indifferents" some things that are "**preferred**" (life, health, etc.) from other things that are "**dispreferred**" (death, illness, etc.), **Diogenes Laertius** VII.101–5.

ADIKIA. Injustice. According to **Aristotle**, if a person does something wrong, knowing that it is wrong, that person does an unjust act. If, on the whole, the person prefers to do unjust acts than just acts, that person is an unjust person. *See also DIKĒ.*

AELIUS ARISTIDES (117–181 CE). Greek orator afflicted with a mysterious disease; his *Sacred Discourses* recount his many attempts to discover a cure, revealing a great deal about the practice of medicine (*iatrikē*) and paramedicine in the second century CE. His ideas were subjected to a critique by **Sextus Empiricus**.

AENESIDEMUS (1st century BCE). Born in Crete, trained as a skeptical Academic, he broke with the **Academy** when it became more dogmatic and less skeptical. Aenesidemus moved to **Alexandria** and founded his own school, claiming **Pyrrho** as its inspiration. He is the author of the 10 "**tropes**" or ways of arguing to skeptical conclusions, preserved in **Sextus Empiricus**, *Outlines of Pyrrhonism*, and elsewhere. *See also SKEPTIKOS.*

AĒR. Air, the fundamental material for **Anaximenes** and **Diogenes of Apollonia**, is also assumed by them to be the basis for life and intellection. This idea was ridiculed by **Aristophanes** in the *Clouds* but continued to be influential through the "*pneumatic*" theory of the soul (*psychē*) and the idea that the *aithēr* or pure upper air is the abode of divine beings.

AETIUS (c. 100 CE). A rather shadowy **doxographer**, reconstructed by Hermann Diels in the 19th century; the reconstruction has recently been criticized by Jaap Mansfeld. Diels-Kranz credit "Aetius" as the source for many of the fragments and testimonia printed in their *Fragmente der Vorsokratiker*. A treatise sometimes attributed to him is included in the **corpus** of the works of **Plutarch of Chaeronea**; called the *Placita*, it is a summary of opinions of various philosophers, relying extensively on the work of **Theophrastus**. Those who are unsure of the attribution call the author "pseudo-Plutarch." Somewhat similar passages occur in **Stobaeus,** attributed to the same source by Diels.

AFFECTION. *See PATHOS.*

AFFINITY. *See OIKEIŌSIS.*

AGATHON. Good. The primary form (*eidos*) in **Plato**'s *Republic*. For **Aristotle**, one of three general objects of pursuit, along with *kalon* and *hēdyn*. While *hēdyn* clearly means "pleasurable," the distinction between *agathon* and *kalon* is not clear-cut. *Kalon* has more of a connotation of "**beauty**" or "nobility" and *agathon* has a connotation, in some contexts, of exchange value. The standard word for "gentleman" in **Athens** in **Aristotle**'s day was "*kalokagathos*," someone who was both *kalos* and *agathos. See also EIDOS; KALOKAGATHIA.*

AGENT INTELLECT. *Nous poiētikos.* In *de Anima* III, **Aristotle** distinguishes between the passive aspect of mind (nous), capable of accepting information from the senses, and the active aspect of mind, capable of creating concepts and initiating intelligent action. It is characteristic of ancient Greek philosophy to use the idea of mental activity to describe the nature of **God**. From **Xenophanes** through the unmoved mover (*akinēton kinoun*) of Aristotle to the God of the **Stoics**, God is an active mind.

AGNŌSTOS. Unknowable. For **Protagoras**, questions about the **God**s were too difficult and life too short. That line of thought leads to skepticism, which teaches that you cannot even be confident that knowledge is impossible.

Although most ancient Greek thinkers had confident positive theologies, in later Greek philosophy negative theologies appeared more frequently. Such theologies asserted that God is beyond comprehension, knowledge, and description—somehow, saying that God is beyond being is taken to be quite different from saying that God does not exist.

In another sense, **Socrates** in the *Theaetetus* (202b) points out that if you define knowledge as analysis of complexes into simples, then the simples themselves are unknowable.

AGRAPHOS NOMOS. Unwritten law. *See NOMOS.*

AGREEMENT. *See HOMOLOGIA.*

AĪDIOS. Everlasting. In principle, this word is used for unending time rather than timelessness, although ancient philosophers were no more careful about that distinction than more recent thinkers.

AIŌN. In early Greek thought, an individual person's life span, or "age." **Parmenides** suggests a contrast between time (***chronos***) and the timelessness of **being**, to which he applies the word *aiōn*. Thus, the word comes to mean "timeless eternity" (**Plato** *Tm* 37d); in that guise it plays an important role in **Neoplatonism**.

AIR. *See AĒR.*

AISTHĒSIS. Perception, sensation. **Presocratic** thinkers tended to suggest materialist theories of perception—for example, streams of particles from the perceived item to the sense organ. **Theophrastus** wrote a book, *On the Senses*, intended to present and critique the views of earlier philosophers; he suggests that there are two general sorts of Presocratic theories: those that suppose that "like is known by like" (**Empedocles** is a good example of someone who held this sort of theory); and those who suppose that contrast is essential for perception—as Theophrastus sees it **Anaxagoras** counts as having this sort of theory.

Plato analyzes *aisthēsis* rather carefully in the *Theaetetus*, ostensibly to refute the claim that "knowledge (***epistēmē***) is perception" but effectively constructing a theory that allows perception to contribute to knowledge. "Knowledge is not in the perceptions, but in putting together an account (***syllogismos***) about them" (186d).

Aristotle attempted to develop the conceptual structure of the understanding of perception further in the *de Anima* and *Sense and Sensible Objects*. His definition of *aisthēsis* is reception of the sensible form without the **matter**. This reception is done by the various sense organs, which can be understood as possessing a proportionality or *logos* of the material elements that permits the required receptivity.

AITHĒR. "Ether." In early Greek thought, including the poets, *aithēr* is the purer air breathed by the **Gods** on the mountaintops or the realm of light in the heavens. For **Aristotle**, *aithēr* is the "fifth element" after **earth**, **water**, **air**, and **fire**; it is the material substrate of astronomical entities, and it naturally moves in a circle. It is also, for Aristotle, the **medium** for the transmission of light. And he suggests some sort of affinity between *aithēr* and *pneuma*, the special material instrument of the soul (*psychē*) in his *Generation* and *Movement of Animals* (*GA* II.6).

AITION, AITIA. Responsibility, cause. In legal contexts, this word means "legal responsibility." **Aristotle** adopts the word to designate the answers to his four sorts of demand for explanation. What is it? What is it made out of? What brought it into being? What is it for? Aristotle's account of explanation differs in several ways from modern philosophy of science accounts. For one thing, it is meant to be close to ordinary language explanations and thus needs to accommodate explanations appealing to intention and choice (*proairesis*) on the one hand and to luck (*tychē*) and chance on the other (see, e.g., *Physics* II). For another, Aristotle regularly allows simultaneous parallel explanations, appealing to **matter** and movement (*kinēsis*) as one sort of explanation of some state of affairs and at the same time allowing a teleological and formal explanation of the same state of affairs. He resolutely resists reductionist accounts, in particular the sort of explanation called "mechanical" since the 16th century. *See also ARCHĒ; EIDOS; TELOS.*

AITION AUTOTELĒS. Complete cause. In **Stoic** philosophy, this phrase is roughly equivalent to "sufficient condition."

AKATALĒPTON. In **Stoic** epistemology, non-cognitive, as applied to sensory impressions received when one is in an abnormal state, for example, mentally ill or under the influence of drugs.

AKINĒTON. Unmoved, immovable. According to **Parmenides, being** is "unmoved, immovable." In the *Timaeus*, **Plato** says that **earth** is *akinētotatē*, "most immobile" (55e1), although in another way the cosmic deities are immobile (40b3) in the sense that they are changeless other than their circular movement.

AKINĒTON KINOUN. Unmoved Mover. **Aristotle** pursues that thought and argues that the ultimate cause of the entire universe is the *akinēton kinoun*, the "immovable" (*Metaph*. XII.6, *Phys*. VIII. 6). In fact, Aristotle distinguishes three senses of *akinēton*: totally incapable of being moved, moved with difficulty, or movable but not currently in motion (*Phys*. V.3, 226b). The "unmoved mover" is, of course, immovable in the first sense, not the sort of thing that could be moved at all since it is non-spatial.

AKOLASIA, AKOLASTOS. Licentiousness, intemperance, the vice opposed to *sōphrosynē*. The word literally means "uncorrected, undisciplined." **Socrates** uses that implication to good effect in arguing with **Callicles** in the *Gorgias* (505bff): Callicles wants to pursue unlimited bodily pleasures but also wants to remain "in control," and thus not *akolastos*. When Socrates makes him aware of the incompatibility of these goals, Callicles tries to break off the discussion.

    Aristotle discusses *sōphrosynē* and *akolasia* in *EN* III.10–12. The *akolastos* intentionally pursues bodily pleasures to excess. He notes that the word is also applied to undisciplined children; where it occurs with that usage, English translators typically use the word "naughty" in that place.

AKOLOUTHEIN, AKOLUTHEIA. To follow; consequentiality.

AKOUSMATA; AKOUSMATIKOI. Literally, things heard; eager hearers. The word *akousmata* is applied to a group of somewhat mysterious **Pythagorean** sayings apparently learned and studied by new initiates to the Pythagorean way of life. The word *akousmatikoi* is applied to those initiates.

AKRASIA, AKRATEIA; AKRATĒS. *Akrasia* and *akrateia* are alternate spellings of the word meaning "lack of power, debility, lack of self-control." The *akratēs* is the person who exhibits a lack of control. The word is used in the **Hippocratic corpus** to denote physical disability; in **Plato**'s *Timaeus* (86d) the word is used for a propensity for sexual overindulgence and is described as a physical disease. Similarly, male and female homosexual intercourse are attributed to *akrateia* at *Laws* I, 636c. The idea of *akrateia* fits readily into Plato's psychology, since he represents the soul (*psychē*) as divided into parts that could be in conflict with each other—think of the *Phaedrus* **charioteer** struggling and perhaps failing to control the horses.

Aristotle discusses *akrateia* at length in *EN* VII.1–11. Since *akolasia* is the vice of excess related to the virtue *sōphrosynē*, one might wonder whether *akrateia* and *akolasia* are really the same thing, distinguished only by the fact that the *akolastos* is honest about what he is doing, while the *akratēs* tries to make excuses for his behavior. Aristotle tries to make a space for *akrasia* by arguing that some who profess good intentions might really not have control over their actions in all circumstances. He makes that point partly by arguing that people do not always consciously mean what they say—they might be mouthing the words without really grasping their import, like the person who recites the verses of **Empedocles** when he is drunk (*EN* VII.3, 1147b12). He also compares the condition of people who suffer from "beastliness" (*thēriotēs*)—they lack control over their actions to the point where they do things that human beings would not normally even *want* to do.

The akratic person, Aristotle believes, entertains practical syllogisms that are inconsistent in the present instance: "Eat sweet things—this chocolate cake is sweet—eat this cake" and "Eat healthy things—this chocolate cake is not healthy—do not eat this cake" and then proceeds to eat the cake, while professing to believe, intellectually, the second syllogism.

Aristotle calls people who, as we say, "lose their temper," akratic in a qualified sense (*EN* VII.4, 6); it may be reasonable to be angry with someone but not to the extent of taking a poke at him.

AKRON, AKRA. Extremity. This term is used in geometry to speak of the ends of a line, for example; in everyday conversation, the ends of the fingertips. **Atomists** talk about the "extremities" of atoms that touch each other. **Aristotle** uses *akra* of the "terms" of a syllogism; *akroi* is also used of the best people, somewhat as we say "tops" in English.

ALBINUS. *See* ALCINOUS.

ALCINOUS (Second century CE). Author of the extant *Didascalicus*, a handbook of **Platonic** philosophy. The author of this text has sometimes been called "Albinus" (known as a teacher of **Galen**), but that attribution has been disproved.

ALCMAEON OF CROTON (c. 570–490 BCE). Some believe that Alcmaeon was an early member of the **Pythagorean** School. If that is so, he is unusual in his focus on biology and medicine (*iatrikē*). He believed that health depends on a balance of various "powers" (*dynameis*) in the body. He seems to have been the first in the Greek philosophical tradition to attribute cognition to the brain, and he developed an early version of the argument for immortality of the soul (*psychē*), which appears in **Plato**'s *Phaedrus* at 245, that the soul is the ultimate cause of change, and the ultimate cause of change cannot itself be destroyed.

ALĒTHEIA. Truth. **Parmenides** divided his poem into the *Way of Truth* and the *Way of Opinion*; the *Way of Truth* tells of "what is" while the *Way of Opinion* tells what people believe. **Protagoras**, in contrast, in a book that might have been called "The Truth," wrote "Human beings are the measure of all things, of what is, that it is, and of what is not, that it is not." **Plato** sides with Parmenides in closely associating *alētheia* with **being**, while **Aristotle** favors a more syntactical definition of truth in *Metaphysics* IV.

In the Hellenistic period, philosophers sought a "canon" (*kanōn*, standard) or criterion (*kritērion*) of truth. **Epicurus** argued that perceptions (*aisthēseis*), preconceptions (*prolēpseis*), and feelings (*pathē*) are criteria of truth. For Epicurus, the primary feelings involved are pleasure (*hēdonē*) and pain (*lypē*); the perceptions are either immediate individual perceptions or generalizations based on perception. Epicurus believed that immediate perception is infallible. "Preconceptions" or *prolēpseis* are crucially important to the epistemological position, since they are the general notion of a particular kind of experience; for example, we may have a preconception of body, or of space, or of number, making possible experience of a particular kind.

The **Stoics** attempted to distinguish between cognitively reliable and cognitively unreliable perceptions; correct *prolēpseis* make some perceptions cognitively reliable. There are significant discussions of these issues in **Cicero**'s *Academica* and **Sextus Empiricus'** *Against the Professors*.

ALEXANDER OF APHRODISIAS (Second to third centuries CE). Alexander was appointed to a chair of **Peripatetic** philosophy, possibly in **Athens**, by the emperors Septimius Severus and Caracalla between 198 and 209. Alexander wrote extant commentaries on **Aristotle**'s *Prior Analytics* I, *Topics*, **Metaphysics**, *Meteorologica*, and *Sense*. His extant "original" works include *On the Soul*, *Problems*, *On Fate*, and others. Regarded as the most reliable commentator on Aristotle in subsequent centuries, his works (including many now lost) were often incorporated into the commentaries of others.

ALEXANDER OF MACEDON (356–323 BCE). Aristotle's most famous student. Philip of Macedon, Alexander's father, engaged Aristotle as Alexander's tutor in about 343 BCE; the teacher-student relationship seems to have lasted only a year or two. When Alexander became king after the death of his father in 336, he moved fairly quickly to consolidate his hold over Greece; in his peace treaty with **Athens**, apparently one of the terms was that Aristotle, not a citizen of Athens, would be permitted to open a school in that city. While Alexander was a warrior, not a philosopher, the effect of his conquests was the opening of the Middle East to Greek ideas—and Greece to Middle Eastern ideas—with many important consequences over the next thousand years.

ALEXANDRIA. Capital of the Ptolemaic rulers of **Egypt**, home of the famous **Museum (Museion) and Library**, center for scientific and philosophical investigation from the late fourth century BCE until the martyrdom of **Hypatia** in 415 CE. Philosophical teaching in Alexandria was revived by **Hermeias** toward the end of the fifth century; his successors **Ammonius** and **Olympiodorus** continued his teaching, instructing **John Philoponus**, a Christian commentator on **Aristotle**, and others, who continued a Christian philosophical tradition until the city was taken by a Muslim army in 641.

ALEXINUS OF ELIS (Late fourth to early third century BCE). Dialectician, successor of **Eubulides**, noted for his critique of **Zeno the Stoic**, using parodies of Zeno's arguments.

ALGOS. **Pain** of body or mind. The more frequently used word is *lypē*.

ALIENATION. *Allotriōsis.* In **Stoic** philosophy, the opposite of *oikeiōsis*, **appropriation**.

ALLĒGORIA. Speaking in such a way as to be interpreted other than literally; interpretation of speech or text other than literally. **Plato**'s image of the Cave in the *Republic* is usually referred to as an "allegory," and in general most readers take his "myths" to be allegorical in character. But he does not use the word "*allēgoria*"; he uses the word *hyponoein* (*Rep.* II, 378b–d; *cf. Laws* III, 679c). Allegorical interpretations of literary and philosophical texts became very much in vogue in late antiquity. *See also MYTHOS.*

ALLEGORY. *See ALLĒGORIA.*

ALLOIŌSIS. Qualitative change, i.e., the same entity becoming qualitatively different while remaining the same entity (see *Phys.* V. 2, 226b1). One of **Aristotle**'s examples is a person getting a tan. In *de An.* II.5, 417b15, Aristotle distinguishes two senses: from absence to presence of a quality, and change of the *hexis* (condition) and *physis* (nature).

ALTERATION. Alteration is another term for qualitative change. *Alloiōsis* is **Aristotle**'s standard word for qualitative change; *heteroiōsis* occurs only a couple of times. *See also KINĒSIS, METABOLĒ.*

AMBIGUITY. *See AMPHIBOLIA.*

AMELIUS (Third century CE). Neoplatonist, student of **Numenius** of Apamea and **Plotinus**. He functioned as a secretary to Plotinus, making copious notes of his teachings. He wrote several works of his own that do not survive except as reports in later writers. At the death of Plotinus, he moved (back) to Apamea in Syria.

AMMONIUS (First century CE). Platonist, teacher of **Plutarch of Chaeronea**.

AMMONIUS (c. 440–c. 520 CE). Head of the **Neoplatonist** school in **Alexandria**, he focused attention on the works of **Aristotle**. Ammonius was the son of **Hermeias**, who had studied with **Syrianus** in **Athens**. In turn, Ammonius was the teacher of **Olympiodorus, Damascius** (the last **Scholarch** in Athens), **John Philoponus**, and **Asclepius**. There are extant commentaries by Ammonius on the *Categories, On Interpretation*, and *Prior Analytics*, The commentaries on **Aristotle** of Asclepius and Philoponus reflect his teaching.

AMMONIUS SACCAS (c. 175–242 CE). He merits the title of "the first **Neoplatonist**." The teacher of **Plotinus, Clement**, and **Origen**, he tried to synthesize the teachings of **Plato** and **Aristotle** with the religious and philosophical teachings from the cultures with which he was familiar.

AMPHIBOLIA. Ambiguity. **Chrysippus** wrote extensively on the varieties of ambiguity. According to **Galen**, he distinguished eight different kinds of ambiguity, some of them developments of **Aristotle**'s distinctions between synonymy, paronymy, and homonymy, in the *Categories*, but some of them are interesting observations of the ways in which the Greek language can be abused.

ANAGKĒ, ANANKĒ. Necessity. Early Greek philosophy is regularly concerned with what happens of necessity and, to a lesser extent, what necessarily does not happen. **Anaximander** asserts that things that come to perish again into the indefinite "by necessity" (f. 1); for **Parmenides**, "mighty Necessity" holds **being** in the bonds of limits (f. 8, line 30); **Leucippus** says, "Nothing happens at random, but everything happens for a reason and by necessity" (f. 2).
    In **Plato**'s *Timaeus*, Timaeus' mythic **cosmology** is divided into three sections, the works of reason (*logos*), the works of *anagkē*, and the cooperation of reason and necessity. The "*anagkē*" section features the receptacle (*hypodochē*)—the space-time continuum or the ground of otherness of sensibilia. It is important to recognize that for Plato in the *Timaeus*, the "necessary" is not the predictable and orderly but is

the unpredictable and disorderly that becomes orderly only when subjected to the ordering of mind (*nous*) and reason.

Aristotle distinguishes simple (*haplōs*) necessity from conditional (*ex hypotheseōs*) necessity. Those processes are simply necessary that always happen in the same way: astronomical processes would be a good example. But most natural processes do not *always* happen in the same way. These can be understood by looking at how and to what degree they serve some end. For example, the growth of teeth in such animals as dogs and cats is "conditionally" necessary, since their teeth enable them to get their nutrition, and without them they would not be able to survive. Both of these senses of necessity are contrasted with the "forced" (*biaion*), where a process thwarts some natural end (*Phys.* IV.8, 215a3). This "unnatural" necessity actually accords more with the most frequent popular uses of the term *anagkē*. In non-philosophical contexts, "necessity" is usually "dire" and contrary to inclination and desire.

Although we may see the fragment of Leucippus cited above as an anticipation of the modern concept of "mechanical" necessity, neither Plato nor Aristotle has much time for what we would call "mechanical" necessity.

Epicurus, however, takes seriously the **atomist** assertion of universal causality, and attempts to make room for "free will" by asserting that there is some element of randomness in the movement of the atoms, a "**swerve**," that gives some room for human self-determination.

The **Stoics** asserted an absolutely universal determinism; everything that happens, happens of necessity, to such a degree that when everything that can happen has happened, it all happens again, in exactly the same way. In later antiquity, the debate turned on the concept of "fate." *See HEIMARMENĒ*.

ANALOGIA. Proportion, Analogy. Mathematically, an *analogia* is an equality of ratios (*logoi*). **Aristotle** famously applies proportionality to the idea of justice in *EN* 5.3, where he distinguishes discrete from continuous proportions, geometrical from arithmetic. Aristotle also speaks of different "unities": one in number, one in species, one in genus, and analogically one (*Metaph.* V.6, 1016b30).

In **Epicurean** and **Stoic** epistemology, analogy is one of the ways that concepts arise from perception (*aisthēsis*) (DL VII.53, X.32). **Ci-**

cero argues that the range of our application of the word "good" comes from an application of analogy, a thought that might well go back to Aristotle, *EN* I.6, 1096b28.

ANALOGY. *See ANALOGIA.*

ANAMNĒSIS. Recollection. **Plato**'s **Socrates**, especially in the *Meno, Phaedo, Phaedrus,* and by implication *Timaeus,* uses the **Pythagorean** doctrine of metempsychosis to argue that human knowledge is made possible by experiences of truth (*alētheia*) that souls have between lives. Since the empirical world is not true (not real), it can at best remind us of whatever reality and truth we experienced between lives. Such "recovered memories" may enable us to gain some provisional understanding of sensory experiences, but the objective is to recover as much as possible of the original experience of reality.

ANAPODEIKTON. Unproven, indemonstrable, inconclusive. **Aristotle** talks of the "unproven" opinions of experienced people as valuable evidence in ethical contexts (*EN* VI.11, 1143b12). In the *Prior Analytics,* he notes that some **syllogisms** are "inconclusive" (e.g., II.1), and **Chrysippus** follows that usage and develops it for the propositional calculus for which **Stoic** logicians are famous.

ANAXAGORAS OF CLAZOMENAE (c. 500–428 BCE). Born in Ionia, Anaxagoras moved to **Athens** in the 460s where he became the personal friend and advisor of Pericles. In about 434, he was accused of impiety and was forced to return to Clazomenae. He was notable for his scientific investigations: investigating a meteorite, he concluded that at least some of the astronomical bodies had to be earthy in character; observing fossils of shellfish on the tops of hills, he concluded that the sea must have covered that land at some time. Anaxagoras had a rather unique **cosmological** theory: all sorts of materials are infinitely divisible, and there is a portion of everything in everything. A cosmic Mind (*nous*) sets up a rotation, a vortex, (*dinē*) that tends to separate out similar materials, giving rise ultimately to the various things that we see in the universe. Both **Plato** and **Aristotle** complain, in different ways, about Anaxagoras' failure to give an account of complex entities, so we might conclude that his focus is on the generation of basic materials.

ANAXIMANDER OF MILETUS (c. 610–545 BCE). He wrote a prose book that seems to have been primarily geographical in intent, but the book began with **cosmological** speculations, and it was those that captured the imagination of some of his successors. **Theophrastus** quoted a bit of his text, and that quotation was later preserved by **Simplicius**. Anaximander said that the origin of everything is the *apeiron*, or "indefinite" and that all the "heavens and universes" come to be from it and ultimately necessarily return to the indefinite. "For they give justice and reparation to each other according to the arrangement of time." Anaximander believed that the **earth** is cylindrical in shape, that we live on one of the "flat" (or rather a bit concave) surfaces, and that the earth is in the middle of the universe because there is no reason for it to go anywhere else.

ANAXIMENES OF MILETUS (c. 585–528). Younger contemporary of **Anaximander**, he envisioned the world as enclosed by a membrane that is full of air. He seems to have thought that the contents of the world are all derived somehow from air (*aēr*), by condensing into water and then solidifying. He is quoted as saying, "As our soul, being air, rules and holds us together, so breath and air encompass the whole universe" (DK13b2). He thought of the **earth** as flat and thin, held up by the air like a floating leaf.

ANDREIA. Courage, literally "manliness." Analyzed by **Socrates** in **Plato**'s *Laches*, and *Protagoras* and by **Aristotle** in both the *Eudemian* and *Nicomachean Ethics*.

ANDRONICUS OF RHODES (First century BCE). Andronicus is credited (by **Porphyry**, in the first instance) with editing the works of **Aristotle**, putting them in their current arrangement. He is otherwise said to have been the teacher of **Boethus**.

ANEPIKRITOS. Undecidable, in a fundamental sense. The Skeptics argued that there was no ground or basis for judging . . . anything. *See also SKEPTIKOS.*

ANGEL. *Angelos* in classical Greek is simply a "messenger." The translators of the Septuagint adopted the word to avoid using the word *daimōn*, a word with far too much pagan freight. Incidentally, **Aristotle** remarks at *Progression of Animals* 11, 711a1, that the representation of *Erōtēs* (cupids) with two legs, two arms, and two wings, is biologically impossible; unnatural. That would hold for the standard representation of angels as well.

ANIMA. Latin translation of *psychē*, "soul."

ANIMAL. *See ZOŌN.*

ANOMIA. Lawlessness. **Plato**, *Rep.* IX, 575a, notes the "lawlessness" of the "tyrannical" constitution.

ANTECEDENT CAUSE. *See PROĒGOUMENON AITION.*

ANTHRŌPOS. Human being. This word is often translated "man" but it must be recognized that *anthrōpos* is gender-neutral; the gendered word for "man" would be *anēr*.

ANTIKOPĒ. Collision. In **Epicurean** physics, a collision of **atoms**. If all of the atoms were moving in the same direction at the same speed to start with, why are they moving in all directions today? Two reasons: first, the **swerve**, and second, collisions. *See also PHYSIS.*

ANTIOCHUS OF ASCALON (c. 130–c. 68 BCE). He studied with the **Stoic** Mnesarchus and with **Philo of Larissa** in the **Academy**. He broke with Philo at about the time of Sulla's invasion of **Athens**; after that, he set up his own "Academy" where he taught **Cicero** in 79 BCE.

ANTIPATER OF TARSUS (c. 200–c. 130 BCE). Head of the **Stoic** school in **Athens** between **Diogenes of Babylon** and **Panaetius**. He defended Stoic principles against the skeptical attacks of **Carneades**.

ANTIPATER OF TYRE (1st century BCE). He taught **Stoicism** to Cato in Rome.

ANTIPHON (OF RHAMNOUS?) (c. 479–411 BCE). Sophist who may or may not be the same person as the Athenian orator Antiphon of Rhamnous. One or more individuals with the name Antiphon attempted to square the circle, interpreted dreams and offered psychotherapy, wrote a book *On Truth* that is extant in fragmentary form, wrote and published forensic speeches (several are extant), wrote plays, and was convicted of complicity with the oligarchy and was executed in 411 (thus, the death date cited).

Antiphon the Sophist (author of *On Truth*) contrasts nature and convention (***physis*** and ***nomos***), defending the thesis that convention or law is repressive, but by nature all human beings are free and in principle equal; it is law that makes people unfree and unequal. Some think that those sentiments are inconsistent with the known oligarchical political stance of Antiphon of Rhamnous.

ANTISTHENES OF ATHENS (c. 440–370 BCE). Some take him to be the founder of the **Cynic** school of philosophy. He is said to have studied first with **Gorgias** and then with **Socrates.** Antisthenes was notable for wearing exceedingly ragged and dirty clothing to demonstrate his disdain for material things. Philosophically, he emphasized the centrality of virtue (***aretē***). Antisthenes was the teacher of **Diogenes of Sinope**, who has a better claim to be the first **Cynic**. Some of Antisthenes' ideas reappear in doctrines of the older **Stoics**.

AOCHLĒSIA. Unperturbedness, the goal of life according to **Speusippus** and the **Epicureans**. *See also ATARAXIA.*

AORISTON. Indefinite. In **Stoic** logic, used of a sentence with an indefinite article as subject or predicate. *See also LOGIKĒ.*

APATHEIA. Condition of being unaffected. For **Aristotle**, it is important that the mind (***nous***) is "unaffected," in contrast to the sense organs, which are affected by external causes (*de An.* III.4–6). For the **Stoics**, ***pathē*** are unnatural physical processes that interfere with rational behavior; thus, a condition of *apatheia* is much to be desired.

APAXIA. **Stoic** term for "disvalue."

APEIRON. Literally, "without limit" or "without definition." **Anaximander** says that "the *apeiron*" is the origin of all things; **Theophrastus** understands him as meaning that the *apeiron* is a material substrate that as yet has no characteristics. Some later writers took Anaximander as meaning that the *apeiron* is indefinitely extended space and time.

The idea of infinity in Greek philosophy took a large step forward in the fifth century BCE with the paradoxes of **Zeno of Elea**. He argued, for example, that if space is infinitely divisible, one would have to make an infinite number of moves to go any finite distance, so motion is impossible. **Melissus, Empedocles, Anaxagoras**, and **Democritus** all seem to have believed the universe to be spatially infinite.

Aristotle, in contrast, denied that the universe is spatially infinite. The **Stoics** accepted Aristotle's finite universe but asserted an infinite void outside the universe. **Plato**'s use of "limit" and "unlimited" (*peras* and *apeiron*) in the *Philebus* led to more elaborate conceptual structures based on this contrast in **Neoplatonic** philosophy. The identification of "The One" with the **Form** of the **Good**, on the one hand, and indefinite multiplicity with **matter** and absence of good, on the other, lends a negative evaluative slant to the concept of "indefiniteness" in some late Greek thinkers.

APODEIXIS. Exposition, demonstration, proof. In the *Phaedo*, at 73a, Cebes asks **Socrates** for *apodeixeis* that the soul (*psychē*) has pre-existed this present life. For **Aristotle**, the word tends to be used as a technical term for drawing a conclusion from true premises in a valid **syllogism** (*APo* I.17, 81a40). The word also has this sense for the **Stoics**.

APOGEGENĒMENON. Development. An **Epicurean** term for emergent properties of concatenations of atoms (*atoma*).

APOKATASTASIS. Restoration. In **Stoic** philosophy, the periodic new beginning of the universe after the universal conflagration (*ekpyrosis*); in some **Neoplatonic** philosophers (notably **Proclus**), the reunion of the individual soul (*psychē*) with the **World Soul**; in the **Christian** philosophy of **Origen**, the reconciliation of all parts of the universe with God.

APOLLONIUS OF RHODES (d. 247 BCE). Alexandrian poet, author of *Argonautica*, and head of the Library in **Alexandria**. *See also* MUSEUM AND LIBRARY OF ALEXANDRIA.

APOLLONIUS OF TYANA (2 BCE–98 CE). Probable founder of the **Neopythagorean** movement. His life and teachings are recorded in an extant work by **Philostratus**. This work is so full of claims of miracles performed by Apollonius that modern scholars are tempted to discredit everything said in the book, leaving us with a legend rather than a person. Still, we know that he wrote on a range of subjects, including (apparently) some letters still extant, and that his writings were collected and copied at the command of the Emperor Hadrian (76–138 CE) for wide distribution through the Empire, so it is reasonable to believe that his thought was influential from at least the end of the first century through the second century CE. Indeed, Hierocles (proconsul of Bithynia), in the third century, was still arguing that Apollonius was better than Jesus Christ. Apollonius has continued to attract attention from occultists and mystics from time to time.

APOPROEGMENA. In **Stoic** philosophy, "things dispreferred." *See also ADIAPHORA.*

APORIA. "No path"; puzzle. **Socratic** questioning is designed to lead people to discover that they did not know what they thought they knew, i.e., to an *aporia.* **Aristotle** tends to attack an area of inquiry by gathering the various puzzles surrounding the topic as well as the various opinions of "most people, or the wise, or most of the wise." Generally, Aristotle, unlike **Plato**'s Socrates, sooner or later proposes solutions to most or all of the puzzles posed at the beginning of the inquiry.

APOTELESMA. Literally, "completion," **Stoic** word for the effect of causes.

APPELATIVE. *See PROSEGORIA.*

APPETITE. *See EPITHYMIA.*

APPROPRIATE. The English word is used ambiguously to refer to two different **Stoic** concepts: *kathēkon*, one's moral duty, and *oikeion*, what is proper to oneself, one's own.

APULEIUS OF MADAURA (c. 123–c. 180 CE). Born in North Africa (modern Algeria), he is most widely known for his novel, *The Golden Ass* (*Metamorphoses*). His more philosophical works include "On the God of **Socrates**," "On **Plato**'s Teachings," and "On the Universe." He is counted among the "**middle Platonists**."

ARCESILAUS OF PITANE (c. 316–c. 241 BCE). Scholarch of the **Academy** after **Polemon** and **Crates**; he initiated the period of Academic Skepticism. *See also SKEPTIKOS.*

ARCHĒ. Origin, beginning, source, rule. **Heraclitus** says (f. 70), "In a circle, the beginning (*archē*) and end are common." **Alcmaeon** says (f. 2), "People are unable to connect the end with the beginning." From an Aristotelian point of view, the early Greek philosophers were seeking the "origin" of all things, for the most part the *material* origin. When **Aristotle** distinguishes the senses of the word, he begins from immanent starting points (the heart of a living being, for example) and external origins (the parents of the child, for example). In another sense, it means the ruling authority. Importantly, the basis on which something is known is the *archē,* so not only the material and moving causes are *archai,* but in a way all the causes, including formal and final (Aristotle, *Metaph.* III.1). *See also AITION.*

ARCHĒ KINĒSEŌS. The Aristotelian cause with which *archē* is most closely associated is the *moving* cause, since **Aristotle**'s most normal way of referring to it is *archē kinēseōs,* or "beginning of movement." *See also KINĒSIS.*

ARCHELAUS OF ATHENS (?) (Fifth century BCE). He is thought to be a student or associate of **Anaxagoras,** mentioned most explicitly by **Diogenes Laertius** and **Hippolytus.** If he was indeed an Athenian, he was the first of the city to become a philosopher. His views include the opinion that Mind (*nous*) is closely associated with Air (*aēr*), an idea going back to **Anaximenes** and shared with **Diogenes of Apollonia**. The "air" theory of the soul (*psychē*) and mind (*nous*) is put into the mouth of **Socrates** in **Aristophanes'** *Clouds*, suggesting that in the popular mind, Socrates was associated with one or both of these cosmologists at the time of the production of the play (423 BCE).

ARCHIMEDES OF SYRACUSE (287–212 BCE). Mathematician, scientist, and inventor. Although not normally counted among the standard "philosophers," his theoretical mathematical work had, and in some ways continues to have, implications for theoretical physics and **cosmology**. His *Sandreckoner*, for example, presents a way of representing symbolically the number of grains of sand it would take to fill up the known universe (of his time), 8×10^{63} in modern notation. He also significantly improved the accuracy of the calculation of the calculation of π.

ARCHYTAS OF TARENTUM (Late fifth to mid-fourth century BCE). Archytas was a **Pythagorean**, roughly contemporary with **Plato**. As political leader of Tarentum, he rescued Plato from Dionysius II of Syracuse in 361 BCE. While it is difficult to know just how much of the work attributed to him is really his, it does seem clear that he made significant advances in mathematics and is a significant source of the "Pythagorean" aspects of Plato's philosophy. *See also MATHĒMA.*

ARETĒ. Virtue, Excellence. The **Sophists** claimed to instruct their students in *aretē*, which meant for them any teachable human excellence, but particularly those which would help their students to become social and political leaders. Skill in persuasion and public speaking, and techniques of leadership, were among their promised outcomes.

Plato's **Socrates** repeatedly challenged their practice and the assumptions upon which it rests, calling attention to the moral dimension of each conventional human excellence and of the general concept of human excellence. Although individual virtues are examined in one dialogue or another—temperance or moderation (*sōphrosynē*), courage (*andreia*), piety (*hosiotēs*), justice (*dikaiosynē*), wisdom (*sophia*)—they always seem to be systematically interrelated and are most likely all dependent on wisdom, but a wisdom that often seems beyond the possibility of instruction.

Aristotle, however, tries to provide individual accounts of the virtues (in *Nicomachean Ethics* III–V) that hold out the possibility of successfully exhibiting some of the virtues without necessarily having them all. Many of the virtues are represented as a mean between extremes. For example, courage is a mean between foolhardiness and cowardice, so it seems possible that someone might more or less hit the mark with some virtues and not with others. The **Stoics** return to the Socratic ideal with a vengeance, since they propose that there is a theoretical person who is completely wise (*sophos*) and consequently has *all* of the virtues—and no one else really has any of them, since when it comes to perfection, a miss is as good as a mile.

ARGUMENT. *See LOGOS.*

ARISTARCHUS OF SAMOS (c. 310–230 BCE). Astronomer and mathematician, he studied with **Strato of Lampsacus** in **Alexandria**. He asserted a heliocentric solar system (anticipating Copernicus) and made a serious attempt to calculate the distance of the moon, sun, and stars from **earth** on the basis of careful observations, preserved in *On the Sizes and Distances of the Sun and the Moon*. That he was not believed by other ancient scientists should not detract from his accomplishment.

ARISTIPPUS OF CYRENE (c. 435–356 BCE). Aristippus was a disciple of **Socrates** and founder of the **Cyrenaic school** (Cyrene is near Benghazi, in modern Libya). As an ethical hedonist, Aristippus anticipated **Epicurus**. He was succeeded as **Scholarch** by his daughter Arete (probably the first woman to direct an ancient philosophical school) and his grandson Aristippus. The stories told about Aristippus in **Diogenes Laertius** sound a bit like attempts to show dramatically that hedonism is a shameful theory, but some of them might nevertheless be true. *See also HĒDONĒ.*

ARISTO OF CHIOS (Mid-third century BCE). Aristo was a **Stoic**, a student of **Zeno of Citium**. Aristo seems to have taken a hard line, limiting philosophy to moral issues and favoring some **Cynic** positions.

ARISTOPHANES (c. 448–380 BCE). Aristophanes was a comic poet, the author of 11 surviving plays, the only complete pieces of "old comedy" from **Athens** still extant. Several of his plays reflect philosophical discussion current in his society. The *Clouds* presents **Socrates** as a major character, propounding a mixture of views attributed by historians of philosophy to **Anaxagoras**, **Diogenes of Apollonia**, **Protagoras**, and **Prodicus**. In **Plato**'s *Apology*, Socrates is represented as obliged to disavow the opinions expressed in that play, written some 25 years before his trial. The play clearly shaped public opinion about philosophy in general and Socrates in particular; if taken at its word, it provides a good deal of evidence that Socrates had clearly "un-Athenian" religious opinions, and that he corrupted the young, the character Pheidippides in particular.

Aristophanes reflects ongoing philosophical discussion also in the *Ecclesiasuzae*, for example, with its utopian communitarianism anticipating Plato's *Republic*. Aristophanes appears as a character himself in Plato's *Symposium*, where he is represented as presenting an especially vivid myth designed to explain various sexual preferences. It is likely that Plato was influenced by Aristophanes' dramatic techniques in his composition of the dialogues.

ARISTOTLE OF STAGIRA (384–322 BCE). Ancient Stagira was on the coast of the Chalcidike, northwest of Mount Athos; there is a modern village of Stagira inland. Aristotle's father, Nicomachus, was court physician of the Macedonian king, Amyntas II, the father of Philip II and grandfather of **Alexander**. Both Nicomachus, and Aristotle's mother, Phaestis, were from Aesclepiad families; both died when Aristotle was young. His guardian, Proxenus, sent him to **Plato**'s **Academy** at age 17; Aristotle remained there as a student and teacher for 20 years, until nearly the time of the death of Plato in 347.

Around the time of the death of Plato, Aristotle traveled to visit Hermias, satrap (subsidiary ruler under the Persians) of Atarneus in what is now northwest Turkey. He was accompanied by **Xenocrates** and joined Erastus and Coriscus; the whole group settled for a time in Assos, a town across from the island of Lesbos, home of **Theophrastus**; the group moved at some point to Lesbos. During this time Aristotle met Pythias, who would later become his wife. He also carried out a good deal of biological investigation and probably wrote some of his critiques of Platonism.

In 343, Aristotle returned to Macedonia, invited by Philip II to be tutor of Alexander, who was 13 at the time. In 340, Alexander became regent, ending the educational relationship. It is not clear whether Aristotle remained in Macedonia, or went to Stagira, or returned to Lesbos until 335, when, under pressure from Alexander, the Athenians agreed to allow the non-citizen Aristotle to operate a school in **Athens**.

During this period Pythias died, and Aristotle began a relationship with Herpyllis which continued until his death. He opened his school in the **Lyceum** and operated it for the next 12 years. At the death of Alexander in 323, anti-Macedonian feeling in Athens led to charges being made against him and he retired to Chalcis, where he died in 322.

The body of Aristotle's writings, known collectively as the **Corpus** Aristotelicum, was organized in antiquity according to topic and in some cases according to indications left by Aristotle himself in the text. The first group of writings is known collectively as the *Organon*, or "Tool"; it includes the *Categories*, *On Interpretation*, *Prior Analytics*, *Posterior Analytics*, *Topics*, and *Sophistical Refutations*. At its most basic level, the *Organon* is a study of language; from that perspective, the *Categories* examines predication, specifically the kinds of predicates there are; *On Interpretation* looks at declarative sentences and their potential truth value; the *Prior Analytics* develops an account of syllogistic reasoning; and the *Posterior Analytics* looks at how we find the premises for **syllogistic** arguments. *Topics* is a study of where to find arguments, and *Sophistical Refutation* is a study of bad arguments.

From the *Organon*, one could proceed to any part of Aristotle's philosophical work; in a way, a natural direction would be to the study of *Rhetoric* and *Poetics*, but those works are tucked in at the end of the Corpus. Instead, the Corpus proceeds to Natural Philosophy. The *Physics, Generation and Corruption, On the Heavens, Meteorologics*, for what we would call the "inorganic" world; then we have *On the Soul*, several short psychobiological treatises known as the *Short Natural Treatises* (*Parva Naturalia*), and several frankly zoological books: *History of Animals, Parts of Animals, Generation of Animals, Movement of Animals*, and *Progression of Animals*. If we count up the total number of pages, the biological part of Aristotle's work is a very significant proportion—nearly a third of the entire corpus.

After the books on natural philosophy, we find a longish treatise, in 14 books, called the **Metaphysics**. In the *Metaphysics*, as in several of his other works, Aristotle locates his philosophical position in relation to his predecessors and constructs a systematic interpretation of many of the issues that had vexed earlier philosophers.

The *Metaphysics* is followed by several works on **ethics** and politics—the *Nicomachean Ethics*, the *Eudemian Ethics*, and a work called the *Magna Moralia*, as well as the *Politics*. The *Nicomachean* and *Eudemian Ethics* partially overlap, as if one were a partial revision of the other, although there is no complete agreement about which came first. The *Nicomachean Ethics* has been the one most usually studied ever since a commentary was constructed by several Greek writers, and the whole thing translated into Latin by Robert Grosseteste (1170–1253 CE) and his helpers. Also, the *Nicomachean Ethics* is closely tied to the *Politics*, almost as if they were one continuous work.

The series of treatises continues with the *Rhetoric* and the *Poetics*, full of recommendations on how to construct effective literary compositions. Added to the Corpus in the late 19th century was a "Constitution of **Athens**," accepted by many as written by Aristotle himself and by others as the work of a colleague in the **Lyceum** at the same period as Aristotle. Several more works are traditionally included in the Corpus but are not generally regarded as by Aristotle, and there are a number of compositions not listed here that exist only in fragmentary form.

Systematically, Aristotle's philosophy is based on his revised conception of what exists primarily, *ousia*. Rejecting the apparent tendency of most early Greek philosophers to take "**matter**" as primary existence, and the explicit position of the **Pythagoreans** and **Plato** to assert the primacy of form (*eidos*), Aristotle follows the lead of the Greek language in asserting that the sorts of things that are named as subjects of normal declarative sentences are most likely to count as primary existences—individual persons and animals, and natural kinds, are the best candidates. Natural kinds have the virtue of being clearly definable, and that definition can state clearly what sorts of things can belong to that natural kind.

Since natural kinds are primary existences, Aristotle turns to the examination of nature (*physis*), defining it as "source or cause of changing or not changing in that to which it belongs primarily." The causative aspect of nature may be according to any one or more of the four "causes" (*aitia*), **matter** (*hylē*), mover (*kinoun*), form (*eidos*), and end (*telos*).

Paradigmatic of natural things are *living* things, entities with a soul (*psychē*); the soul is the cause of the body in the sense of mover, form, and end. And the paradigm for living beings is the human person. The soul is defined as the first level of **actuality** of a natural living body with organs; the various functions of the soul are present in the organic parts as their activity. The only possible exception to that rule, according to Aristotle, is the mind (*nous*), which appears to enter in "from outside" and to be in some way independent of any particular organic part.

Just as each organic part has its function, so (Aristotle believes) the whole person has a function, namely "virtuous activity." That activity must, of course, be carried out in a social context. Human beings are language-using animals, and the primary function of language is to enable people to function within a social environment. Achievement of the best possible functioning is, for Aristotle, *eudaimonia*, human happiness.

Similarly the society (*polis*) that maximizes the opportunities for its members to achieve the greatest human functioning of which they are capable is the happiest society.

ARISTOXENUS (c. 370–300 BCE). Aristoxenus was a student of **Aristotle** who wrote on music, preserved in a work called *Elementa Harmonica*. He also wrote biographies of various philosophers, preserved in fragments.

ARITHMOS. Number. **Pythagoras** is reputed to have brought the theory that everything is composed of numbers from **Egypt**. There may be some truth to the tale, for the Egyptians did indulge in some number-mysticism. At any rate, the Pythagoreans developed the concept of number and its application in many areas, only some of which make sense to us today. First, one must recognize that "*arithmos*" has not only ordinal and cardinal meanings (as the English word "number") but also refers readily to quantity. Further, the Pythagoreans tended to identify cardinal numbers with geometrical figures. If "three" is the triangle, then it might be concluded that "two" is the line, and "one" is the point (*stigmē*). Going in the other direction, "four" may be the tetrahedron, the first three-dimensional figure that can be constructed out of straight lines and flat surfaces.

Early Pythagoreans also interested themselves in mathematical ratios, e.g., in musical harmonies and overtones, supporting the thesis that the world is fundamentally arithmetical or geometrical in nature (cf. **Aristotle** *Metaph.* I.5, 985b23ff). Aristotle finds it odd that the Pythagoreans went on to assert that things like Justice (*dikaiosynē*), Mind (*nous*), and Opportunity are also "numbers" in some way.

In *Metaphysics* I, and elsewhere, Aristotle says that **Plato** followed the Pythagorean lead, particularly in asserting that the Forms (*eidē*) are in fact numbers. There is not a lot of evidence supporting that assertion in the dialogues, but Aristotle knew Plato for 20 years, so we have to assume that he knew what he was talking about. For Aristotle, numbers are not *ousia* but are rather predicates in the category of quantity. That is, the things that are measured or counted pre-exist the measuring and counting.

Plotinus asserts that numbers do belong to the intelligible world, but he rejects the Pythagorean number-mysticism that had become popular (again) in his time, *Enn.* VI.6.

ARIUS DIDYMUS OF ALEXANDRIA (Before 70–after 9 BCE). Arius was a well-known philosopher in **Alexandria** when Augustus defeated Cleopatra in 30 BCE; Augustus invited him to become the court philosopher of newly Imperial Rome. Arius seems to have written *On Sects* and *Epitome*, both **doxographies,** possibly different parts of the same book. His goal seems to have been to highlight points of agreement among the various philosophical positions. **Stobaeus** includes many passages of Arius' work, particularly sections on **Stoic** and **Aristotelian ethics**.

ARRIAN. Lucius Flavius Arrianus (c. 92–c. 175 CE). Known to historians of philosophy primarily for his nearly stenographic reports of the *Discourses* of **Epictetus,** he also wrote a very important account of the campaigns of **Alexander of Macedon**, the *Anabasis Alexan-*

dri, and a report of the voyage back from **India** of the Macedonian fleet under Nearchus, the *Indica*. In addition to his literary career, Arrian also was active as a military and political leader; his written accounts of his military campaigns continue to be of interest to military historians.

ART. There does not seem to be much of a concept of "art" distinct from "***technē***" in antiquity. That is, *technē* denominates a learnable skill; to the extent that products (***poiēseis***) are attributed to divine inspiration there seems to be no ground for either praising or blaming the "artist" who has been, after all, only the medium for the work of the Muses (*see **mousikē***). That is the point of view of most philosophers from **Plato** (*Ion, Republic*) onward. At the same time, some writers were rather confident that the skills involved could be analyzed and taught; **Aristotle**'s *Poetics* bears witness to that confidence.

ARTEMIDORUS OF EPHESUS (Second century CE). Author of *Onirocriticon*, or the *Interpretation of Dreams*, an extant text. An earlier (c. 100 BCE) person with the same name was a geographer, quoted by **Strabo**.

ASCLEPIUS. The Greek **God** of healing and medicine (***iatrikē***). Asclepius was credited with founding the guild of ancient physicians. Throughout antiquity temples of Asclepius were favored goals for pilgrimages by people in ill health. The most famous Asclepeion was at Epidaurus; another was on Cos, associated with **Hippocrates**.

At least by the Hellenistic era, and possibly earlier, the Greek deity was identified with the Egyptian deity Imhotep. In that guise, Asclepius plays an important role in several of the treatises included in the Hermetic **Corpus** (*see* HERMES TRISMEGISTUS).

When **Socrates** says to Crito at the end of the *Phaedo* that they must sacrifice a cock to Asclepius, it is not entirely clear whether he has only the Greek deity in mind.

ASCLEPIUS OF TRALLES (465 CE–?). Student, in **Alexandria**, of **Ammonius son of Hermias;** his notes from two courses taught by Ammonius survive: on **Aristotle**'s *Metaphysics* and on **Nicomachus'** *Elements of Arithmetic*.

ASŌMATON. Without body, disembodied, incorporeal. **Plato** clearly believed that the Forms (*eidē*) are incorporeal, and that souls (*psychai*) can be separated from body, and can be incorporeal, but he rarely used the word *asōmaton*. One place where it does occur is in *Sophist* 246ff, in the passage called the Battle of Gods and Giants; the "Giants" are those who claim that only that which is bodily is real, while the "Gods" hold that some incorporeal things exist.

Aristotle is committed to the existence of *asōmata* (*Metaph.* I.8), although he is not very explicit about what the incorporeals are. Judging from *Physics* IV, one would conclude that at least place and time are incorporeal. For the **Epicureans**, the only incorporeal is empty space or the void; the **Stoics** list four "incorporeals": *lekta* (sayables), *kenon* (void), *topos* (place), and *chronos* (time).

ASPASIA (c. 469 BCE–?). Ionian-born mistress of Pericles, she was given much credit—and blame—for introduction of Ionian ideas, and young women, into **Athens**, and for advising Pericles. In **Plato's** *Menexenus*, **Socrates** credits her with teaching him oratory and with writing both Pericles' famous funeral oration and the alternative version included in that dialogue.

ASSENT. *Synkatathesis.* In **Stoic** epistemology, one gives one's assent to a reasonable perceptual presentation; this is a matter of accepting the presentation as veridical.

ASTRA. Stars. (The singular is either *astēr* or *astron*). Judging from later **doxographers**, the **Presocratic**s tended to have a variety of opinions about the stars in particular. For one thing, there was a difference of opinion about whether the stars (fixed stars, as distinguished from planets) were all located on the inside surface of one great sphere surrounding the rest of the astronomical entities, with the **Earth** (or solar system) in the center, or were scattered at different distances through an indefinitely large space. The former was the majority opinion in antiquity, including both **Plato** and **Aristotle**; the latter was the view of the **atomists** and may have been the view of **Anaximander**.

Another difference of opinion concerns whether the stars are living divine beings or inanimate material entities. The author of the

Epinomis, ascribed to Plato, and Aristotle in *Metaphysics* XII, sub-scribe to the "living deity" theory; **Anaxagoras**, along with the atom-ists, gets credit for the inanimate theory. *See also* ASTRONOMY.

ASTROLOGIA. As a Greek term, this word at first simply means "**as-tronomy**"; there is a disambiguating Greek term, *astromanteia*, that signifies the art of foretelling the future by observation of the stars. Still, after the time of **Aristotle** (more or less) until quite modern times it is rather difficult to distinguish "astronomy" from "astrol-ogy" since a major source of income for people who studied the stars was the provision of predictions supposedly based on their studies. We should note that the Hellenes gained a great deal of their knowl-edge of astronomical phenomena from the **Egyptians**, Babylonians, and other peoples of North Africa and the Middle East, and for all of those cultures the motivations for investigation were often as much astrological as anything else.

Both **Cicero** and **Sextus Empiricus**, to mention only two, recog-nized that the pretenses of astrological predictions did not make sense.

ASTRONOMY. Much ancient speculation was inspired by contempla-tion of the sun, moon, stars, and planets. A fairly complex astronom-ical theory can already by attributed to **Anaximander**. Even **Hera-clitus** and **Parmenides**, better known for other issues, are cited by ancient **doxographers** for their astronomical views. Heraclitus says, "The limit of East and West is the Bear; and opposite the Bear is the boundary of bright Zeus" (f.120). Parmenides says of the moon, "Shining by night with borrowed light, wandering round the **Earth**," "Always straining her eyes to the beams of the sun" (f. 14 and 15).

Plato's *Timaeus* reflects **Pythagorean** astronomical views. **Eu-doxus of Cnidus**, an associate of Plato in the **Academy**, made seri-ous studies attempting to explain the movements of the planets; his astronomy is, in part, reflected in **Aristotle**'s *Metaphysics* XII. **Her-aclides of Pontus**, Aristotle's younger contemporary, suggested that Earth rotates and that Venus and Mercury orbit the Sun.

Aristarchus of Samos (310–230 BCE), at the Library of **Alexan-dria**, wrote *On the Sizes and Distances of the Sun and the Moon.* **Hip-parchus** of Nicaea increased the accuracy of those distances rather considerably and calculated the length of the year to an accuracy within 6.5 minutes. **Claudius Ptolemy** of Alexandria synthesized all previous astronomy in his work known as the Almagest. *See also AS-TROLOGIA.*

ATARAXIA. Freedom from disturbance, tranquility of the soul (*psychē*). Among Greek philosophers, *ataraxia* was widely supposed to be true *eudaimonia.* This thesis was attributed to **Democritus** by **Arius Didymus** (DK I.129) and is well attested for **Pyrrho of Elis**, the Skeptic, and **Epicurus.** The sentiment, if not the word, is also **Stoic.** For the Skeptics, *ataraxia* is achieved by suspension of judgment. *See also SKEPTIKOS.*

ATAXIA. Disorder. Primarily used to mean lack of discipline in a military unit, since *taxis* is primarily military order, this word is applied by **Plato** to the social disorder that **Socrates** would find in Thessaly, were he to accept Crito's offer of an escape plan (*Crito* 53d), and by **Aristotle** to the supposed "anarchy" of a radical **democracy** (*Pol.* V.3, 1302b28).

ATHANATOS. Immortal, Deathless. **Heraclitus** says, "Mortals are immortals (*athanatoi*) and immortals are mortals, the one living the other's death and dying the other's life" (f.62).

In early Greek thought, there are approximately four different kinds of theory that would allow for some sort of immortality. One common early Greek notion was that the **God**s, and some others specially favored by the Gods, do not die, but most people do; that is behind the statement of Heraclitus in f.62. A variant of that idea, known to at least some Greeks, was the **Egyptian** idea that some favored individuals could be bodily resurrected.

A second kind of theory proposed that some material principle, widespread in the universe, provides the basis of life and mind (*nous*). The aēr of **Anaximenes**, for example, would provide a certain immortality but not individual immortality.

Third, the Pythagorean/Orphic idea of *metempsychosis* offered individual immortality via rebirth in a new person (or animal or plant); this process of rebirth was seen (as it continues to be seen today in Buddhism, for example) as a consequence of the defects of the individual soul (*psychē*). **Empedocles** provides particularly poignant details of this sort of immortality.

Fourth, the mind (*nous*) of **Anaxagoras** or **Aristotle**, since un-mixed with **matter**, appears to be "deathless."

Socrates in the *Phaedo* provides several arguments for the im-mortality of the soul; the kinship of the soul with the Forms (*eidē*) is a particularly Platonic argument.

In later Greek philosophy the **Epicureans** totally rejected the idea of immortality, actually presenting the mortality of the soul as a kind of "gospel" in that one need not worry about possible punishment af-ter death or in some other reborn life. Orthodox **Stoics** also did not believe in immortality of the soul. **Neoplatonists**, on the other hand, had no doubt at all about immortality.

ATHENS. Although not the location where Greek philosophy began — that honor belongs to Miletus and second prize to southern Italy and Sicily — by the mid-fifth century Athens was the center of Greek cul-ture, mainly as a consequence of Athens' leadership against the Per-sian invasions of 490 and 480/79 BCE. Philosophically sophisticated **Sophists** from Ionia and Italy/Sicily arrived in Athens, and soon Athenians were taking the lead intellectually — **Archelaus**, **Socrates**, and **Plato**, for three. The establishment of permanent schools by **An-tisthenes**, **Isocrates**, and Plato, and later by **Aristotle**, in the fourth century, solidified Athens' leadership, since now students were drawn from the whole Greek world, and beyond.

Athens' role as an intellectual center very largely outlived its role as a political powerhouse. With the invasion of Sulla in 86 BCE, Athens became totally dependent on Rome, from a political perspec-tive, but continued to be a leading educational center until 529 CE, when the last philosophical school was closed by order of the Em-peror Justinian. *See also* ACADEMY; GARDEN; LYCEUM; STOA.

ATOM. *See ATOMON.*

ATOMISM, ATOMIST SCHOOL. Leucippus, **Democritus**, and the **Epicureans** believed that the world divides into indivisible entities. The theory may be seen as a response to the **Eleatic** thesis that being is one and thus that there is no real change. The Atomists held that since being is many, change does indeed occur, fundamentally in terms of the relative positions of atoms to each other. Interestingly,

Plato never names either Leucippus or Democritus, although he may refer to them obliquely sometimes as those who claim that nothing is real except that which one can lay one's hands upon.

Aristotle understands the Atomists as the most consistent, and radical, of earlier materialists and consequently refers to them frequently as proponents of one of the two major theories in opposition to his own, the other being the formalism of the **Pythagoreans** and Plato. *See also* MATTER.

ATOMON, ATOMA. Atom, the uncutable smallest bit of **matter** according to **Democritus** and other ancient Atomists. Atoms are internally changeless, partless, ungenerated, and undestroyed. Complex entities are formed by many atoms sticking together in various ways. **Epicurus** presents his version of the atomic theory in the *Letter to Herodotus*, primarily. An extensive account is presented in **Lucretius**, *de Rerum Natura*.

ATTENTION. In **Epicurean** epistemology, *epibolē*.

ATTEST. *EPIMARTYREIN.* "Attestation" is a primary criterion (*kritērion*) of **truth** in **Epicurean** epistemology.

ATTICUS (Late second century CE). Leading **Platonist** in **Athens** after **Taurus**; possibly the first occupant of the Chair of Platonism established by the Emperor **Marcus Aurelius** in 176 CE. We have from him a radical attack on Aristotelianism, preserved by **Eusebius**, in the *Praeparatio Evangelica*. "Atticus" means "of Athens"; as a proper name it suggests some relationship to the Atticus family. *See also* HERODES ATTICUS.

ATTRIBUTE. In the sense of "predicate," this is one of the ways that *symbebēkos* is translated into English.

AUGUSTINE, BISHOP OF HIPPO (354–430 CE). Saint (Aurelius) Augustinus was born in Tagaste (now in Algeria) and educated at Madaura and Carthage. He joined a group of **Neoplatonists** in Milan; according to his *Confessions*, his conversations there led him away from his interest in **Manicheanism**, and under the influence of his mother, he converted to **Christianity**.

His most famous works are the *Confessions* and the *City of God*, although his critique of Academic Skepticism in *Against the Academicians* has considerable philosophic interest as well. His extensive writings are available in the original Latin and in translation. *See also SKEPTIKOS*.

AULOS. An ancient Greek musical instrument with a single or double reed; the *aulos* was very commonly played in pairs, attached to the same mouthpiece. The closest thing to a classic *aulos* seen and heard today would be the chanter on a bagpipe, minus the bag of course; a double *aulos* is even closer to a bagpipe, since the performer can play a rudimentary duet. This entry is included because the *aulos* appears several times in philosophical texts, and English translators persist in translating it as "flute," failing to make sense of the passages in question. In *Republic* III, 399d4, **Plato** bans the *aulos* from the ideal state but turns around and permits the pan-pipe, which is really rather similar to a "flute." But the *aulos* is a Dionysian instrument, regarded a suitable for Bacchic revels, *orgiastikē*, as **Aristotle** says at *Pol.* VIII.7, 1342b. Aristotle also says, at *EN* X.5, 1175b3, that it is hard to do philosophy while listening to someone playing the *aulos*. Think bagpipe, not flute.

AULUS GELLIUS (c. 125–after 180 CE). Author of *Attic Nights*, recounting after-dinner discussions in Athens in the mid-second century. This work is a significant source of information about intellectual life, including philosophy, in the period.

AURELIUS, ANTONINUS MARCUS (121–180 CE). Emperor of Rome from 161 to 180, author of the work known as *Meditations*, an application of **Stoic** principles to the problems of his life.

AUTARKEIA. Self-sufficiency. Many Greek philosophers regarded *autarkeia* as a major life goal. As **Aristotle** puts it *(EN* I.7, 1097b7), "The complete good is thought to be self-sufficient." Thus, the theoretical life is regarded as the best, partly on the ground that it is most self-sufficient (*EN* X. 7, 1177a27). On a more mundane level, **Democritus** tells us (f. 246), "Living in foreign lands teaches self-sufficiency: black bread and snow are the sweetest cures for hunger and pain." That virtue (*aretē*), or the virtuous person, is self-sufficient, is a normal part of Hellenistic and Imperial ethical theories. **Epicurus**, *Letter to Menoeceus*, 130; for **Stoics**, DL 7.127; **Plotinus** *Enn.* I.4.3. Even in the New Testament we find the argument that **God** can provide for your *autarkeia*: *Second Letter to the Corinthians* 9.8.

AUTOMATON. Self-moved. *To automaton* is, for **Aristotle**, a name for random events, those that happen *kata symbebēkos*. (*See* ACCIDENT.) In a related sense, Aristotle believes that some plants and animals are generated not by parents of the same species, but "spontaneously." He uses the word *automata* of such "self-generated" entities.

"Automata" in the modern sense, mechanical devices that appear to have the capacity of self-movement, occur as conceptual ideas in ancient philosophical texts. **Plato** refers to the idea that Daedalus constructed self-moving statues (*Meno* 97d, *Euthyphro* 11b); Aristotle talks of the "marvelous self-moving puppets" *(tōn thaumatōn tautomata)* (*Metaph.* I.2, 983a14; *GA* II.1, 734b10; *Movement of Animals* 7, 701b2). The self-moving puppets are used to illustrate the point that if there are many built-in potentialities, it takes only a small initial cause to bring about many large changes. Modeling of this kind has contributed to the development of scientific thought. *See also* ACCIDENT.

AUXILIARY (CAUSE). *See SYNERGON.*

AXIA. Worth, value. Both **Plato** and **Aristotle** use this word both of the monetary "value" of something, and of worth or value in less tangible respects. The **Stoics** tend to use it of moral worth particularly.

AXIŌMA. Axiom, basic principle. **Aristotle** uses this word for propositions that are fundamental for demonstrations, both in philosophical and mathematical arguments. This usage was picked up by the **Stoics**, and has been standard ever since.

– B –

BASIL OF CAESAREA (330–379 CE). With **Gregory Nazianzus** and **John Chrysostom**, Basil is one of the three Cappadocian Fathers who are regarded by the Eastern Orthodox Church with special respect. A student of **Origen**, Basil wrote what Christians take to be the definitive defense and explanation of the divinity of the Holy Spirit (*Hagion Pneuma*).

BEAUTY. *To Kalon* is often translated as "Beauty" in **Plato** translations. Thus, the famous "**Form** of the **Good**" is also the "**Idea** of Beauty." The identification of "Good" with "Beauty" becomes especially close in the *Symposium* and *Phaedrus* when **Socrates** interprets erotic attraction as ultimately aimed not at this individual person but at the abstract "beauty itself" in which this attractive person participates or which he or she imitates in his or her body (*sōma*) and soul (*psychē*). *See also EIDOS; IDEA; KALON.*

BECOMING. In **Plato** and some other ancient philosophers, becoming is contrasted with "**being**." According to perspective, there are two sorts of things that we can investigate, those that are involved in change, or "becoming," and those that do not change at all, and are (timeless) "being." The fullest account of this relationship in Plato is in the *Timaeus*. **Aristotle**, in contrast, tries to show how being (*ousia*, in terminology that he shares with Plato) is directly involved in becoming, how, for example, a living thing can both be an entity (*ousia*) and have come to be and be the origin of other living things that come to be, in a process of *genesis* or generation, for example by sexual reproduction. *See also GENESIS.*

BEGINNING. *See ARCHĒ.*

BEING. The closest equivalent to the word "being" in ancient Greek is *to on*, the present participle of *einai*, to be (*ON, ONTA*). The first part of **Parmenides'** poem has as its focus *esti*, the third person singular of *einai*, and *to eon*, the equivalent of *to on* in Parmenides' dialect. For Parmenides, "being" (*to on*) is one, timeless and changeless, and this, he says, is "the **truth**"; all talk about plurality and change is "opinion" (*doxa*), and not the truth about "being."

Since *to on* and *ta onta* are, in ordinary Greek, often used as stand-ins for names of one or more individual things, other Greek philosophers looked for other locutions to talk about "being" in ontologically loaded contexts. One of **Plato**'s favorite locutions to refer to the forms (*eidē*) is *to ontōs on*, using the adverb made from the participle to intensify its meaning, literally, "the beingly being," but typically translated into English as "the really real." *Ontōs* was in common use to mean, roughly, "really" or "actually" or "in fact" but combining it with the participle seems to be Plato's coinage.

Plato also adopts the abstract noun built on the same participle, *ousia*, the stem *ont*—plus the abstract noun ending—*sia*. In ordinary Greek, this word must have some of the resonance that "existence" has in ordinary English, but it is most often used, outside of philosophical contexts, to talk about property or wealth or about important personal characteristics. In English translations of Plato's dialogues, the word *ousia* is sometimes rendered "Reality" and sometimes "being," while in English translations of **Aristotle** the word "being" fairly reliably translates "*to on*," and *ousia* is typically translated "substance" or "entity" (*see OUSIA*).

Thus, in those of Plato's dialogues where the forms play a role the distinction between being and becoming is equivalent to the distinction between forms and phenomena (*phainomena*), or between Object of knowledge (*epistēmē*) and object of opinion (*doxa*).

Aristotle does not use the locution *to ontōs on*; apart from his exceedingly widespread use of the word *ousia*. we may note the locution *to on hē on*, typically translated "being qua being," and *to on haplōs* (that which simply is). More generally, Aristotle frequently talks of the many senses of "being": in one way, "being" (*to einai*, the infinitive, or *to on*) has as many senses as the categories (i.e., 10), but there is also a distinction between potential and actual being, between essential and **accidental**, and an equation of being and truth.

The **Stoics** tend to use the word *hyparchein* for both existence and predication.

BELIEF. *See DOXA; PISTIS.*

BELONG. *See HYPARCHEIN; OIKEION;* PREDICATE.

BENEFIT. *See ŌPHELĒMA.*

BIOS. Life. "The name of the Bow is 'life' but its work is death" (**Heraclitus** f. 48); the distinction depends on which syllable is accented. *Bios* is distinguished from *zōē* in that *zōē* is primarily "animal" life, while *bios* is simple survival, or a way of life (way of surviving). In a striking phrase, **Aristotle** says of the pre-quickening fetus that it "lives the life of a plant," *zēn phytou bion*. At the other end of things, so to speak, Aristotle talks in the *Politics* of the "lives" of different peoples, such as nomadic, agricultural, fishing, hunting, and so on. In the *Nicomachean Ethics* Book I, he focuses on the "best" kind of life, and how it is a comparison between the life devoted to maximizing pleasure versus the life devoted to achieving fame and honors versus the life of the mind (***nous***) (the life of money-making regarded only as a means to one of these). It is not surprising that the Philosopher affirms that the theoretical life (*bios theoretikos*) is the best, and the community life (*bios politikos*) second best.

BLEND. *See KRAMA; KRASIS; MIGMA; MIXIS; SYNTHESIS.*

BODY. *See SŌMA.*

BOETHIUS (Anicius Manlius Severinus Boethius, c. 480–524/6 CE). Boethius wrote *The Consolation of Philosophy* and quite a few theological and philosophical treatises. He took upon himself the task of translating into Latin and commenting on the works of **Aristotle** and other classical Greek philosophers but had done only the *Categories* and *On Interpretation*, plus **Porphyry**'s *Isagoge*, when his translating career was brought to an abrupt end by his imprisonment on religious and political grounds, followed some time later by his execution at the hands of Theodoric the Great (454–526). We do have his studies of much of the rest of the *Organon*, perhaps on the way to translating them, including *Introductio ad syllogismos categoricos, De syllogismos categoricos, De hypotheticis syllogismis, De diuisione, In Topica Ciceronis comm., De Differentiis topicis.*

For the Latin west for the next several hundred years, direct knowledge of Aristotle's philosophy was to a large extent limited to the two short treatises that Boethius had translated.

BOETHUS (First century BCE). Peripatetic commentator on the *Categories*. There was also a **Stoic**, roughly contemporary, known as Boethus of Sidon, with whom Boethus the Peripatetic is often confused.

***BOULĒSIS*. Wish.** *Boulē* is the basic word, meaning will, determination, counsel, deliberation. In **Athens**, the *Boulē* was a select legislative body, a Senate. **Plato** and **Aristotle**, especially, use the word *boulēsis* and the associate verb *boulesthai* for a "wish," i.e., a mentally framed desire for something that might actually be quite impossible (*EN* III.4, 1111b22).

BOULEUSIS*. Deliberation.** Also built on *boul-*, the verb *bouleuein* refers primarily to the activity of a deliberative body, like a *Boulē* (*see BOULĒSIS*). **Aristotle** makes the abstract noun into a technical term in his moral psychology in *EN* III.3—our consideration of how to bring about a feasible goal. He defines "choice" (proairesis***) as "either deliberative desire (***orexis***) or desiderative deliberation."

BREATH. *See PNEUMA*.

– C –

CALCIDIUS (sometimes written Chalcidius) (active c. 350 CE). Calcidius translated a good bit of **Plato**'s *Timaeus* into Latin and did a commentary on the part translated. This was the only translation of a dialogue of Plato available in Latin in the earlier Middle Ages, although **Cicero** had done a kind of paraphrase of the *Timaeus*, also extant.

CALLICLES. A character in **Plato**'s *Gorgias* (represented as a fairly young adult who had studied with **Gorgias**) who some have argued to have been a historical person. The ethical position that he defends has been taken as an anticipation, in some respects, of that of Friedrich Nietzsche.

CANON. *See KANŌN.*

CARNEADES (214–129/8 BCE). Born in Cyrene, he joined the **Academy** and became **Scholarch** during part of the Skeptical period. He was a member of the delegation representing **Athens** in Rome in 155 BCE. We know of his philosophy through **Cicero** and **Sextus Empiricus**. He was reputed to be adept at arguing both sides of issues. *See also* ACADEMY; *SKEPTIKOS.*

CATEGORIES. *See KATEGORIAI.*

CATHARSIS. *See KATHARSIS.*

CAUSE, CAUSATION. *See AITION; APOTELESMA.*

CELSUS, AULUS CORNELIUS (wrote in the period 14–37 CE). He composed an encyclopedia of which primarily eight books on medicine (*iatrikē*) survive. The introductory section is especially interesting for its discussion of the philosophical grounding of medicine; the entirety is of great interest to historians of medicine.

CELSUS (Second century CE). Platonist anti-Christian polemicist. His work, written about 173 CE, is known primarily through the reply by **Origen**, written in 248 CE.

CHALDEAN ORACLES (Second century CE). A (fragmentary) collection of verses assembled by **Julian the Theurgist**, perhaps with contributions by his father, Julian the Chaldean. Julian claims that the basis of the work is material that came from Babylonia (known alternatively as Chaldea), and some have subsequently attributed the materials to **Zoroastrian** sources (Babylonia was then under Persian rule), but modern scholarship finds the contents to be more typical of Alexandrian speculation. Julian is a contemporary of **Numenius**, and there are many similarities between the fragments of the Oracles and the text of Numenius. **Porphyry**, **Iamblichus**, and

Proclus wrote (no longer extant) commentaries on the *Oracles*, and some Byzantine writers also took an interest, for example Michael Psellus and Pletho.

CHANCE. *See KATA SYMBEBĒKOS; TYCHĒ.*

CHANGE. *See ALLOIŌSIS; GENESIS; KINĒSIS; METABOLĒ.*

CHARA. Joy, used especially by the **Stoics** to mark a distinction between their views and those of the **Epicureans**, who made pleasure (*hēdonē*) the centerpiece of their moral psychology. New Testament writers follow the Stoic usage, frequently using *chara* and rarely *hēdonē*.

CHARACTER. *See ETHOS.*

CHARIOT; CHARIOTEER. In the *Phaedrus*, **Socrates** describes the immortal soul (*psychē*) as a chariot with a charioteer driving two horses, one noble, representing the "spirited" part of the soul, the other ignoble, representing the "appetitive" part of the soul. The charioteer is of course Reason. This vivid image often reappears in later Greek philosophy. *See also OCHĒMA.*

CHARISMA. A New Testament word meaning the gift of God's grace.

CHOICE. *See HAIRETON; PROAIRESIS.*

CHŌRA. Place; Space. In *Timaeus* 52, **Plato** identifies the receptacle (*hypodochē*) with "space." The implication of the passage seems to be that space pre-exists, in some sense, the appearance of phenomena (*phainomena*) in space. In *Physics* IV.1, **Aristotle** argues for "place" (*topos*) rather than "space," i.e., there is no pre-existing or independently existing continuum, it is the existence of spatiotemporal entities that define whatever "places" exist. Still, he does continue to use the word *chōra* in the everyday sense of "space," even of astronomical "space" (e.g., *Meteor.* I.7, 345a9). Both **Epicureans** and **Stoics** use *chōra* for "space" in their physical writings. *See also PHYSIS.*

CHŌRIS, CHŌRISTON. Separate; separable. A big issue for **Plato**'s theory of forms (*eidē*) is that they are said to be "separate" (*chōris*) from the things of which they are forms. *Parm.* 130 ff explores the implications of that idea. It is also true that for Plato the soul (*psychē*) is "separable" from the body (*sōma*) (*Phaedo* 67d). The *Phaedrus* presents a charming image of souls separated from body going on a tour, guided by a deity, of the forms, separated from the phenomena (*phainomena*).

Aristotle does not buy it (for forms, *Metaph.* XIII.11, 1086b9; for souls, *de An.* I.3, 407b15 ff), but he does have a "separability" problem of his own, namely the Mind (*nous*). Aristotle deals with that by making a distinction between separability "*kata topon*" or spatially, versus separability "*kata logon*," or conceptually. Since the mind does not occupy space, it cannot be spatially separable, only conceptually (*de An.* III.4). But then could not Plato use the same argument for the forms?

CHRISTIANITY. The story of the relationship between ancient Greek philosophy and the development of the Christian religion is long and complex. The Christian religion arose in the context of a struggle among the Jewish people between those who wanted to adhere closely to tradition and those who embraced various elements of the Greek culture that surrounded them, especially since the conquests of **Alexander of Macedon**. The audience of Jesus was primarily the less educated, less international members of the Jewish community, and his message does not reflect Greek philosophical conceptualization.

After the crucifixion, the apostles reached out first to the Jewish Diaspora, symbolized by the story of Pentecost, and then to non-Jews. That dissemination quickly involved addressing current philosophical movements. That address is neatly symbolized by Paul's sermon on the Areopagus; the effects on the development of early Christian teaching can be seen in the Gospel of John and in many of the Epistles. Paul often seems to be aware of addressing his message to people who were already, to one degree or another, followers of an **Epicurean** or **Stoic** way of life. Indeed, we know that he spent a fair amount of time with Festus, the philosophically sophisticated brother of the great Roman **Stoic Seneca**.

It took a little longer for the Greek-speaking philosophical community to take significant notice of Christianity. **Philo of Alexandria** demonstrated how to bring together Judaic and Greek conceptualizations: the philosophical sensibilities that he brought to the task were predominantly **Platonic** in inspiration, and as Christians became philosophers or philosophers became Christians, it was most often a form of Platonism that formed the transitional vehicle.

The most important Christian philosopher of antiquity was **Augustine**, but there are many others: **Origen**, (pseudo) **Dionysius**, and **Boethius** to mention a few.

As Christianity gained political ascendancy, tensions mounted between the demand for conformity to the accepted teachings of the religion and the tradition of free inquiry and tendency toward skepticism of the philosophers. For three or four centuries after the Hadj, the Islamic world was a better place to study philosophy than the Christian. *See also* HYPATIA; JUDAISM; SIMPLICIUS; *SKEPTIKOS*.

CHRONOS. Time. Some early writers synthesize this word with *Kronos*, the father of Zeus (cf. DL 1.119). This synthesis may be operating in the fragment of **Anaximander**. The **Pythagoreans** and **Plato** supposed time to exist independently of the physical world, a separate regulator of change (*Timaeus* 37 ff). Plato also identifies a cosmic time intrinsic to regular processes; for **Aristotle**, that concept of time was sufficient. Time is a consequence of the circular movements of the astronomical bodies (*Phys.* 218–233); it is the numbering of motion (*Phys.* 219). **Plotinus** returns to a (purified) Platonic conception, asserting the priority of **eternity** (*aiōn*) and making time the process of souls (*psychai*) changing from one condition to another.

CHRYSIPPUS OF SOLI (280/76–208/4 BCE). Chrysippus was the third **Scholarch** of the **Stoic** school, after **Cleanthes**. He also studied in the **Academy** and was known as a master of dialectical argument. He wrote a very great deal, but no complete treatises survive—only extensive fragments, especially as quoted by **Plutarch** and **Galen**. Many of the Stoic concepts, definitions, and arguments cited elsewhere in this Dictionary ultimately stem from the work of Chrysippus.

CHRYSOSTOM, JOHN (347–407 CE). Famous Christian preacher of the late fourth and early fifth centuries. "Chrysostom" is an honorary title meaning "Golden-Mouthed." He tended to avoid **allegorical** interpretations. A series of eight sermons, gathered under the title "Against the Judaizers," has historically been a favored lode from which to mine (possibly out of context) anti-Semitic comments.

CICERO, MARCUS TULLIUS (106–43 BCE). Roman politician and man of letters, Cicero was the most important conveyer of Greek philosophy into the Latin tradition. When he was very young, he studied with **Phaedrus the Epicurean**; when he was about 19, he heard **Philo of Larissa**, **Scholarch** of the **Academy** while Philo was visiting Rome; then **Diodotus,** a **Stoic,** lived with his family, and Cicero studied with him. After 79 BCE, Cicero lived in **Athens** for a period of time, studying with **Antiochus of Ascalon** and others, and visited Rhodes, where he met the Stoic **Posidonius.**

Cicero actively pursued a political career, although he found time while active in politics to produce three works on rhetoric and politics: the *De Oratore*, the *De Re Publica*, and the *De Legibus*. In 46 BCE, he withdrew from political life and turned to (mainly) philosophical writing. *On Stoic Paradoxes, Academica, De Finibus, Tusculan Disputations, The Nature of the Gods, On Divination, On Fate, Topics*, and *On Duties* all come from a period of about two years between the ascension of Julius Caesar to power in 46 and his assassination in 44. At that point, Cicero returned to the political arena, which led to his own assassination in 43.

Much of the Latin vocabulary of technical philosophical terms was invented by Cicero; English-language philosophical vocabulary is in turn largely indebted to those Ciceronian translations. Furthermore, because Cicero was so much a part of the normal academic curriculum in western Europe and America for such a long time, his formulations of philosophical issues and conceptualizations often seem to be the natural or intuitive understandings.

CLEANTHES OF ASSOS (?331/0–230/29 BCE). Second **Scholarch** of the **Stoa**, from 261. Cleanthes studied with **Zeno**; he is best known for his *Hymn to Zeus*. During his lifetime, he was in competition with

Aristo of Chios, who was less orthodox than Cleanthes, and was strongly supported by his student and successor **Chrysippus**.

CLEMENT OF ALEXANDRIA (d. 205 CE) (Titus Flavius Clemens). Christian theologian and philosopher. His *Stromateis* ("Miscellany") is an important source of quotations ("fragments") of earlier philosophers.

COGNITION. *See DIANOIA; KATALĒPSIS; NOĒSIS; NOUS.*

COHESION (logical). *See SYNARTĒSIS.*

COLLECTION. *See SYNAGOGĒ.*

COLLISION. *See ANTIKOPĒ.*

COMMANDING FACULTY. *See HĒGEMONIKON.*

COMMON SENSE. *AISTHĒSIS KOINĒ: See AISTHĒSIS.*

COMPLETE CAUSE. *AITION AUTOTELĒS. See AITION.*

COMPOSITE. *See SYNTHETON.*

CONCEPT. *See ENNOĒMA; ENNOIA.*

CONCOMITANCE, CONCOMITANT. *See PARAKOLOUTHĒSIS, PARAKOLOUTHOUN.*

CONCLUSION. *See EPIPHORA.*

CONTEMPLATION. *See THEŌRIA.*

CONTINUITY. *See SYNECHEIA.*

CONVINCING. *See PITHANOS.*

CORPUS. Latin for "body," this word is applied, for example, to the "body" of the extant works of ancient authors. Thus, the extant works of **Aristotle** are known as the Corpus Aristotelicum, the extant works of **Hippocrates** are known as the Corpus Hippocraticum, and so on.

COSMOS (*KOSMOS*), COSMOLOGY. The original sense of *kosmos* is "good order" (e.g., **Homer** *Od.* 8.179). It is also used to refer to ornaments and decorations, particularly of women (*Il.* 14.187). The **Presocratics** applied the word to the world order. **Heraclitus**, f. 30, says: "This *kosmos*, the same for all, was made by neither men nor Gods, but always has been, is, and will be, everliving **fire**, igniting by measures and extinguishing by measures."

Cosmology, or the study of the universe as a whole, is often a part of ancient philosophy, from **Anaximander** through the **Pythagoreans** and **Plato**'s *Timaeus* to **Aristotle**'s *de Caelo* and *Metaphysics* XII, to the **Stoics** and **Lucretius** the **Epicurean**.

Greek cosmologists can be divided into those who thought of the universe as spatially and temporally unlimited and those who thought of it as limited. Anaximander and the atomists seem to be on the "unlimited" side, and **Empedocles**, **Anaxagoras**, Plato, Aristotle, and the Stoics on the "limited." Anaximander speaks of "all the *kosmoi* and *ouranoi* within them" and that everything comes from "the unlimited." The atomists explicitly think of an indefinitely large number of atoms (*atoma*) in an indefinitely large space; whatever order there might be is in a sense **accidental**, and illusory.

Those who opt for a limited universe also have some principle or origin of the order in the universe. For Empedocles, the opposed principles of "love" and "strife" bring about opposed "orders" in which the elements are all separated out or all combined together into an organic whole. For Anaxagoras, mind (*nous*) sets up a "whirl" that works a bit as a centrifuge, separating out materials that somehow belong together. The early Pythagoreans seem to have expected to find mathematical principles at work in the universe as unifiers and orderers.

The Pythagorean lead was followed by Plato in the *Timaeus*; there, we learn of an ordering deity, the *Demiourgos*, who looks at the forms (*eidē*) and creates the visible universe out of geometrically defined materials, putting order into disorder, life into the lifeless, and mind (*nous*) into the mindless. It is not entirely clear whether Plato is truly committed to an actual creation—certainly he did not believe in a creation out of nothing—but in the *Timaeus* the universe as it exists turns out to be a single living **being** whose regular movements define time (***chronos***).

Structurally, the *Timaeus* cosmos is geocentric, with the heavenly bodies moving in circles. The major circles are the "Circles of Same and Different," motions in the celestial equator and the ecliptic. The account of the motion of the planets is tantalizing but truncated (*Tm* 36c, 38c).

While Aristotle agrees with Plato that the visible universe is a single and unique entity, he does not think of it as an "imitation" of eternal and transcendent forms, although the source and principle of its movement, the Unmoved Mover (***akinēton kinoun***), is eternal and transcendent. For Aristotle, the Cosmos, taken together with the Unmoved Mover, is the ultimate reality.

Aristotle's universe is also geocentric, with the sun, moon, and planets described as "moving themselves" in circular orbits, although in order to account for the "peculiarities" of the motion of the planets, from a geocentric perspective, it was necessary to posit multiple rotating spheres in which the center of one sphere is on the surface of another. In ***Metaphysics*** XII, Aristotle suggests that there are perhaps 55 such self-moving (rotating) spheres to account for the motions of the heavenly bodies.

For the **Stoics**, the order of the universe is the direct consequence of the immanence of **God** and the mind of God throughout the universe at all levels of complexity. There is a certain identity between God and the Cosmos—God may be spoken of as the Mind of the Universe and the Cosmos as the body of God.

The Stoics also believe in a great cycle of time in which the entire universe periodically turns to fire (the ***ekpyrosis***) and starts over again.

COURAGE. *See ANDREIA; ARETĒ.*

CRANTOR (c. 336–276/5 BCE). From Soli, Cyprus, he studied in the **Academy** with **Xenocrates** and **Polemon**. Crantor's interpretation of **Plato**'s *Timaeus* was influential with later Platonists. According to **Proclus**, he took the Atlantis story as historical rather than allegorical. Also, Crantor did not take the creative activity of the ***Demiourgos*** as having occurred at a specific moment in time but as something continuous. **Plutarch** relied heavily on Crantor for his interpretation of the generation of the **World Soul** in the Timaeus. Apparently Crantor's essay *On Grief* was admired and imitated by **Cicero** and **Plutarch**.

CRATES OF ATHENS (d. c. 265 BCE). Academic philosopher, colleague, and probably lover of **Polemon**.

CRATES OF THEBES (c. 368–288 BCE). Cynic, follower of **Diogenes of Sinope**. He is noted for his cynical marriage to **Hipparchia** and for being a teacher of **Zeno of Citium**.

CRATYLUS OF ATHENS (Probably born in the mid-fifth century). Cratylus represented himself to be a follower of **Heraclitus**, but judging by what we learn of Cratylus from **Plato** and **Aristotle** there are some significant differences. Plato's dialogue the *Cratylus* focuses on the tension between natural and conventional theories of language, tending to indicate that Cratylus was concerned about the inadequacies of language in conveying information about the sensory world. For one thing, Cratylus is represented as saying that Heraclitus was wrong to say that you cannot step into the same river twice— you cannot step into the *same* river even *once*. For another, Aristotle says that Cratylus eventually gave up talking altogether and just waggled his finger. Aristotle tells us that Plato studied with Cratylus and was persuaded by him of the inadequacies of language for talking about sensory experience.

CRITERION OF TRUTH. *See ALĒTHEIA, KRITĒRION.*

CRITIAS OF ATHENS (1) (c. 520–429). He appears in **Plato**'s *Timaeus* and *Critias*, where he would have been a very old man (over 90).

CRITIAS OF ATHENS (2) (c. 460–403). He appears in **Plato**'s *Charmides* and *Protagoras*, as well as in **Xenophon**. Critias (2) was both a writer of elegant poetry and prose and a bloodthirsty member of the 30 Tyrants—leading to his death at the hands of the democrats. He tends to be counted as a **Sophist**, although unlike most Sophists, he did not teach. A number of fragments of his works remain.

CRITOLAUS OF PHASELIS (2nd century BCE). Scholarch of the **Lyceum**, member of the delegation of **Athenian** philosophers to Rome in 155 BCE.

CUT. *See TEMNEIN, TOMĒ.*

CYNIC. *Kynikos* literally means "doglike." **Diogenes of Sinope** (c. 410–c. 323) acquired the nickname for his shameless public behavior. Some say that Diogenes studied with **Antisthenes** (445–365), the associate of **Socrates,** and thus that Antisthenes deserves credit as founder of the Cynic manner of philosophizing. But Diogenes is the one whose behavior was regarded as "doglike." He favored a life according to nature, and pursued that by living as simply as possible.

While Cynicism is mainly about a way of life, it has repeatedly influenced the history of philosophy. Diogenes' most famous student was **Crates of Thebes** (368–288), who in turn was a teacher of **Zeno of Citium**, the founder of the **Stoic** school. The Stoics retained some cynical elements in their philosophy, especially allegiance to a "life according to nature."

Many people claimed to be cynics, or to have been influenced by the cynics, throughout antiquity — its anarchic stance provided a convenient counterpoint to emperors from **Alexander of Macedon** to the end of the Roman Empire.

The most famous female cynic was **Hipparchia**, who fell in love with Crates and shared his austere and public life.

CYRENAIC SCHOOL. Aristippus of Cyrene (435–355), a follower of **Socrates** also influenced by **Protagoras**, returned to his native city and founded a school that remained in the family for perhaps 100 years. His daughter Arete directed the school after his death, and her son Aristippus the younger followed her. The Cyrenaic school seems to have been primarily concerned with moral psychology; they share a commitment to one form or another of hedonism, believing that the maximization of pleasure would bring about happiness or *eudaimonia*. After the founding and spread of **Epicureanism**, the two schools eventually became indistinguishable from each other. *See also HĒDONĒ.*

– D –

DAIMŌN, DAIMŌNION. In classical Greek religious belief, a *daimon* was most often a personal divine **being**, appointed to look out for an individual person; the belief is critiqued, for example, by **Heraclitus** when he says *ethos anthrōpōi daimōn*, a person's character is his *daimōn*. The most famous *daimōn* or *daimōnion*, as he prefers to say, is that of **Socrates**, referred to several times in **Plato**'s dialogues and discussed at some length in **Xenophon** *Mem*.1, 1, 4.

In later centuries, semi-divine beings in other religious traditions, such as Persian and **Egyptian**, are interpreted as *daimones*, so that by the time of **Plutarch** (*de def. orac*. 414–417) there is a fairly complex hierarchy. Christian religious imperialism made *daimones* into demons and took over a good deal of the hierarchy but called these entities "**angels**."

DAMASCIUS OF DAMASCUS (c. 462–after 538 CE). Damascius was the last **Scholarch** of the **Neoplatonic** school of **Athens**. Originally a teacher of rhetoric, he studied philosophy with the successors of **Proclus**, **Marinus**, and **Isidore** and was the teacher of **Simplicius**. When Justinian closed the school of Athens in 529, he went into exile in Persia along with Simplicius and others. He apparently moved to **Alexandria** in 532. Many fragments and some complete works survive, notably *On First Principles*, a commentary on the *Parmenides*, and a (fragmentary) *Life of Isidore,* also known as the Philosophical History.

DAMON OF ATHENS (Mid fifth-century BCE). Damon was a friend and advisor to Pericles, and best known as a musical theorist. **Plato** speaks approvingly of his work, for example, at *Rep*. III, 400b.

DAVID. Name attached to several sixth century CE works of philosophy, including lecture notes for an introduction to philosophy and a commentary on **Porphyry**'s *Introduction*. There is a commentary on the *Categories* also attributed to **Elias**. Although the name might indicate that "David" was a Christian, some of the opinions expressed in his writings are not very orthodox.

DEDUCE. *See SYNAGEIN.*

DEDUCTION. *See SYNAGŌGĒ.*

DEDUCTIVE. *See SYNAKTIKOS.*

DEFINE. *See HORIZEIN.*

DEFINITION. *See HORISMOS; LOGOS.*

DEIXIS. Literally, "indication," or "demonstration." **Aristotle** uses the word to refer to a mode of argument, in the *Rhetoric* (1408a26) and *Prior Analytics* Book I. In **Stoic** philosophy, the word might be translated "demonstrative reference" or "indication." For the Stoics, a valid **syllogism** must have a "demonstrative reference" to something that actually exists.

DELIBERATION. *See BOULEUSIS.*

DELINEATION. *See TYPOS.*

DEMETRIUS OF PHALERON (d. 280 BCE). Demetrius was a student of **Aristotle** and **Theophrastus**. From 317 to 307, he was in charge of ruling **Athens** under the authority of Cassander; when Demetrius I (son of Antigonus) took Athens in 307, Demetrius of Phaleron went to **Alexandria**, where he became the founding intellectual leader of the **Museum and Library**, under Ptolemy I. When Ptolemy Philadelphus came to the throne in 285, Demetrius went into exile again.

DEMIOURGOS. Literally, someone who works for the city; the implication is close to the idea of "civil engineer" in American English. **Plato** uses this word to refer to the deity responsible for putting the **cosmos** in order, in the *Timaeus* and *Statesman*. Plato does not make the *Demiourgos* omnipotent; the world is not created out of nothing but out of disorder (*Tm* 30), and the *Demiourgos* makes the world as good as he can, given the undependable materials available. Further, mortal creatures such as human beings were not created by the *Demiourgos*; that job was delegated to lesser deities (*Tm* 41c).

Some later Platonists, influenced by **Stoic** or **Aristotelian** ideas, ascribed the arrangement of the world order to *Logos* (e.g., **Philo of Alexandria**) or *Nous* (**Plotinus**). In any case, the Platonic tradition is committed to some version of "intelligent design."

DEMOCRACY. *See DEMOKRATIA.*

DEMOCRITUS OF ABDERA (460–370 BCE). Born in northern Greece, Democritus associated with **Leucippus** and studied with Persian teachers before traveling to **Egypt** and other parts of the Middle East, according to our ancient sources. His many writings are all lost except for fragments and reports of his teaching. Perhaps the best sources are **Aristotle** for his criticisms of Democritus' physical theory, and the frank admiration and imitation of **Epicurus** and Epicureans such as **Lucretius,** who doubtless preserves much of the wisdom of Democritus in his *De Rerum Natura.* Democritus believed that everything is made out of atoms (*atoma*) or "**beings**," separated by empty **space**, or "nothing." We too are conglomerations of atoms. Our perceptions (*aisthēseis*) of the world are consequences of atoms of various kinds colliding with our sense organs; our interpretations of those collisions are "conventional." "By convention (*nomos*) sweet, by convention bitter, by convention hot, by convention cold, by convention color, but in reality, atoms and void" (DK 68B9).

DEMOKRATIA. "Rule by the people." In classical Greece, "democracy" meant *direct* popular rule by the (male) citizens. Thus, a viable democratic state was limited in size to the number of people who could assemble on a regular basis. In ancient democracies, most government positions were assigned by lot, for relatively short terms (one year is common); military leaders and others requiring specialized knowledge were elected by the assembly and were subject to instant recall by the assembly. **Plato** disliked this form of government; for one thing, the Athenian democracy executed **Socrates. Aristotle** combined democratic institutions with aristocratic institutions in his favored form of government. The entire discussion became somewhat moot, however, with the Macedonian establishment of an imperial monarchy and the subsequent Roman Empire.

DEMONSTRATION. *See APODEIXIS; DEIXIS.*

DESIRE. *See EPITHYMIA; ERŌS; HORMĒ; OREXIS; THYMOS.*

DEVELOPMENT. *Apogegenēmenon,* an **Epicurean** term for an emergent property of a concatenation of atoms (*atoma*).

DEXIPPUS (Early fourth century CE). Dexippus was a **Neoplatonist**, a student of **Iamblichus**. Part of his commentary on **Aristotle**'s *Categories* survives.

DIAIRĒSIS. Division, distinction. **Plato** examines the relationship between forms (*eidē*) by means of a process that he calls "collection and division." While we see an application of the method at *Phaedrus* 265b, it takes over completely in the *Sophist* and *Statesman*. **Aristotle** finds that the practice of *diairesis* demonstrates the incoherence of the theory of forms, since if we divide the genus "animal" into "horses" and "human," how many forms do we have? One ("animal")? Two ("horse," "human")? Or three? And how many forms does Socrates participate in, qua human? One, two, or more? (*Metaphysics* VII.13, 1039a). Of course, Aristotle's own frequent use of *diairesis* resulting in genera and species would not be susceptible to the same criticism, since the real existents, the *ousiai*, are the individual animals (for example) which may belong to as many classes as one likes, since those are just predicates. He provides some recommendations on how to carry out *diairēseis* most effectively in *APo* II.13 and compares his method with the Platonic as applied to biology in *PA* I.2–4.

The **Stoics** applied the method of division to the definition of terms, a practice developed from the Platonic and Aristotelian uses, but for them focused on language in itself.

DIALECTIC, *DIALEKTIKĒ.* The basic definition of "dialectic" is "discussion by question and answer." According to **Aristotle, Zeno of Elea** made dialectic a philosophical method (DL IX.25), but it was very much extended by **Socrates**. In its basic form, the philosophical method of dialectic starts from premises offered by one's opponent and argues that those premises lead to unacceptable, even self-contradictory, conclusions. Thus Zeno, in order to demonstrate that "**being** is one," starts from the premise, "there are many beings (*polla estin*)," and argues that on any interpretation of *polla estin*, the thesis is incoherent. Thus for Zeno, it seems to be a method of indirect proof.

For Socrates, dialectic is a standard part of the *elenchus*, or examination of the views of his interlocutor. When confronted with someone who claims ethical knowledge of some kind, he asks them (usually) for a definition of holiness (*Euthyphro*), virtue (*aretē*) (*Meno, Protagoras*), **temperance** (*Charmides*), or the like, and proceeds to show that the definer has other views that are inconsistent with that definition. It is not always easy to tell what positive view Socrates might be aiming at, or even if he has one. In that sense, the Socratic dialectic often appears to be exploratory or heuristic.

In the *Republic*, **Plato** proposes dialectic as an important part of the education of the future philosopher ruler; it is still heuristic, but there is an expectation that dialectic will indeed lead to knowledge (*epistēmē*) of the forms (*eidē*) (*Rep* VI, 511c–e, in the Line passage). In the *Phaedrus, Sophist, Statesman*, and *Philebus*, dialectic is identified with the method of "collection and division," which often appears to be a proposal that knowledge is to be gained by taxonomic investigations.

Aristotle examines dialectical method at length in the *Topics*, focused on potential uses of dialectic, especially rhetorical uses. But in comparison with "philosophy," a typical Aristotelian assessment occurs in *Metaphysics* IV.2, 1004b25. "Dialectic is merely critical where philosophy claims to know, and sophistic is what appears to be philosophy but is not." He says that because in his view philosophy aims at the construction of demonstrative **syllogisms** based on well-established premises, while dialectic is a critical examination of generally accepted opinions. Ironically, Aristotle's own methodology is very frequently dialectical, starting from a critical examination of *endoxa*; *EN* VII is a good example.

While **Epicurus** appears to have rejected dialectic (DL 10.31), the **Stoics** put a good deal of emphasis on dialectic. **Alexander of Aphrodisias**, in his commentary on the *Topics*, says that the Stoics define dialectic "as the science of speaking well, taking speaking well to consist in saying what is true and what is fitting, and regarding this as a distinguishing characteristic of the philosopher, use it of philosophy at its highest. For this reason, only the wise man is a dialectician in their view." **Chrysippus**, especially, is said to have been highly skilled in dialectic.

DIALECTICAL SCHOOL. The term "Dialectical School" is applied to several philosophers who emphasized the use of dialectical arguments; these people used to be attributed to the **Megarian school**, but recent scholarship has, to some extent, distinguished the two groups. **Diodorus Cronus** and **Philo the Logician** are the leading members of the Dialectical School. Synchronous with the establishment of the **Stoic** school, the logical studies of the Dialectical School influenced the development of Stoic logic. *See also* DIALECTIC; *LOGIKĒ*.

DIANOIA. Reasoning: "*dia*" through, "*noia*" thinking. In the "Line" passage, *Rep*. VI, 510–511, **Plato** applies it particularly to hypothetical-deductive reasoning, particularly as practiced by mathematicians. **Aristotle** tends to apply the word to thinking in general. *Metaphysics* VI.1, 1025b25. "*Dianoia* is either practical or productive or theoretical." *See POIĒSIS; PRAXIS; THEŌRIA.*

The Stoics identify *dianoia* with the *hegemonikon*, or governing part of the soul (*psychē*). Sometimes *dianoia* can best be translated "understanding" or even "the rational faculty."

DIAPHORA. Difference. In **Aristotle**'s concept of definition (*horismos*), a species (*eidos*) is defined by providing the genus (*genos*) and the specific "difference." It is important that the "difference" be a characteristic that is "essential" or causative of the nature of the species in order that the definition be truly adequate. One of his examples of a good definition is "Thunder is the noise of fire being quenched in the clouds." The genus would be "noise of fire being quenched" and the difference would be "in the clouds." *APo* II.8. *See also DIAIRĒSIS.*

DIARTĒSIS. Disconnection. According to the **Stoics**, one kind of logical fallacy is *diartēsis*. **Sextus Empiricus** gives an example: "If it is day, it is light, but wheat is sold in the market, therefore it is light."

DIASTĒMA. Interval, Dimension, Distance. Regularly used to denote musical intervals. According to the **Stoics**, time (*see chronos*) is "the dimension of movement," either of all movement, or of the movements of the heavens. *Diastaton* is that which is extended, or has extension, particularly in three dimensions, thus equivalent to "body" (*sōma*).

DIATHESIS. Disposition, character, state, defined in **Aristotle *Metaphysics*** V.19, 1022b1, as "an arrangement of that which has parts, in respect either of place or of capacity or of kind." According to the **Stoics**, virtue (***aretē***) is a *diathesis*, choiceworthy for its own sake (DL 7.89). They use the word *diathesis* of characteristics that cannot be changed, or cannot be changed easily; so saying that virtue is a *diathesis* emphasizes its permanence, once acquired.

DIATRIBĒ. Literally, "pastime." Starting at least with **Plato**, the word gets the sense of a philosophical discourse (*Apol.* 37d), especially a popular lecture presentation of philosophical theories. This usage is especially pronounced among the **Cynics** and **Stoics,** many of whom made a point of popularizing their teachings. In many cases, surviving *diatribai* were copied down by students and survive—this is true for those of **Musonius Rufus** and of **Epictetus**, for example.

DICAEARCHUS OF MESSENE (c. 350–285 BCE). Dicaearchus was a student of **Aristotle** who gained a reputation as a mathematician, historian, geographer, and ethicist. He established the idea of the world as a globe with latitude and longitude and discussed various forms of music.

DIEZEUGMENON. This is a **Stoic** technical term for what we might, in English, call a "disjunctive proposition." An example would be: "Either it is day, or it is night."

DIKĒ, DIKAIOS, DIKAIOSYNĒ. Justice. In **Homer**, *dikē* means something like "proper procedure," the practice and judgment of kings, that which is right as opposed to that which is compelled. A *dikaios* person is observant of customs and rules, a well-ordered righteous person. *Dikaiosynē* is the abstract noun for justice.

By the time of **Herodotus**, "injustice" is roughly of two sorts: *pleonexia*, or getting more than one's fair share, and *anomia*, not following proper procedure. Already in **Anaximander**, the "pleonexia" sense is operational in a philosophical setting: he says, of the things that come to be, "they give *dikē* and reparation to each other for their *adikia* according to the order of time." **Heraclitus** has the procedural sense, f. 94: "The sun will not overstep his bounds; if he does, the Erinnyes, allies of *dikē*, will find him out." One more **Presocratic** bit, from **Antiphon** the **Sophist** (from f. 44): "Justice (*dikaiosynē*) therefore is not violating the rules (*nomima*) of the city in which one is a citizen. Thus, a person would best use justice to his own advantage if he considered the laws (*nomoi*) important when witnesses are present, but the requirements of nature (*physis*) important in the absence of witnesses."

Plato explored the idea of justice in detail in the *Republic*; **Socrates** in the dialogue argues that there is a justice of the individual person, and a justice of the *polis*, analogous to each other. The *polis* is composed of productive people, protective people, or **Guardians**, and rulers. The characteristic motivation of the productive people is *epithymia*, or appetite; the virtue (*aretē*) that enables them to be productive is *sōphrosynē*, or temperance. The characteristic motivation of the Guardians is *timē*, or honor, and the virtue that enables them to gain honor is *andreia*, or courage. The characteristic motivation and virtue of the ruler is *sophia*, or wisdom; thus the **appropriate** ruler is the lover of wisdom, or *philosophos*. Justice, *dikaiosynē*, in the *polis*, Socrates argues, is all the classes of citizens doing their proper job according to their proper virtue. But what then is justice in the individual person? The soul (*psychē*) or human personality has each of these three parts: the appetite, the spirit, and the mind; when all three parts of the soul have the appropriate virtues: temperance, courage, and wisdom, then the person is *dikaios*.

In the *Nicomachean Ethics*, **Aristotle** presents an account of justice that is more in line with the pre-Platonic traditions. That is, he distinguishes justice as fair shares from legality and then establishes each on what he takes to be an appropriate footing. Starting from the **Pythagorean** idea of proportionality, he gives some structure to the idea of fair distribution, and like Heraclitus, he supposes that there is one universal law that is in a way the basis of legislated law (*EN* V.7).

The **Epicureans** argued that justice derived from social utility: "Justice was never anything in itself but a contract of not harming or being harmed" (**Epicurus**, *Principle Doctrines* 31). The **Stoics** understood justice as the art of distributing what is appropriate to each person, but is also part of natural law. *See also NOMOS*.

DINĒ. Vortex. Although such phenomena as eddies in rivers and tornados were commonly called *dinai*, for some of the **Presocratics** this physical phenomenon was a model for cosmological explanations. **Empedocles** B35 has a vortex that marks the transition between the rule of Love and the rule of Strife; **Anaxagoras** says that Mind (*nous*) gets the vortex going in the first place: (f. 9) "as these things are thus rotating and being separated off by both force and speed, the speed causes the force, and their speed is like the speed of nothing now found among humans, but altogether many times as fast." (f. 12): "And Mind ruled the entire rotation, so that it rotated in the beginning." **Plato**, **Aristotle**, and their successors tended to limit the application of *dinē* to terrestrial—or rather aquatic and meteorological—phenomena.

DIO CHRYSOSTOM (c. 40–120 CE). From Prusa, in Bithynia, Dio was an orator who became influenced by **Cynic** and **Stoic** philosophies. Eighty of his discourses are extant. He was banished from Rome by Domitian; he was again in favor under Nerva and became a friend of Trajan. Since he traveled widely during his period of banishment, some of his discourses have valuable information about lesser-known parts of the Empire around 100 CE.

DIODORUS CRONUS (Late fourth to early third centuries BCE). Diodorus was a **Dialectical** philosopher from Iasos in Caria. He was a teacher of **Philo the Logician** and **Zeno of Citium**, founder of the **Stoic** school. Diodorus is known for his "Master Argument," an argument that appears to support a deterministic thesis, or Fate.

DIOGENES LAERTIUS (fl. 200 CE). Diogenes is the author of "The Lives and Opinions of the Philosophers," the only extant ancient history of philosophy. Diogenes tends to group philosophers by "schools," tracing student-teacher relationships back to founders. His account of each philosopher is about as good as whichever source he happens to be using at the moment, although he tends to throw in a bit of his own rather bad poetry from time to time. His Life of **Zeno**

of Citium includes an excellent summary of early **Stoic** philosophy; his life of **Epicurus** includes extensive quotations from the works of Epicurus that are not otherwise available. One test of his reliability is to compare what he says with the works of **Plato** and **Aristotle**. Diogenes' summary of Plato's philosophy, while very different from what modern writers would say, is not too bad; he probably had some decent general introduction to go on, something like **Alcinous** for example. For Aristotle, his summary is considerably less perceptive and less complete but nevertheless does give us an idea of how Aristotle was understood by non-specialists in that period. Another test of his reliability is to compare what he says about **Socrates** with what Plato tells us about Socrates. What Diogenes tells us about the trial of Socrates, for example, is both inconsistent with the *Apology* and internally inconsistent, leading us to conclude that it is hazardous to rely very much on what Diogenes says; on the other hand, most of the time we do not have any alternative source, so we have to accept Diogenes, but with a large grain of salt.

DIOGENES OF APOLLONIA (Mid to late 5th century BCE). The views of Diogenes were parodied in **Aristophanes'** *Clouds*. Like **Anaximenes**, he made air *(aēr)* the first principle; he argues that air is also the principle of life and intelligence, against the implied dualism of **Anaxagoras**. **Aristotle** quotes his description of the system of blood vessels (*HA* III.2, 511b30–512b10).

DIOGENES OF BABYLON. *See* DIOGENES OF SELEUCIA.

DIOGENES OF OENOANDA (Second century CE). Oenoanda is an ancient site in south-central Turkey where a massive inscription of **Epicurean** philosophy was found in 1884. The inscription was set up in the second century CE, and Diogenes is the author. The reconstruction of the inscription has been one of the major sources of information about Epicureanism in the Christian era.

DIOGENES OF SELEUCIA (or BABYLON) (c. 228–140 [or earlier] BCE). Diogenes was a student of **Chrysippus** and of **Zeno of Tarsus** and was the fifth director of the **Stoic** school; he taught **Panaetius** and others. In 156/5 BCE, he was a member of the delegation of philosophers from **Athens** to Rome and thus helped introduce Stoicism to this fertile soil for its further growth and development. **Cicero** often cites him as an authority.

DIOGENES OF SINOPE (c. 410–c. 322 BCE). Diogenes was the original "**Cynic**," so-called because of his "dog-like" behavior, living according to nature, shamelessly. Rejecting civilized life, he attacked all political and social conventions, all sexual, racial, and class distinctions, and all kinds of intellectual speculation, all claims to authority. He wrote a *Politeia*, apparently something of a spoof of **Plato**'s *Republic*, and supported all forms of human equality. It is no surprise that he is the subject of numerous stories, some of them appreciative, others critical.

DIONYSIUS THE AREOPAGITE. The original Dionysius was converted by Paul (*Acts* 17.34), and according to church history became a bishop and was martyred in 95. Much later (late fifth or early sixth century), a **Christian Neoplatonist** writer represented his own philosophical work as having been produced by that earlier martyr. Thus, the philosopher is often referred to as "Pseudo-Dionysius." His surviving work comprises 4 treatises and 10 letters. The treatises are: *On Divine Names*, *On the Celestial Hierarchy*, *On the Ecclesiastical Hierarchy*, and *Mystical Theology*. His influence on **Christian** theology, though significant in the West, is far more important on Eastern Orthodox writers.

DIOTIMA OF MANTINEA. In **Plato**'s *Symposium*, **Socrates** gives a speech about the nature of Love, claiming that what he says was learned from the Priestess Diotima. Most readers have assumed that this was a mere literary trope, that Diotima was fictional and that all of the ideas presented in this speech are in fact Plato's, put into the mouth of Socrates. Others have, not unreasonably, supposed that Diotima really existed and that Socrates might actually have learned something from her. In any case, it is significant that in response to a conversation that has focused mainly on male homosexual relationships, Plato's Socrates chooses to represent a woman as the source of the true understanding of love.

DISCONNECTION. *See DIARTĒSIS.*

DISCOURSE. *See LOGOS.*

DISJUNCTIVE PROPOSITION. *See* DIEZEUGMENON.

DISORDER. *See ATAXIA.*

DISPOSED. *Pōs echein* is one of the **Stoic** categories; the term would be literally translated "having how." "Disposed" is a conventional translation of the phrase.

DISPREFERRED. *See APOPROĒGMENA.*

DISSOI LOGOI. An anonymous **Sophistic** text included in the manuscripts of **Sextus Empiricus**, first published in 1570 under the name *Dialexeis*. The phrase *Dissoi Logoi*, or "Double Arguments," appears repeatedly in the text, lending support to the current title. Scholars think that the work was written sometime between 400 and 380 BCE. The general trend of argument in the treatise is that words like "good" and "bad," "beautiful" and "ugly," "just" and "unjust," "true" and "false," differ in meaning according to the person and circumstances in which they are used. The treatise thus illustrates sophistic relativism very clearly. At the same time, the author does take stands opposing selection of officials by lot, claiming that the person skilled in **dialectic** is the best statesman, and recommending the cultivation of a good memory.

DISVALUE. *See APAXIA.*

DIVINATION. *See MANTIKĒ; THEURGY.*

DIVINE. *See DEMIOURGOS; GOD; THEOS.*

DIVISION. *See DIAIRĒSIS.*

DOCTRINE. *See DOGMA.*

DOGMA. Teaching, opinion. **DOGMATIKOS.** Doctrinaire, opinionated. **Aristotle** uses *dogma* apparently as a synonym for *doxa*. In *Phys.* IV.2, 209b15, Aristotle refers to the *agrapha dogmata*, **unwritten**

teachings, of **Plato**, on the subject of **space** and **time**. In Hellenistic philosophy, **Epicureans** and **Stoics** were proud of their *dogmata*, while Pyrrhonian Skeptics were equally proud of avoiding all *dogmata*. *See also SKEPTIKOS*.

DOXA. Opinion, expectation. **Parmenides' Goddess** distinguishes between the **Truth** and the "opinions of mortals in which is no true belief" (f. 1., line 30). For **Plato,** apprehension of the perceptible world is *doxa*, contrasted with the *epistēmē* available to those who make **dialectical** contact with the forms (*eidē*). In the **Sun-Line-Cave** passage of the *Republic*, *doxa* is distinguished into *pistis* and *eikasia*, a confidence based on some understanding of the material nature of the perceived object versus conjecture based on attention to the appearances alone. In the *Theaetetus*, the hypotheses that knowledge might be "true belief" (*alēthē doxa*) or "true belief plus an account" (*logos*) are discussed and refuted, but at the same time, *doxa* is accorded a positive epistemic role, fleshing out the outline provided in the *Republic*.

For **Aristotle**, we have *doxa* of contingent facts and *epistēmē* of necessary facts. For **Epicurus**, *doxa* is a movement akin to but different from *aesthesis*; *doxa* can go beyond the evidence of the senses and thus be erroneous.

Parallel to, and somewhat separate from, these epistemological uses of the term is the sense of "repute"; in the Septuagint and New Testament, *doxa* sometimes has the sense of praise, honor, or glory. *See also ENDOXA*.

DOXOGRAPHY. Several ancient writers collected the opinions of various philosophers, giving generally brief and often comparative descriptions of their views. Some of those texts are our only evidence for the opinions of some of the ancient thinkers, or the only evidence for a significant portion of their work. *See also* AETIUS; ARIUS DIDYMUS; CLEMENT OF ALEXANDRIA; DIOGENES LAERTIUS; HIPPOLYTUS; STOBAEUS; THEOPHRASTUS OF ERESUS.

DREAM. *See ONEIROS.*

DYAS. Dyad. In **Pythagorean** philosophy, the principle of duality (*see* **Aristotle** *Metaphysics* I.5, 986a). According to Aristotle, **Plato** and his followers generate numbers from the one and the "indefinite dyad" (*Metaph.* XIV.3, 1090b). In *Phys.* III, 206b, Aristotle seems to take the "indefinite dyad" of Plato to be straight-line infinite extension.

DYNAMIS, DYNAMEIS. Power, potentiality, capacity. In early Greek literature, the word is applied to personal strength and to military power. In the **Hippocratic corpus**, *dynamis* is also used of physical capacities, particularly those of medical significance. At *Theaetetus* 185c, for example, **Plato** explicitly moves the significance of a *dynamis* from a physical ability to a mental ability; also in the *Theaetetus*, in describing the theory of perception (*aisthēsis*) at 156, he distinguishes active and passive *dynameis* present in the perceptual process. That is an idea that **Aristotle** developed significantly. Combining the idea of active and passive *dynameis* with the theory of the four causes (*aitia*), **matter** may be identified with the passive potentialities, the capacity of undergoing change, and an entity may serve as a source of change (*archē kinēseōs*) in virtue of its active powers. In general, for Aristotle, if appropriate active and passive powers meet, an activity (*energeia*) or at least some sort of change (*metabolē*) will result.

In *PA* II.1, Aristotle argues that the so-called **elements** (**earth, water, air**, and **fire**) are really compounded of elemental "powers": earth is cold and dry, water cold and fluid, air warm and fluid, fire hot and dry. Thus, the elements can really change into each other; each is "matter" for the other.

For the **Stoics**, however, each element has just one power: fire is hot, air is cold, water is wet, earth is dry; really, there are just two *dynameis*, active and passive, ultimately identifiable as **God** and **Matter**.

In the meantime, the religious traditions had adopted the word to apply to the powers of God and divine beings. If natural **science** can show us how to use the natural powers inherent in material things, then why cannot divine science teach us how to control the supernatural powers inherent in divine things?

– E –

EARTH. GĒ. In addition to the solid ground that we stand on, "earth" is, beginning with **Empedocles** at least, one of the four "elements" (*see **stoicheion***) of which everything is constructed. At *Metaphysics*

I.8, 989a5, **Aristotle** notes that none of the monistic natural philosophers make "earth" the most basic element, though perhaps they should, as do most common people.

Almost all ancient cosmologies, starting with **Anaximander**, agreed that the Earth is in the center of the universe, with sun, moon, and stars revolving around it. Aristotle made that into a principle of explanation of what we call "gravity": it is the nature of Earth to move toward its natural place, the center of the universe, and the nature of water to move to its natural place, on top of the earth, air on top of that, and fire above the air.

Plato's **Pythagorean** physics in the *Timaeus* asserts that atoms (*atoma*) of earth are cubes; one wonders whether observation of salt crystals contributed to that hypothesis. *See also PHYSIS.*

ECHEIN. Literally, "to have," "to be in some condition." One of **Aristotle**'s 10 categories (*see katēgoriai*); see *Cat.* 15b18 for a list of examples. *Pōs echein* and *pōs echein pros ti* (how it is, and how it is in relation to something) are two of the four **Stoic** categories.

EDUCATION. *See PAIDEIA.*

EFFICIENT CAUSE. **Aristotle** distinguishes four "causes" (*aitia*): matter (*hylē*), mover (*kinoun*), form (*eidos*), and end (*telos*); his standard phrase for the second is "*archē kinēseōs*," or source of movement. But sometimes movement results in something being "made," in which case the moving cause is also a "making" cause, *poiētikon* (*GA* I.21, 729b13). So in the medieval Latin commentaries, the general sense is "*causa movens*," while if there is a new entity that comes to be, the source of its coming-to-be is a *causa efficiens*. "*Efficiens*" is Latin for "*poiētikon*." In Aquinas, for example, the existence of **God** is demonstrated both as first "moving" cause (of any change whatever) and as first "efficient" cause (of the coming-to-be of entities). Subsequently, the locution "efficient cause" came to be used to denote all moving causes, although this usage is etymologically inaccurate. *See also AITION; ARCHĒ.*

EGYPTIAN ORIGINS OF GREEK PHILOSOPHY. In some circles, there has been a certain vogue to claim that Greek philosophy was derived from prior Egyptian thought. In favor of that idea, we may note that both **Thales** and **Pythagoras** are reputed to have spent some time in Egypt, as well as **Democritus, Eudoxus** (an associate of **Plato**), and possibly Plato himself. Further, **Isocrates** says in his *Busiris* that philosophy came from Egypt (the context is, however, a bit fanciful). On the other hand, it is hard to discern exactly what philosophical concepts or practices really could have been learned from the Egyptians in view of the fact that surviving Egyptian texts from the period before Thales, as interesting as they may be in other respects, are at best marginally philosophical in character. Of course, once Greek civilization established its beachhead at **Alexandria** at the end of the fourth century BCE, a good deal of cross-fertilization of ideas could and did occur, leading on the one hand to the great philosophical synthesis of **Plotinus** and on the other to such things as **Gnosticism** and the **Hermetic Corpus**.

EIDŌLON. Insubstantial image, as at **Plato** *Sophist* 266b, or illusion, as at Plato *Phaedo* 66c. **Aristotle** uses it in the sense of dream images, *Div. Somn.* 464b. **Epicurus** uses the word *eidōlon* to refer to the set of atoms (***atoma***) leaving the perceived object and coming to the eyes (*Letter to Herodotus* 46 ff), thus a "substantial" image.

EIDOS, EIDĒ. Form, shape, kind, species. Noun built on the verb *idein*, to see. In **Homer** and generally in the poets, *eidos* is "form" or "shape," particularly of a human being. In general, fifth century BCE usage *eidos* also means "kind" or "species." **Plato** adopted the word as one of his two standard words for the forms (the other is ***idea***). In the *Euthyphro* (5–6) **Socrates** proposes that "holiness" is an ***eidos*** that makes everything that is holy, holy. That usage is adopted and developed in *Phaedo* 103e and many other places. What *eidē* are there, according to Plato? Holiness and all other ethical concepts are clearly *eidē*. Further, Plato gives many examples of mathematical *eidē*. *Phaedo* 101b–c talking of largeness and smallness, One and Two, is typical. Plato clearly thinks that there are *eidē* of natural kinds (e.g., *Sophist* 266b) and even of artificial kinds, if we take seriously passages like *Republic* X, 597b, wherein **God** makes the archetypical bed. Problematically, Plato is led to assert forms of relations (e.g., "equality" in *Phaedo* 74a ff) and of negations (ugly, bad, unjust, etc., *Republic* 476a, for example). Putting it another way, one can find examples in the dialogues that appear to commit Plato to the belief that there are *eidē* of items in all of **Aristotle**'s 10 **categories**.

One supposes that Plato is led to that because he is convinced that the forms are necessary for the **being**, knowability, and sayability of anything in the phenomenal world, so there must, in principle, be forms for anything that is, is known, or can be truly said. Still, there is clearly a hierarchy of Forms that lies behind much of what Plato says in the dialogues. In the *Republic*, the Good is the "Sun" that illuminates all the other forms; in the *Phaedrus*, the **Charioteer** sees some forms and not others; in the *Timaeus* the **Demiourgos** looks at a structured set of forms to create the universe. The occupants and structure of the world of forms must have been a lively topic in the early **Academy**, since we get reports of quite different accounts attributed to **Speusippos** and **Xenocrates**.

Aristotle accepted the use of the word *eidos* as picking out a natural kind but rejected the notion that the *eidos* could exist independently of the individual material members of that kind. The word works in tandem with the word *genos*; in any analysis of kinds of things, the larger class is a *genos* and the subgroups of the *genos* are *eidē*. In a definition, according to Aristotle, there is a *genos* term and a *diaphora*, difference.

EIKASIA. In the **Sun-Line-Cave** passage in **Plato**'s *Republic*, the epistemic condition corresponding to the lowest part of the line, and thus to the prisoners in the Cave, is said to be *eikasia*. Since this is also said to be the epistemic condition of most people most of the time, there is some discussion concerning what, precisely, Plato means to say about this condition by using this word. While the word is obviously related to *eikōn*, it has a pre-Platonic life with the sense "conjecture, guesswork." We might also note that we are told that *doxa* is divided into *pistis* and *eikasia*: we might parse this distinction by saying that beliefs are either well grounded or poorly grounded, with *eikasia* denoting the second. In the same vein, at *Meno* 98 **Socrates** uses the verb form (*eikazein*) to refer to opinions that might wander off, like the statues of Daedalus, if not tied down by an **appropriate logos**.

Aristotle occasionally uses the verb with the meaning "conjecture," for example at *EN* II.6, 1106b30, where the **Pythagoreans**

"conjecture" that evil belongs to the class of unlimited, and good to the limited.

EIKŌN. Image. In **Plato**'s mode of thinking in terms of *mimēsis*, the "imitation" of the real entity is an *eikōn*. The cave-dwellers, in the **Sun-Line-Cave** passage in the *Republic*, are in an epistemic state of *eikasia*, all they are aware of is images, imitations. Of course any representational art that begins from these images is one more step away from reality (*Rep.* X). But at a higher level, so to speak, the visible world is the *eikōn* of the intelligible world (*Tm.* 30), time is the moving *eikōn* of eternity (*Tm.* 37d).

EKPYROSIS. Conflagration. According to the **Stoics**, the entire universe periodically all turns to **fire** and then starts over again. The fire that it turns into is at the same time **God**, that is, in the *ekpyrosis*, the entire universe is literally one living rational being; that being then recommences the process of creating a varied universe.

EKSTASIS. Literally, displacement. **Aristotle** uses it for physical displacements, normally; a psychological sense appears in the biological context (*PA* II.4, 650b30ff), where bulls and boars are *ekstatikos*, "excitable." At least once, Aristotle uses the word to talk of insanity at *Cat.* 10a1 (*ekstasis manikē*). The word occurs fairly frequently in the *New Testament*, e. g., *Luke* 5.26, usually to mean something like "amazement." In **Plotinus**, it is used of the ultimate mystical union, *Enn.* VI.9.11.

ELEATIC SCHOOL. The noted members of the Eleatic School are **Parmenides of Elea, Zeno of Elea,** and **Melissus of Samos.** Sometimes **Xenophanes of Colophon** is cited as at least a precursor of the school, if not directly a teacher of Parmenides. We may add a fictional member of the school, the "Eleatic Stranger," who appears in **Plato**'s *Sophist* and *Statesman*. The Eleatic School is notable for its uncompromising argumentation that **being** is one and that change and multiplicity are illusory.

ELEMENT. *See STOICHEION.*

ELENCHUS. This word literally means "examination." In the context of Greek philosophy, it is used primarily of **Socrates'** method of questioning. Typically, the people with whom Socrates discusses commit themselves to believing some proposition, very often the definition of some personal quality, or at least a characterization of such a quality; by persistent questioning, these people come to admit also to believing something inconsistent with that original proposition. In some cases, Socrates' interlocutors propose amended hypotheses that are again in turn "examined" and again are shown to be inconsistent with other beliefs of the interlocutor. The entire process may be construed either as an examination of a belief or chain of beliefs, or as an examination of the person himself: for example, the *elenchus* of Meno in the *Meno* or of **Protagoras** in the *Protagoras* is not just an examination of possible understandings of the meaning of the word "virtue" (*aretē*) but also an examination of the character of Meno or of Protagoras himself.

ELEUTHERIA. Freedom, as opposed to slavery.

ELEUTHERIŌTĒS. Liberality, generosity: the virtue (*aretē*) of acting like a free person as opposed to acting slavishly.

ELIAN SCHOOL. School of philosophy founded by **Phaedo of Elis**; it was succeeded by the **Eretrian School** at the time of **Menedemus**, who moved the school from Elis to Eretria. Since Phaedo was a disciple of **Socrates**, the school is assumed to be roughly "Socratic" in character. The Elian School should not be confused with the **Eleatic School**, based in Elea, in southern Italy. Elis is in the western Peloponnesus.

ELIAS. Name associated with a commentary on **Porphyry's** *Isagoge*, a commentary on **Aristotle's** *Categories*, and some comments on Aristotle's *Prior Analytics*, produced, as it seems, in the sixth century CE in **Alexandria**.

EMPEDOCLES OF ACRAGAS (c. 492–432 BCE). Empedocles wrote two poems (or one poem with two parts), *On Nature* and *Purifications*.

We have more than 150 fragments of his poetry. Starting from **Pythagorean** and **Eleatic** insights, Empedocles claimed that there are four material elements (*stoicheia*): **earth**, **water**, **air**, and **fire**, and two cosmic forces that act on those elements: Love (*Philia*) and Strife (*Neikos*). When Strife gains absolute ascendance, the four elements are separated out into concentric spheres; as Love gains ascendancy, the elements join together to form organic unities, including living beings; in the total ascendancy of Love, the **cosmos** is one great spherical living being. Both of the extreme conditions are unstable, and indeed the processes of coming to be and passing away that we observe in the world are local examples of this cosmic cycle. Empedocles applies his ideas to a wide range of natural phenomena, including, prominently, his observations of physiological processes.

Empedocles' religious ideas seem to be essentially **Pythagorean**, asserting that human beings have the souls (*psychai*) of fallen **angels** (*daimones*) that are paying for some obscure sin by living repeated lives in many life forms. Since human souls can inhabit animal bodies, and even some vegetables, Empedocles believes that the consumption of meat is a sin for which we pay by even more cycles of rebirth, and that we should also avoid bay leaves and beans.

The theory of the four elements is generally taken to be, in part, a response to **Parmenides**, since they are characterized as in themselves permanent and unchanging, as Parmenides asserted **being** to be. Empedocles goes on to try to explain how complex beings, including (especially) living things, are constructed of the four elements. Part of that story is a kind of abbreviated evolutionary account which proposes that some forms that have been generated have perished, leaving what we see today. *See also STOICHEION.*

ENANTIA. Opposites. Several different ancient Greek physical theories supposed that change involved some tension or alternation between opposite characters. **Heraclitus** is an obvious example: "Things taken together are whole and not whole, brought together and brought apart, in tune and out of tune, out of all things there comes a **unity** and out of unity all things" (f. 10). The **Pythagoreans** constructed a list of oppositions, cited by **Aristotle** in *Metaphysics* I.5 thus:

Limited	Unlimited
Odd	Even
One	Plurality
Right	Left
Male	Female
At Rest	Moving
Straight	Bent
Light	Darkness
Good	Evil
Square	Oblong

Empedocles had "love" (*philia*) and "strife" (*neikos*); **Plato**, in the *Timaeus*, makes the "circles of the same and different" part of the fundamental **cosmology**. For Aristotle, the lowest level of **matter** is not really **earth**, **water**, **air**, and **fire** but the pairs of opposites that characterize those elements: hot and cold, fluid and solid (*Parts of Animals* II.1, 646a17). *See also DYAS; STOICHEION.*

ENARGEIA. The self-evidence of perceived facts, in Epicurean philosophy: **Epicurus**, *Letter to Herodotus*, 82. The "transparent clarity" of immediate perception (*aisthēsis*) is already noted by **Socrates** at *Theaetetus* 179c6, without conceding that it is knowledge (*epistēmē*). The **Stoics** and later **Academics** also note the "self-evidence" of some perceptions; whether one should take that self-evidence as tantamount to some sort of knowledge was a matter for discussion throughout the Hellenistic period.

END. *See TELOS.*

ENDOXA. Accepted opinions. **Aristotle** often begins the study of a topic by summarizing the *endoxa*, with the apparent goal of critiquing those he must and incorporating into his position as many as he can. "*Endoxa* are opinions that seem true to all or to the majority or to the wise" (*Topics* 1, 100a). The procedure is a kind of **dialectical** argument that is in some ways similar to that used by Plato, for Plato's dialogues often begin with some statement of common opinions. But there is a difference of emphasis, since Plato is most often concerned with refuting the opinions stated at the beginning, and Aristotle explicitly expects to find something reliable derived from the history of human thought. After Aristotle, collections of opinions are often used in a skeptical way: given that so many wise people have thought such disparate and indeed contradictory things, perhaps we are best off suspending our belief entirely. *See also DOXA*.

ENERGEIA. "Activity," or **actuality**," made into a technical term by **Aristotle**, defined in detail in ***Metaphysics*** IX.6–9. The word is based on **ergon**, meaning "work" or "function." For Aristotle, a process, such as life, that is valuable in itself is an *energeia*, an actualization of potentials for such an activity to occur. **Dynameis**, potentials or powers, are passive or active; if an active power works on the **appropriate** passive power an *energeia* results. Aristotle gives many examples of this form of analysis: if the active power present in the male semen comes into contact with the passive potentiality present in a developing chicken egg, the activity of embryological development of a chick results. If an active carpenter chooses to work with a pile of passive lumber, the activity of housebuilding may result. The *energeia* participates in the end (*telos*). *See also ENTELECHEIA*.

ENKRATEIA, ENKRATĒS (EGKRATEIA, EGKRATĒS). Self-control, a self-controlled person, often opposed to *akrateia* (or **akrasia**), *akrates*. In *Republic* IV, 430–31, **Socrates** argues that self-control is an incoherent concept, on the ground that the person controlling and the person controlled are presumably one and the same, while the idea of "control" is intrinsically binary. Presumably a truly unitary personality would simply do the right thing, effortlessly. By implication, however, *akrateia* IS possible, if one's personality is divided and at war with itself.

    Aristotle discusses *enkrateia* specifically at *EN* VII.1–11. He distinguishes it from temperance, **sōphrosynē**, in that the **sōphrōn** habitually chooses correctly concerning bodily pleasures, presumably with no great effort once the good habits are established, while the *enkratēs* overcomes temptation in order to act correctly with regard to those same pleasures.

ENNEADS. The writings and teachings of **Plotinus**, as recorded, edited, and arranged by **Porphyry**. There are six books, each divided into nine tractates: thus the name "enneads," which means "nines." These numbers, as well as their product, 54, doubtless had esoteric meaning for Porphyry.

ENNOĒMA. Concept. **Aristotle** uses the term in *Metaph.* I.1, 981a6, as a product of experience. In **Stoic** epistemology, there is a distinction between *ennoia* and *ennoēma*: the *ennoēma* is particular, the *ennoia* is general.

ENNOIA. Concept or idea; literally, something in the mind (*nous*). In **Plato**, the usual word for this is *noēma* (*see noēsis*). **Aristotle** uses both words. *Ennoia* becomes a technical term in **Stoic** philosophy, where "common concepts" or *koinai ennoiai* are an important criterion (*kritērion*) of truth, a fundamental part of the epistemological system. *See also ENNOĒMA.*

ENTELECHEIA. Word invented by **Aristotle** suggesting the actual presence of an end—a Greek could understand the word as "having an end in it." There is a closely similar word, already in use before Aristotle's time, *endelecheia*, with a "d" instead of a "t," meaning "continuity" or "persistence," and Aristotle is doubtless using that connotation as well. One of the more famous places where Aristotle applies the word is in his definition of the soul (*psychē*) as "the first *entelecheia* of a natural organic body," going on to explain that the soul is the actual presence of capacities (*dynameis*) of performing life functions. *See also ENERGEIA.*

EPAGŌGĒ. Literally, bringing up, proposing, and thus to a method of persuasion. In **Plato**, *Statesman* 278a, for example, it means a way of educating someone. **Aristotle** makes it something of a technical term, which we translate normally as "induction." "*Epagōgē* is a passage from **particular**s to universals." Comparing "induction" to "deduction," Aristotle says that "induction is more convincing and clear; it is more readily learnt by the use of the senses and is applicable generally to the mass of people, but deduction is more forcible and more effective against contradictious people" (*Top.* I.12, 105a10). The quick justification of induction in Aristotle's thought is, "The universal is present in the clearly known **particular**" (*see KATHOLOU*). Plato sometimes uses the word *synagōgē* for a process rather similar in some respects to Aristotelian induction.

EPAISTHĒSIS. Sensory recognition. The **Epicureans** argued that perception can be reliable; the fact that we "recognize" items in our sensory field without any need to reason about it is one indication of that reliability.

EPH' HĒMIN. Up to us, in our power. Although the **Stoics** are rigid determinists, they also say that when the causal chain goes through us, the consequences are "up to us," "in our power." As **Epictetus** puts it (I.1.7), it is a matter of how we use our impressions, how we think about things.

EPIBOLĒ. In **Epicurean** epistemology, focus of **attention** on the perceptual given; attention. This concept functions a bit as a fourth criterion (*kritērion*) of truth (*alētheia*), in addition to sensations, preconceptions (*prolēpseis*), and feelings.

EPICTETUS (c. 50–135 CE). Born into slavery in Hieropolis, Phrygia, Epictetus learned **Stoic** philosophy from **Musonius Rufus**. Freed from slavery, he set up his school in Nicopolis (Epirus, in northwest Greece). His student **Arrian** copied down his major teachings in a book called the *Encheiridion* (Handbook) and many of his **diatribes**, available in a largish volume called, in English, *Discourses*.

EPICURUS AND EPICUREANISM. Epicurus was born about 341 BCE and lived in Samos and various places in Ionia; about 307, he moved to **Athens** and purchased the home and **Garden** where his friends and followers gathered; he died in about 270. Of his many writings, three complete *Letters* and two collections of his sayings survive, as well as numerous fragments and some papyrus from Herculaneum, probably from the library of Phildemus, an Epicurean philosopher. Otherwise, the major sources for the philosophy of Epicurus are the biography in **Diogenes Laertius** X, the great poem of **Lucretius**, *De Rerum Natura*, and the inscriptions of **Diogenes of Oenoanda**.

The immediate followers of Epicurus included (among others) **Hermarchus**, **Metrodorus of Lampsacus**, and Polyaenus, who also wrote texts available in antiquity. The school included several women, and Epicurus tried to make his teachings accessible to everyone, regardless of level of education or culture.

Epicurus, as an **atomist** in his physical theory, followed the teachings of **Leucippus** and **Democritus** but added the idea of the **swerve**—that atoms (*atoma*) would occasionally move randomly rather than predictably. The "gospel" of Epicurus is that there is no life after death, consequently no punishment or suffering after death, so the best we can do is to concentrate on making our present life as happy as possible. Epicurus was both a psychological and ethical hedonist. *See also TETRAPHARMAKON.*

EPIEIKEIA. Reasonableness, Equity; defined by **Aristotle**, *EN* V.10, 1137a32ff, as "the just, but not the legally just but a correction of legal justice" where the universality of the law does not deal correctly with individual cases. The word is used somewhat ambiguously of equitable states of affairs and of equitable people.

EPIMARTYREIN. Attest. In **Epicurean** epistemology, true opinions are those that are "attested" and uncontested by self-evidence.

EPIPHORA. Term used by **Chrysippus** to denominate the conclusion of a **syllogism**.

EPISTĒMĒ. Knowledge, particularly knowledge of necessarily true propositions, derived from the verb *epistasthai*, to stand upon. The **Presocratics** do not usually use the word *epistēmē*; they prefer *sophia, gnomē*, or *gnōsis*. One place where the verb form occurs is **Heraclitus** f. 41. "Wisdom is one thing: it is to know (*epistasthai*) the thought that steers all things through all things." **Stobaeus** cites **Democritus** as saying (f. 181), "Thus a person becomes simultaneously courageous and right-thinking in virtue of understanding and knowledge (*epistēmē*) of correct action." In **Plato**, *epistēmē* is regularly about the forms (*eidē*), whether in the *Meno, Phaedo, Republic, Sophist*, or *Timaeus*. In the *Theaetetus*, the hypotheses that *epistēmē* is the same as perception (*aisthēsis*), true opinion (*alēthē doxa*), or true opinion with an account (*logos*), are all refuted.

For **Aristotle**, *epistēmē* is about the causes, represented in syllogistic deductions (*Posterior Analytics*). In *Metaphysics* VI, Aristotle says that *epistēmē* may be distinguished into practical, productive, and theoretical, and that theoretical knowledge may be distinguished into mathematical, physical, and theological. In translations of Aristotle, *epistēmē* is often and reasonably translated as "**science**."

Zeno the Stoic, according to **Cicero** (*Academica* 2.145), spread out his fingers of one hand and said "An impression is like this"; then he brought his fingers together a little and said "Assent is like this." Then, making a fist, he said that this was *katalēpsis*; and bringing his other hand and wrapping it strongly around his fist, said that this was *epistēmē* and that only the wise man possesses it.

EPITHYMIA. Appetite, desire. For **Plato**, the *epithymētikon*, or desiderative part of the soul (*psychē*), is characteristic of the productive classes in the *Republic*, and the relevant virtue (*aretē*) is temperance (*sophrosynē*). For **Aristotle**, *epithymia* is the *orexis* for **pleasure**.

EPOCHĒ. Suspension of judgment. The recommendation that one suspend judgment in order to live more happily characterizes Pyrrhonian skepticism (DL IX.61–62). The Academic skeptics would, I think, suspend judgment even about that proposition. *See also SKEPTIKOS*.

EQUITY. *See EPIEIKEIA*.

ERASISTRATUS (from Iulis on Ceos) (c. 315–240 BCE). Erasistratus was a physician, said to have connections with the **Peripatos**. He practiced medicine (*iatrikē*) both in Antioch and in **Alexandria**. **Pliny** claims that Erasistratus was the grandson of **Aristotle**, via Aristotle's daughter Pythias. Erasistratus is attested to have dissected human cadavers, and **Celsus** says that he vivisected condemned criminals provided by the Alexandrian court. Erasistratus took special interest in the nervous and circulatory systems; his dissections advanced the understanding of both, although he thought that the nerves were hollow (with psychic *pneuma* inside them), and that the arteries had "vital" *pneuma* in them. Although **Galen** criticized him, he also followed much that Erasistratus said.

ERATOSHENES (c. 276–194 BCE). Originally from Cyrene (Libya), Eratosthenes was Head of the Library in **Alexandria** after **Apollo-**

nius of Rhodes, from about 247. Although he studied with the Stoic **Aristo of Chios**, he is best known as a geographer; he accurately calculated the circumference of the **Earth**. He also worked at stabilizing Hellenic chronology by compiling a list of Olympic victors with the years of their victories.

ERETRIAN SCHOOL. The **Eretrian School** was a continuation of the **Elian School**, founded by **Phaedo of Elis**, transferred to Eretria by **Menedemus**. The school is assumed to have been **Socratic** in some sense.

ERGON. Work, function. **Heraclitus** f. 48: "The name of the bow is life (*bios*), but its *ergon* is death." **Aristotle** distinguishes different senses: the activity and the goal (*EE* II.1, 1219a13ff). So the *ergon* of the art of medicine (*iatrikē*) is both the process of curing and the ultimate state of health. In other cases, the activity IS the goal, as seeing, contemplating, and indeed living. *Ergon* is the basis for Aristotle's technical term *energeia*.

ERIS. Strife, with *Philia* (friendship), one of the **Empedocles'** two cosmic motivating principles, though he somewhat more frequently uses the word *neikos* for strife. In **Heraclitus**, *eris* is one of the words for the opposition of opposites: f. 80: "We must know that war is common to all and strife (*eris*) is justice, and that all things come into being through strife necessarily."

ERISTIC. *Eristikē.* Verbal competition aimed at victory, not necessarily understanding. **Plato** and **Aristotle** distinguish "eristic" from "**dialectic**," accusing some **Sophists** of willfully using patently bad arguments competitively. Plato's *Euthydemus* and Aristotle's *Sophistical Refutations* both present many such arguments.

ERŌS. Love or desire—especially sexual; personified as the **God** of love. **Parmenides**: "First of all the Gods she contrived *Eros*" (f. 13). Two of **Plato**'s most famous dialogues focus on understanding *eros*, the *Symposium* and the *Phaedrus*. Plato's true or best *eros* is a desire for union with the beautiful that leads those with more enlightened souls (*psychai*) to seek the forms (*eidē*). Inferior *eros* leads to an attempt to satisfy physical desires, particularly sexual. Plotinus also speaks of *eros* as motivating union with the one: *Enn.* I.6. *See also PHILIA*.

ESOTERIC PHILOSOPHY. *See EXŌTERIKOI LOGOI.*

ESSENCE. *"Essentia"* is **Cicero**'s translation of **Aristotle**'s phrase, *to ti ēn einai*. The Greek phrase literally means something like "the what it would be to be (something)" or "the to be what is." Cicero's translation reasonably enough takes the infinitive and the participle of the Latin verb meaning "to be": *esse* and *ens*, plus the abstract ending, *-tia*, to make an abstract noun meant to convey the sense of Aristotle's phrase. The essence, or "the what it is to be x," corresponds with the definition of the *eidos*: thus, if "thunder" is defined as "the noise of **fire** being quenched in the clouds" that set of words conveys the essence of thunder, it tells you what thunder is (*Top.* 102a3). In *Metaphysics* VII.4–6, Aristotle makes it clear that we can distinguish between essential and non-essential properties: if Roger is human, then it belongs to Roger's essence that he is a language-user; but the shade of his skin is not part of Roger's essence, although it is part of his *ousia* as an individual thing. *See also BEING; TI ESTI.*

ESTI. "IS," the third person singular of the verb *einai*, to be. It is the word of truth that the **Goddess** brings to **Parmenides** (f. 2, 3). *See also OUSIA; TI ESTI.*

ETERNITY. *See AIŌN.*

ETHER. *See AITHĒR.*

ETHICS. Aristotle, inventor of the word "ethics" (see next entry), says that "in the time of **Socrates**, people turned from inquiry into nature, and philosophers turned to political studies and the useful virtues" (*PA* I.2, 642a30). An overly strong reading of that statement would suggest that there was no "moral philosophy" before the late fifth century BCE. Of course there was some, but in terms of degree of emphasis, it is fair to say that there was a philosophical shift. **Heraclitus**, the **Pythagoreans**, and **Empedocles**, all had things to say about how one ought to live; even more, the poets often had much to say about the good life—or the bad life, depending on the poem and the poet.

But in a way, Aristotle is right in that philosophical *discussion* of morality largely begins "in the time of Socrates" and most especially with the challenge to traditional morality posed by the **Sophists** and with Socrates' counter-attack.

Ancient philosophers, from that time on, often focused primarily on how one ought to live one's life; the **Epicureans** taught that living apart from the world, undisturbed, was the path to happiness, the **Stoics** obeyed the dictates of cosmic reason in their lives.

ĒTHIKE ARETĒ. Moral virtue. The phrase is **Aristotle's**, distinguishing excellences of character and habit from physical health, on the one hand, and virtues of skill and intelligence, on the other. He emphasizes courage (*andreia*) and temperance (*sophrosynē*) but includes the virtues of liberality (*eleutheriōtēs*), magnificence (*megaloprepeia*), proper pride (*megalopsychia*), **appropriate** ambition, even-temperedness, sociability, honesty, wittiness, and tact in his discussion in *EN* IV. Aristotle also distinguishes (in *EN* V) several personal qualities centered around justice: being a "just" person both in the sense of fair and in the sense of law-abiding (*see dikaiosynē*), and equitableness (*epieikeia*).

Plato discusses some of these virtues, without calling them "ethical," in various dialogues. The *Laches* focuses on courage, the *Charmides* on temperance, and the *Republic* on both of those plus justice. It is interesting to note that Aristotle has nothing to say about "piety" or *hosiotēs*, the topic of Plato's *Euthyphro*.

ĒTHOS. Character. **Heraclitus** f. 119: "*ēthos anthropōi daimōn*," "For a human being, character is destiny." Virtue **ethics**, whether **Socratic**, **Aristotelian**, or **Stoic**, is in a sense about "character"—"*ēthikos*," as in the title of Aristotle's *Nicomachean* and *Eudemian "Ethics*," is the adjective form of the noun. **Zeno the Stoic** is quoted as saying "*Ēthos* is the spring of life from which actions individually flow" (SVF I.50).

EUBULIDES OF MILETUS (Fourth century BCE). Megarian philosopher, successor of **Euclides** as head of the school. He is credited with formulating the "Liar" paradox, the "Bald Man" paradox, and several others of the sort. *See also* MEGARIAN SCHOOL.

EUCLID OF ALEXANDRIA (fl. c. 300 BCE). Geometer, supposed to be the author of the *Elements*, *Sectio Canonis*, *Phenomena*, *Optics*, and *Data*. These works were fundamental for the study of mathematics for more than 2,000 years. Euclid is thought to have been a **Peripatetic** in his philosophical leanings. *See also* MATHĒMA.

EUCLIDES OF MEGARA (c. 450–380 BCE). Socratic, founded a school in Megara. Euclides is in the "frame" dialogue of the *Theaetetus*; he claims that he wrote down the dialogue as **Socrates** told it to him. He is listed as present in the *Phaedo*. **Diogenes Laertius** says (3.6) that **Plato** and other associates of Socrates visited Euclides after the death of Socrates. Diogenes also says that Euclides rather liked **Parmenides'** philosophy (DL 2.106). *See also* MEGARIAN SCHOOL.

EUDAIMONIA. Happiness; literally, the condition of having a good **angel**, widely regarded as the ultimate goal of human existence. **Democritus** B171 gives a good summary of the popular philosophical understanding:

> Happiness does not dwell in flocks of cattle or in gold. Happiness, like unhappiness, is a property of the soul (*psychē*). And it is right that men should value the soul rather than the body (*sōma*); for perfection of soul corrects the inferiority of the body, but physical strength without intelligence does nothing to improve the mind. Men find happiness neither by means of the body nor through possessions but through uprightness and wisdom.

The conclusion of **Plato** *Rep.* I, against **Thrasymachus**, is that it is the just person who is happy (*Rep.* I, 354); that thesis is, in a sense, defended throughout the rest of the *Republic*. In *EN*, **Aristotle** defines *eudaimonia* as "virtuous activity of the soul" and makes it the goal of human existence, as if everyone, at least in principle, agreed with that thesis. For the **Stoics**, *eudaimonia* is not the end of life (that would be virtue itself) but is a concomitant of the virtuous life). For the **Epicureans**, happiness is the maximization of pleasure (*hēdonē*) and minimization of pain (*lypē*).

EUDEMUS OF RHODES (Late fourth century BCE). A student of **Aristotle**, he founded an Aristotelian school in Rhodes. He seems to have taken copies of (many of) the books in the **Lyceum** library; according to ancient accounts, those copies are the ultimate source of much of the Aristotelian **corpus** we have today. His major contributions were in logic, mathematics, and the history of these and related fields. **Alexander of Aphrodisias** and other later authors cite him rather frequently; for example, he is thought to have argued that "existence" is a predicate. He was credited with the *Eudemian Ethics* at one time, but it is now thought that this was simply the version of Aristotle's *Ethics* present in the library of Eudemus.

EUDORUS OF ALEXANDRIA (First century BCE). Eudorus was a Platonist, a contemporary of **Arius Didymus**. He wrote a *Concise Survey of Philosophy*, apparently arranged by subject matter rather than chronologically; significant pieces and reports of his writings are preserved by **Stobaeus**. His interest in **Pythagorean** thought anticipates the flourishing of **Neopythagoreanism** over the next several centuries; his anti-Aristotelian stands also anticipate the views of many subsequent Platonists.

EUDOXUS OF CNIDUS (c. 408–355 BCE). In antiquity he was counted as a **Pythagorean**. He studied with **Archytas** in Tarentum and traveled to **Egypt** to study mathematics and **astronomy**. He also studied with **Plato**; he is reported both to have had his own school and to have been associated with Plato in the **Academy**. His mathematical discoveries are reported (and included) in **Euclid**; his astronomical explanations influenced those of **Aristotle** in *Metaphysics* XII. Aristotle also attributes to him a hedonistic ethical theory (*EN* X.2, 1172b). *See also MATHĒMA.*

EULOGOS. Reasonable, sensible, probable. The adverbial form, *eulogōs*, also occurs frequently enough.

EUNAPIUS OF SARDIS (c. 346–after 414 CE). Eunapius was the author of *Lives of the Philosophers and Sophists*, a book of biographies of **Neoplatonists** beginning from **Plotinus**, contemporary rhetoricians (**sophists**), and a few physicians with philosophical or rhetorical education. Eunapius, a committed pagan, provides an interesting perspective on the interaction between **Christianity** and paganism in the intellectual world of the fourth century CE.

EUPATHEIA. The state of having positive feelings about something (see **Aristotle** *EN* VIII.9, 1159a21); the condition of having innocent emotions, in **Stoic** philosophy.

EUSEBIUS OF CAESAREA (c. 275–339 CE). Christian apologist and church historian; his account of the conflict between Arians and Athanasians is particularly informative. He was a major contributor to the formulation of the canonical Christian Bible.

EUTHYDEMUS OF CHIOS. Sophist, appears in **Plato**'s dialogue named after him, with his brother Dionysodorus. **Aristotle** cites him a couple of times for sophistic arguments that do not appear in the dialogue.

EVERLASTING. *See AIDIOS.*

EVIL. *See KAKON.*

EXISTENCE. *See OUSIA, HYPARCHEIN.*

EXŌTERIKOI LOGOI. Literally, "exterior accounts." **Aristotle** uses the phrase several times, and scholars have puzzled over what precisely it means. What or whose *logoi* would those exterior *logoi* be? In two *EN* passages (*EN* I.13, 1102a26; VI.3, 1140a3), it would be easy to take the reference to be to non-Aristotelians or to non-specialists in philosophy; at *Pol.* III.6, 1278b30 and VII.1, 1323a21, the reference is clearly to *Aristotle's own* popular presentations. Similarly, at **Metaphysics** XIII.1, 1076a28, it makes more sense to suppose that he is referring to his own "external *logoi*." Are any of the works that survive in the **Corpus** Aristotelicum *exōterikoi logoi*? Some scholars of Aristotle would respond, "probably not."

A possible source of confusion for those who are not familiar with the Greek language is the use of the phrase *esōterikoi logoi* by **Galen**, some **Stoics**, and some **Neoplatonists**. This phrase means "*interior* accounts." "*Exō-*" means "outside," "*esō-*" means inside. Probably the phrase was coined to contrast "exterior" and "interior" accounts—naturally enough, if Aristotle says in the **Ethics** and *Politics* that there are some other works that are "exterior," the works in which that locution occurs must be "interior" (**Lucian**, *Vit. Auct.* 26). From there, it is an easy step to calling teachings that are keep secret from the general public, like oral teachings of the **Pythagorean** school, "esoteric," as **Iamblichus** does. The **Gnostic** and **Hermetic** movements were in principle esoteric, in that sense, since they tended to keep their teachings within the school. *See also* UNWRITTEN TEACHINGS.

EXPERIENCE. *See AISTHĒSIS.*

EXPERTISE. *See TECHNĒ.*

EXPLANATION. *See AITION.*

EXPRESSION (LINGUISTIC). *See LEXIS.*

EXTREMITY. *See AKRA, AKRON.*

EXTENSION. *See DIASTĒMA.*

– F –

FACULTY (OF THE SOUL). *See DYNAMIS.*

FALSE. *See* PSEUDOS.

FAMILIAR. *See PAR' HĒMIN, OIKEION.*

FATE. *See ANAGKĒ, HEIMARMENĒ.*

FEELING. *See PATHOS.*

FIGMENT (OF IMAGINATION). *See PHANTASMA.*

FIGULUS, PUBLIUS NIGIDIUS (d. 45 BCE). Friend of **Cicero** who attempted to revive **Pythagorean** philosophy and **magic**. He may be credited with anticipating the **Neopythagorean** movement, which really got rolling about 100 years after his death.

FINAL CAUSE. *See TELOS.*

FIRE. *See PYR, STOICHEION, TECHNIKOS.*

FIRST MOVER. *See ARCHĒ KINĒSEŌS, PRŌTON KINOUN.*

FIRST PHILOSOPHY. *See PRŌTĒ PHILOSOPHIA.*

FORM. *See EIDOS; IDEA; MORPHĒ.* For a brief discussion of **Plato**'s Theory of Forms, *see EIDOS.*

FORMAL CAUSE. Aristotle distinguishes four "causes" (*aitia*) or modes of explanation: matter (*hylē*), mover (*kinoun*), form (*eidos*), and end (*telos*). The formal cause corresponds to the answer of the question, "what is it?" Although he sees some of the ideas of his predecessors as anticipations of his theory of the formal cause, he is quite definite that none of them really "got it." Two anticipations are particularly instructive, those of **Democritus** and **Plato**. Democritus says that everything is made of atoms (*atoma*); the differences between things at the gross level are consequences not only of differences in shape of the atoms of which they are composed but also in the way that they are arranged and connected to each other (*Metaphysics* I.4, 985b14–19). That sort of explanation might work at the molecular level but does nothing for entities of a higher degree of complexity.

Plato, in contrast, has "forms" (*eidē*) at whatever level one might need for explanation, but from an Aristotelian point of view he perversely separates them from the entities they are meant to explain. If we ask, "what is Dobbin?" the right answer cannot refer to something located elsewhere than in Dobbin.

If we say that Dobbin is a horse, that is its *eidos*. If we ask, "what's a horse?" the answer could be placing that sort of entity within a larger class and telling how this sort of **being** differs from other sorts within that class. So we might say that "horse" is "solid-hoofed maned animal," from which we could reasonably conclude that Dobbin has solid hooves and a mane. Further pursuit along this line could lead us in anatomical, zoological, ecological, or even agricultural directions, but ultimately it all refers back to Dobbin. So, to pursue this example further, Aristotle tells us that horses are viviparous quadrupeds, herbivores with consequent peculiarities in dentition; that there are interesting differences between horses and related species. He adds details about their mating and generally about their reproduction and so on. But all of these details refer back to what we know about individual horses.

Aristotle believes that his theory of the formal cause is original also because it is at the same time a teleological theory. That is, Aristotle starts from the assumption that the existence of entities and the continued existence of species is a good thing. Thus, the characteristics of Dobbin that are most important are those that enable Dobbin to continue to survive and to reproduce. So the formal cause of any living being includes whatever capacities it has that enable it to survive and reproduce, the soul, or ***psychē***.

Very often, people explain Aristotle's theory of the four causes by using the example of a statue—the matter is marble, the mover is the sculptor, the form is the shape of Apollo, the end is to be a beautiful thing. While the example is not totally wrong, it is not truly Aristotelian either, since Aristotle focuses primarily on *living* things, characterized by hierarchical orderings of complex arrangements of material. So the horse (to continue with that example) is a complex arrangement of tissues and organs with emergent properties that make it a horse rather than a cow, for example. *See also GENOS; OUSIA.*

FREEDOM. *See ELEUTHERIOTĒS.*

FREEDOM FROM DISTURBANCE. *See ATARAXIA.*

FRIENDSHIP. *See PHILIA.*

FUNCTION. *See ENERGEIA; ERGON.*

– G –

GALEN OF PERGAMUM (129–after 210 CE). "The best physician is also a philosopher" (title of a treatise by Galen). Son of a successful architect who sent him to philosophers to be educated, Galen began as a 'student of Gaius' (a well-known **Platonist**), at age 14. At 16 or 17 he took up medicine (*iatrikē*) in addition, and continued his philosophical education with Albinus, another Platonist, in Smyrna (modern Izmir) along with his medical studies. From 152–157 CE, he studied in **Alexandria**, returning to Pergamum to become the resident physician of the gladiatorial school. In 162, when he was in his early 30s, Galen moved to Rome where he rapidly made a name for himself as much by his combative public confrontations with the medical people most in favor at the time as by his medical practice. Four years later, Galen left Rome for a time but apparently was recalled by the Emperor **Marcus Aurelius**, who may well have been attracted by Galen's interests, since Marcus believed that the best *emperor* is also a philosopher. Although Marcus wanted Galen to accompany him on campaign, Galen persuaded him that he should remain in Rome and serve as physician to the heir, the future emperor Commodus. He continued to serve as physician to Commodus during his reign and lived on, probably mainly writing, during the reign of the Emperor Septimius Severus.

We know all this (and much more) about Galen because we have a great many of his writings, more than of any other classical Greek writer, and because some of his writings are autobiographical. Even though he tells us that a good many of his philosophical writings were destroyed in a fire at the Temple of Peace in Rome in 191, we can certainly learn a great deal about his philosophical views from the thousands of his pages that we still possess.

Galen's contributions to philosophical thought need to be discussed in relation to two somewhat distinct parameters: the philosophical schools and the medical "sects" of the second century. One of Galen's primary goals was to develop an adequate theoretical foundation for medical practice. He had to adapt and to adopt whatever he needed from the philosophical traditions available to him and then to construct a theory that would be able to withstand the criticisms coming from alternative positions held by other physicians of his time.

The predominant philosophical schools (or tendencies) of the second century were Platonism, **Aristotelianism**, **Stoicism**, **Epicureanism**, and **Skepticism**. The medical sects (or tendencies) were Empiricist, Methodist, and Dogmatic (or Rationalist). There is no simple correspondence between the philosophical groups and the medical groups, and Galen, despite his various protestations, can be shown to have drawn significantly from all of the philosophical schools and all of the medical sects. He is most explicit about having drawn from **Plato** philosophically and from **Hippocrates**, medically. Galen bases that connection on the positive references to Hippocrates in Plato's writing (*Protagoras* 311b, *Phaedrus* 270c and, by implication, *Charmides* 156e), and on his belief that the medical parts of the *Timaeus* are consistent with the teachings of the Hippocratic **corpus**.

There is a large dose of Aristotelianism in Galen's synthesis, inevitably, since Aristotle's biological works are a great deal more extensive and detailed on matters touching on medicine than Plato's *Timaeus*. Galen, like Aristotle, never tires of saying "nature does nothing in vain" when explaining the functional relationships of the parts of the body. Indeed, one could argue that at the level of natural teleology the philosophies of Plato and Aristotle are not all that opposed to each other, that the distinctions between them turn on issues like the ontological status of the forms (*eidē*) and the immortality of the soul (*psychē*), issues that Galen generally avoids as not directly relevant to establishing a philosophical foundation for medicine. Possibly the most obvious disagreement between Galen and Aristotle concerns the function of the heart, since Aristotle made that organ the center of sensation, movement, and cognition, and Galen delighted in demonstrating experimentally that animals continued to respond to stimuli for a time after their heart was removed but not at all with their brain removed. Of course, Galen had to thank the physicians of Alexandria who discovered the nervous system for this point, but he continued to meet philosophers who had not yet understood the significance of that discovery.

Galen is even more bitingly critical of Stoic philosophy, particularly of **Chrysippus** (in *Opinions of Hippocrates and Plato*, notably), but here, too, we may find influences, mainly unacknowledged. For example, in "On the Passions of the Soul" and "On the Errors of the Soul," Galen gives what amounts to a straightforwardly Stoic analysis of "sickness of soul."

As for the Epicureans and Skeptics, among the philosophers, it is more convenient to see how their doctrines played out among the medical schools of thought. The "Dogmatic" school of medicine was really characterized by their primary opponents, the "Empiricists." Essentially, the Empirical movement in medicine was based on a blanket criticism of medicine as it was practiced in antiquity—the Empiricists held that practicing medicine on the basis of a general philosophical theory of the causes of diseases and of their treatments was unjustified and insupportable, that one should base the practice of medicine solely on experience, never on theory. The Empiricists characterized every medical practice that relied on theory as "Dogmatic" or "Rationalist," in effect pretty much all medical writers since Hippocrates. To be sure, one can distinguish both "Empiricist" and "Rationalist" tendencies even within the Hippocratic corpus: the *Epidemics* are mainly "Empiricist," not offering any causal hypotheses, just describing; while treatises like *On Ancient Medicine* and *Airs Waters Places* are obviously "Rationalist" or "Dogmatic." In its expression in Galen's day, Empiricism was a kind of skepticism about medical knowledge; philosophical skeptics doubted all the traditional philosophical explanatory schemata and medical skeptics doubted all the traditional medical explanatory schemata.

Galen notes with amusement that Empiricists use the treatment modalities devised by Rationalists—once they have seen them work effectively—and Rationalists use the treatment modalities devised by Empiricists—once they have seen them work effectively. The worst sort of medicine, according to Galen, would be one that rejected empirical investigation without having an adequate rational understanding of health and disease; at least the Empiricist will be able to treat those conditions with which he has had adequate experience.

The third medical school, Methodism, is attributed in its inception to a physician who is characterized as philosophically an Epicurean, Asclepiades of Bythynia, from the first century BCE. The Methodist approach was based, in principle, on Epicurean **atomism**, and to that extent it resembled a "Dogmatic" approach, but the crucial distinction of Methodism from the other schools was its insistence on paying attention specifically to the disease and devising a standardized treatment (a "method") for treating identifiable diseases.

Galen took over the four-element (*stoicheion*) theory, going back to **Empedocles**, that the world is composed of **earth, water, air**, and **fire**, or (as Aristotle would have it) of four elementary powers, hot and cold, fluid and solid, and applied it in as subtle and nuanced a way as he was capable of developing. It finds a physiological expression in the theory of the four "humors" that Galen claims to have found in Hippocrates: blood, phlegm, black bile, and yellow bile: health is a balance of these fluids in the body, and disease is an imbalance. That is perhaps the most "dogmatic" aspect of his medical philosophy; otherwise, Galen repeatedly emphasizes careful observation, anatomical and physiological study, and a general recourse to purposive explanations. Galen was a diligent student of formal and informal logic, often using his linguistic skill to score points against his adversaries; he expected physicians to use logic and scientific methodology in trying to understand the illnesses with which they were confronted and in developing treatment plans. Philosophically, perhaps his greatest contribution was to the development of a theoretical foundation for medicine, and more generally, to the development of scientific method and theory of knowledge.

Galen's influence in the ancient Greco-Roman world was at first not predominant; for some time, other medical writers also gained the attention of physicians and the reading public. But by about 350, Galen's synthesis had gained quite general acceptance. Thus, it is not surprising that many of his works were translated into Arabic (primarily by Hunayn Ibn Ishaq), and inspired the "Canon" of Ibn Sina. Indeed, some of his works are known today only in their Arabic translation. The use of Galen by medical people continued more or less unabated in the Greek-speaking eastern empire, into Byzantine times, and doubtless accounts for the fact that we have as many manuscripts as we do of his work.

Although some of Galen's works were known in Latin translation in the early Middle Ages, his influence became much greater with the transmission of Arabic and Byzantine medicine to western Europe after about 1000 CE. For centuries thereafter, Galen's medical philosophy was nearly always seen as a major player in discussions of the understanding of health and disease; his more general philosophical opinions have most often been ignored or rejected—not always as bitingly as by

Maimonides, who called him "ignorant of most things about which he speaks except the medical science." *See also LOGIKĒ.*

GARDEN. Nickname of the **Epicurean School**, parallel with **Stoa** and **Peripatos**. The name does convey a sense of the school's goal of tranquility. It gained that name from the fact that the school was physically located in the home of **Epicurus**, and the home was surrounded by a garden. Epicurus bought the property, between the Dipylon Gate and the **Academy**, in 305 BCE; it was handed down to his successors, although we do not know for how long.

We may note that the places properly called "**Lyceum**" and "Academy" were in fact largely public gardens; the structures that we hear about, whether *gymnasia* or *peripatoi*, were adjacent to tree-shaded areas. Plato had, in addition, a private garden (*kēpos*) in the vicinity of the Academy public space.

GĒ. See EARTH.

GENESIS. **Anaximander**, f. 1: "From that from which things have their *genesis*, to that again is their destruction, according to what must be." *Genesis* is "coming into **being**." After **Parmenides** had denied that genesis could exist (*agenēton*, f. 8, line 3; *genesis* has been driven far off, line 27), subsequent Greek philosophers tried to determine how *genesis could* occur. The materialist solution was that the elements (*stoicheia*) could be rearranged—whether **earth, water, air**, and **fire** (**Empedocles**) or the **atoms**—to make new complex entities, with no "real" becoming, since the elements remained what they were. **Socrates**, at *Phaedo* 96, takes up the issue of *genesis* in the context of a discussion of the immortality of the soul (*psychē*), but we mainly learn of his dissatisfaction with the materialist line of thought. In the *Timaeus*, however, **Plato** attempts a full-scale account of *genesis* in the phenomenal world, depending on **Pythagorean** mathematical models, on the figure of the creative *demiourgos*, and on the introduction of the receptacle (*hypodochē*) that provides a matrix for the appearance of phenomena without any permanent being at the level of the phenomenal world. Thus the Parmenidean ontology turns out for Plato to be true of the forms (*eidē*), and not applicable to the phenomena, which belong to the second part of Parmenides' poem.

For **Aristotle**, this was not a satisfactory solution. For him, the paradigmatic examples of "beings" (*ousiai*) are the universe as a whole and living things, whose being is life and thus simultaneously process. So being and becoming are not mutually exclusive, as they were for Plato, but are both true of the same things. For Aristotle, *genesis* is primarily the coming-into-being of new entities. In any process of *genesis*, there is a pre-existing material that has the potentiality of becoming that which is generated and a source of movement and change that has in itself somehow the form that will come to be in this material; the process of generation is "for the sake of" that which is generated and also in a sense for the species of which it is a member.

Thus, the bricks and lumber can be made into a house by the builder who has in mind a plan of construction, for the sake of shelter. A chicken egg has the possibility of developing into a new chick if fertilized by the rooster, which contributes a source of movement and a crucial element of form for the sake of the existence of the new chick and the species chicken.

From an Aristotelian perspective, *genesis* is distinguished from other sorts of change by the fact that it results in the existence of a new *ousia*. Any philosophical position that holds that all *ousiai* are permanent and none are generated, in effect denies that *genesis* occurs: that would be true of both Platonism and **Atomism**, from Aristotle's point of view. *See also* BECOMING; *STOICHEION*.

GENOS. The basic sense of this word is "offspring," "descent," or more generally a hereditary group of some kind. The word was appropriated as a classificatory term without genetic significance, as "square" belongs to the *genos* of "plane figure" (**Aristotle *Metaphysics*** V.28, 1024b1). So in a proper Aristotelian definition, the *genos* is the larger class to which the ***eidos*** being defined belongs. In this example, "square" is the *eidos*, "plane figure" is the *genos*. The relationship between *eidos* and *genos* varies readily up and down; that is, we might define "dog" as "domesticated canine," where "dog" is the *eidos*, and "canine" is the *genos* (and "domesticated" the *diaphora*). But we can also say that "Laconian hound" is an *eidos* of the *genos* "dog," or that "canine" is an *eidos* of the *genos* "viviparous quadruped."

In the *History of Animals*, Aristotle sometimes talks of "very large (*megista*) *genē*" of animals, but generally these lists are not exhaustive and not always consistent—for example, at *HA* I.6, he mentions birds, fishes, and cetaceans, then shellfish, soft-shells, and shell-less mollusks, and insects. Returning to what we would call vertebrate animals, he mentions viviparous and oviparous. Later, he distinguishes "animals with blood" (essentially our "vertebrates") from "animals without blood" (invertebrates, more or less), at *HA* II.15, 505b26. Aristotle does not have taxonomy as a major goal; rather, the classifications of animals that he does present are constructed as a convenience for exposition of characteristics shared by a number of different sorts of animals.

The **Stoics** apply the word *genos* yet more broadly, so that the largest *genos* is whatever exists (and the smallest *eidos* is the individual entity). They also seem to take the **categories** as genera of **being**, and reduce the number of categories to four.

GNŌMĒ. One of the words for the faculty by which one knows or opines; thought, judgment, opinion. This word is especially prominent in **Presocratic** texts: for example, in **Anaxagoras**, Mind (*nous*) has *gnōmē* of all things (B12). **Democritus** says that there are two kinds of *gnōmē*, "legitimate and bastard." The "bastard" *gnōmē* is that of the senses; the "legitimate" is the one that reveals to us atoms (*atoma*) and the void (DK 68B11).

In **Plato**, the word is relatively rare and tends to mean "opinion" in a non-technical sense. **Aristotle** defines *gnōmē* in the *Rhetoric* (II.21) as "a general statement about questions of practical conduct"; it is thus translated "maxim" at this place in the Oxford Aristotle. In the *Nicomachean Ethics*, at VI.11, *gnōmē* is defined as "the right discrimination of the equitable." A person of *gnōmē* is said to be forgiving, because equitable.

GNŌRIMOS, GNŌRIMON. Well-known; intelligible. *gnōrimōteron*. Better known. *gnōrimōtaton*. Best known. This adjective can refer to "well-known" people; **Aristotle** especially tends to use the neuter form of well-known facts. He often distinguishes between things that are better known "in themselves" or "by nature" or "by reason" and things that are better known "to us." Good **syllogisms** have premises that are "better known" than the conclusions; the definite is "better known" than the indefinite—the comparative form is much the most common.

GNŌSIS. Knowledge by acquaintance; cognition. **Heraclitus** says, "People are deceived about the *gnōsis* of obvious things" (f. 56). **Plato** uses this specific noun relatively rarely, although he does use it of knowledge of the beautiful itself at *Republic* V.476c2. **Aristotle** says that all animals share in some kind of *gnōsis* because they all have the faculty of perception (*aisthēsis*) (*GA* I.23). In the New Testament, *gnōsis* often appears with the sense of "spiritual knowledge," e.g., at *First Letter to the Corinthians* 1.5. In later Greek writers, it is used especially of esoteric knowledge. *See also GNŌSTIKOS.*

GNOSTICISM. Modern scholars have grouped together several philosophical-religious movements of late antiquity under this general heading. General features of these movements include emphasis on self-understanding, a dualistic worldview, and a religious intensity.

GNŌSTIKOS. Cognitive. **Plato's Eleatic** Stranger uses this word in the *Statesman* (258e ff) to refer to "theoretical" as distinguished from "practical" knowledge. This adjective is not normally used to describe esoteric knowledge in ancient texts, although it would be a natural extension from *gnōsis*.

GOD, GODS. Classical Greek religion is notoriously polytheistic and for the most part anthropomorphic. The Olympian deities are well known: Zeus, Hera, Apollo, Ares, Aphrodite, Athena, Poseidon, Demeter, and there are many more divinities that appear in **Hesiod** and elsewhere. At the same time, several of the earliest Greek philosophers strongly criticized the traditional religion. **Xenophanes** charged that not only do the Gods vary to resemble the ethnic groups that portray them, "But if oxen and horses and lions had hands or could create works of art like those made by people, horses would draw pictures of Gods like horses, and oxen of Gods like oxen, and they would make the bodies in accordance with the form that each species itself possesses." So Xenophanes argues that there is one supreme deity, not anthropomorphic at all. Similarly **Heraclitus** says, ". . . .they talk to these statues as if one were to hold conversation with houses, in ignorance of the nature of both Gods and heroes," "One alone is wise, unwilling and willing to be called by the name of Zeus." We are told that **Anaxagoras** was put on trial for impiety, perhaps because he said that at least some heavenly bodies are rocks (on the basis of examining a meteorite), but we also know that he puts Mind (*nous*) in the place of a cosmic deity and seems to leave no place for the traditional Gods. **Protagoras** is quoted saying that he has nothing to say about the Gods, because the question is too large and life is too short. **Socrates** was, of course, convicted and executed on a charge of not respecting the Gods.

We see in Plato and Aristotle and in most Hellenistic philosophers a kind of uneasy truce between a philosophically driven monotheism and the traditional and popular polytheism that continued to dominate the popular imagination in the Greek and, later, the Greco-Roman world. Philosophical monotheism stems from the thought that if the universe is a **unity**, it must have one ultimate causative principle. Plato repeatedly talks about the "*demiourgos*"; in modern terms, the "Intelligent Designer." Aristotle famously argues for the existence of an Unmoved Mover (*akinēton kinoun*), adding a tag line from **Homer**, "The rule of many is not good, one ruler let there be." The **Stoics** have a system that depends upon the unity and omnipotence of God; **Neoplatonists** have a supreme principle that is a One that is Beyond **Being**. At the same time, Plato has the *Demiourgos* create the traditional Greek deities (in the *Timaeus*), and has lots to say about the Gods (plural) throughout the dialogues, and especially that we ought to worship them (this especially in the *Laws*). Aristotle argues explicitly in **Metaphysics** XII that not only is the Unmoved Mover divine, but so are the movers of the celestial entities, the primum mobile, the planets, the sun, and the moon. He even seems to save a place for the traditional deities, at least in the political sphere.

While the **Epicureans** recognize the existence of the traditional Gods, they do not play any important explanatory role in the Epicurean picture of the universe. While the Stoics might sometime seem to be pantheists, one of the most famous Stoic texts is **Clean-**

thes' "Hymn to Zeus," and that seems to be both within orthodox Stoicism and within the mode of expression expected in a polytheistic culture. On the other hand, apart from a passing reference to "the Gods" in the next to last line, the entire poem looks like it would be acceptable in a Jewish, Christian, or Islamic context, with the substitution of "God," "Adonai," or "Allah" for "Zeus."

Perhaps starting with Stoicism, but surely with dual-culture philosophers like **Philo of Alexandria**, the Hellenic concept of God came up against the Semitic concept of God, and each influenced the other during the confrontation of **Judaism** and **Christianity** on the one hand, and Greco-Roman patterns of thought on the other, until the ultimate victory of the monotheists over all forms of polytheism in the Mediterranean world. *See also THEOS.*

GOOD. *See AGATHON, KALON.*

GORGIAS OF LEONTINI (485–373 BCE). Gorgias is regarded as one of the leading early **Sophists,** though he prided himself on being a teacher of rhetoric and not a "philosopher." His show speeches, "Defense of Helen" and "Palamedes," are extant, and he appears several times in **Plato**'s dialogues, especially in the dialogue named for him. **Sextus Empiricus** gives us a very interesting summary of the arguments presented in a treatise called "On What Is Not." He defended the following theses: "Nothing exists"; "If anything were to exist, one could not know it"; "If one did know something, one could not communicate it to anyone else." It is possible that this is directed very specifically against the book of **Melissus**. Perhaps once Gorgias has shown that **Eleatic dialectic** could be turned against itself, he loses faith in the possibility of reliable conclusions from philosophical argument, and turns instead completely to the art of rhetorical persuasion. *See also RHETORIKĒ.*

GRAMMATIKĒ (TECHNĒ). Writing, the art of writing. At the beginning of Greek philosophy, the process of writing was a relatively novel phenomenon in the Greek world; the development of philosophy shows the signs of being a participant in the transition from oral to literate culture. The teachings of **Thales, Pythagoras,**

and **Socrates** were transmitted originally only in oral form; **Plato**'s dialogues are designed to preserve many of the characteristics of face-to-face oral dialogue.

The **Sophists** often focused on techniques of writing, for example the meanings of words, and the different kinds of linguistic expressions. **Aristophanes'** *Clouds* gives a good, if perhaps somewhat exaggerated, impression of the sorts of "grammatical" concerns of the Sophists. Plato reflects those preoccupations, sometimes to satirize them, sometimes to use them for his own purposes. The *Phaedrus*, from 258 to the end, reviews the linguistic interests of the Sophists, and transforms them; the *Cratylus* is full of etymologies.

Aristotle makes the study of language fundamental for the study of philosophy, beginning in the *Categories* with an analysis of predicates, and in *On Interpretation*, with a study of declarative sentences. He often returns to grammatical studies, for example in the *Rhetoric* and *Poetics*. **Theophrastus** seems to have pushed the analysis of written language a bit further (see fragments 681 ff in Fortenbaugh, ed., *Theophrastus*).

The **Stoics,** particularly **Diogenes of Babylon** (see DL 7.55–59), advanced the study of written language, a practice taken up by the Alexandrian school, and later the Romans, including **Cicero** and others.

In late antiquity, there was a recognition that regulation of the written language and making that regulated language normative tended to preserve a unity and hegemony of the educated elite; while Attic Greek and Classical Latin eventually were no longer common spoken tongues, it is to the credit of the ancient grammarians that acquaintance with the formal structure of these languages is still recognized as one way that a scholar may demonstrate erudition.

GREGORY NAZIANZUS (329–389 CE). Trained as a rhetorician, he became Bishop of Constantinople and wrote defending the Trinity and specifically the divinity of Jesus Christ.

GREGORY OF NYSSA (c. 335–394 CE). Christian theologian, brother of **Basil of Caesarea**. He applied **Neoplatonic** concepts to the defense of Christian concepts—for example, he used the principle of the identity of indiscernibles to defend the Trinity, and was the first Christian theologian to argue for the infinity of **God**, on approximately Plotinian grounds (the limitlessness of the One).

GUARDIANS (*PHYLAKES*). The "protective" class in **Plato**'s *Republic*; motivated by honor (*timē*), their characteristic virtue (*aretē*) is courage (*andreia*). Much of books II–V of the *Republic* is devoted to outlining the education and other arrangements concerning the Guardians.

GYMNASION. "Gymnasium." Fundamentally, a structure designed for physical exercise, as the word continues to be used in English today, but extended to mean, roughly, "school," especially a school for *epheboi*, ephebes, teenagers. In **Athens**, the three major gymnasia were the **Academy**, the **Lyceum**, and the Cynosarges. In the fifth century BCE, all three were favored venues for the **Sophists**, looking for likely students. In the 390s, **Antisthenes** established himself in the Cynosarges; **Isocrates** established his school in his own home; **Plato** took over the Academy; **Aristotle** eventually took over the **Lyceum**. Two additional gymnasia were built in Athens toward the end of the third century BCE: the Diogeneion and the Ptolemaion; the latter included a public library.

Apparently the *gymnasia* continued to be used for other purposes, including physical education, while used by rival schools for philosophical education, until all of them were destroyed or severely damaged by Sulla in 86 BCE.

GYMNOSOPHISTAI. The Greek name for the Hindu wise men of their day; the word means "naked sophists." **Pyrrho of Elis** is reliably said to have encountered them when traveling with the army of **Alexander of Macedon**. It is possible that there were philosophical contacts between **India** and Greece before Pyrrho—at its height, the Persian Empire included parts of both the Greek and Hindu/Buddhist worlds. But after the conquests of Alexander contacts were usually much easier, and the evidence shows that they increased.

– H –

HABIT. *See HEXIS.*

HAIRETON. In **Epicurean** and **Stoic** philosophy, "choiceworthy."

HAMARTĒMA. Error, failure, fault. In *EN* V.8, 1135b18, a *hamartēma* is between an **accident** and an act of injustice. It is wrongdoing that stems from ignorance, but the wrongdoer should have known better. It is an accident when the person who did the action could not have known the relevant fact, and it is an act of injustice if the person knew it was wrong but did it anyway. In the New Testament, this word is translated "sin," a good deal stronger than the sense it has in classical authors.

HAPHĒ. Touch, the sense of touch, the point of contact between bodies. For a materialist, touch is the primary sense; **Democritus** (consistently) makes all the senses variations of touch, since all of the senses operate by coming into contact with atoms (*atoma*). **Plato,** in contrast, models his epistemology on vision—the **Sun-Line-Cave** story is all about vision, bodily and intellectual, as is the *Phaedrus* **chariot** ride. **Aristotle** tends to put the senses on a more or less equal basis by arguing that all of them require a **medium** that conveys the sensible form between sensed object and sense organ; in the case of touch, the medium is the flesh. But at the same time, the sense of touch is the "most necessary," the only one that belongs to all animals, primarily sensitive of the basic qualities of **matter**: hot and cold, fluid and solid (*de An.* II.11).

At *GC* I.6, 322b29ff, Aristotle discusses the necessity of moving causes to be in *contact* with objects moved.

HAPPINESS. *See EUDAIMONIA.*

HARMONIA. **Heraclitus**, f. 51 says, "People do not know how what is at variance agrees with itself. It is a *harmonia* of opposite tension, like that of the bow and the lyre." According to **Aristotle**, and to later writers such as **Iamblichus**, the **Pythagoreans** believed the world to be "numbers and harmonies" (*Metaphysics* I.5, 986a2–12); Aristotle took them to be saying, furthermore, that the motion of the sun, moon, and planets, generate what we would call a harmonious sound (*Cael*. II.9, 290b12ff). In **Plato**'s *Phaedo* (85), Simmias proposes the idea that life is (nothing but) a "harmony" of the parts of the body. Although Simmias is described as a Pythagorean, this cannot be a Pythagorean theory in this form since, as **Socrates** demonstrates in the dialogue, the harmony theory is inconsistent with the idea of an immortal and transmigrating soul (*psychē*). The harmony theory is also inconsistent with the idea that the soul is a source of movement; thus both Socrates and Aristotle reject it on that ground (*Phaedo* 93, *de Anima* I.4, 407b34). Of course denying that life IS a harmony in no way detracts from the idea that life should have harmonious attributes. As **Cicero** puts it in *de Fin*. 3.17.22, "harmony of conduct" is part of the highest end for a human being.

HEART. *See KARDIA.*

HECATAEUS OF ABDERA (c. 350–290 BCE). Hecataeus wrote on **Homer** and **Hesiod**, about the "Hyperboreans" (far northern people) and "The Philosophy of the **Egyptian**s," all lost except fragments. He seems to have been associated with **Democritus**, his fellow Abderite and near contemporary.

HECATAEUS OF MILETUS (c. 550–490 BCE). Traveler and geographer, he wrote a book called *Description of the World*, and produced a map of the world representing an advance on that of **Anaximander**. A fair number of fragments survive, especially information about **Egypt**, including some descriptions of Egyptian animals (not always very accurate). **Herodotus** uses much of his information, while also criticizing.

HĒDONĒ, HĒDYN. Pleasure, the pleasurable. *Hēdys, hēdyn*, is the adjective meaning sweet, pleasant. Consequently *to hēdyn* is "the pleasant," one of the three natural objects of pursuit, along with the noble (*to kalon*) and the good (*to agathon*), according to **Aristotle**. *Hēdonē* is an alternative noun form. **Heraclitus** f. 111: "Sickness makes health pleasant and good, hunger satiety, hard work rest." In the *Protagoras* (353c ff), **Socrates** argues that courage (*andreia*) is a form of wisdom on the ground that a wise person will be able to carry out a hedonic calculus that will recommend the courageous act; some have felt that this and some other passages indicated that the historical Socrates may have been some form of hedonist. In the *Gorgias*, in contrast, Callicles defends a form of hedonism that holds that pleasure (*hēdonē*) occurs as a consequence of "replenishment," a thesis that Socrates is able to reduce to ridicule by arguing that showing the happiest person is some sort of sieve. In other dialogues, Socrates argues that the desire for pleasure attaches the soul (*psychē*) to the body (*sōma*), and interferes with the activity of the mind (*nous*) (e.g., *Phaedo* 64d ff). The settled Platonic position on pleasure appears to be that pleasure is a "process" (*kinēsis*), and no process is really good in itself. At *Philebus* 65ff, a ranking of "goods" puts the measured first, the beautiful (*kalon*) second, reason (*nous*) third, knowledge (*epistēmē*) and the arts fourth, and pure pleasures fifth.

Meanwhile, **Aristippus** and the **Cyrenaic School** were defending a hedonistic position. **Eudoxus**, a colleague of Plato in the **Academy**, also defended a form of hedonism. **Aristotle** was inspired to discuss pleasure twice in the *Nicomachean Ethics*, once in the latter part of Book VII and the other in the first part of Book X. While the two accounts are subtly different, we can say that Aristotle holds that pleasure is a part of the happy life, although not the whole of it. Pleasure, he believes, arises through good functioning of human capacities, and that good functioning itself contributes to happiness, with or without the accompanying pleasure.

As is well-known, the **Epicureans** focused on the maximization of pleasure and minimization of pain (*lypē*). The **Stoics** make a distinction between *hēdonē* and *chara*, or "joy," claiming that "pleasure" is an irrational *pathos*, while *chara* is rational (DL 7.116). The distinction seems to depend on just what it is that you are enjoying.

HĒGEMONIKON. In **Stoic** philosophy, the "directive" aspect or power of the soul (*psychē*). A *hēgemōn* is a leader. Consider the image of the soul in the *Phaedrus*: there are a **charioteer** and two horses; obviously the charioteer is the "leader" (cf. *Phaedrus* 252). The Stoics talk a lot about the various aspects of the *hēgemonikon*, including the obvious idea that **God** is the *hēgemonikon* of the entire universe.

HEIMARMENĒ. Fate. The word is actually the perfect passive participle of the verb *meiromai*, to allot or distribute, thus it means, basically, that which has been allotted, and is related to the word *moira*, also translated "fate." **Socrates** says, "like a tragic actor," that it is his *heimarmenē* day just before he drinks the hemlock in *Phaedo* 115a. Cf. **Aristotle** *Poetics* 16, 1455a11, speaking of characters in a play who had figured out their "fate," that they were going to die. The Stoics put a lot of emphasis on *heimarmenē*, essentially because they are determinists, so they identify "fate" with the Reason (*logos*) of the **Cosmos** and **God** (SVF II.264 ff). **Alexander of Aphrodisias**, a leading Aristotelian, wrote a book *Peri heimarmenes*, essentially critiquing the Stoic concept of fate. *See also ANAGKE; MOIRA.*

HEN. One. From the time of **Parmenides**, who asserted the absolute **unity** of **being**, Greek philosophy was concerned with finding the proper location for the idea of unity. A major objective of **Plato**'s theory of forms (*eidē*) is to find a unity as an object of thought that makes meaningful the multiplicities of the phenomenal world. The larger part of Plato's *Parmenides* is occupied with a **dialectical** examination of the relationship between one and many, being and nonbeing. Plato, perhaps following a **Pythagorean** suggestion (**Aristotle** *Metaphysics* I, 986a), seems to have made "The One" a primary ontological principle and identified it with The Good (*agathon*) (*Metaphysics* XIV, 1091b); his early successors in the **Academy** seem to have followed that lead. Aristotle distinguishes several senses of unity in *Metaphysics* V.6 and X.1 and argues that the Pythagorean-Platonic position on "The One" depends on failing to make the necessary distinctions (*Metaphysics* I.9, 992b).

For **Plotinus**, The One is "beyond being" and without qualification (*Enn.* VI.9.3).

HENAS, HENADOS. Henad, **Unity.** At *Philebus* 15a, *Plato* uses this word to say that a human being, an ox, the beautiful, and the good, are all "unities." How many "unities" are there? There is a tension between unity and multiplicity. Although the word is rare in the interim, late **Neoplatonists (Proclus, Damascius)** picked upon this locution and built it into their systematic *Metaphysics. See also HEN.*

HERACLIDES OF PONTUS (c. 388–c. 310 BCE). Student and colleague in the **Academy**, where he associated significantly with **Aristotle**. Heraclides failed in his bid to become **Scholarch** at the death of **Speusippos**. There are significant fragments of his astronomical and physical treatises and of his work on the **Pythagoreans**.

HERACLITUS OF EPHESUS (fl. c. 500 BCE). We have fairly extensive fragments of Heraclitus partly because his writings were so quotable and partly because he was extensively quoted by **Hippolytus**, Bishop of Rome, in aid of his attack on a heresy called Donatism that Hippolytus thought resembled or was derived from the philosophy of Heraclitus. Heraclitus focused on principles of **unity** in change, expressed in an "account," the *logos*. Heraclitus often expresses himself in paradoxical or ambiguous ways, giving him the reputation of being "obscure." Unity in change is symbolized by Heraclitus most vividly by the image of "everliving fire," for a flame exists only because change is happening. Everliving fire is also associated with the soul (*psychē*), for a "dry soul is wisest and best."

HERILLUS OF CARTHAGE (Third century BCE). Stoic, student of **Zeno of Citium**, noteworthy in his city of origin. **Diogenes Laertius** provides a very brief vita.

HERMARCHUS OF MYTILENE (330s–250s BCE). Co-founder of the **Epicurean School**, successor of **Epicurus** as its leader. He wrote works critical of **Plato**, **Aristotle**, and **Empedocles**; *Against Empedocles* is the source of most fragments. He defended killing animals for socially useful purposes.

HERMEIAS (Fifth–sixth centuries CE). Hermeias studied **Neoplatonic** philosophy in **Athens** with **Syrianus** and moved to Alexandria, where he revitalized the Alexandrian philosophical school. **Ammonius** and **Olympiodorus** continued his teaching, instructing, among others, **John Philoponus**, a Christian commentator on **Aristotle**.

HERMES TRISMEGISTUS. "Thrice-greatest Hermes," or Thoth, to whom many of the so-called Hermetic texts are attributed by their authors. There are 17 Greek-language treatises in the collection called the *Corpus Hermeticum*, a Latin treatise called the *Asclepius*, a significant number of fragments in Stobaeus, three texts in Coptic found at Nag Hammadi, a text in Armenian, and some technical (magical) treatises. The earliest treatises, specifically some of the technical treatises, may date to the third century BCE, but the philosophical treatises seem to have appeared in the second century CE.

The Hermetic treatises represent themselves as **Egyptian**, although most of them seem to have been written in Greek; they emanate from an Egyptian religious tradition with ties to the religious movements known as "**Gnostic**."

The goal of the philosophic Hermetic texts is to gain knowledge of **God** and of the universe in order to become one with God. There is an inner source of knowledge; cultivating that inner source leads to liberation of the spirit.

HERMODORUS OF SYRACUSE (Fourth century BCE). Member of **Plato**'s **Academy**, he possibly followed Plato back from Syracuse after one of Plato's visits. His biography of Plato, although lost, was one of the sources for later writers on Plato. He seems to have emphasized Plato's ties to **Pythagoreanism**.

HERMOGENES OF ALOPECE (c. 445–after 392 BCE). He appears in **Plato**'s *Cratylus*, was present in the *Phaedo*, and is credited with being the source of much of the information used by **Xenophon** about the last part of **Socrates**' life. According to **Diogenes Laertius**, Plato associated with him and **Cratylus** after the death of Socrates; Diogenes claims that he was an enthusiast of **Parmenides**, but there is little independent confirmation of that.

HERO OF ALEXANDRIA (c. 10–70 CE). Aristotelian or **Atomist** inventor and mathematician. A significant number of his works are extant, including some that describe precisely how to produce some rather remarkable machines. For example, he described a working steam engine some 1,700 years before steam engines were put to industrial use.

HERODES ATTICUS (c. 101–177). Very wealthy Athenian who had studied philosophy and rhetoric and took up a life combining public service and teaching under Hadrian. Antoninus Pius brought him to Rome as the tutor of **Marcus Aurelius**. He was instrumental in the establishment of the Aurelian chairs of philosophy in **Athens**, and was a part of the Second Sophistic, along with **Philostratus**.

The theater that he had constructed on the south slope of the Acropolis in Athens is still used for theatrical performances.

HERODOTUS OF HALICARNASSUS (c. 484–c. 425 BCE). Historian of the Persian wars. He names **Thales** and **Pythagoras** and often cites ideas that we can find also in various **Presocratic** philosophical writers. The text of Herodotus was well known to the classical philosophers who often rely on him, usually without attribution. Herodotus is the most reliable extant source for attempting to trace non-Greek sources for ideas that flourish in the context of early Greek philosophy.

HEROPHILUS OF CHALCEDON (c. 330–260 BCE). Medical writer in **Alexandria**; along with **Erasistratus**, he carried out dissections of cadavers, and studied the nervous system and human reproduction.

HESIOD (fl. about 700 BCE). A poet from Boeotia, he wrote the extant *Theogony*, or "Birth of the **Gods**," and *Works and Days*, a more practical poem about farming, and about justice and injustice. *Theogony* was seen by ancient philosophers as a kind of precursor to the philosophical tradition, in that it made a serious attempt to give reasonable explanations of a wide range of phenomena. Even though the rhetoric is "religious" or "theological," a kind of conceptual structure emerges from the relationships of the deities, who are often really nothing but various abstract concepts personified. One example among many possible: "Deadly night holds in her hands sleep, the brother of death."

HETERON. "The Other," otherness, difference. In **Plato**'s *Sophist* and *Timaeus*, the "other" is a major ontological principle: the **World Soul** is composed of Existence, Sameness, and Difference (*Tm* 35a). In **Plotinus**, "The Other" is the principle of production of **matter** (*Enn.* II.4.5).

HEXIS. This is an abstract noun built on the verb *echein*, to have. In a general sense, a *hexis* is a "having" (*Metaphysics* V.20, 1022b4). In the context of moral psychology, a *hexis* is a disposition to act in a certain way, should the occasion arise; a habit. In *EN* II.5, 1105b19ff, **Aristotle** distinguishes *pathē* (emotions), *dynameis* (capacities), and *hexeis* (dispositions), on his way to arguing that ethical virtue (*aretē*) is a *hexis* rather than either of the other two.

The **Stoics** thought that virtue is a *diathesis* rather than a *hexis*. They used the word *hexis* to refer to the supposed power of *pneuma* to "hold" things, particularly things like stones and logs, together; thus this word is typically translated "tenor" when it occurs in Stoic contexts. They do use *hexis* in psychological or moral contexts but for denominating non-moral dispositional characteristics, like being able to play a musical instrument or being good in sports.

HIEROCLES (in Stobaeus) (Early second century CE). Stoic, cited several times by Stobaeus, and mentioned by Aulus Gellius (*Attic Nights*, 9.5.8). A papyrus discovered in 1901 has been shown to be part of his work on **ethics**—the bits that we have discuss *oikeiōsis* in relation to animal instincts. The bits in Stobaeus are concerned with the *kathēkonta*, or **appropriate** actions.

HIEROCLES OF ALEXANDRIA (Fifth century CE). Neoplatonist, student of **Plutarch of Athens**. His commentary on the *Carmen Aureum*, an introduction to philosophy, and some fragments of his work *On Providence* are extant. He is seen as part of the transition in Neoplatonism between **Iamblichus** and **Proclus**.

HIERONYMUS OF RHODES (Third century BCE). Peripatetic, cited fairly frequently for historical information about earlier philosophers, and for contributions to **Aristotelian ethics**.

HIPPARCHIA OF MARONEIA (b. 340–330 BCE). A Cynic, married to **Crates,** as recounted in DL 6.96–98. Hipparchia is one of the better known women philosophers in the ancient Greek philosophical world.

HIPPASUS OF METAPONTIUM (first half 5th century BCE).
Pythagorean, credited by Aristotle for making fire the primary element (**Metaphysics** I.3, 984a7). **Iamblichus** tells us that Hippasus claimed credit for (or publicized) the inscription of the dodecahedron in the sphere, and was "lost at sea" (drowned?) as a result (*Life of Pythagoras* 247).

HIPPIAS OF ELIS (c. 470–385? BCE). Sophist, a generation younger than **Protagoras.** He is notable for his claim to have mastered all of the arts, so that he appeared at the Olympic Games decked out entirely in clothing and adornments of his own manufacture. **Plato** wrote two dialogues named after him; Hippias also appears in the *Protagoras*, in something of a conciliatory role. Plato regularly mentions mathematics in connection with him, so he is likely the Hippias who invented the quadratrix, used for trisecting an angle; he also tried to square the circle with it, according to **Proclus** (DK 86b21). *See also MATHĒMA.*

HIPPO (Second half of the fifth century BCE). Hippo was a physical philosopher who seems to have revived some of the viewpoints of **Thales. Aristotle** calls him "superficial" (*de Anima* I.2, 405b2) for saying that the **soul** is **water**.

HIPPOCRATES OF COS (c. 460–370 BCE). The founder of a school of medicine (*iatrikē*) in Cos, Hippocrates was already famous in his lifetime, as we learn from **Plato**'s *Protagoras* and *Phaedrus*. Eventually, he was credited with the composition of more than 50 medical works known today as the "Hippocratic **Corpus**." He could not possibly have been the author of all of them, not least because they are stylistically and conceptually incompatible with each other. Still, he may have been the author of some of the works in the Corpus; candidates might include *On Ancient Medicine, Airs Waters Places,* and *On the Sacred Disease.* The author or authors of those works, and of some of the other treatises in the collection, was/were aware of the philosophical trends of the fifth century BCE, and used them to encourage a more "empirical" approach to understanding health and disease than had been common before his/their day. Later, **Galen** took many of the treatises to be authentically by Hippocrates himself and argued that the medical theories of Hippocrates and the physical theories of **Plato** in the *Timaeus* were in concert with each other and were essentially correct.

HIPPOLYTUS, BISHOP OF ROME (d. c. 236 CE). Author of *Refutation of All Heresies*, one of the major sources of fragments of **Heraclitus** and some other **Presocratics**. His extant writings are quite extensive, more than any other pre-Constantinian church father.

HISTORIA. Investigation, inquiry. Although it is true that **Herodotus** calls his work about the Peloponnesian War a *Historia* (7.96), **Aristotle**'s account of the structure and habits of animals is a *Historia*, and **Theophrastus'** description of the various sorts of plants is a *Historia* as well. At *Phaedo* 96a, **Socrates** talks of his early temptation to pursue *historia peri physeōs*, or "investigation about nature," a phrase that we are tempted to translate "natural **science**." The sense "systematic investigation" still appears in modern medical usage.

HOLON. Whole, organic **unity**, universe. On the one hand, from the beginning of Greek philosophy, a *"holon"* is typically an organic unity composed of parts; on the other, also from the beginning of Greek philosophy, *to holon* is the universe as a whole. Those senses come together in the famous fragment of **Xenophanes**, that there is one **God** that "sees as a whole, thinks as a whole, hears as a whole" (f. 24) more or less identical with the universe (**Aristotle *Metaphysics*** I.5, 986b10). According to **Parmenides** (8.38), Fate has chained **being** "so that it remains whole and immovable." But with the **atomist** response to the **Eleatic** philosophy, only the atoms (*atoma*) appeared to remain as "wholes"; the wholeness of living things, say, was compromised, let alone the wholeness of the **cosmos**. The **dialectic** of whole and part is explored in detail in the second part of **Plato**'s *Parmenides*. Aristotle distinguishes several senses of *holon*: he recognizes the usage of this word for the entire universe (*Metaphysics* XII.10, 1075a11); he often emphasizes organic unities—indeed, he uses the related word *synolon* for the combination of **matter** and form (*eidos*) that is a **particular** entity (*ousia*). For anything that is claimed to be a whole of parts, the question is, what is the cause of the unity? *Metaphysics* VII.17, 1041b. But the universe has a cause (*aition*), the first mover, so the universe, too, is a unity. (*Metaph*. XII.10)

HOMER. Author of the *Iliad* and *Odyssey*, written down about 750 BCE. Starting at least with **Heraclitus** and continuing through **Plato**, Homer's poems are an indispensable backdrop and foil against which ancient philosophy develops. "Homer deserves to be expelled from the contest and flogged" (Heraclitus f. 42; **Xenophanes** f. 11). Homer sometimes describes the **Gods** as immoral; in the *Republic*, **Plato** develops an extended argument why children should not be taught Homer in school. **Aristotle** is more tolerant of the Homeric epics, and **Stoics** such as **Chrysippus** tend to quote large chunks of Homer in support of their arguments.

HOMO MENSURA. This Latin phrase points out the statement of **Protagoras** that "human beings are the measure" of all things. Is each individual the measure of all things, as **Plato** takes Protagoras to mean in the *Theaetetus*, or are human beings collectively, perhaps as social groups, the measure of what is and is not? Judging from the representation of Protagoras in the *Protagoras*, he is more likely to have believed the social interpretation than the individualistic interpretation.

HOMOIOS. Similar, like. There is a persistent tendency for Greek philosophers to believe that "like is known by like"; thus, there is a search for aspects of the knower that are similar to the objects perceived and known. **Empedocles** is very explicit, saying that we know the elements in virtue of the fact that we are composed of them. Aristotle jokes that according to Empedocles, **God** is less intelligent than human beings, since God does not have any strife in his makeup and thus cannot know strife, but we can. (*Metaph* II.4, 1000a32). Still, in Plato the possibility of interpreting the world appears to turn on the prior presence in the soul (*psychē*) of recollectable knowledge (*epistēmē*) of the forms (*eidē*) to which the events in the world are similar. This leads, in Plato, to the expectation that objects in the phenomenal world are "similar" in some respect to the forms (*see mimēsis*), which in turn leads to various antinomies explored in the *Parmenides*. Also for Plato, "similarity" is a major category of the understanding. See, for example, *Theaetetus* 185d, where the mind (*nous*) contributes to judgments of "existence, similarity and difference, one and many, identical and non-identical." We should also note that in the *Timaeus*, the **World Soul** is composed of "cycles of similar and different."

Aristotle finds several senses of "similar" (e.g., *Metaph.* X.3, 1054b3ff). There are differences in degree or quantity, or in the number of shared **attributes**, for example. And in the *Ethics*, he finds that many (not all) friendships are based on "similarity" of the friends.

The **Epicurean**s posited "similarity" (*homoiotēs*) as a method for gaining knowledge; to critics, that looked rather like a hasty generalization.

HOMOIŌSIS. Literally, a process of making similar. **Plato,** at *Theaetetus* 176b, says that we should do our best to escape this **earth** and go to heaven, and that is done by becoming like **God**, *homoiōsis theōi*. **Plotinus** picks up this idea at *Enn.* I.6.6, "The Soul's becoming a good and beautiful thing is its becoming like to God."

HOMOLOGIA, HOMOLOGOUMENOS. Agreement, agreeing. The *telos* of life in **Stoic ethics** was "living in agreement with **Nature**."

HOMONYMOI. If a word is used for two different things and the definition of the word varies between those uses, those things are called *homonymoi*, according to **Aristotle** in *Categories*. This usage is a bit different from the usual English usage, in which the "homonym" is primarily the word rather than the things picked out by the word.

HONOR. *See TIMĒ.*

HONORABLE. *See KALOS.*

HORISMOS. Definition. *HORIZEIN*. To delimit, define. A *horos* is a boundary or limit; in fact, the word "*horos*" is sometimes used of a limiting term in a **syllogism**, or the like, or even definition. So *horismos* is the process of delimitation. The metaphysical significance of definition is explored by **Aristotle** in *Metaphysics* VII.10, 1034b20ff, for example. In a famous passage at the beginning of the *Metaphysics*, Aristotle says (987b) that **Socrates** did not concern himself with the whole of nature but sought the universal about ethical things, "fixing thought for the first time on definitions (*horismoi*)."

HORMĒ. Noun derived from *ornumi*, to rouse, stir up, awaken, excite. Readily translated as "drive" or "instinct" (it occurs in this sense several times in both **Plato** and **Aristotle** but not as a key technical term); *hormē* became a basic concept in **Stoic** moral psychology. All living things have a basic *hormē* for self-preservation; in most circumstances this is not problematic, but if *hormē* comes into conflict with **reason**, that causes problems, and if a *hormē* is excessive, it becomes a *pathos*. That, for the Stoics, is to be avoided.

HOSIOTĒS. Piety, holiness. This "virtue" (*aretē*) is examined by **Socrates** in **Plato**'s *Euthyphro*. Socrates was tried and convicted for "impiety" on the putative grounds that he did not believe in the **Gods** of the state but had introduced new and alien *daimones*. The *hosion* is that which is sanctioned by divine law, so apart from Plato's discussion of the word, *hosiotēs* would normally mean a disposition to obey divine law.

The relationship between philosophy and religion in Greek thought has been complex from the start. Classical Greek religion, as a polytheism, tended to be more tolerant of differences in religious opinion than many monotheistic faiths, and that opened a space for several of the earlier philosophers to introduce innovations — the *metempsychosis* of **Pythagoras**, the austere fiery *Logos* of **Heraclitus**, the swirl-inducing Mind (*nous*) of **Anaxagoras** are readily remembered.

Although **Protagoras** professed to have nothing to say about the Gods, on the ground that the question is too big and life is too short, and several philosophers were reputed to be "atheists," it is doubtless fair to say that the quasi-theological metaphysical speculations of Plato and **Aristotle**, the intensely theocentric philosophical synthesis of the **Stoics**, and the strongly mystical tendencies of philosophers of many schools in late antiquity resulted in a general presupposition in the ancient world that philosophers were, on the whole, a pious if often unorthodox lot.

HOU HENEKA. "On account of what," one of **Aristotle**'s locutions for picking out final causes. *See also TELOS.*

HYLĒ. Literally "lumber," this is **Aristotle**'s preferred term for "**matter**," whatever something is made out of. In fact "materia" is an excellent literal translation of *hylē* into Latin. Aristotle believed that the **Presocratics**, the people he calls "*physiologoi*," were proposing various alternative views of the material principle—**water, air, fire**; the four **elements**; atoms (*atoma*) and the void—but that you cannot have an adequate concept of matter until you have an adequate correlative concept of form, and that the *physiologoi* generally lacked. Outside seriously **Peripatetic** circles, the most likely equivalent word for "matter" is probably *sōma*.

A phrase that might give some trouble is *prōtē hylē*, or "first matter." Material reductionists seduced by Aristotelian vocabulary but unconverted to Aristotelian ways of thought tend to think of "first matter" as the most fundamental level of matter, e.g., the elements (**earth**, water, air, fire) or the atoms. But Aristotle, while allowing that that is one possible way that the phrase can be used, also insists on thinking of it as the "first" matter from the perspective of a **particular** entity, so for a bronze statue, the bronze is the "first matter" (*Metaphysics* V.4, 1015a7). Thus in *GA* I.20, 729a32, when Aristotle says that the menstrual fluid is a kind of *prōtē hylē*, he of course means *proximate* matter. *See also HYPOKEIMENON; STOICHEION.*

HYPARCHEIN. Be, Belong. This verb is used especially by the **Stoics** to denominate both existence and predication. These uses can be found in **Plato** and **Aristotle** as well, but the Stoics emphasize their correspondence theory of truth (*alētheia*) by applying this word.

HYPATIA OF ALEXANDRIA (d. 415 CE). An erudite teacher of philosophy and mathematics in **Alexandria** (**Egypt**). Her father is listed as the last director of the **Museum** of Alexandria; that shows which way things were going. A pagan and on the wrong side in a political dispute, Hypatia was seized on the street by Christian monks and beaten to death. She has become a heroine and a symbol for women philosophers.

HYPEROUSIA. Literally, "beyond **being**"; transcendence. This is a **Neoplatonic** word, particularly associated with **Proclus**.

HYPHISTASTHAI. Subsist. In **Stoic** ontology, it is recognized that there some words with clear definitions that do not correspond with physical (material) entities. "Time" and "Centaur" subsist rather than exist.

HYPODOCHĒ. Receptacle. **Plato**'s name for the space-time continuum in *Timaeus* 48e–52d. **Plotinus** makes the *hypodochē* a kind of **matter**, *qua* pure extension, *Enn*. II.4.

HYPOKEIMENON. Literally, "underlying," typically translated "substratum." For **Aristotle**, it is that which persists through radical change (*Phys*. I. 190a–b). In *Metaphysics* VII.3, Aristotle considers the claim of *hypokeimenon* to be *ousia*, on the ground that it is that of which everything else is predicated. But there is an ambiguity in the use of the word *hypokeimenon*, between the logical and the physical senses. Logically, the subject of predications "underlies" those predications; but if we abstract all the predications, what are we ultimately left with? Simply a logical place-holder. Similarly physically, the "ultimate substratum" "is of itself neither a **particular** thing nor of a particular quality nor otherwise positively characterized, nor yet negatively, for negations also will belong to it only by **accident**" (*Metaph*. VII.3, 1029a25). So the substrate, and **matter**, cannot be *ousia*, because *ousia* must be separable and individual, and the ultimate substrate is surely neither. *See also LOGIKĒ.*

HYPOLAMBANEIN. Suppose. **HYPOLĒPSIS.** Supposition. The **Stoics** use this term for belief that is not necessarily veridical, in contrast to *katalēpsis*, which is supposed to be veridical.

HYPOSTASIS. Literally, "standing under." There is a whole range of metaphorical senses, from lying in ambush, to sediment, to a thick soup; philosophically, the word is used by various authors to refer to the subject matter of a disquisition, to the duration of time, to "reality." This is the Greek word most closely related to the Latin "substantia," whence we get "substance" in English. Oddly, **Aristotle** does not use *hypostasis* in this sense, though the word "substance" has been foisted off as the most frequent translation of his word *ousia*. Aristotle generally uses the word *hypostasis* either for a support (e.g., of one's feet) or for a sediment, some solid material that settles to the bottom. In **Neoplatonism**, *hypostaseis* are the most general ontological principles: The **One**, Mind (*nous*), and **Soul** (**Plotinus** *Enn.* II.9.1; **Proclus**, *Elements of Theology,* Proposition 20).

HYPOTHESIS. Literally, something that is "put under." Widely used for all sorts of "proposals." In the *Meno* (86e), **Socrates** describes (somewhat obscurely) a hypothetical method used by geometers and then suggests a parallel method for examining "virtue" (*aretē*) that involves the supposition that if virtue is knowledge (*epistēmē*), then it can be (or is) taught. In the *Phaedo* (100–101), Socrates again resorts to a hypothetical method that involves asserting a plausible hypothesis and examining its consequences until one finds that it leads to a contradiction. In the *Republic* (VII.533c, in the "Line" passage), **dialectic** is said to be the art that "eliminates hypotheses and proceeds to the first principle." In the *Parmenides*, **Parmenides** describes the method of dialectic as examining both the hypothesis and its negation (136).

Aristotle uses the word hypothesis to refer to a fundamental presupposition; for example, he says that "The *hypothesis* of a democratic constitution is freedom" (*Pol.* VI.2, 1317a40). He also often uses the word in a logical sense, either for a postulate (undemonstrated first principle) or for a proposition that is "proposed" for proof or refutation. Finally (in this rapid summary), in his discussion of **necessity**, hypothetical or conditional (*ex hypotheseōs*) necessity is contrasted with "simple" necessity (*Phys.* II.9, 199b34; *PA* I.1, 639b24).

– I –

IAMBLICHUS OF CHALKIS (c. 245–325 CE). (This "Chalkis" was in the Beqaa valley of Lebanon.) Iamblichus was a **Neoplatonist** philosopher who probably studied with **Porphyry** and **Amelius**. In 304, he founded his own school in Apamea in Syria (really the continuation of the schools of **Numenius** and Amelius). His surviving works include part of his large work bringing together the evidence for **Pythagorean** philosophy (including *On the Pythagorean Life* and the *Protrepticus*), *On the Egyptian Mysteries*, *The Theology of Arithmetic*, and fragments of his commentaries on several of the works of **Plato** and **Aristotle**. Iamblichus placed significant emphasis on the Pythagorean aspects of Platonism, including mathematical interpretations of fundamental ontological concepts. He also favored the practice of theurgy, religious rituals and practices intended to improve the relationship between human beings and the **Gods**. Some of his students, for example **Dexippus**, continued to operate his school after his death. **Plutarch of Athens,** who reestablished instruction in Platonism in Athens, seems to have studied with the successors of Iamblichus in Apamea. *See also THEOURGIA.*

IATROS, IATRIKĒ. Physician; the art of medicine. The Greek words mean literally "healer" and "the art of healing." From nearly the beginning of Greek philosophy medicine and philosophy were often intertwined: **Empedocles**, for example, focuses his philosophy on healing both the body (*sōma*) and the soul (*psychē*); several of the treatises in the Hippocratic corpus are as philosophical as they are medical—"On Ancient Medicine" and "On the Sacred Disease" are good examples. Indeed, **Socrates** cites his near contemporary **Hippocrates** with approval (*Charmides* 156e, *Phaedrus* 270c, *Protagoras* 311b).

Although **Plato** is sometimes a little suspicious of some medical practice, he often represents Socrates using medicine as an art analogous to philosophy (notably in the *Gorgias* and *Republic*) and develops a theory of physiology and applies it to a range of medical issues in the latter part of the *Timaeus* with so much success that **Galen**, hundreds of years later, would give it very high marks.

It has often been noted that **Aristotle**'s father was physician to the Macedonian court; although Nicomachus died when Aristotle was very young, it may be that early experiences with a medical point of view contributed to Aristotle's consuming interest in biological phenomena and his extension of the biological perspective throughout his philosophical system.

After the time of Aristotle, several individuals combined the roles of philosopher and physician, though none in antiquity with quite the distinction of **Galen**.

In subsequent centuries, the model of the philosophical physician often led to remarkable revivals of classical learning in the guise of furthering medical therapy—Ibn Sina, Maimonides, Paracelsus, and Harvey are a few names that come immediately to mind.

IDEA. Visible form. **Xenophanes** f. 15. "Yes, and if oxen and horses or lions had hands, and could paint with their hands and produce works of art as people do, horses would paint the forms (*ideai*) of the **Gods** like horses, and oxen like oxen, and make their bodies in the image of their several kinds." **Protagoras** f. 4. "About the Gods, I am not able to know whether they exist or do not exist, nor what they are like in form (*idea*); for the factors preventing knowledge are many: the obscurity of the subject, and the shortness of human life." For **Plato**, this is one of the two most common words used to refer to "the forms" (the other is *eidos*). It is not entirely clear why he uses one word and then the other; they have similar origin (both come from the verb *idein*, to see). **Aristotle** frequently uses the word in the sense of "visible form," or as a synonym for *eidos*, which for him means kind or species; he also very commonly uses it to refer to Plato's forms, e.g., in *Metaphysics* I.9, and in fact wrote a treatise, *Peri Ideōn*, attacking the theory of forms in detail. For more discussion of Plato's forms and Aristotle's species, *see EIDOS*.

Another ancient book, also entitled *Peri Ideōn*, was written by the rhetorician Hermogenes, dealing with the elements of rhetorical style.

The modern English word "idea" is not a good translation of the Greek word *idea*; "form" is probably best. The ancient Greek equivalent of the modern "idea" would perhaps be *ennoia*.

IDIŌMA. Peculiarity, specific property, unique feature. For the **Epicurean**s and **Stoics**, this word is applied to uniquely distinguishable perceptual experiences; it is later used in the context of discussion of rhetorical style.

IDION. That which belongs to the individual, private. **Aristotle** uses the word for characteristics that belong to a **particular species** as distinguished from other species in the **genus**, *Top.* I.5.

IMAGE. *See EIDŌLON; EIKŌN; MIMĒSIS; PHANTASIA.*

IMAGINATION. *See PHANTASIA.*

IMITATION. *See MIMĒSIS.*

IMMORTAL. *See ATHANATOS.*

IMPASSIVITY. *See APATHEIA.*

IMPRESSION. *See AISTHĒSIS; TYPŌSIS.*

IMPULSE. *See HORMĒ.*

INDEFINITE, INFINITE. *See AORISTON; APEIRON.*

INDEMONSTRABLE. *See ANAPODEIKTON.*

INDIA—Philosophical Influences. The Vedas and early Upanishads predate the development of Greek philosophy; Gautama Buddha was a contemporary of **Pythagoras**, **Heraclitus**, and **Xenophanes**. At what point did the Greek philosophical tradition become aware of their colleagues in India, and what parts of the Indian tradition could have influenced their thought? For the Milesians, we can only point to tantalizing parallels—the plurality of universes in **Anaximander**, as in the Upanishads, the primacy of breath and air in **Anaximenes**, as in the Rig Veda—but we do not have enough information even to speculate about connections. In the case of Pythagoras, there are late texts (especially **Iamblichus** "Life of Pythagoras") that tell us that Pythagoras spent time in the Persian capital of Susa when the Persians had extended their empire into India, and of course Pythagoras' ideas about the soul (*psychē*) are very reminiscent of Indian concepts, but seemed novel to the Greeks. In any case, relationships between Indian and Greek intellectual traditions in the period before the Persian Wars continue to be very speculative in the absence of significant evidence one way or the other.

During the period of conflict between Greeks and Persians, from about 490 BCE, travel to India was very difficult for Greeks, but as the level of conflict between Greeks and Persians diminished, facility of travel may have increased. Contacts between Greek and Indian philosophers could have occurred in the fourth century BCE, before the time of **Alexander**—the Persian Empire at its height included both Greeks and Indians, and some non-philosophers traveled to India in that period. Definite philosophical contacts resume with **Pyrrho of Elis** (c. 360–270 BCE), founder of the Skeptical line of philosophy, who traveled to India in the company of **Alexander of Macedon** and visited with philosophers known to the Greeks as *gymnosophistai*. From the 320s BCE onward, it was often possible for Greek intellectuals to visit any of the lands conquered by Alexander, or for intellectuals from those lands to visit the Greek-speaking world. King Ashoka (273–232 BCE) claims to have sent (Buddhist) missionaries to several places in the Greek world, for example.

One extremely interesting text extant in Pali is the "Milinda Pañha," or "Questions of Menander." Menander was a Greek who controlled a good bit of India (155–130 BCE); the work represents him in discussion with a Buddhist sage named "Nagasena" who might be the same as the famous Nagarjuna. The work represents Menander asking questions, sometimes along recognizably typical Hellenistic philosophic lines, and then at the end converting to Buddhism. *See also* AMMONIUS SACCAS; *GYMNOSOPHISTAI;* PYRRHO; *SKEPTIKOS.*

INDIFFERENT. *See ADIAPHORAN.*

INDIVIDUAL. *See HEN; KATH' HEKASTON; TODE TI.*

INDUCTION. *See EPAGŌGĒ; SYNAGŌGĒ.*

INSTINCT. *See HORMĒ.*

INTELLECT. *See NOĒSIS; NOUS; PHRONĒSIS.*

INTELLIGIBLE. *See GNŌRIMON.*

INTUITION. *See NOUS.*

ISIDORE OF ALEXANDRIA (Fifth century CE). Successor of **Marinus** as **Scholarch** of the Platonic school in **Athens**, he was a teacher of **Damascius**, who wrote a biography of him; some fragments remain.

Isidore was eased out of his position in Athens; he moved to **Alexandria** where, according to Damascius, he married the ill-fated **Hypatia**.

ISOCRATES OF ATHENS (437–338 BCE). Student of **Gorgias,** possibly of **Socrates**. His school, opened in his home in 392 BCE, anticipated in its organization the schools of **Plato** and **Aristotle**. Although he started as a Rhetorician, and his school is sometimes called "Sophistic," he himself claimed that he was teaching *philosophia*. He clearly had a philosophy of education, and of other practical areas. There is a fairly significant number of writings extant (three volumes in the Loeb series)—speeches that he wrote early in his career, for others to deliver; a critique of the **Sophists**; an essay called the *Busiris* in which among other things he claims that philosophy originated in **Egypt**; and his *Panegyric* and *Antidosis*, essays in which he defends his political perspective.

ISONOMIA. Equality of political rights. **Plato** refers to *isonomia* between men and women as a characteristic of the democratic state, *Republic* VIII.563b.

– J –

JEROME (347–420 CE). Eusebius Sophronius Hieronymus, translator of the Bible into Latin.

JUDAISM. Although some ancient authors devised fanciful chronologies and scenarios in an attempt to demonstrate that **Pythagoras** and/or **Plato** was familiar with the Torah, or even with Moses himself, the first really clear connection between Greek philosophy and Judaism is in the person of **Philo of Alexandria**, who combined knowledge of both traditions with the desire to show that they were consistent with each other. To be sure, the Hebrew Bible had been translated into Greek in the third to second centuries BCE, according to legend, at the request of Ptolemy Philadelphus, for inclusion in the **Library** of **Alexandria**.

For the most part, the Jewish intellectual tradition tried to avoid contamination by Greek philosophy, and the Greek philosophical tradition responded by not paying much attention to the Jewish intellectual tradition.

In the Medieval period, particularly in the Islamic lands, further synthesis of Jewish and Greek philosophical ideas did occur, but that is outside the scope of this Dictionary.

JUDGMENT. *See DOXA.*

JULIAN THE APOSTATE (331–363 CE). Flavius Claudius Iulianus, brought up Christian, converted to paganism; as Emperor (361–363) he attempted to restore pagan practices in the Empire. Before becoming Emperor, he had studied **Neoplatonism** and was particularly favorable to the Theurgy (*theourgia*) of **Iamblichus**.

JULIAN THE THEURGIST (fl. 173 CE). He introduced the *Chaldaean Oracles* to the world, having, as he says, saved them from a rainstorm in a military camp in 173 (thus the date). Julian claims that they derive from ancient pronouncements of the deities of Chaldaea (Iraq), though modern scholars find them rather reminiscent of the **Neoplatonic** philosophy of **Numenius**, an older contemporary of Julian. Some say that the *Oracles* were composed by Julian the Theurgist's father, a person known as Julian the Chaldaean. In any case they were destined to become rather popular with late **Neoplatonists**, and again in Byzantine times. *See also THEOURGIA.*

JUSTICE. *See DIKAIOSYNĒ; DIKĒ.*

– K –

KAKIA. Vice, but in general the abstract noun formed from *KAKOS*. *See also ARETĒ* (virtue).

KAKOS, KAKĒ, KAKON. Adjective meaning bad, ugly, lowborn, cowardly, unskilled; evil. All these senses are common in nonphilosophical Greek. The Goddess tells **Parmenides** (f. 1) that no *kakē moira*, evil fate, has brought him to her. *To kakon* (the bad) is opposed to *to agathon* (the good). Why does evil exist in the world?

The **Pythagoreans** believed that evil was closely related to the *apeiron*, or indefinite; following that line of thought, at *Timaeus*, at 41c, **Plato** explains the imperfections of human beings by the fact that the fashioning of their bodies was delegated to lesser deities, and he attributes the imperfections of the perceptible world to the fundamental randomness that pre-existed the activity of the *Demiourgos* (48a). At *Laws* 10, 896e, however, the Athenian Stranger asserts that there is both a good **World Soul** and a bad World Soul, reminiscent of **Empedoclean** dualism between the two cosmic principles of *Philia* and *Eris*. **Aristotle** rejects this sort of dualism at *Metaphysics* IX.9, 1051a18ff. "The bad does not exist apart from bad things, for the bad is posterior to the potentiality (*dynamis*). And therefore we may also say that in the things that are from the beginning, i.e., in eternal things, there is nothing bad, nothing defective, nothing perverted." For Aristotle, there is no positive principle of evil; not even **matter** plays this role. **Plutarch**, in *On Isis and Osiris*, follows a dualistic line, asserting the existence of both good and evil deities; **Numenius** identifies the principle of evil as "matter," assuming the identification of the receptacle (*hypodochē*) of the *Timaeus* with Aristotle's matter. This identification is fundamental for **Gnosticism**; it is rejected by **Plotinus**, who insists that evil is simply the absence of good (*Enn.* 1.8.11). **Proclus** asserts that evil in the world is brought about by bad choices (*De mal. Subst.*).

KALLIPOLIS. Plato uses this word just once, at *Rep* VII, 527c2, to refer to the ideal city of the *Republic*; it has become a convenient tag to refer to that utopia.

KALOGATHIA. The condition of having all of the social virtues proposed by **Aristotle** as a summative virtue (*aretē*) in *Eudemian Ethics* VII.15.

KALON. Beautiful, noble, good. In general, *kalon* is used to designate that good which is desired for itself and not for the sake of anything else. *Agathon* sometimes has an implication of exchange value or utility. **Plato** tends to use *kalon* and *agathon* more or less interchangeably, whereas **Aristotle** tends to keep them distinct, as two different objects of choice, along with the third, the pleasurable (*hē-*

dyn). *To Kalon* is, in some of Plato's dialogues, the highest existence, perhaps indistinguishable from *To* **Hen**, The One; later **Platonists**, especially **Plotinus**, focused on this aspect of Plato's thought to form a basis for systematization.

KANŌN. Canon, standard, measure. Used in geometry for a straight edge, the word was introduced into philosophical usage by **Democritus**, who applied the word to a book on logic or philosophy of language, as did **Epicurus** subsequently. Polyclitus the sculptor had written a book called "The Canon" stating the ideal proportions of body, and made a statue illustrating his ideas. Thus a "Canon" is also an ideal standard or arrangement. *See also KRITĒRION.*

KARDIA. Heart. For **Aristotle**, the location of the governing part of the soul (*psychē*), including thought.

KATALAMBANEIN. To grasp, to cognize.

KATALĒPSIS. In **Stoic** epistemology, this is the act of "grasping" an impression; the standard translation is "cognition." The Stoics distinguish between cognitive (*kataleptikon*) and non-cognitive impressions. Similarly *katalambanein,* the verb from which these other words are derived, is translated "cognize." *See also ALĒTHEIA; KRITERION; PHANTASIA.*

KATĒGORIAI. Categories. In normal Greek, *katēgorizein* is to accuse someone of something. **Aristotle** appropriates the word in order to talk about *predication.* The first treatise in Aristotle's works as constituted since antiquity is on the *Categories*, or predicates of normal declarative sentences. Aristotle figures that normal sentences in Greek talk about things that there are (*ousiai*, typically translated "substances"), or kinds of *ousiai.* If you assert that something is a member of a class, you are in fact predicating something in the "category" of *ousia.* e.g., "Fido is a dog." He distinguishes nine more sorts of predicates: quality (*poion*), quantity (*poson*), relation (*pros ti*); action (*poiein*) and passion (*paschein*) (for active and passive verbs); time (*pote*) and place (*pou*), possession (*hexis*) and disposition (*diathesis*). The last two make it pretty clear that the paradigmatic sentences are in fact about people, since "possession" is illustrated with "has a hat on" and "disposition" is illustrated with "is sitting." Aristotle suggests that **being** has as many senses as there are categories (*de Anima* I.5, 410a13; *Metaph*. V.7, 1017a24).

The **Stoics** reduced the number of categories to four: substratum (*hypokeimenon*), quality (*poion*), state (*pōs echon*), and relation (*pros ti pōs echon*). **Plotinus** also reviews the theory from an ontological standpoint (*Enn*. VI.1).

KATH' HEKASTON. **Aristotelian** technical term for "individual," literally "according to each," contrasted with *katholou*. *See also TODE TI*.

KATHARSIS. Purification, catharsis. **Aristoxenus** is quoted as saying, "The **Pythagoreans** practiced purification of the body by means of the medical art, and of the soul by means of music" (DK 1.468, 20). Medically, *katharsis* tends to mean ridding the body of something, whether by a laxative or emetic; a woman's menstrual flow is also called a *katharsis*. In the *Phaedo* (67c), **Socrates**, talking to two Pythagoreans, says that the separation of the soul (*psychē*) from the body (*sōma*) in death is a *katharsis*. In the *Sophist*, 226ff, the **Eleatic** Stranger's analysis of the different senses of *katharsis* leads to the conclusion that there is a cleansing of the soul by means of philosophical *elenchus*; in the context there is a rather coy comparison of Socratic practice, which could be described this way, and that of the **Sophists**, who are unlikely to want to rid their interlocutors of error. In *Pol*. VIII.7, 1341b20ff, **Aristotle** discusses with approval the Pythagorean theory that music can cleanse the soul, criticizing Socrates of the *Republic* as too limited in the forms of music he accepts. Famously, Aristotle in the *Poetics* says that tragedy performs the function of the *katharsis* of pity and fear (6, 1449b25). Putting the two Aristotelian passages together, one may conclude that "purification" in this context is not exactly totally ridding the individual of the emotions in question, but rather restoring balance and direction among the emotions.

KATHĒKONTA. In **Stoic** moral theory, *kathēkonta* are **appropriate** actions or proper functions, i.e., moral duties. DL 7.108 lists "honoring parents, brothers, and country, spending time with friends." **Cicero**, *de Fin*. 3.60: "When a man has a preponderance of the things in accordance with nature, it is *kathēkon* to stay alive; when he has or foresees a preponderance of their opposites, it is *kathēkon* to depart from life."

KATHODOS. "The road down." Used of the descent of the soul (*psychē*). **Empedocles** f. 115: (W. E. Leonard translation)

> There is a word of Fate, an old decree
> And everlasting of the **gods**, made fast
> With amplest oaths, that whosoe'er of those
> Fair spirits, with their lot of age-long life,
> Do foul their limbs with slaughter in offense,
> Or swear forsworn, as failing of their pledge,
> Shall wander thrice ten thousand weary years
> Far from the Blessed, and be born through time
> In various shapes of mortal kind, which change
> Ever and ever troublous paths of life.
> For now Air hunts them onward to the Sea;
> Now the wild Sea disgorges them on Land;
> Now **Earth** will spue toward beams of radiant Sun;
> Whence he will toss them back to whirling Air—
> Each gets from other what they all abhor.
> And in that brood I too am numbered now,
> A fugitive and vagabond from heaven,
> As one obedient unto raving Strife.

Similarly, the **Pythagoreans** believe that the soul is incarnated as punishment for some unspecified sins; in **Plato**'s version (e.g., *Phaedo, Phaedrus*), the soul is drawn down into the body (*sōma*) because of desires for bodily things. *See also METEMPSYCHOSIS.*

KATHOLOU. As an adverb, "in general." With the definite article, *to katholou* is a technical term in **Aristotle**'s philosophy, generally translated "universal": "I mean by universal that which is naturally predicated of several things; the individual is not" (*Int.* 7, 17a39). Aristotle continues: "human" is a universal, "Callias" is an individual.

KATORTHŌMA. Literally, that which is straight, correct. In **Stoic** philosophy, it is a word for morally correct action. Other schools picked up on this terminology, granted that they thought it a bit easier to accomplish than did the Stoics.

KEISTHAI. One of **Aristotle's** 10 categories (*katēgoriai*), in English, "position." His examples at *Cat.* 2a1 are "is lying, is sitting." *See also* THESIS.

KENON. Empty, void, vacuum. **Democritus** and **Epicurus** use this word for the "void" of space. **Aristotle**, and some other ancient philosophers, denied the existence of such a void, *Physics* IV.6–9.

KINĒSIS. Movement. This abstract noun is made from the verb *kinein*, to move or change. Cautionary note: one of the tricky things about Greek verbs is that in addition to active and passive voice, there is a "middle" which indicates that the subject of the verb does (whatever) for itself or on its own behalf. In the case of *kinein*, the middle and passive forms in the present are indistinguishable, so that *kineitai* means either "is moved" or "moves itself."

Zeno of Elea's paradoxes problematized *kinēsis* by presenting arguments that seem to show that movement cannot occur. **Atomism** is, for one thing, a response to those paradoxes.

Plato, according to **Aristotle**, was persuaded by the **Heraclitean Cratylus** that the sensory world is constantly in all sorts of movement, and is consequently not intelligible (*Metaph.* I.6, 987a32). We see the effects of that stance in the *Theaetetus*, where the combination of the positions of **Protagoras** and **Heraclitus** yields the **hypothesis** that "everything is movement," *to pan kinēsis ēn* (*Tht* 156).

Aristotle has a great deal to say about *kinēsis*, especially in the *Physics*. Movement is an actualization of a potentiality; some movements are toward an end, but in other cases, the movement is itself the **actuality** and end. In principle, *kinēsis* can occur in respect of any of the categories: thus change in *ousia* is either *genesis* or *phthora*; change in quality (*to poion*) is *alloiōsis*; change in place is *phora*; change in quantity is, for example, growth or diminution; and so on.

KINOUN, TO. Participle of the verb "to move," *to kinoun* means "that which causes motion; mover." That which is moved is called *to kinoumenon*. In **Aristotle**'s analysis of motion and change there must be a source of movement, probably a series of intermediate "moved movers," and something at the end of the process which is moved but does not move anything else. The ultimate source of all movement must be *to prōton kinoun akinēton*, the first unmoved mover. *See also AKINĒTON KINOUN; ARCHĒ KINĒSEŌS; PRŌTON KINOUN.*

KNOWLEDGE. *See EPISTĒMĒ; GNŌSIS; NOĒSIS.*

KOINŌNIA. Community. **Socrates** talking to **Callicles** in the *Gorgias* (508) says that where there is no *koinōnia* there is no friendship (*philia*): "Yes, Callicles, wise men claim that *koinōnia* and *philia*, orderliness, self-control (*sōphrosynē*), and justice (*dikaiosynē*) hold together heaven and **earth**, **Gods** and humans, and that is why they call it a "whole" (*holon*)." **Aristotle**, more down-to-earth in the *Politics*, defines a *"polis"* as a *"koinōnia* of families and villages in a complete and self-sufficient life, i.e., a happy and honorable life" (III.9, 1281a1).

KOSMOS. See COSMOS; COSMOLOGY.

KRAMA, KRASIS. Blending mixture. Everything that there is, is a *krasis* of the elements, according to **Empedocles** (f. 22). **Alcmaeon** said that "health is a proportionate *krasis* of the qualities" (DK 24B4). **Aristotle** distinguishes a *krasis* from a *synthesis* at *GC* 328a6. If the components are preserved in small particles, it is a *krasis*. In a *synthesis*, the elements are transformed, and could not be divided out, even theoretically. *Krama* is the **Epicurean** word for "blend" of atoms (*atoma*) affecting our perception (*aisthēsis*). **Chrysippus** argues that a drop of wine would blend with the sea in such a way that that drop would extend through the entire ocean. (See SVF 2.473, 480). *See also MIGMA; MIXIS; STOICHEION; SYNTHESIS.*

KRITĒRION. Criterion, basis of judging. **Plato,** at *Theaetetus* 178b, says that when **Protagoras** says that "the human being is the measure," that means that he has "the criterion within himself." Similarly **Aristotle**, in *Metaphysics* XI.6, 1063b, talking about the same thesis of **Protagoras**, says that people perceive the same perceptible qualities similarly unless someone has a sense organ "perverted or injured." In that case, the person with the sense organ intact must be the "criterion" of the quality. What should be the criterion or criteria of truth becomes a big topic of discussion in Hellenistic philosophy. **Epicurus** proposes sensations, preconceptions, and feelings as the criteria. The **Stoics** countered with the idea that only some impressions are cognitive. **Carneades** and the Academic Skeptics argued that there is *no* criterion of truth, thus we do not know the truth. *See also SKEPTIKOS.*

KYNIKOS. *See* CYNIC.

– L –

LACYDES OF CYRENE (3rd century BCE). Skeptic, Scholarch of the **Academy** from 241/40 BCE. Student of **Arcesilaus**, Lacydes seems to have made skepticism the official position of the school.

LANGUAGE, THEORY OF. *See LEXIS; LOGOS; ONOMA.*

LAW. *See NOMOS.*

LEKTON. Literally, something said, or sayable. In **Stoic** philosophy, the ontological status of *lekta* is a most interesting issue: although the Stoics are, in principle, materialists, *lekta* are not material entities, yet they subsist somehow. *Lekta* are not simply what we call "propositions"; non-propositional "things said" are also *lekta*.

LEUCIPPUS OF ABDERA (c. 480–400 BCE). He is said to have written two books, *The Great World System* and *On Mind*. It is probable that Leucippus devised the atomic theory in response to the **Eleatic** philosophy that there is exactly one **being** and no real change. By positing an indefinitely large number of "beings" in the Eleatic sense, and allowing them to move in empty space in relation to each other, empirically discernable change becomes intellectually possible. *See also ATOMON.*

LEXIS. Speech, style of speech, diction, word, expression, text. In **Aristotle**, *lexis* is the speech performance, or written expression, whereas *logos* is about the thought behind the utterance. This distinction is pursued by the **Stoics**, who are prepared to call a nonsense word like *blituri* a *lexis*, but not a *logos*.

LIFE. *See BIOS, ZOĒ.*

LIMIT. *See PERAS.*

LOCOMOTION. *See PHORA.* *Phora* means motion from one place to another; "locomotion" is used by translators to capture the distinction between this sort of motion and others that ancient authors might be mentioning.

LOGIC. *See KANŌN; LOGIKĒ.*

LOGIKĒ. Logic. While the adjective *logikos* can mean simply possessed of the power of speech or reason (*anthrōpos* is defined as *zōion logikon*), it gains, particularly in the feminine, the sense of a branch of intellectual endeavor focused on language, as distinguished from *physikē*, focused on nature, and *ethikē*, focused on morality.

In a sense, the **Eleatic** philosophers, **Parmenides** and **Zeno**, called attention most dramatically to logic by offering arguments that look like they are about the meaning of the verb "to be" or the relationship between **unity** and plurality, and quickly turn to conclusions about what must be (or not be) the case about the world. **Plato**'s **Socrates** also frequently turns logical arguments to important conclusions; for example, in *Theaetetus* (186d), when he shows that "knowledge is not in the experiences but in the process of reasoning (*syllogismos*) about them."

Still, **Aristotle** is often credited with the creation of formal logic, specifically in the *Prior Analytics*, where he offers a formal theory of validity. He distinguishes several kinds of reasoning—deductive, inductive, and dialectical—and in the course of his collection of works called the *Organon* presents a methodology for each.

At the same time, other schools of philosophy inspired by Socrates pursued investigations into logical method; we may mention particularly the **Megarian** and **Dialectical** schools in this connection. After the time of Aristotle, the **Stoics** developed logic in new ways: for example, they interpreted Aristotelian syllogistic premises (like "all human beings are mortal") as conditionals ("if anything is a human being, then it is mortal") and developed a kind of propositional calculus.

Galen eventually showed that Aristotelian and Stoic logical systems are consistent with each other.

LOGISMOS. Calculation, Reasoning. Although the word is widely used of doing arithmetic, **Aristotle** extends it to cover rational activity in general.

LOGISTIKON. In a narrow sense, the word means skilled in calculation (**Plato** *Tht*. 145a), but both Plato and Aristotle apply the word to mean the rational part of the soul (*Rep*. 439d, *de An*. 432a25).

LOGOS. The word "*logos*" is perhaps the most used, and crucial, word in ancient Greek philosophy. Based on the verb *legein*, to speak, to say, or to count, in various contexts it may be translated word, account, ratio, definition, proposition, discourse, language, and doubtless other things besides. The emphasis on *logos* begins perhaps with **Heraclitus**, f. 1: "Although this *logos* always exists, people fail to understand it, both before they hear it, and when they first hear it. For everything happens according to the *logos*, people seem not to have experienced them when they try the word and works such as I present, dividing each thing according to its nature and telling how it really is. But other people do not notice what they are doing when they are awakened, just as they forget what they do when asleep." Already *logos* is ambiguous between the account that Heraclitus provides, and the principles on which that account is presumably founded.

In **Plato**'s "Socratic" dialogues, *logos* may have any of its senses, but perhaps most often it refers to the whole discussion, or to a specific argument presented by one of the participants. At *Phaedo* 75B a close connection is made with knowledge (*epistēmē*): it is regarded as self-evident that the person who knows is able to provide a *logos* of what he or she knows. One might say that that is a major objective of **Socrates**' questionings, to get people to provide an adequate *logos* of what they claim to know. While one might, with **Aristotle**, want to say that Socrates is looking for a definition (*see horismos*), what Socrates asks for is perhaps a bit broader than simply a definition.

In the *Theaetetus*, the last definition of *epistēmē* examined is "true belief plus a *logos*," and while no explanation of the meaning of *logos* in this context turns out to be satisfactory, the reader is given the impression that we are, by the end of the dialogue, at least *approaching* a satisfactory account of knowledge. If we put that passage in conjunction with the **Sun-Line-Cave** passage in the *Republic*, we see that in the *Republic*, the top segment of the Line, called dialectic, is characterized by the person who practices this art being able to give a *logos* of the being (*ousia*) of each thing. We can then see where the *Theaetetus* definition falls short—the *logos* there was not of the *ousia*.

Of the many other Platonic places we might mention, let us stick to just one more: in the *Timaeus*, the accounting of the work of the **Demiourgos** is often called The Works of *Logos*, usually translated "Reason," in contrast with the Works of Necessity (*Anagkē*), the part that tells of randomness and the irrational. The large third section of the Timaeus is called The Cooperation of *Logos* and *Anagkē*. The *Demiourgos* models the world "after that which is changeless and is grasped by *logos*" (*Tm* 29a).

Aristotle uses the word *logos* for a wide range of language-related items: language, word, speech, story, prose, talking, and so on; but it also takes on technical philosophical senses, as in Plato, and in some ways, beyond the Platonic senses. For example, he very often uses *logos* to mean the verbal formula that expresses the **essence** of some species, i.e., a real definition. Yet the expression "the *logos* of the *ousia*" seems often to have a wider signification for him than just definition.

The roughly definitional sense of *logos* easily slips into using it to mean something like concept or thought; *logos*, he says, is of the universal, while perception (*aisthēsis*) is of the **particular** (e.g., *Metaph.* VII.10, 1035b35ff). Thus, he can say of the mind (*nous*) and body (*sōma*) that they are one in terms of location, they can be separated *kata logon*, which we might translate as "conceptually" (*de An.* III.4).

Logos is also used by Aristotle as a word for the rational faculty as such: the soul (*psychē*), he says, may be divided into the part that has *logos*, and that which is *alogon* (e.g., *EN* I.13, 1103a28); the "rational" part may again be divided into that which obeys the *logos*, and that which thinks the *logos* (e.g., *EN* I.6, 1098a3).

Many of these distinctions continued to be used by subsequent philosophers. The **Stoics** are cited for defining "*logos*" as "a meaningful sound sent out from **reason (*dianoia*)**; articulate meaningful sound" (SVF III.213ff). But beyond that, the *logos* is the immanent ordering principle of the universe, an idea that they traced to Heraclitus (see above). The dissemination of the *logos* throughout the universe occurs by means of the *spermatikoi logoi*, the seeds of the *logos*.

Philo of Alexandria places a great deal of emphasis on the notion of *logos*, making it the mediating principle between **God** and the World. There is a kind of proto-trinity in Philo's thought: God, *Logos*, and **World Soul**. Unlike the Stoics, Philo ensures the transcendence of God by distinguishing God both from the life of the universe, and from its inherent rationality.

This structure was not lost on the author of the *Gospel of John*, who writes, "In the beginning was the Logos, and the Logos was with God, and the Logos was God" (I.1), "And the Logos became flesh and dwelt among us, full of grace and truth" (I.14). So John identifies Jesus with the principle of rationality in the universe.

A final point: **Plotinus** goes at least one better than Philo by clearly distinguishing the *Logos* from *Nous* (Mind) in *Enn*. III.16.

LOVE. *See ERŌS; PHILIA.*

LUCIAN OF SAMOSATA (c. 120–180 CE). Lucian was a sophist and satirist who made philosophy a subject of comedy. His *Philosophers for Sale* imagines how various classical philosophers would behave were they put on the slave market. His *True Story* includes, among other fanciful adventures, a trip to the moon, thus anticipating "science fiction." His *Auction of Lives* (or *Auction of Wisdom*) introduces the word "esoteric" to the philosophic vocabulary. There are many other extant works (eight volumes in the Loeb edition), well worth reading.

LUCRETIUS (c. 90–c. 50 BCE). Titus Lucretius Carus, Roman poet and **Epicurean**. His *De Rerum Natura* is the most complete and detailed ancient presentation of Epicurean philosophy extant. **Cicero** may have had some role in bringing this work to the attention of the public. Lucretius has probably had his greatest influence since the 17th century, after rediscovery of his poem in the Renaissance.

LYCEUM. In the fifth century BCE, the Lyceum was the location of a large wrestling school, named after the adjoining temple of Apollo Lykeios; it was a favorite hangout of **Sophists** and others (see **Plato**, beginning of the *Euthydemus*, cf. the beginning of the *Lysis*). **Isocrates** taught there in the earlier part of the fourth century. In 335, **Aristotle** acquired the building as a location for his school. He taught there until shortly before his death in 323. It gained the alternative name, the Peripatos, due to the covered walkways in the structure where Aristotle often taught while walking around (*see* PERIPATETIC SCHOOL).

The school continued to operate under successor **Scholarchs: Theophrastus**, **Strato of Lampsacus**, and **Lyco**, until some time after 225, when Lyco left the school to the entire group of scholars rather than to one individual. In fact at that point it was in serious decline, since the **Museum** of **Alexandria** had proven to be a much livelier location for Aristotelian research. Some sources tell us that **Aristo of Ceos** succeeded Lyco; we know that **Critolaus** was the leading Peripatetic in 155 BCE, as he was a member of the Athenian embassy of that year to Rome. We hear that Diodorus of Tyre succeeded Critolaus, and Erymneus succeeded Critolaus, which takes us to about 100 BCE.

There were known Peripatetics during the first century BCE, but the Athenian school itself seems to have collapsed before 86 BCE, when Sulla attacked **Athens**. According to one story, Apellicon of Teos had acquired (possibly stolen) the library of the Lyceum, and Sulla shipped it off to Rome, where it was the basis of the edition of the **Corpus** Aristotelicum produced by **Andronicus of Rhodes** (**Plutarch**, *Life of Sulla* 26). **Cicero** spent nearly two years in Athens (79–77 BCE) and does not mention visiting the Lyceum; in his opinion the contemporary Peripatetics were indistinguishable from Stoics.

A kind of revival of the Lyceum occurred in Athens when **Marcus Aurelius** funded a Chair of Aristotelian Philosophy, but the precise location of resulting instruction is not at all clear.

LYCO OF TROAS (d. 225 BCE). Successor of **Strato of Lampsacus** as **Scholarch** of the **Lyceum**, apparently succeeded by **Aristo of Ceos**.

LYPĒ. Bodily pain, opposed to bodily pleasure. **Anaxagoras** says that every perception (***aisthēsis***) is attended by pain (*lypē*), according to **Theophrastus** in *Physical Opinions*, frag. 23. **Plato** discusses the relationship between pleasure and pain in *Philebus* 31cff; **Aristotle** in *EN* VII.12–15.

LYSIS. Solution, seeing free, deliverance. **Aristotle** uses this term for the solution of a problem, or the resolution of the plot in a play. At *Phaedo* 67d, **Plato**'s **Socrates** uses it of the separation of the soul (***psychē***) from the body (***sōma***) at death.

– M –

MACROBIUS (AMBROSIUS THEODOSIUS MACROBIUS) (fl. 395–423 CE). Grammarian and **Neoplatonist**, author of *Saturnalia*, an extensive text explaining the origin and meaning of the festival that is now known as Christmas, and a commentary on **Cicero**'s *Dream of Scipio*, influential in the medieval West.

MAGIC. Two Greek words are closely associated with this English word. The one is *mageia*, the theory and practice of the "Mages" or priests of the Persian deity **Zoroaster**. For example, **Theophrastus** uses this word as the practice of the Mages, and magic, in *Historia Plantarum* 9.15.7. The other word is *manganeia* (and various related words) meaning "trickery," e.g., **Plato** *Laws* X, 908d. The form of "magic" most closely associated with the philosophical tradition is theurgy (***theourgia***).

MAGNITUDE. *See MEGETHOS, DIASTĒMA.*

MANIA. Madness. In the *Phaedrus* (254a), **Socrates** distinguishes several sorts of *mania*; first, there is bad madness and good madness, and of the good madness there are four varieties: that of oracles and prophets; the sort that leads to purifications of long-standing plagues; the mad inspiration of poets; and the madness of the philosophical lover. Similarly in the *Symposium* (218a), Alcibiades talks about all the people around Socrates "sharing in the Bacchic frenzy of philosophy." After **Plato**, philosophers tended to be a fairly sober lot, avoiding talk of philosophical madness. For example, Aristotle says that the person who stands on a high spot during a thunderstorm is crazy, not brave (*EE* III.1, 1229b27). According to the **Stoics**, everyone but the wise person is insane (SVF III.166). *See also MANTIKĒ.*

MANICHEANISM. Religion founded by the Persian Mani (216–276 CE), strongly dualistic between "good" and "evil"; it combined Zoroastrian, Christian, and Buddhist ideas (and severely rejected Jewish ideas) and became extremely popular and widespread. **Augustine** was a follower for several years before becoming a **Platonist** and **Christian**. Augustine came to believe, with the Platonists, that "evil" is simply the absence of good, that there is no irreducible evil power in the universe. Orthodox and Roman Christians, and subsequently Muslims, did their best to eliminate Manicheanism. When they succeeded, the name became something of an insult to be thrown at one's religious opponents. *See also JUDAISM; ZOROASTRIANISM.*

MANILIUS, MARCUS (1st century CE). Author of *Astronomica,* a long poem presenting **astronomy** and astrology with a Stoic slant. *See also ASTROLOGIA.*

MANTIKĒ. Divination, prophecy. **Plato**, at *Phaedrus* 244c, relates the word etymologically to *mania*, or madness, suggesting that prophets and diviners are inspired but are out of their minds. **Socrates** is represented as calling the messages from his *daimōnion* "*mantikē*" (*Apol.* 40a). At the same time, *mantikē* is sometimes represented as an art or craft (*technē*), e.g., at **Aristotle** *Politics* 1274a28.

Cicero, in *De Divinatione*, distinguishes the "inspired" form of divination from the "craft" variety; the "inspired" sort operates either through prophets as described by Plato, or by way of dreams (*see oneiros*), the technical sort uses the flight of birds or the entrails of sacrificial animals, for example, as indications of the future.

MARCUS AURELIUS. *See AURELIUS.*

MARINUS (c. 450–500 CE). Successor of **Proclus** as **Scholarch** of the Platonic school of **Athens**. His biography of Proclus survives.

MARTIANUS CAPELLA (MARTIANUS MINNEUS FELIX CAPELLA) (Early fifth century CE). His one known work, *Satyricon*, or *De Nuptiis Philologiae et Mercurii et de septem Artibus liberalibus libri novem* ("On the wedding of Philology and Mercury and of the Seven Liberal Arts, in Nine Books"), was a favored inspiration of the organization of education in the medieval West.

MATHĒMA, MATHĒMATA; TA MATHĒMATIKA. A *mathēma* is something that can be learned. *Ta mathēmata*, the plural, is especially applied to what we would call "mathematical" knowledge: arithmetic, geometry, and **astronomy** (**Plato** *Laws* 817e), with the later addition of harmonics. **Aristotle**, at *Physics* II.2, 194a8, distinguishes abstract mathematical studies from mathematics in nature, which includes (for example) optics, harmonics, and astronomy. In that same context, he uses the phrase *ta mathēmatika* to refer to "mathematical" entities such as odd and even, point, line, and surface considered separately from bodies, and so on.

Mathematical knowledge was fundamental at the beginning of ancient Greek philosophy. **Thales** is credited with developing (or borrowing from elsewhere) the method of triangulating to calculate the distance of a ship at sea, or the height of a pyramid, for example. **Pythagoras** asserted a mathematical, specifically geometrical, understanding of reality, developed by his followers.

While **Egyptians** and Babylonians had a great deal of advanced understanding of mathematical principles, the ancient Greeks are usually given credit for the idea of a rigorous mathematical proof of theorems.

MATHĒMATIKOI. Serious students, individuals who want to learn. **Iamblichus**, in his account of early **Pythagoreanism**, uses this word of the more scientifically and mathematically inclined of the master's disciples.

MATTER. It is well known that in **Aristotle**'s opinion, most of the earliest Greeks whom we now call "philosophers" were interested primarily in figuring out what the world is made of. Thus a quick Aristotelian summary of much of early Greek philosophy looks like this. **Anaximander**—the *apeiron*; **Thales**—water; **Anaximenes** and

Diogenes of Apollonia—air; **Heraclitus**—fire; **Empedocles**— **earth**, water, air, and fire; **Anaxagoras**—"like-parts"; **Leucippus** and **Democritus**—atoms (*atoma*) and the void. Similarly, **Plato**, according to Aristotle, imagined that the receptacle (*hypodochē*), or space, was that out of which everything is made. But in a sense, the idea of matter is itself an Aristotelian invention; that is, Aristotle took the word *hylē*, original sense "lumber," and applied it to whatever anything is made out of. Our word "matter" comes from **Cicero**'s translation of *hylē* as *materia*, which also meant (before he used it this way) "lumber."

For Aristotle, there are four basic sorts of questions that you can ask about anything. What is it? What is it made out of? How did it come to be what it is? What is it for? "*Hylē*" is the general answer to "What is it made out of?" For Aristotle, the *proximate* matter is a much more informative answer than a more remote level of material. For example, it is much more informative to say that the house is made of bricks and mortar, wood and nails, than to say that it is such and such a percentage of silicon, oxygen, carbon, iron and so on, to put it into modern vocabulary. But even that is more informative than saying that it is made out of atoms (*atoma*) of various shapes and sizes (which are too small for us to observe) as the atomists suggest, or that it is made out of the possibility of the othering of perceptibility afforded by the space-time continuum, as Plato appears to suggest.

After Aristotle, both the **Epicurean** and **Stoic** schools were, in their different ways, thoroughly materialistic. The Epicureans were atomists; the Stoics were also reductionist. **Peripatetic**s tended to be more reductionist than Aristotle himself. Only the **Platonists** remained deeply suspicious of explaining things in terms of what they were made out of. *See also HYLE; HYPOKEIMENON; STOICHEION.*

MEAN. *See MESON.*

MEDICINE. *See IATROS, IATRIKĒ.*

MEDIUM OF PERCEPTION. **Aristotle** argues that the perceptible form must be transferred from the perceived object to the perceiving organ by means of a "medium" (*de An.* II.7ff). Light is transported instantaneously through the *aithēr*; air (*aēr*) or **water** is the medium for sound and smell; the flesh is the medium for taste and touch. *See also AISTHĒSIS; MESON; METAXY.*

MEGALOPREPEIA. Magnificence, as a personal quality. In **Plato** *Rep.* VI, 486a, it is assumed to be a quality of the "true philosopher." In **Aristotle** *EN* IV.2, 1122a19ff, it is limited to the **appropriate** expenditure of money by the wealthy person.

MEGALOPSYCHIA. "Great-souled-ness" or pride, as a personal quality. In *EN* IV.3, 1123a34ff, **Aristotle** struggles to convey a sense of the quality of an individual who is a paragon of the virtues, and is appropriately aware of his greatness, but not excessively. Some of his description looks like an attempt to explain what later became known as *charisma*. Of course, there is a serious danger of someone going beyond the evidence, so to speak, in thinking of himself as a *megalopsychos*. In the *Second Alcibiades* (a dialogue not written by **Plato**), **Socrates** says that *megalopsychia* is a euphemism for stupidity (140c, 150c).

MEGARIAN SCHOOL. Said to have been founded by **Euclides of Megara**, associate of **Socrates** and enthusiast of **Parmenides**. Others said to be associated with the Megarian School include **Stilpo**, **Diodorus Cronus**, **Philo the Logician**, **Eubulides**, and others. Several sophistic paradoxes are associated with the name of Eubulides. **Aristotle** critiques the Megarian School at *Metaphysics* IX.3; the Megarians apparently denied potentiality, claiming that something *can* act only when it is actually acting. If the Megarians were followers of the **Eleatic** philosophy, that would be consistent with a denial of potentiality.

MEGETHOS. Size, magnitude. **Zeno of Elea**'s paradoxes include the dilemma: if there are many things, and they have magnitude, then the many things are potentially indefinitely divisible, so there is an infinite number of things; if there are many things, and they do not have magnitude, then nothing with a finite magnitude can be constructed of them. **Leucippus** is not worried: he seems to have said that space (***to kenon***) is indefinite in terms of size (*megethos*), and the atoms (***atoma***) indefinite in terms of number (*plethos*).

In *Metaphysics* V.13, **Aristotle** says that a *megethos* that is continuous in one dimension is a length, a *megethos* that is continuous in two dimensions is breadth, and a *megethos* that is continuous in three dimensions is depth; if these are limited in extent, they are line, surface, and solid.

MEIGMA. Mixture, compound. Alternate spelling for *MIGMA*.

MELISSUS OF SAMOS (Born before 470 BCE). He commanded the Samian fleet that defeated the Athenian navy in 442 BCE, according to **Plutarch**, *Life of Pericles*. Melissus wrote a book supporting and in some ways extending the **Eleatic** philosophy of **Parmenides** and **Zeno**, asserting the **unity** and eternality of **being** and the consequent illusoriness of the observed perceptible world. While Parmenides says that being is "like a well-rounded sphere," implying that it is finite in extent, Melissus asserts the spatial infinity of being. **Aristotle** was very critical of Melissus (*Metaph.* I.5, 986b25-27, *Phys.* I.2, 185a9-12); we have fairly extensive fragments, preserved by **Simplicius**, that present a **dialectical** argument in support of the Eleatic position as Melissus understood it. Simplicius also presents a summary of the arguments presented by **Gorgias** in a book that looks to be a use of Melissus' style of argument turned against him. If that is correct, the main lines of Melissus' argument would be to show, first, that "Being Is"; second, that "Being is the Object of Knowledge"; third, that "Being is the Referent of Speech." *See* GORGIAS for what he does with that.

MENEDEMUS OF ERETRIA (c. 340–265 BCE). He studied with **Stilpo** in **Athens** and at the **Elian** School, founded by **Phaedo**. He is supposed to have moved the school to Eretria. Like Phaedo, he is assumed to be "Socratic" in some sense.

MENELAUS OF ALEXANDRIA (c. 100 CE). Mathematician and astronomer whose work *Sphaerica*, lost in Greek, is preserved in Arabic, and in Hebrew and Latin translations of the Arabic version.

MENIPPUS OF GADARA (First half 3rd century BCE). A **Cynic**, associated with **Crates**, Menippus wrote a good deal (now lost) that influenced later writers of satire.

MĒ ON. Non-being. After the work of **Parmenides**, who said that you cannot talk about non-being because it is not there to be talked of, Greek thinkers had some trouble with negations. Or fun, as in the case of **Gorgias**. **Plato** deals with false (***pseudos***) propositions, which might be taken to be "about" non-being, by saying that both the subject and predicate exist (as Forms, ***eidē***) but are not actually related as the sentence states (e.g., "Theaetetus is flying"). **Aristotle** pointed out that denying that some predicate belongs to some subject is in fact talking about something that exists, namely that subject; we do not need Forms for that, or even for the predicate, which is supposed to be a "**universal**" in one of the **categories**. *See also* **BEING;** *ON*.

MESON, MESOTĒS. Mean, middle, medium. *Meson* is the adjective, it can be made into a concrete noun with the addition of the definite article (*to meson*); *mesotēs* is the abstract noun. Among the "local" senses, there is a cosmic sense (the middle of the universe). **Parmenides** f. 12. ". . . in the *meson* . . . is the **Goddess** who steers all things. . . ." The **Pythagoreans** tend to use the word in a mathematical sense (as mathematical mean); they see the mean, or middle, as a "limit" and thus good. It is easy to go from that to a metaphorical sense, as in **Plato** *Republic* X.619a5. "We must always know how to choose the *meson* and how to avoid either of the extremes, as far as possible, both in this life and in all those beyond it. This is the way that a human being becomes happiest." **Aristotle** defines the "ethical virtue" as "the habit of choosing the action lying in the *meson* relatively to us, according to the right rule as determined by the person of practical wisdom." The *meson* is also, for Aristotle, the "middle" term of a **syllogism**, the one that ties the first two premises together and yields the conclusion. *See also METAXY*.

METABASIS. Transition, "going across." **Aristotle** uses this word for the change of the **elements** into each other (*Cael*. III.7, 305b27ff); he also uses it in a famous passage on the continuity of living kinds:

> Nature proceeds little by little from things lifeless to animal life in such a way that it is impossible to determine the exact line of demarcation, nor on which side thereof an intermediate form should lie . . . there is observed in plants a continuous *metabasis* to the animal (*HA* VII.1, 588b11).

The **Epicureans** use the word for "regress," i.e., they deny that there is a regress or reduction of physical magnitudes ad infinitum—there is no *metabasis* of the atoms (*atoma*) at a certain point. The **Stoics** use the word *metabasis* for arguments by analogy that emphasize the continuity of the cases. *See also STOICHEION.*

METABOLĒ. **Aristotle**'s most general word for "**change**." Change of **matter** into an **entity** is *genesis*, and destruction of an entity is *phthora*; qualitative change is *alloiōsis*; change in location is *kinēsis*; quantitative change may be growth or diminution. Sometimes Aristotle uses the word *kinēsis* in a broader sense, almost equivalent to *metabolē*. Aristotle's general account of change begins in *Physics* V. 1.

METAPHYSICS, TA META TA PHYSICA. This word was first used of **Aristotle**'s treatise, in 14 books, that he himself variously calls "First Philosophy," "The Science of **Being** qua Being" or "Theology." Because the prefix *meta-* in Greek can mean either "after" or "beyond" (i.e., superior to), some have said that the name refers in the first instance to the location of the scrolls on the shelf in the **Lyceum**. At any rate, this treatise provided the initial definition of this philosophical field of study. As analyzed by the Italian scholar Giovanni Reale, Aristotelian metaphysics includes four complementary sorts of study: ousiology, or the study of entities (*ousiai*); aitiology, or the study of causes (*aitia*); axiology, or the study of axioms (*axiomata*); **theology**, or the study of **God** and the Divine. From that perspective, ancient Greek philosophy was heavily involved in metaphysical investigation from the start.

Pre-Aristotelian documents that are crucially "metaphysical" in character include but are not limited to the Poem of **Parmenides**, and **Plato**'s *Phaedo*, the **Sun-Line-Cave** passage in the *Republic*, the *Parmenides*, and the *Sophist* (for a start).

The Hellenistic philosophers did not pick up on the word "Metaphysics" as a field of philosophical study. For example, as the **Stoics** saw it, philosophers should be interested in Logic (*logikē*), Physics (*physikē*), and **Ethics**. They did plenty of metaphysics, but called some of it Logic and some of it Physics. The development of a distinct field of investigation called "metaphysics" probably owes most to the commentators on Aristotle's writings. **Alexander of Aphrodisias** wrote the fundamental commentary on the *Metaphysics* from a **Peripatetic** perspective; subsequent ancient commentaries on the *Metaphysics* were written by **Neoplatonists**. For Western philosophy, the commentary on the *Metaphysics* by Averroes (Ibn Rushd), translated into Latin, played a role, as did the careful study and commentary by Thomas Aquinas. But that takes us out of the focus of this Dictionary.

METAXY. Between. One of **Zeno of Elea**'s more puzzling arguments is the one that holds that if there are more than one being in the world, then additional beings can be inserted "between" the beings that there are, but that process can be continued indefinitely, so if there exist more than one being, there must be an infinite number of beings, which is impossible (reported by **Simplicius**, *in Phys.* 140, 27).

On a somewhat different note, **Aristotle** accuses **Plato** of having "intermediate" knowable objects, between the Forms (*eidē*) and the phenomena, at *Metaphysics* I.6, 987b15. These "intermediates" are, he says, the "objects of mathematics." It would be possible to gather something on that order from the **Sun-Line-Cave** passage, *Rep.* VI, 510b-c, though it would be more attractive to consider that *dianoia* would not be *limited* to mathematical calculations.

For Aristotle, *to metaxy* is the "medium" of any of the senses, that which conveys the sensible form from the sensed object to the sense organ (*de Anima* II). He also uses it as a synonym for several of the senses of *meson, mesotēs*. *See also* MATHĒMA.

METEMPSYCHOSIS. This is the late Greek (starting second century CE) word for the idea that souls (*psychai*) leave the body (*sōma*) of people (and perhaps animals) at death, and are reborn in new individuals (people or animals). This is of course a standard part of Hindu and Buddhist belief; **Pythagoras** is credited with bringing it to Greece—**Herodotus** suggests from **Egypt**, where it was not at all part of the standard belief. **Xenophanes** tells the story that when Pythagoras came upon someone beating his puppy, he told him to stop, because he "heard the voice of a friend" (f. 7). *Metempsychosis* is an important part of **Empedocles'** theory of the soul: "For before now I have been at some time boy and girl, bush, bird, and a mute fish in the sea," f. 117. It is a central part of the argument of **Plato**'s *Phaedo* and *Phaedrus*, and appears in the *Republic*. We should also note that the Orphic cult in Greece also believed in *metempsychosis*, but there appears to be no evidence of that cult before the time of Pythagoras.

In some authors, the word *palingenesis* is a synonym for *metempsychosis*. *Palingenesis* literally means "regeneration," and is used by the **Stoics** for the rebirth of the world after the period conflagration (*ekpyrosis*). In the *New Testament*, it is applied both to the status of having been "born again" through baptism and to the resurrection.

In modern usage, the word "transmigration" is applied to the Pythagorean form of *metempsychosis*, in which souls may go from animal to human or human to animal form; the word "reincarnation" is sometimes restricted to the sort of *metempsychosis* in which human souls always return to another human life.

METHEXIS. This is a Platonic word, translated "participation"; it is one of the metaphors for describing the relationship between Forms (*eidē*) and Phenomena (*phainomena*). In the *methexis* model, phenomena "have some of" or "share in" the form. **Plato** is well aware of the potential paradoxes of the model; in fact he explores them in the first part of the *Parmenides*. **Aristotle** assures us that it is Plato's coinage in this sense. A typical non-metaphysical use of the word occurs at *Pol*. III.5, where Aristotle talks of aristocracies that limit who can have a "share" of honors.

METRODORUS OF LAMPSACUS (331–278 BCE). Cofounder of the **Epicurean School**. He remained a close associate of **Epicurus** throughout his life, writing a great deal that contributed to the popularity of the school. His sister and two brothers also joined the school, and he had two children with the ex-prostitute Leontion, who had joined the school; one of those children was named Epicurus.

METRODORUS OF STRATONICEA (Late second century BCE). Academic skeptic, student of **Carneades**. **Diogenes Laertius** says that he was an **Epicurean** before going to Carneades. *See also SKEPTIKOS*.

MICROCOSM. Democritus is credited with saying that a human being is a "*micros kosmos*," a small universe. The phraseology was new, but the idea was not, since one could argue that earlier thinkers had thought that the universe is a big person (see, for example, **Xenophanes**, **Anaxagoras**).

MIDDLE PLATONISM. The first followers of **Plato**, the Old **Academy**, tended to engage in metaphysical speculation (see **Speusippos**, **Xenocrates**, **Polemon**), but after Polemon, the Academy became a center for Skepticism (*see SKEPTIKOS*). **Antiochus of Ascalon**, who had joined the Academy and studied with **Philo of Larissa**, broke with Philo after the destruction of the Athenian schools by the attacks of Mithridates and Sulla (88 and 86 BCE). From Philo's perspective, there was an essential unity of the **Academic**, **Peripatetic**, and **Stoic** philosophies, and that a positive dogmatic position could be constructed. **Cicero** reports the resultant position in *Academica*. At the same time, the Stoic **Panaetius** was synthesizing **Aristotelian** and Stoic theories, and the Stoic **Posidonius**, who had studied with Panaetius, tended to synthesize Stoicism and Platonism. In **Alexandria**, **Eudorus** developed a dogmatic and syncretistic Platonism, with a neo-**Pythagorean** twist. We do not have enough text to be totally sure of the details of his teaching, but in the case of **Philo of Alexandria** we have quite a lot of text; he was concerned to synthesize what he took to be the best of Greek philosophy, the dogmatic Platonism that he knew, and bring it into line with the Hebrew Bible.

In the next century in **Athens**, we know of a dogmatic teacher of Platonism, **Ammonius**, and a great deal about his most famous student, **Plutarch of Chaeronea**. Others who should be counted as Middle Platonists include **Alcinous** (sometimes known as Albinus), **Apuleius**, **Galen**, and others.

The period of "middle Platonism" may be said to end at the time of **Ammonius Saccas**, the teacher of **Plotinus**, who is credited with initiating **Neoplatonism**. It would also be possible to argue that the distinction between "Old Academy," "middle Platonism," and "Neoplatonism," is more temporal than doctrinal, since all of them thought that they were true to the text of Plato.

MIGMA. Mixture, compound. **Aristotle** reports that according to **Empedocles** and **Anaximander**, things come to be by differentiation from a previous "mixture" (*Metaph.* XII.2, 1069b23). **Anaxagoras**, too, has a persistent "mixture" of the various component parts of things. According to Aristotle's *Generation of Animals*, the beginning of a new individual animal occurs by means of a *migma* of the male semen and the female menstrual fluid (*GA* I.19, 726a32).

MIMĒSIS. Imitation. "The **Pythagoreans** say that **being**s exist by imitation of **numbers**, and **Plato** by **participation**, changing the name" (**Aristotle** *Metaphysics* I.6, 987b10). In fact, according to the Cave part of the **Sun–Line–Cave** story of the *Republic*, the objects of hypothetical-deductive reasoning are already imitations of the Forms (*eidē*) (they are like reflections in pools of water); material things are definitely imitations, since they are represented by the models carried back and forth in front of the fire, in the cave, and our perceptions (*aisthēseis*) of the world are again imitations of them, for they are like the shadows cast on the wall of the cave. In *Rep.* X, Plato applies this "continuous analogy" to the detriment of representational art, which turns out to be essentially an imitation of the shadows on the wall of the cave and therefore one more step away from reality (598c). In the *Timaeus*, the *Demiourgos* imitates the Forms in creating the world. But if imitation is not of the Forms, from a Platonic point of view, one is going away from being toward unreality. In the *Sophist*, there is an extensive analysis of the various sorts of *mimēsis*, with the "Sophist" turning out to be a particularly perverse sort of practitioner of *mimēsis*.

Aristotle says of *technē* that it partially imitates nature, partially completes what nature cannot finish (*Phys.* II.8, 199a15).

MIND. *See NOUS (NOOS).*

MIXIS. Mixture, blending, sexual intercourse. **Empedocles**, f. 8, says (in part):

> there is no birth
> Of all things mortal, nor end in ruinous death;
> But *mixis* only and interchange. . .

Thus Empedocles explains all generation by the various ways that the **elements** are blended.

Aristotle discusses *mixis* at *GC* I.10, 327a30ff. He argues, against Empedocles and others, that various materials have the potentiality to undergo change, so that once that change has occurred, the constituent parts can no longer be disassembled from the whole. The Empedocles "mixture," Aristotle says, is really just a "juxtaposition" or *krasis*, not a real mixture. *See also STOICHEION.*

MIXTURE. *See KRASIS; MIGMA; MIXIS; SYNTHESIS.*

MNESARCHUS OF ATHENS (c. 170–88 BCE). Stoic philosopher, student of **Diogenes of Seleucia** and **Antipater of Tarsus. Cicero** mentions him as a leading Stoic in the beginning of the first century BCE (*Acad.* 2.22.69).

MODE. *See TROPOS.*

MODERATION. *See SŌPHROSYNĒ.*

MODERATUS OF GADES (c. 50–100 CE). Neopythagorean, contemporary with **Apollonius of Tyana**. His *Lectures on Pythagoras* is cited by **Porphyry**.

MOIRA. Allotment, Portion, Fate. The Goddess tells **Parmenides** that no *kakē* moira has brought him to her (f. 1); **Heraclitus** says that those with "greater deaths" have "greater *moirai*" (f. 25); **Anaxagoras** says that there is a *moira* of everything in everything (f. 11). In **Plato**'s *Phaedo* 133e5, the *moira* of incurably evil souls is to be thrown into Tartarus, never to be seen again. The word rarely occurs in **Aristotle**; one place where it does is *EN* I.9, 1099b10, where he notes that some have thought that *eudaimonia* comes as a consequence of divine *moira*. This is not Aristotle's own opinion. *See also ANAGKĒ; HEIMARMENĒ.*

MONAS. One, unit. **Plato** talks about "ones" and "twos" at *Phaedo* 101c, in a roughly **Pythagorean** way. **Aristotle** critiques the Pythagorean / Platonic idea that the "unit" can exist without being something other than a unit (*Metaphysics* XIV.2, 1089b35). **Nicomachus**, *Introduction to Arithmetic*, develops the **Neopythagorean** concept of units and numbers. *See also DYAS; HEN.*

MONIMUS OF SYRACUSE (4th century BCE). A **Cynic**, with skeptical tendencies. **Diogenes Laertius** (VI.3, 82–83) tells us that he had been the slave of a banker, and that he feigned madness to be able to become the follower of **Diogenes the Cynic** and **Crates**. He is noted for his statement that "every supposition is a delusion."

MORPHĒ. Shape, form. Unlike *idea* and *eidos*, which are explicitly related to *visible* form, *morphē* tends to imply touchable shape. Consequently, **Aristotle** often combines it with *eidos* in referring to the "form" of something: the carpenter imparts "*morphē* and *eidos*" to the wood when he builds, so too the male semen to the female contribution to generation (*GA* I.22, 730b14).

MOTION. *See KINĒSIS; PHORA.*

MOUSIKĒ. The arts of the Muses. While there are several different versions of stories about the Muses, the standard or official version says that there are nine, with following sponsorships.

Calliope	Epic Poetry
Clio	History (i.e., empirical investigation)
Erato	Love Poetry
Euterpe	*Aulos* Music
Melpomene	Tragedy
Polyhymnia	Sacred Poetry
Terpsichore	Dance
Thalia	Comedy
Urania	**Astronomy**

Thus, *mousikē* potentially covers a wide range of artistic and intellectual endeavor.

Plato often refers to the muses; in fact in the Greek anthology, there is an epigram attributed to him that claims that Sappho should be counted as the 10th muse (Cooper, *Plato*, p. 1745; H. Beckby, *Anthologia Graeca* 1957, #12). In the *Phaedrus*, **Socrates** not only invokes the muses before launching into his inspired speech, he later claims that poets who try to compose without having been maddened by the muses are doomed to failure (245), and tells a charming myth that the cicadas are spies of the muses (259).

In the *Republic* (403), *mousikē* is one of the three parts of basic education; the other two are **grammatikē**, or writing, and *gymnastikē*, or physical exercise. At *Politics* VIII.3, 1337b24, **Aristotle** says that some add *graphikē* or drawing to the list of subjects that are required for a basic education. He goes on to defend the inclusion of *mousikē* in education, clearly thinking of it as a combination of what we call music and poetry.

Aristotle also uses the adjective *mousikos* as a standard example of an **accidental** (as opposed to essential) **attribute** of a person (e.g., *Metaphysics* V.6, 1015b15).

MOVER. *See KINOUN.*

MUSEUM (*MUSEION*) AND LIBRARY OF ALEXANDRIA. Ptolemy II of **Egypt**, with the help and advice of the Aristotelian **Demetrius of Phaleron**, established a shrine to the muses (*see mousikē*) that served as an educational and research center; it included a library. The Ptolemies initiated a unique tax on books—every book introduced into **Egypt** had to be copied for inclusion in the library. Throughout the Ptolemaic period this institution served as an intellectual center, and it helped to establish **Alexandria** as a continuing intellectual center throughout antiquity.

This legendary institution was so great that there are more or less credible stories of its destruction on three separate occasions. The first occasion was the invasion of Egypt by Julius Caesar, in his war against Cleopatra and Mark Antony, in 47/8 BCE; the evidence supports the idea that there was a serious fire, perhaps total destruction, of the Royal Library of the Ptolemies at that time.

The second occasion was in about 391 CE; Theophilus is said to have destroyed the Serapeion at that time as part of an attack on paganism. Some scholars (notably Edward Gibbon) have claimed that this attack resulted in the destruction of (the remains of?) the Alexandrian library, housed in the Serapeion, which was indeed destroyed. The evidence is mixed on this point.

The third time has to do with the Caliph Omar, who took Alexandria in 640 CE. The story goes that his troops asked him what to do with the library, and he responded, "either those books disagree with the Koran, and are heretical, and thus should be burned, or they agree with the Koran, and are duplicative, and thus may also be burned, so burn them all." It is a great story, but it is unlikely that there was any significant library left in Alexandria after the fanatical Christians had finished with it. *See also* HYPATIA.

MUSONIUS RUFUS (c. 30–100 CE). Of Volsinii (Bolsena) in Etruria; **Stoic**. Part of the opposition to Nero, he was exiled to the Greek island of Gyaros (incidentally, this island was used again in the 20th century for exiling opponents to the Greek government). Recalled to Rome, he was eventually again exiled for protesting the use of the theater of Dionysus in **Athens** for gladiatorial games. Musonius taught philosophy wherever he was; his two most famous students were **Epictetus** and **Dio Chrysostom**. His students copied down many of his lectures, known as "diatribes"; 21 survive, all on ethical and political topics. One diatribe that has gained some recent notice is "That Women Too Should Study Philosophy."

MYTHOS. Although this word was often used of any verbal performance, whether in speech or writing, it came to have the connotation of "fiction," or at any rate something that is contrasted with a rational verbal account, a *logos*. **Socrates** makes this contrast explicitly at the beginning of the *Phaedo* (61b), when he says that poets write *mythoi*, not *logoi*.

    Plato has an ambiguous relationship with "myths," since he mercilessly attacks many of the "myths" most popular in his culture, most notably in the early books of the *Republic*, yet he also recounts his own myths, including the Myth of Er in the *Republic*, the myth of the afterlife in the *Phaedo*, the **charioteer** myth in the *Phaedrus*, another myth of judgment after death in the *Gorgias*, and quite a few others. In fact the dialogue taken by later **Platonists** as the definition of Plato's cosmological opinions, the *Timaeus*, represents itself as a *mythos*. One way to understand that would be to suppose that *logos* can take you just so far, and if you want to go farther, you will have to rely upon *mythos*.

    Aristotle uses the word *mythos* much as we use the word "story" in English, that is, without necessarily judging whether the story is true or false. Sometimes there is an implication that a *mythos* is an allegory or parable—he refers to the *mythoi* of Aesop, for example

(*Meteor.* II.3, 356b11, *Rhet.* II.20, 1393a30). In **Metaphysics** XII.8, 1074b1, he says that humankind has handed down the "myth" that the sun, moon, planets, and stars are **Gods**, "and that the divine encloses the whole of nature." Aristotle believes that that part is true. He goes on to say that the rest of the details of religious teaching have been added "in mythical form" to persuade the people and for legal and utilitarian expediency.

In post-Aristotelian philosophy there was an increasing tendency to construct allegorical interpretations of traditional myths; the **Stoics** were particularly interested in such interpretations, as we can see from **Cicero**'s *On the Nature of the Gods*.

– N –

NAME. *See ONOMA.*

NATURAL LAW. *See NOMOS; PHYSIS.*

NATURAL PHILOSOPHER. *See PHYSIKOS.*

NATURE. *See PHYSIS.*

NAUSIPHANES OF TEOS (Late 4th century BCE). Nausiphanes was a follower of **Democritus** and **Pyrrho**, and teacher of **Epicurus**. We surmise from the references in **Diogenes Laertius** that he accepted atomism but was otherwise skeptical.

NECESSITY. *See ANAGKĒ (ANANKĒ).*

NEIKOS. Strife, as opposed to friendship (**philia**) in the **cosmology** of **Empedocles**. Empedocles uses this word more frequently than its synonym **eris**. *Neikos* is a **Homeric** word for battle, and is also used for the conflict between opposing sides in a legal trial.

NEMESIS. Literally, a distribution (from the verb *nemein*). In fact the word always means "retribution," especially in righteous indignation at having been unjustly treated. **Aristotle** *EN* II.7, 1108a35 extends it to indignation on behalf of others who have been unjustly treated.

NEMESIUS OF EMESA (4th century CE). Nemesius was a Christian bishop known mainly as the author of "On the Nature of Man," a work full of information about the theories of the soul (*psychē*) of many ancient thinkers.

NEOPLATONISM. "Neoplatonism" is a modern designation for the form of **Platonism** initiated by **Ammonius Saccas** and developed into its highest expression by his student **Plotinus**, as preserved in the *Enneads*. Neoplatonism may be characterized by its adoption of conceptual structures from the wide range of religious traditions present in the Greco-Roman world in the first few centuries CE but always referring its interpretations to the text of **Plato**, primarily, and secondarily to **Aristotle**, **Theophrastus**, and other classical philosophers. Neoplatonism may also be characterized as the *defense* of Platonism and philosophy generally against the inroads of **Christian**, **Gnostic**, **Manichaean**, and other religious movements.

Ancient Neoplatonism, although begun in **Alexandria**, was developed in several parts of the ancient world. From 245 until his death in 270, Plotinus taught in Rome, primarily. Two of his most important students there were **Porphyry** and **Amelius**. We do not know where Porphyry was located after the death of Plotinus (some say Rome); his editing of the *Enneads* was of course crucial for the development of the movement and some of his writings were translated into Latin, influencing the course of Western philosophy. **Marius Victorinus** and **Augustine** were both influenced by Porphyry's version of Neoplatonism.

Amelius, who had studied with **Numenius** in Apamea (Syria), returned to Apamea after the death of Plotinus and became the teacher of **Iamblichus.** The Syrian school continued for some time; the successors of Iamblichus seem to have instructed **Plutarch of Athens**, who reestablished the teaching of Platonism in **Athens**, which continued under the leadership of **Syrianus**, **Proclus**, **Marinus**, **Isidore**, and **Damascius**, until the Athenian school was closed in 529 CE.

Syrianus was teacher of both Proclus and **Hermeias**; Hermeias moved to Alexandria, where he seems to have revitalized the Alexandrian school. His son **Ammonius** continued his tradition and was the teacher of **Olympiodorus**, **John Philoponus**, a Christian Neoplatonist commentator on Aristotle, and others.

The Eastern Orthodox church fathers were, many of them, educated as Neoplatonists; perhaps the most extreme examples of Christian

Neoplatonic texts are the works of the (pseudo)-**Dionysius the Areopagite**. But Neoplatonism had a strong foothold in many places in the east, and as it turned out, it was transferred easily to Islamic philosophers.

In the West, **Augustine** had learned his Neoplatonism from **Marius Victorinus** and became in turn the leading theologian of the Roman church until the time of Thomas Aquinas—who was also influenced by Neoplatonic interpretations of Aristotle.

For central doctrines of Neoplatonism, *see* PLOTINUS.

NEOPYTHAGOREANISM. Pythagoras established his philosophical and religious community toward the end of the sixth century BCE; it seems to have been to some degree a secretive and closed community, but nevertheless we hear of a significant number of people who were first and second generation Pythagoreans, during the fifth century. Indeed, Cebes and Simmias, present at the death of **Socrates**, are said to have been students of **Philolaus**, in Thebes.

In the first half of the fourth century, **Plato** encountered Pythagoreans in Sicily, and presented a Pythagorean **cosmology** in the *Timaeus*. After the *Timaeus*, it is difficult to make any philosophical or conceptual differences between "Platonism" and "Pythagoreanism." After the time of **Archytas** (d. c. 350 BCE), we hear less about an independent Pythagoreanism. **Aristotle** writes of "those who call themselves Pythagoreans" (*hoi kaloumenoi Pythagoreioi, Metaph.* I.5, 985b23). One of his contemporaries, **Heraclides of Pontus**, seems to have written a fairly detailed account of Pythagoreanism, judging from the citations in later authors.

For perhaps 300 years it is difficult to discern any actual practicing Pythagoreans, as distinct from Platonists, though Hellenistic writers continued to have a historical interest in the Pythagorean School, and there may have been attempts to revive classical Pythagorean practices and ideas.

The first named individual associated with an attempt to revive Pythagoreanism in the Greco-Roman period is probably **Figulus**, a Roman, and friend of **Cicero**. A robust revival came in the first century CE with the activity of **Apollonius of Tyana**, **Moderatus of Gades**, **Nicomachus of Gerasa**, and later on, in the second to third centuries, **Numenius of Apamea**. **Iamblichus**, counted by us as a

Neoplatonist, thought of himself as a (Neo)-Pythagorean; in many respects his writings established a way of reading the history and character of the Pythagorean way of philosophy.

NICOMACHUS OF GERASA (c. 60–120 CE). Nicomachus was the author of the extant works *Introduction to Arithmetic* and *Manual of Harmonics*. There are also considerable fragments of his *Theology of Arithmetic* and his *Life of Pythagoras*. Nicomachus was a **Neopythagorean**; these are some of the major texts of Neopythagoreanism. Modern historians of mathematics find him somewhat careless as a mathematician. *See also MATHĒMA.*

NOĒSIS, NOĒMA, NOĒTON. Words formed on the verb *noein*, to think, and the noun *nous*, or mind. *Noēsis* is a Platonic term for thinking directed at **being** (*Republic* 534a), contrasted in the *Republic* with **dianoia**, there taken to be derivative or deductive reasoning. *Noēma* is a word used fairly widely meaning "a thought." *Parmenides* B8, line 34: "*noein* and that for the sake which a *noēma* exists are the same." In **Plato**'s *Parmenides*, 132b, **Socrates** briefly suggests that the Forms (*eidē*) might be *noēmata*, but that is quickly refuted. The *noēton* is that which is "thinkable," usually as distinguished from the *aisthēton*, that which is perceptible (cf. **Aristotle** *EN* X.4, 1174b34).

NOMOS. Law; convention. Noun formed from *nemo*, "distribute; "*nemesis*" is another noun based on the same verb. There is some tension in the way this word is used in Greek philosophy and literature. On the one hand, the *nomoi* are clearly the laws governing the organization of the state; **Plato**'s longest dialogue, outlining the constitution of an ideal state, is called the *Nomoi* (*Laws*). By extension, the rules governing human behavior universally, possibly as decreed by the **God**s, are often called *agraphoi nomoi*, unwritten laws (**Xenophon** *Mem.* IV.4, 5–25; Sophocles *Oed. Tyr.* 863–871, et al.). As **Heraclitus** says (f. 114, in part), "All human *nomoi* are nourished by the one divine (*nomos*)." On the other hand, legislated laws tended, at least by the fifth century BCE, to be seen as arbitrary and variable from one society to another. Thus, some introduced the idea of a contrasting Nature (*physis*) that was not subject to social variability. **Antiphon** provides a particularly good example of a writer who emphasizes this contrast (DK87A44). **Plato** often represents the **Sophists** arguing on the basis of this contrast. **Thrasymachus** in *Republic* I, **Callicles** in the *Gorgias*, and **Protagoras** in the *Protagoras*, are just a few examples. **Democritus** took the contrast back into the scientific context, at least in epistemological terms, when he said. "By convention (by *nomos*) sweet by convention bitter, by convention hot by convention cold, in reality atoms and void."

The **Stoics** supposed that nature operates according to divine reason, or *Logos,* so that the tension or dialectic between nature and law is resolved: physics (*physikē*) and **ethics** are both part of the same rational system, the thought of God. Stoics argued that we could discover "natural law" of a normative sort in much the same way as we discover descriptive or explanatory natural law. Possibly the clearest exposition of this Stoic position is in **Cicero**'s *de Legibus* II.

NON-BEING. *See* BEING; *MĒ ON.*

NOUS (NOOS). Mind. Classical Greek philosophy is characterized by, as much as anything else, the discovery of the mind. **Xenophanes** says of **God**, "Always he remains in the same place, moving not at all, nor is it fitting for him to move now here now there, but without toil he makes all things shiver by the impulse of his mind" (f. 25–26). **Anaxagoras** talked so much about mind that comic poets joked about it.

Plato's **Socrates** repeatedly emphasizes the centrality of the mind in his philosophy from the immortality of the soul (*psychē*), envisioned primarily as the mind, in the *Phaedo*, to the argument that the virtue (*aretē*) of the mind, wisdom (*sophia*), is the proper source of both moral and political governance in the *Republic*, and of course beyond. Plato goes on to argue for a cosmic mind, in the tracks of **Xenophanes** and Anaxagoras, in his *Timaeus* (30b), *Philebus* (30d) and *Laws* (875, 897, 966).

Aristotle, too, makes mind central in his philosophy, from the beginning of the *Metaphysics*, where he says that all human beings by nature desire to know and to understand, to the last book of the *Nicomachean* **Ethics**, where the activity of the mind is the highest happiness for a human being, to the 12th book of the *Metaphysics*, where

God is said to be mind thinking itself (*ho nous autos auto noei*). In the *de Anima*, mind alone is said to be separable (***choriston***) from the body (***sōma***). Similarly in *GA*, mind alone of the psychic functions is said to come into the developing human being "from outside" (***thyra-then***). In *de An.* III. 4–6, Aristotle distinguishes a function of the mind that acquires knowable forms from perception, the *nous pathētikos* from the active or creative faculty of mind, *nous poiētikos*. Since the superior function of mind is the active and creative, that is the function that we attribute most readily to God, who is consequently a mover, indeed the first and unmoved mover (***akinēton kinoun***) of everything in virtue of being active intellect (***nous***).

The **Stoics** identify mind with what they call the ***hegemonikon***, or directive part of the soul, and they assert that it exists as much in the universe as a whole as it does in us as individuals (DL VII.138).

In **middle Platonism**, the cosmic mind becomes the source of all good in the universe (**Alcinous** X.1–4). For **Plotinus**, the cosmic mind is the ***energeia*** and ***logos*** of the **One** (*Enn.* V.1.6).

NUMBER. *See ARITHMOS.*

NUMENIUS OF APAMEA (fl. 160–180 CE). Apamea is in northern Syria. Numenius is counted as a "**middle Platonist**," though his teaching is directly connected to the **Neoplatonist** tradition that follows. He was the teacher of **Amelius**, who functioned as secretary to **Plotinus** in Rome and returned to Apamea on the death of Plotinus. Considerable fragments remain of Numenius' book *On the Good* and of his history of the **Academy**, *On the Divergence of the Academics from Plato*. Numenius believed that Plato's teaching was **Pythagorean**, and not only that, but that it derived from **Indian** Sages (Brahmins), Persian Magi, **Egyptian** Priests, **Chaldean Oracles**, and Jews; **Numenius** supported those ascriptions by interpreting traditional texts allegorically.

NUTRITIVE SOUL. *Psychē threptikē*. In **Aristotle**, this is the part or faculty of the soul concerned with maintaining the bodily life of the individual, shared by all living things, including plants. Aristotle says that this part of the soul is also responsible for generation of new individuals of the species: *de Anima* II.4, 416a19. *See also PSYCHĒ.*

– O –

OCHĒMA. Literally, carriage or vehicle. **Parmenides** rides in an *ochēma* to see the Goddess, in the prologue of his poem; in **Plato**'s *Phaedrus*, the soul (*psychē*) is envisaged as a **charioteer** driving an *ochēma* drawn by two horses, symbols of the psychic powers of appetite and ambition. This powerful image naturally leads to speculation about the nature of the chariot itself. A strong tradition going back at least to **Anaximenes** held that the physical basis of the soul is *pneuma*, or breath, and that this *pneuma* has some affinity for or relationship to the element from which the stars are composed (**Aristotle** *GA* II.6). Plato suggests, in the *Timaeus*, that each soul is related to an individual star, as to an *ochēma* (41d-e). All of these themes come together in **Neoplatonism**, especially in **Proclus**, where each individual human soul has *three* bodies: an immortal astral body, a spiritual (pneumatic) body that is mortal, and the flesh and bone body it inhabits while on **earth** (*Commentary on Timaeus* 111, 236, 298; *Platonic Theology* 111, 125). Each of these is a "vehicle" for the soul in different contexts.

OENOMAUS OF GADARA (Second century CE). Oenomaus was a **Cynic**, possibly identical with the Abnimus mentioned in the Talmud as a friend of the Rabbi Meir (2nd century). Significant fragments survive of his sarcastic attacks on divination, in a treatise called "Unmasking the Magicians." *See also* MAGIC.

OIKEION. In everyday Greek, that which belongs to one's household; personal property; anything that is "one's own." It becomes something of a technical term in **Stoic** philosophy for what is proper to or belonging to oneself.

OIKEIŌSIS. Appropriation. In ordinary Greek, this word could mean making a friend of someone, or (going back to the original sense of *oikos*, "home") to include someone in one's household. For the **Stoics,** this word has a lot of significance: Starting from the instinct of self-preservation and self-consciousness, going on to our natural positive feelings toward our family, friends, and community, and ultimately to the whole universe, we make our relationships our own (See, e.g., **Cicero** *de Fin.* 3.62–8).

"OLD OLIGARCH." Among the extant writings attributed to **Xenophon** is a "Constitution of the Athenians"; Xenophon could not have written it because it must have been written either before Xenophon was born, or when he was still a young child. (The treatise was written between 446 and 424, and Xenophon was born in about 430.) In view of the political point of view espoused in the document, its author has come to be known as "The Old Oligarch."

OLYMPIODORUS (Before 510–after 565 CE). Neoplatonist Alexandrian commentator on **Plato** and **Aristotle**. His commentaries on *Alcibiades* I and *Gorgias* give a good picture of philosophical education in **Alexandria** in late antiquity, near the end of non-Christian instruction in that city.

ON, ONTA. **Parmenides** problematized **being**; **Plato** focused on a solution to the problem of being that distinguished the static and timeless *ontōs on* ("beingly being," usually translated "really real) from the changing *genesis*. **Aristotle** describes the task of his book that we call the *Metaphysics* as the study of *to on hē on*, being qua being. Being, he says, is primarily *ousia*, and in a secondary sense whatever is referred to in the other nine **categories**. For **Plotinus**, the One is beyond being; all being is somehow derivative from the One.

ONE. *See HEN.*

ONEIROS. Dream. In **Homer**, at *Od.* XIX, 560ff, there is a distinction between dreams that come through the gates of ivory, and those that come through the gates of horn; the first are phantasies, the second are portents, if we know how to interpret them. Dream interpretation has long been in demand (consider Joseph and Pharaoh, *Genesis* 41); **Antiphon** the Sophist wrote a book on dream interpretation (DK 2.367ff). The temples of **Asclepius** invited the ill to sleep in their precincts, where they might be visited in their dreams by Asclepius, providing a cure for their ailments. Others thought of dreams as belonging to pure subjectivity (**Heraclitus** f. 89. "The waking have one common world, but the sleeping turn aside each into a world of his own"). **Plato**'s **Socrates** often refers to dreams taken as veridical, perhaps most seriously at *Phaedo* 60e, but sometimes as a rhetorical trope, for example at *Theaetetus* 201e. At *Timaeus* 71a–72b, Plato tries to explain how dreams occur by involving the liver in the process.

Aristotle wrote a short treatise *On Dreams*, providing a physiological explanation of how dreams occur, and another short treatise, *On Divination in Sleep*, which takes somewhat seriously the possibility that there might be veridical dreams. Rejecting the thesis that dreams are sent by **God**, Aristotle supposes that dreams might have a causative relationship with various events, or be signs of those events; for example, physicians take particular sorts of dreams to be diagnostic of particular illnesses, and that totally makes sense to Aristotle. But, he argues, "most dreams are mere coincidences" (463a32). **Cicero**, *On Divination* 62, 127–8, largely follows the Aristotelian direction. Still, many people continued to believe that some dreams are prophetic: **Iamblichus** *Vit. Pyth.* 65, **Aelius Aristides** *Sacred Discourses*, **Artemidorus of Ephesus**, *Oneirocritikon*.

ONOMA. Name, noun. **Heraclitus** fr. 24: "They would not have known the name of justice if these things did not exist." **Parmenides** f. 8, lines 39–40: "All these things are but names which mortals have given, believing them to be true—coming into being and passing away, being and not being, change of place and alteration of bright color." Ever since Odysseus told the Cyclops that his name was "*Oudeis*," which means "Nobody"—and subsequently the Cyclops ran out screaming to his neighbors, "Nobody has blinded me," the ancient Greeks were concerned with the possibility that words, and particularly names, might fail to communicate the truth (*Od.* IX, 364). The extreme position is that of **Gorgias**, DK 82B3, that there is no connection between names and things.

Are there natural names, or are all names conventional? The **Sophists** clearly talked about these issues, a lot; **Prodicus** and **Protagoras** more than others perhaps. In **Aristophanes'** *Clouds* (875), **Socrates** is represented as arguing that the words we use for male and female chickens are wrong; we can translate the argument as saying that we really ought to call roosters "Chickers" and hens "Chickesses." The *Cratylus* is entirely devoted to a discussion of the correctness of names, whether words have a natural or conventional origin. Since for **Plato**, words in principle correspond with Forms (*eidē*), their "correctness" is a matter of some importance.

At the beginning of *On Interpretation*, **Aristotle** says, "Spoken sounds are symbols of affections in the soul (*psychē*), and written marks symbols of spoken sounds. And just as written marks are not the same for all people, neither are spoken sounds. But what these are in the first place signs of—affections of the soul—are the same for all; and what these affections are likenesses of—actual things—are also the same." He goes on to define (*Int.* 2) an *onoma* as "a spoken sound, significant by convention (*nomos*), without time, none of whose parts is significant in separation. . . . No name is a name naturally but only when it has become a symbol."

The theory that language is natural did have significant support: **Herodotus** tells the story of the Pharaoh "Psamtik" who had some children raised by deaf-mutes; when the children were brought before him, they said something like "ba," which he took to be the Phrygian word for bread. Herodotus also points out that the children got their milk from goats. Of philosophers, **Epicurus** believed that the origin of language was natural, that the sounds made by animals and babies are the beginning of language (*Letter to Herodotus*, 75–87; **Lucretius** V.1028–90).

The **Stoics**, in contrast, believed that language stems from *logos*, reason, and that consequently only human beings have true language. Following the lead of Socrates in the *Cratylus*, the Stoics paid a great deal of attention to etymology (*etymon* actually means "true"), attempting to find the "true" meaning of words.

ŌPHELEIN, ŌPHELĒMA. To owe a debt, the debt itself (**Aristotle** *EN* IX.2, 1165a3). In **Stoic ethics**, the obligation is construed as advantage, or benefit, and since you "ought" to be virtuous, it turns out to be that which is good in itself.

OPINION. *See DOXA.*

OPPOSITES. *See ENANTIA.*

ORDER. *See COSMOS, TAXIS.*

OREXIS. Often translated "desire," sometimes translated "intention," this is the noun form of *oregō*, "I reach out (my hand)." In **Aristotle**'s moral psychology, *orexis* is the capacity of initiating movement shared by all living beings capable of local movement. The **Stoics** preferred to use the term "*hormē*."

Aristotle characterizes "choice" (*prohairesis*) as "deliberative orexis."

ORGANON. Literally, "tool." A knife or an axe is a common example of an *organon*. At least from the time of **Plato** the word was applied to instrumental parts of the body (the eye is the *organon* of vision, *Rep.* VI, 508b, for example). **Aristotle** of course devotes much of his biological investigation to the understanding of the *organa* of the body. Organs have their meaning only as parts—a severed hand is no longer a hand, it is no more a hand than a carved stone *aulos* is really an *aulos*. More generally, he defines *organon* as whatever exists for the sake of something else, even to the point of saying that "A slave is a living tool, a tool is a non-living slave," *EN* VIII. 11, 1161b4.

We should also note that the books on logic that begin the Aristotelian **Corpus** are collectively known as the *Organon*. It may be that this denomination came from the remark of **Alexander of Aphrodisias**, that logic (*logikē*) "has the role of a tool" in philosophy (*in Top.* 74.29).

ORIGEN (c. 185–254/5 CE). Christian **Neoplatonist** philosopher who studied with **Ammonius Saccas** (also the teacher of **Plotinus**). His work "On First Principles" (*de Principiis*) is a fundamental exposition of Christian Platonism; his "Against **Celsus**" is a detailed refutation of a pagan attack on the Christian religion. He also wrote significant extended commentaries on books of both the Old and the New Testament.

Influenced by his reading of the Jewish philosopher **Philo of Alexandria**, and the **middle Platonist Numenius**, Origen constructed an intellectually sophisticated doctrine of the Trinity, defended human free will, and argued for an eventual reconciliation of the entire universe with **God**, the *apokatastasis*.

Neither the Orthodox nor the Roman Catholic branch of **Christianity** has been entirely comfortable with Origen. Their complaints have been: Origen's allegorical interpretation of Scripture could readily be abused; in his doctrine of the Trinity he appears to subordinate Jesus Christ and the Holy Spirit to the Father; the *apokatasta-*

sis was not accepted by either church, since inconsistent with the doctrine of everlasting damnation of the unforgiven. It is hard to know precisely how far Origen went in any of these respects since we do not have much of the original Greek of the *de Principiis*; rather we have a Latin translation by Rufinus that probably tones down unorthodox positions.

ORIGEN (Third century CE). There seems to be another "Origen" roughly contemporaneous with the famous Christian philosopher, a pagan **Neoplatonist** who also studied with **Ammonius Saccas**, and taught **Porphyry** in **Athens** before Porphyry joined **Plotinus** in Rome. **Proclus** ascribes to him the view that the first principle is intellect (*nous*), denying that the first principle is the One beyond **being**.

ORIGIN. *See ARCHĒ.*

ORPHIC RELIGION. Cult religion originating in the sixth century BCE, loosely connected with **Pythagoreanism** by some similarities of belief. Like the Pythagoreans, the Orphics believed in *metempsychosis*, and lived in religion-based communities. Adeimantus in the *Republic* says of them (364b–365a): "They produce a whole collection of books of ritual instructions written by Musaeus and Orpheus, and they persuade not only individuals but whole communities that, both for living and dead, remission and absolution of sins may be had by sacrifices and childish performances, which they are pleased to call initiations, and which they allege deliver us from all ills in the next world, where terrible things await the uninitiated." Orphic religious practices seem to have continued into the Christian era.

OU MALLON. Literally, "no more" (no more this than that), this common phrase became a shorthand expression for a way of arguing, during the Hellenistic period. In Pyrrhonian skepticism, especially, it implies "determining nothing, and suspending judgment" (DL 9.76). *See also SKEPTIKOS.*

OURANOS, OURANIA. Sky, heaven; heavenly. Is there one *Ouranos* or more than one? Is the *Ouranos* identical with the *Kosmos*? **Anaximander** talks of an indefinite from which are generated "the *ouranoi* and the *kosmoi* within them" (f. 1), implying a plurality of both, and a non-identity of the two. It became more usual in Greek philosophy to assert the **unity** of *Ouranos* and *Kosmos*; indeed, according to **Aristotle, Xenophanes** "contemplated the *Ouranos* and concluded that the One is **God**" (*Metaph*. I.5, 986b23).

The *ouranioi* are the entities that exist in the sky, and they are very commonly, in Greek philosophy, considered to be living divinities. One heaven, one deity, may be the source of all the others, but there is a plurality of lesser celestial deities, starting from the sun, the moon, and the planets or the deities that move those celestial entities around. Aristotle clearly believed that this was the fundamental religious understanding for all humanity, that anthropomorphic deities were a later invention (*Metaph*. XII.8, 1074b1ff).

It is an easy step from astral religion to astrology, a step widely embraced in antiquity, but roundly rejected by the **Epicurean** tradition, particularly **Lucretius** (V.110–145). *See also ASTROLOGIA; ASTRONOMIA;* COSMOS.

OUSIA. Abstract noun built on the participle *on, ontos* (**being**) plus an abstract ending. Consequently, the most obvious translation into English would be "beingness." In non-philosophical Greek, *ousia* means "wealth," especially "real estate." The typical translation of *ousia* in English versions of **Plato** is "reality," which tends to remove the word from its origins in the verb *einai*, to be. Similarly the Platonic phrase, closely related to *ousia* in the texts, *to ontōs on*, literally "the beingly being," is normally translated "the really real." In English translations of **Aristotle**, the most usual translation of *ousia* is "substance," a word that really translates the Greek word *hypostasis*. It is arguable that the right translation would be "entity" since that is formed on the Latin *ens, entis*, plus the Latin abstract ending cognate with the Greek one in *ousia*.

In any case, in philosophical usage the word *ousia* is used to designate whatever it is that exists primarily. That usage may well have started with Plato, when he applied it to the Forms (*eidē*) (e.g., *Phaedo* 70d and many other places). Aristotle attributes to the **Presocratics** the belief that *ousia* is **matter** on the ground that they appear to believe that one or more of the elements (*stoicheia*) (water, air, fire), or all four, or the atoms (*atoma*), are what exist primarily

(*Metaphysics* I.3, 983b6ff). Given that **Democritus** says, "By convention sweet, by convention bitter, by convention hot, by convention cold, by convention colored, but in existence (*eteēi*) atoms and void" (B9), that ascription seems justified.

Aristotle does accept that as one sense of the word *ousia*, in that, in a way, matter does exist primarily; and, in a way, the form of anything is also *ousia*, especially of a living thing, its soul (*psychē*) is its *ousia*, since that is what it *is* (Cf. *Metaph.* V. 8, 1017b16). But for Aristotle the primary sense of *ousia*, that is, that which primarily exists, is the compound of matter and form, the individual thing, or a definable class of things.

In *Metaphysics* XII, Aristotle distinguishes entities (*ousiai*) into sensible and unchangeable, and the sensible into permanent and perishable. Almost everything that we know is in the class of perishable sensible things; only the astronomical beings are permanent and sensible. And there seems to be just one unchangeable entity, the unmoved mover (*akinēton kinoun*).

In post-Aristotelian philosophy, the **Epicureans**, to the extent that they were concerned about metaphysical issues, believed the atoms to be that which primarily exists, following the lead of Democritus. The **Stoics** use the word *ousia* to denominate the underlying substrate, i.e., as *hypokeimenon*. Of course, if we ask, "what exists primarily," the Stoics would *also* say **God**, or Reason, so that in a way there is just *one* entity in Stoic philosophy: everything. **Plotinus** is critical of the whole Aristotelian enterprise concerning *ousia* (*Enn.* VI.1), in that it makes a multiplicity of what Plotinus believes to be a **unity**. He is also critical of the Stoic position, in that it makes of God a material entity.

– P –

PAIDEIA. Education: reading, writing, and the arts. The **Sophists** focused on advancing education; a major conflict between **Socrates**, the Sophists, and popular culture as represented by **Aristophanes**, for example, concerned the nature of that education. The Sophists taught skills, primarily but not exclusively rhetorical skills, generally maintaining a "value-neutral" pose. Socrates urged his young admirers to search for fundamental values, but usually avoided promulgating any of his own value beliefs in any didactic manner. Popular culture, as defined by Aristophanes' *Clouds* and the judgment of the jury in the trail of Socrates, determined that Socrates' failure to inculcate traditional values was as dangerous as the Sophistic avoidance of values entirely.

The organized schools that came into existence after the death of Socrates tended to make room for both training in the skills required by social leaders and at least acquaintance with the ethical expectations of the society into which the products of these schools would enter.

In subsequent centuries organized educational institutions continued to function in many cities of the ancient world: some of the cities with more or less stable educational establishments providing instruction in philosophy for extended periods of time included **Athens**, **Alexandria**, Rhodes, Pergamum, Apamea of Syria, Rome, and others. *See also* ACADEMY; EPICUREAN; ISOCRATES; LYCEUM; MUSEUM OF ALEXANDRIA; PERIPATOS; STOIC.

PAIN. *See ALGOS; LYPĒ; PONOS.*

PALINGENESIS. *Palingenesis* literally means "regeneration," and is used by the **Stoics** for the rebirth of the world after the periodic conflagration (*ekpyrosis*). In the *New Testament*, it is applied both to the status of having been "born again" through baptism, and to the resurrection. In some authors, the word *palingenesis* is a synonym for *metempsychosis*.

PANAETIUS OF RHODES (c. 185–109 BCE). Stoic, Scholarch from 129–109 BCE. Panaetius studied with **Diogenes of Babylon** and **Antipater of Tarsus**, and frequently visited Rome, where he associated with Scipio Africanus. His concentration on ethical and social issues led him to adapt Stoic teachings to the needs of the Roman ruling class. As preserved by **Cicero** (*On Duties*), he taught that there are four "personae" or life-roles: generically as a human being, specifically with one's own natural attributes, the position into which one is cast by fate, and the role one has chosen on one's own. He also redefined the cardinal virtues, synthesizing and transforming **Platonic** and **Aristotelian** conceptions into part of the Stoic doctrine.

PAR' HĒMIN. Familiar, "by us." In **Epicurean** epistemology, we tend to accept appearances that are familiar to us. **Stoics** objected that exceptions are always possible; "not so fast."

PARABOLĒ. Comparison, illustration, parable, parody. In **Plato** *Philebus* 33b2, this word is applied to a comparison (between different lives); a typical **Aristotelian** use occurs at *Rhet*. II.20, 1393b23, where the **Socratic** habit of giving examples or illustrations of a point is noted. It is an easy step from that to the New Testament "parable." In **Sextus Empiricus** (*Against the Professors* 9) the word takes on a new twist, being applied to "parodies" of arguments, particularly of the **Stoics**. **Zeno** says, "The rational is superior to the non-rational; nothing is superior to the universe; therefore the universe is rational." To which **Alexinus of Elis** (a **Megarian** philosopher who critiqued Zeno) replied, "The poet is superior to the non-poet; nothing is superior to the universe; therefore the universe writes poetry."

PARADEIGMA. Example, standard. In the **Platonic** dialogues, the Forms (*eidē*) are often said to serve as *paradeigmata* or standards, e.g., the ideal state exists as a *paradeigma* in heaven (*Rep*. IX 592a–b, cf. *Euthyphro* 6e). Although **Aristotle** usually uses the word in the everyday sense of "example," he is sufficiently influenced by the Platonic usage to use it for the **formal cause** a few times, e.g., *Physics* II.3, 194b27.

PARAKOLOUTHĒSIS, PARAKOLOUTHOUN. Concomitance, concomitant. **Epicurus** uses this word to talk about **attributes** that **Aristotle** would have called "**accidents**" (*symbebēkota*); Epicurus does not think that these attributes are "accidental" at all. **Chrysippus** uses the concept to explain various natural inconveniences that were necessary from some other point of view. One of his examples: the cranium bone is rather thin, and thus in danger of breaking; but if it were thicker, your head would be too heavy and there would be less room for your brains (SVF 2.1170).

PARENKLISIS. Swerve. In **Epicurean** physics, the atoms (*atoma*) that compose the universe are thought to be "falling" through limitless space. If nothing were to interfere with that process, there would be no occasion for complexes of atoms to come together. So atoms must deviate from a perfectly straight line. These deviations or swerves are supposed to occur randomly.

From the Epicurean perspective, the existence of random "swerves" of atoms opens a space for "free will" in an otherwise totally deterministic world. *See also PHYSIS.*

PARMENIDES OF ELEA (c. 510–after 450 BCE). Not much is known of his life other than the implication of the introductory section of **Plato**'s *Parmenides*, indicating that Parmenides and **Zeno** visited **Athens** in about 450, and had a conversation with **Socrates**, represented as reported in the dialogue. Parmenides had written a poem, *On Nature*, that seems to have been widely known in the Greek world soon after its composition. Most of those who wrote about "Nature" (*physis*) in the years following its composition tried to respond in one way or another to its challenge. **Simplicius** and others preserve a significant portion of the first part of the poem, so we are able to interpret his thought fairly directly, rather than relying on reports and scattered fragments, as we have so often to do with other writers of the period.

The poem of Parmenides includes an introductory Proem, in which he tells of traveling in a chariot to visit the Goddess; the Way of Truth, in which the Goddess tells him about what IS; and the Way of Opinion (*doxa*), in which the Goddess gives him an account of **cosmology**. The Proem is intact, and we have most of the Way of Truth; there are only a few fragments of the Way of Opinion.

The Goddess tells Parmenides that there are two ways of thinking, one "IS, and not not-is," the other "IS NOT." In Greek, a verb may be used without a noun or pronoun; thus Parmenides writes *esti* (and *ouk esti*) without noun or pronoun. In this case, one tends to read ESTI as "**being** is." The Goddess goes on to say that ESTI is the only way to go, since in the case of "IS NOT" there is nothing to talk about. She also tells him to avoid "is and is-not," where mortals wander around two-headed.

Sticking strictly to IS has consequences: IS is neither generated nor destroyed, is absolutely One, indivisible, immobile, and perfect. There is no generation or destruction, since IS NOT would have to be the source or destination, and that source or destination IS NOT. IS is indivisible, because it would have to be divided by IS NOT, which of course IS NOT. All thought, all speech, in fact refer to IS, since IS is all that exists—NOT IS is not there to be spoken of or thought of. All differentiations—various colors, for example—are "mere names."

The Way of Opinion, characterized by the Goddess as untrustworthy and deceptive, turns on an opposition and mixing of light and night. It is sometimes said that Parmenides is simply reporting a cosmology developed by someone else, perhaps a **Pythagorean**, but we should notice that the few scattered fragments include some real cosmological advances: Parmenides knows that the moon is illuminated by the sun, that the morning and evening star are identical (and thus a planet), and by implication that the **Earth** is spherical. **Anaximander** had thought that the Earth is cylindrical (we live on one flat end), and apparently that the moon shines with its own internal light.

Parmenides' associate **Zeno** is represented as defending the thesis of Parmenides that what is, is one, dialectically, that is, Zeno starts by assuming plurality and shows that that assumption leads to self-contradictions. While Parmenides' thesis may be represented as primarily "logical," **Melissus of Samos** gives it a decidedly material edge.

The **atomism** of **Leucippus** and **Democritus** can be seen as the flip side of the **Eleatic** philosophy—instead of one **being**, in which all relations are internal, they assert many beings, for which all relations are external.

Plato's later philosophy is clearly much indebted to consideration of the implications of the thought of Parmenides; the dialogue *Parmenides*, and the interventions of the **Eleatic** Stranger in the *Sophist* and *Statesman*, include many of Plato's most profound metaphysical ideas, ones that continue to resonate throughout ancient philosophy, and particularly in the **Neoplatonic** synthesis.

PARONYMOI. According to **Aristotle** in the *Categories*, two words are "paronyms" if one gets its meaning from the other, which is regarded as the primary.

PARTICIPATION. *See METHEXIS.*

PARTICULAR. The word "particular" functions in English-language **metaphysics** as the vehicle for a certain fudge-factor. To the extent that "particular" means something like "individual," the following words are the closest equivalents: *HENAD; KATH' HEKASTON; TODE TI.*

PASCHEIN. To be affected, to suffer. **Plato** distinguishes change (*kinēsis*) into active (*poiein*) and passive (*paschein*) (e.g., *Tht* 156a), so that these in a sense exhaust the world of **becoming** (*genesis*) (*Soph.* 248c). As one of **Aristotle**'s 10 **categories**, *paschein* refers to passive verbs in general. For Aristotle as for the **Stoics**, *paschein* is closely associated with **matter**, as *poiein* is closely associated with the origin of movement (*archē kinēseōs*). It is also the verb from which the noun *pathos* is derived.

PASSION. The Latin equivalent of *pathos*. In English, "passion" has come to have a (paradoxical, given its origin) active sense so that it used for such active principles as lust and ambition.

PASSIVE INTELLECT. *See NOUS PATHETIKOS.*

PATHOS, PATHĒ. Noun derived from the verb *paschein*, meaning that which happens to a person (or anything else); experience, either good or bad. **Democritus** B31: "Medicine cures the diseases of the body, wisdom frees the soul (*psychē*) from *pathē*." **Plato** talks of an erotic *pathos* at *Phaedrus* 265b. At *Timaeus* 42a-b, the *pathē* are a consequence of the soul having been implanted in the body (*sōma*). **Aristotle** distinguishes several senses of *pathos* at **Metaphysics** V.21. "We call *pathos:* (1) A quality in respect of which a thing can be altered . . . (2) The already actualized **alterations.** (3) Especially, injurious alterations and movements, and above all, painful injuries. (4) Experiences pleasant or painful when on a large scale are called *pathē*." In *EN*, he gives a somewhat different account, when he distinguishes *pathē* (of the soul) from *dynameis* and *hexeis*. The *pathē* are "appetite, anger, fear, confidence, envy, joy, love, hatred, longing, emulation, pity, and in general the feelings that are accompanied by pleasure and pain" (II.5, 1105b20). The *dynameis* are the possibilities of having these feelings, the *hexeis* determine how much you have these feelings, and toward what. *Pathos* is often translated "emotion," but it is more nearly the case that the whole complex analyses what we mean by "emotion" in English. *Pathē* is often translated "feelings," and in many cases that is a very good translation.

For **Zeno** the Stoic, a *pathos* is an excessive ***hormē***, something that needs to be controlled or gotten rid of. **Chrysippus** takes *pathē* to be "judgments." Given the *hormē*, the **commanding faculty** decides the extent to which it should be pursued, and if that pursuit is excessive, it is a *pathos*. **Galen**, in the *Doctrines of Hippocrates and Plato*, reports that **Posidonius** disagreed with Chrysippus, arguing that the *pathē* arise to some extent independently and in opposition to reason. *See also* PASSION.

PERAS. Limit, end (in the sense of limit). In **Pythagorean** philosophy, at the beginning of the table of opposites (*see ENANTIA*) and associated with the **Good**. Mathematically, the point is the limit of the line, the line the limit of the surface, and the surface the limit of the solid. In **Plato** *Philebus* 23c ff, limit and the unlimited are proposed as metaphysical principles. **Epicurus** (*Key Doctrines* 19–21) stresses the "limits" in human life, both the limits of pain, and the achievability of pleasure when it is within limits. As **Aristotle** says in *Metaph.* V.17, "end (as limit)" has as many senses as ***archē*** (beginning).

PERFECTION. *See ENTELECHEIA; TELOS.*

PERIPATETIC SCHOOL. This is the usual name for the ancient followers of **Aristotle**, taken as a group. The name comes from the alternative name for the **Lyceum**. A school continued to exist in the Lyceum from 345 BCE (when it was founded by Aristotle) until 86 BCE (when it was destroyed or at least closed by Sulla). But it is important to note that when the **Museum of Alexandria** was founded, Aristotelians were prominently involved, and several other Aristotelian schools were founded—in the lifetime of Aristotle, **Eudemus** founded a school at Rhodes. **Theophrastus** was Aristotle's successor at the Lyceum, followed (36 years later) by **Strato of Lampsacus.** Other early Peripatetics include Dicaearchus, **Aristoxenus**, Clearchus, Phaenias. **Demetrius of Phaleron** was a student of Aristotle involved in the founding of the **Museum and Library at Alexandria**. **Erasistratus of Chios** (c. 304–250 BCE) established the study of anatomy at Alexandria; **Aristarchus of Samos** (310–230

BCE) was a student of Strato who established the study of **astronomy** and mathematics on a very firm footing in Alexandria, leading to the work of **Euclid** and **Claudius Ptolemy**. **Arius Didymus** (1st century BCE) and **Hero of Alexandria** (approx. 10–70 CE) were two more Alexandrian Aristotelians.

Strato was succeeded in **Athens** by **Lyco** (d. 225 BCE), followed by **Aristo of Ceos**, and then **Critolaus,** who was in the famous embassy of philosophers from Athens to Rome in 155 BCE.

In the first century BCE, **Andronicus of Rhodes** produced an edition of the **corpus** of Aristotle's works, possibly based mainly on the copies of Aristotle's library brought to Rhodes by Eudemus, or on the remains of the Lyceum library shipped to Rome by Sulla. The Peripatetic school continued to be one of the four major "schools" of philosophy—**Marcus Aurelius** appointed an Aristotelian chair of philosophy at Athens, and **Alexander of Aphrodisias** produced important (and orthodox) commentaries on some of Aristotle's works. In late antiquity and, to a large extent, in the medieval period, there was a strong belief that Plato and Aristotle were in fundamental agreement; the **Neoplatonic** School saw itself as the synthesis of the teachings of both philosophers, and supported that belief by their commentaries on Aristotle's works. How Platonism and Aristotelianism came to be distinguished and put into opposition is a story belonging to late medieval and early modern philosophy, and thus not a subject for this Dictionary. *See also MATHĒMA.*

PHAEDO OF ELIS (Fifth to fourth century BCE). Plato's dialogue recounting **Socrates'** death is named after Phaedo because Phaedo is its dramatic narrator. He apparently wrote Socratic dialogues and is reputed to have operated a Socratic school in his native Elis, known as the **Elian School**.

PHAEDRUS OF ATHENS (c. 444–393 BCE). Main character, with **Socrates**, in the *Phaedrus*; one of the speakers on love in the *Symposium*. He is also present in the *Protagoras*.

PHAEDRUS OF ATHENS (c. 138–70 BCE). An **Epicurean**, leader of the Epicureans in **Athens**; his lectures were attended by **Cicero**.

PHAINOMENON. Passive or middle participle of the verb *phainein*, to appear, a *phainomenon* is consequently that which appears, a phenomenon, an appearance. "*Ta phainomena opsis **adēlon***, phenomena are a glimpse of the unseen" **Anaxagoras** B21. For **Plato**, the perceptible world consists of *phainomena*, always in change, never persistent, while the knowable world is the source both of the **being** and the understanding of the *phainomena*.

While **Aristotle** does not contrast phenomena with Forms (*eidē*), he does contrast phenomena with "truth" or "**being**," in expressions that we would translate "apparent, not real" (*Rhet*. II.24, 25). He also, very often, conjoins *logos* and *phainomenon* in a manner that says that appearances agree (or disagree) with what one would figure from a rational point of view. On the whole, Aristotle agrees with Anaxagoras, that one can gain an understanding of what one cannot perceive on the basis of appearances. In very different ways, the **Epicureans** and **Stoics** also thought that some knowledge could be based on appearances, while the Skeptics (whether Academic or Pyrrhonian) never tired of reminding their audiences that appearances are deceiving. *See also SKEPTIKOS.*

PHANTASIA. Abstract noun built on *phainein*, to appear (related, for example, to *phainomenon*). "Appearance or presentation to consciousness, whether immediate or in memory, whether true or illusory" (LSJ). The word is seriously confusing, especially in **Aristotle**'s usage, because sometimes it means any appearance whatever (as in the LSJ definition), and sometimes it has a more limited sense, either (approximately) the faculty of imagination, or even specifically having *false* appearances. Also, sometimes *phantasia* is the faculty, sometimes the activity of the faculty, and sometimes it is the content or object of the faculty. It is more than usually important that one be aware of the current sense of the word when attempting to interpret Aristotelian passages including the word *phantasia*.

For the **Stoics**, a *phantasia* is an "impression on the soul" that can be grasped (DL 7.149). *False* perceptions they call *phantasmata*.

PHANTASMA. Figment of the imagination.

PHAULOS. Small, insignificant, worthless, bad. Possibly **Plato**'s most common word for "bad" as in "bad person." For **Aristotle**, *phaulos* is the opposite of *spoudaios*.

PHENOMENON. *See PHAINOMENON.*

PHERECYDES OF SYROS (Sixth century BCE). Pherecydes was a theologian–cosmologist credited by **Diogenes Laertius** and others of having been the teacher of **Pythagoras**. **Aristotle** calls him a theologian who mixed philosophical reasoning with **myth** (*Metaph.* 1091b8).

PHILIA. Friendship, love. One of the two cosmic principles of **Empedocles** (the other is "strife"—*eris*, *neikos*). *Philia* is analyzed by **Socrates** in **Plato**'s *Lysis*. The related concept of *erōs* is prominent in the *Phaedrus* and *Symposium*. **Aristotle** discusses *philia* especially in *Nicomachean Ethics* books 8 and 9; the concept is also fundamental for his political theory, since individual affinities ultimately result in a unified and functional society. Friendship is central in **Epicurean** ethics: "Of the things acquired by wisdom for the blessedness of life, far the greatest is the possession of friendship" (*Key Doctrines* 27).

PHILIPPUS OF OPUS (Fourth century BCE). Philip of Opus became **Plato**'s secretary toward the end of Plato's life, and is credited with writing the dialogue the *Epinomis*, included in the Platonic **Corpus** as a kind of appendix to the *Laws*.

PHILO OF ALEXANDRIA (c. 20 BCE–45 CE). A Jewish philosopher, Philo served in the delegation from **Alexandria** to the Emperor Gaius Caligula in 39 CE. Philo thought that **Pythagoras** had learned his philosophy from Moses, and **Plato** from Pythagoras, so Greek philosophy should be consistent with the Torah. He practices allegorical exegesis of the Torah toward the end of making the desired connections. His basic philosophical orientation is Platonic (he is counted as a "**middle Platonist**"), with a significant amount of **Stoic** thought, especially, included. For example, his use of the Stoic version of *logos* in theological contexts, together with the Platonic **World Soul**, provides a philosophical anticipation of the **Christian** doctrine of the Trinity. *See also* JUDAISM.

PHILO OF LARISSA (158–84 BCE). Scholarch of the **Academy** from about 110 BCE, after Clitomachus, until he moved to Rome during the Mithridatic wars. Unlike his immediate predecessors, he seems to have taught the content of Plato's dialogues. **Cicero** was one of his students.

PHILO THE LOGICIAN (Late fourth to early third centuries BCE). Student of **Diodorus Cronus**, leader of the **Dialectical School.** He contributed to the development of formal logic (*logikē*) including modal logic, influencing the development of **Stoic** logic. Philo is sometimes said to be a **Megarian**, but more recent scholarship has distinguished the two schools.

PHILODEMUS OF GADARA (c.110–40 BCE). Epicurean whose writings were discovered, as charred papyri, in the Villa of the Pisones at Herculaneum. He seems to have been particularly adept at adapting the teachings of his school to the needs of his Roman audience.

PHILOLAUS OF CROTON (c. 470–385 BCE). Author of a book presenting many of the **Pythagorean** ideas, probably one of the people **Aristotle** had in mind in talking about "those who call themselves Pythagoreans." He is presented as the teacher of Simmias and Cebes in **Plato**'s *Phaedo*. In the *Philebus*, Plato uses several of Philolaus' philosophic ideas, including the relation of "limit" and "unlimit." Philolaus believed that mathematics (*mathematikē*) was fundamental for understanding the world. He had a **cosmological** theory including a hypothesized "counter-earth" that we could not see because it is always on the other side of the "central fire"; i.e., Philolaus anticipated a heliocentric universe, as Copernicus noted.

PHILOPONUS, JOHN (c. 490–570 CE). Alexandrian Christian commentator on **Aristotle**, he studied with **Ammonius son of Hermeias**; "Philoponus" is a nickname, given him because he liked to work. Several commentaries survive (*CAG* 13–17); he also wrote treatises attacking the Aristotelian idea that the world has neither beginning nor end: he defends the thesis that the world was created, and will be destroyed. There are also several theological treatises, and treatises on **astronomy** and mathematics (*mathematikē*). His views on the Trinity were not regarded as sufficiently orthodox so he was not much studied in Europe until the Renaissance.

PHILOSOPHIA, PHILOSOPHOS. The word "philosophia" is said to have been invented by **Pythagoras**: when some said that he was a *sophos*, or wise man, he demurred, and said that he was rather a lover of wisdom (*sophia*), that **God** alone is wise. Before the time of **Socrates**, the word *philosophoi* seemed to be used primarily to designate people whose intellectual adventures were influenced in some measure by Pythagoras and his school. **Plato**'s dialogues dramatically depict a range of activities that he calls "philosophy" and a range of methodologies that for him deserve the honorific term "philosophical." **Aristotle** broadened the concept of philosophy to make it nearly synonymous with any attempt to gain knowledge (*epistēmē*) and understanding of the world (cf. *Metaph*. I.1). In the ancient world after Aristotle there were writers who distinguished various parts of philosophy, for example "natural philosophy" (i.e., natural **science**), "ethics," and "logic (*logikē*)."

In the ancient world, philosophy had the reputation of encouraging independent thought, of following the argument wherever it would lead. Many ancient philosophers are depicted as unimpressed by money and power, and disinclined to accept religious orthodoxies.

PHILOSTRATUS (Early third century CE). Author of the "Life of Apollonius of Tyana," and of "Lives of the Sophists." Since his writings often read like fiction, scholars do not rely very heavily on them as a source of historical information. He was a part of the movement known as the "Second Sophistic," a revival beginning in the first century CE and continuing throughout antiquity and into the Byzantine period, emphasizing rhetorical style.

PHŌNĒ. Sound. This word may be used of the sounds made by animals, or applied to vowels as distinguished from consonants. The **Stoics** distinguish the "sound" from the *lexis* and *lekton*. **Diogenes of Babylon** argues, according to **Galen**, that since the "sound" proceeds from the chest, and the sound acquires and carries meaning as language, the rational faculty must be located in the chest, not in the head.

PHORA. From the verb *pherein*, to carry, ***phora*** means primarily the act of carrying or that which is carried. **Aristotle** intentionally defines the word as a very general term for local movement, *Phys*. V.2, 226a33. As such, it is the primary form of ***kinēsis*** (*Phys*. VIII.7, 260a20ff), and is either primarily in a straight line or in a circle (*Phys*. VIII.9, 265a14). The circular form of ***phora*** is especially typical of **astronomical** entities (*Cael*. II.12, 292a14). For the four terrestrial elements (***stoicheia***): earth, water, air, and fire, the natural *phora* is toward the element's natural location, and perhaps cyclical motion once arrived at the natural place.

PHRONĒSIS. Abstract noun based on *phronein*, to think, to have understanding, to be prudent. **Heraclitus** f.2: "Although the ***logos*** is common, the many live as if they had a private *phronēsis*." In the *Symposium*, **Socrates** says that the priestess **Diotima** told him that some people are pregnant in their souls with a *phronēsis* that enables them to order cities and households. Although the word appears often enough in the broader sense of rational thought (cf. *Rep*. VI, 505a), it most especially means "practical wisdom," or the intellectual virtue of being able to organize one's life, one's home, one's society, in the best possible way. The concept of *phronēsis* is fundamental for **Aristotle**'s ethical theory, since the definition of any ethical virtue is determined by the person who has *phronēsis*. The concept continues to function along these lines in later Greek ethical theory.

PHTHORA. Destruction, the correlative of ***genesis***. *Phthora* is change that involves the termination of the existence of an entity (***ousia***).

PHYSICIAN. *See IATRIKĒ, IATROS.*

PHYSICS. *See PHYSIS.*

PHYSIKOI, PHYSIOLOGOI. **Aristotle**'s terms for his predecessors who concentrated on the study of nature (***physis***), primarily **Thales, Anaximander, Anaximenes, Empedocles, Anaxagoras, Leucippus,** and **Democritus**. Aristotle tends to consider these people material reductionists, as in *Metaph*. I. In *PA* I.1, 640b4–22, he enlarges that somewhat: he says that "the old philosophers who first studied *physis*" focused on the material principle, and how the universe is generated from that "under the influence of what motion, whether strife or mind (*nous*) or love or chance" and animals and plants are explained the same way. *See also* COSMOS; MATTER; *STOICHEION*.

PHYSIS, HISTORIA PERI PHYSEŌS. Nature; the study of Nature. **Aristotle**'s definition of "nature" is a good place to start: "Source or cause of change or rest in that to which it belongs primarily" (*Phys.* II.1). More elaborately: (1) the coming-to-be of growing things; (2) the principle of growth in the things that grow; (3) the source of change present in the thing in virtue of its **essence**, and the cause of the organic unity of living things; (4) the basic material of which anything is made (so the "nature" of the knife depends on the iron); (5) the *ousia* of a natural thing (*Metaph.* V.4).

It has been argued that one of the greatest contributions of ancient Greek civilization was the development of the concept of nature, a development that has had vast and permanent consequences for the history of human thought. In this entry reference can be made only to one or two starting points for thinking about this issue.

In the *Odyssey*, the word *physis* occurs just once; Hermes tells Odysseus that he must know the *physis* of the plant *moly* so that he can use it to turn his crew back from pigs to people (10.303). **Heraclitus** says (f. 1) that although people do not understand his *logos*, he "distinguishes each thing according to its *physis* and says how it is." He also says, "Nature loves to hide" (f. 123). Later Greek philosophers believed that essentially all the Presocratics were primarily concerned with "nature," that their books could be described as *historia peri physeōs*.

Greek philosophers relate the concept of *physis* to several other leading concepts, notably *technē* and *nomos*. When *physis* is contrasted with *technē*, nature is whatever happens without human intervention, art is what happens *with* human intervention. Of course there is a possibility of *continuity* between art and nature: as Aristotle says in *Physics* II, art partially imitates nature, and partially completes what nature cannot finish.

When *physis* is contrasted with *nomos*, the nature in question is human nature without social intervention, and law or convention is the social intervention that supervenes on human nature. That way of looking at things tends to bracket or elide discourse about divine intervention. But those who believe in divine intervention can readily use this vocabulary to bring it back in: nature can be seen as an expression of divine art and law.

Plato is a good example of a philosopher who takes the contrast between art and nature and breaks it down to the benefit of a more theological perspective. In the *Phaedo*, at 96b, **Socrates** says that he was attracted to *historia peri physeōs*, investigation of nature, but was disappointed that those who pursued this study did not give teleological explanations. Although **Anaxagoras** posited a divine Mind (*nous*), he neglects to show how Mind planned things.

In *Laws* 10.889a4ff, Plato gives a detailed account of the explanation on the basis of "nature and chance," that the material elements (*stoicheia*) give rise to the sun, moon, stars, earth, and that all the cosmological effects we see are simply the result of powers inhering in the material elements. Art, according to that account, is subsequent and inferior, the creation of mortals. Some arts that cooperate with nature, like medicine (*iatrikē*) and agriculture, have much to recommend them, but others, like government, have results that are "quite artificial." That Plato does not agree with this view of nature does not detract from the fact that it was a remarkable intellectual construct with very significant consequences in later centuries. Plato points out in this passage that the naturalist philosophers essentially argued that the **Gods** are human artifacts; as he continues in *Laws* X, he of course argues that the universe is the artifact of God, and ultimately human laws (*nomoi*) depend on divine law as well.

The **Stoic** philosophers took over this idea and developed it further. For them, God is totally present in all of nature, bringing about all natural processes; materially, God is *pyr technikon*, artisanal fire. At the same time, natural laws and divine laws are identical, and comprise both the laws of physics and the laws of morality and government, so *physis*, *technē*, and *nomos* are all contained within God. The battle lines were drawn. *See also AITION; ARCHĒ; EIDOS; TELOS.*

PIETY. *See ARETĒ; HOSIOTĒS.*

PISTIS. Belief. Noun built on the verb *peithesthai*, to persuade. *Pistis* is both the subjective state of having been persuaded, and the evidence that brings about that persuasion. In the **Sun-Line-Cave** passage in the *Republic*, *pistis* is the improved form of opinion (*doxa*) characterizing those who have broken the chains of ignorance and are no longer staring at the wall of the cave. In **Aristotle**, the word occurs most frequently in the context of talking about arguments and the state of having been persuaded by arguments. In religious contexts, *pistis* is religious faith, especially **Christian** faith, as in the *Second Letter to the Corinthians*, II.

PITHANOS. Convincing, inspiring *pistis*. **Chrysippus** distinguished "convincing" from "unconvincing" impressions. We do not believe everything we see, but up to a point, seeing is believing.

PLACE. *See TOPOS.*

PLATO OF ATHENS (424 or 427–347 BCE). His parents were Ariston and Perictione. Plato had two older brothers, Glaucon and Adeimantus (they are featured in the *Republic*), and a sister, Potone (the mother of **Speusippus**). After the death of Ariston, Perictione married Pyrilampes, with whom she had a son named Antiphon (he appears in the frame dialogue of the *Parmenides*). Pyrilampes brought to the marriage a son by a previous marriage, named Demos (mentioned in the *Gorgias* as the object of **Callicles'** affection). It is well attested that Plato believed that his real father was the God Apollo.

According to **Diogenes Laertius**, the name "Plato" is in fact a nickname, meaning "broad," and dating back to his wrestling days, that his actual given name was "Aristocles" after his grandfather. The dating of his birth to 424 (by D. Nails) implies that he would not have served in the military during the Peloponnesian war, because he would have reached the age of 20 right at the end of the war. The traditional dating of his birth to 427 or even a year or two earlier would make it highly probable that Plato *did* serve in the military just at the end of the war.

On the Nails dating, Plato would have been 25 at the death of **Socrates**; according to Diogenes Laertius, Plato then associated with **Cratylus**, an enthusiast of **Heraclitus**, and **Hermogenes**, an enthusiast of **Parmenides**. Diogenes says that at age 28, Plato left with other followers of Socrates for Megara where he visited **Euclides**. In the next few years he seems to have traveled, including possibly to **Egypt**. In 384/3, he, along with other intellectuals, was invited by Dionysius I to visit Syracuse. This would be an indication that he had written some of his dialogues by that time, and that they had been noticed, a reasonable assumption. While in Sicily, Plato became friendly with Dion, a member of the royal family.

This visit to Syracuse ended badly, with Dionysius selling Plato into slavery for 20 minas. Plato was purchased by Anniceris of Cyrene, who set him free and bought for Plato a garden in the vicinity of the **Academy**, enabling him to establish his school.

Dionysius I died in 367; on receiving the news, Plato left for another visit to Syracuse, where Dionysius II was now in power. When Dionysius II and Dion had a falling out, Plato returned to **Athens**. In 361, Plato returned to Syracuse for a third time, and was virtually imprisoned by Dionysius, escaping only with the help of **Archytas**. From that time on, it appears that Plato focused on philosophical discussions in the Academy and writing his dialogues.

Fitting the composition of his dialogues into this biography is a somewhat complex exercise. Plato's dialogues fall fairly naturally into three groups, arguably roughly chronological. The first group of dialogues have Socrates as their major character, regularly presented as challenging beliefs held by his interlocutors by asking them to state clearly and unambiguously what those beliefs are. While some of the people with whom Socrates is talking could be called "experts" in some sense, none, with the exception of a **Sophist** or two, has any philosophical sophistication. Most often, the beliefs in question are, roughly speaking, moral in character, and the questions with which his interlocutors have most trouble are demands for a definition of a key term, or some other explication of a key term. In this group of dialogues there is usually no agreed-upon solution to the problem discussed, although some progress in understanding has been made. No one, including Socrates, seems to have a definitive answer to the crucial issues Socrates has posed. Some dialogues that fit this model would be the *Euthyphro*, the *Laches*, the *Lysis*, the *Charmides*, the *Ion*, the *Euthydemus*, and to some extent the *Protagoras*.

A second group of dialogues has many of those characteristics, but in addition, Socrates is presented as confidently presenting a fair amount of positive doctrine, and some of the people with whom he is speaking have some philosophical sophistication. The *Gorgias* has Socrates talking with a very able Sophist and two of his more clever students, and Socrates does present some positive doctrine. In the *Meno*, Socrates' interlocutors are philosophically rather naïve, but he does present a version of the doctrine of *anamnesis* and by implication at least a version of the theory of Forms (*eidē*). In the *Phaedo*, Socrates argues for the immortality of the soul (*psychē*), and for an ontological and epistemological scheme within which immortality makes sense; his major interlocutors are two students of the Pythagorean teacher **Philolaus**. In the *Republic*, Socrates outlines a theory of justice in the state and in the individual, and in the **Sun-Line-Cave** passage locates that theory within an ontological-epistemological system; in Book I he contended with a Sophist, and in the rest of the book, his discussants are Plato's two older brothers. In the *Symposium* and *Phaedrus*, Socrates presents two versions of a theory of love (*erōs*) that fit his moral psychology into the larger ontological scheme.

The third group of dialogues is unified primarily by the fact that, unlike the dialogues in groups one and two, they seem to emanate from an environment with a strong emphasis on highly technical discussions of philosophical issues. Socrates is not always the protagonist; the lead is sometimes taken by others. The *Theaetetus*, the *Cratylus*, and the *Philebus* do have Socrates as a principal interlocutor, but the topics are rather technical and at least some of the people in these dialogues are philosophically quite sophisticated. In the *Parmenides*, we see a young Socrates getting a lesson in how to do **dialectical** argument from **Parmenides**, and get a very technical lesson in what kind of theory of Forms might work, and what kind not. In the *Sophist* and *Statesman*, we have a visitor from **Elea** taking on the lead role in the argument; in the *Timaeus*, a Sicilian **Pythagorean** presents a detailed **cosmological** theory, followed in the incomplete *Critias*, by a description of the lost island of Atlantis. Finally, the *Laws*, Plato's longest dialogue, has as its protagonist an "Athenian

Stranger," clearly not Socrates, perhaps a stand-in for Plato himself. It is a discussion between three well-informed individuals about the possible legislation for an ideal state.

Plato wrote these dialogues over a period of about 50 years; he traveled out of Athens several times, especially to Sicily, and between trips to Sicily established his philosophical school, the Academy. We can reasonably suppose that Plato's ideas developed and perhaps even changed over that half-century; historians of philosophy have often attempted to trace those developments importantly assisted by philological investigations that provide evidence of changes in Plato's writing style. At the same time, there is a strong tradition that assumes the unity of Plato's thought. Certainly the ancient Platonists believed that Plato always was putting forward the same message.

What message is that? If we focus on the medium, the philosophical dialogue, and ask ourselves, what is the message of this medium, we may respond that it entices us into engaging in philosophical discussion, not necessarily predetermining the outcome of that discussion. Socrates is a philosophical role model, represented by Plato for imitation and admiration.

But the dialogues include many positive philosophical assertions, positions defended, systematic points made. Scattered through this present Dictionary one may find a good many of those positions and arguments; here are a few of the most salient:

- Forms. Plato's Socrates famously defends the thesis that the true objects of knowledge (*epistēmē*) are "forms" (*eidē*) or "ideas" (*ideai*). Things in the phenomenal world are knowable only inasmuch as they "imitate" or "participate in" the forms. The Forms are true reality, and make language meaningful.
- Knowledge of the Forms is gained through **dialectic**. The precise description of the dialectical method varies somewhat from dialogue to dialogue, but it is primarily *critical*; **hypotheses** are tested, and the presumption is that the true hypothesis will remain standing.
- While the theory of Forms is in principle completely general, Plato's Socrates is mainly interested in gaining knowledge of virtues and values. What is courage? Temperance? Justice? Friendship? Love?

- In some dialogues, notably *Meno*, *Phaedo*, and *Phaedrus*, Plato presents a theory that knowledge of the forms is innate, and that learning is a matter of recollecting the forms (**anamnēsis**).
- **Aristotle** says that Plato "in most respects" followed the **Pythagoreans** (*Metaphysics* I.8). Plato surely followed the Pythagorean lead in accepting the idea of **transmigration** of the soul; his frequently repeated reliance on mathematical categories is also strongly similar to Pythagorean speculation in the period—this is especially true of the *Timaeus*. And the Pythagoreans seemed to favor elitist political arrangements, something we see in detail in Plato's *Republic*.

In a sense, Plato's dialogues provide an ostensive definition of the word "philosophy" by demonstrating how it is done, and by asking the questions that count as philosophical. *See also METHEXIS; MIMĒSIS.*

PLEASURE. *See HĒDONĒ; HĒDYN.*

PLEONEXIA. Getting more than one's fair share. As **Aristotle** puts it in *Nicomachean Ethics* V, there are two ways of being unjust: one is to get more than one's fair share, the other is to disobey the law. Obviously the two need not coincide. *See also DIKĒ.*

PLĒTHOS. Plurality, large number, quantity, magnitude. In **Plato**, there is a dialectic between the One (**to hen**) and the Many (*plēthos*) (especially in *Philebus* and *Parmenides*). Since *to plēthos* also means "most people," **Plato** also contrasts the wisdom of the few and the ignorance of the many. Aristotle defines *plēthos* as that which is divisible into non-continuous parts (*Metaph.* V.13). *Plēthos* followed by a plural genitive would often be translated, especially in Aristotle, as "a lot of . . . " as in *HA* IV.8, 534b13, where he talks of "four classes which include *a lot of* the other animals." And in the *Politics*, rule by *to plēthos* is "democracy."

PLOTINUS (204–270 CE). Plotinus was born in Lycopolis, **Egypt**; he studied with **Ammonius Saccas** in **Alexandria**. Encouraged by Ammonius, Plotinus, at the age of 28, joined a campaign led by the Emperor Gordian III aimed at conquering the Persians and perhaps continuing to **India**. Gordian was assassinated in Mesopotamia, and

Plotinus went to Rome and proceeded to teach philosophy there for the rest of his life. In 263, **Porphyry** joined Plotinus in Rome, and proceeded to gather and edit into topical units Plotinus' writings in the work we know as the *Enneads*. Porphyry also wrote an account of the order in which Plotinus wrote these things, not at all the order in which they are included in the *Enneads*.

Plotinus' *Enneads* are taken as the fundamental and inaugural statement of the philosophical movement that is today called **Neoplatonism**. At the center of his philosophy is the idea of an ineffable and transcendent One (*hen*), self-aware and the source of all **being**. All differentiated beings, all pluralities, emanate from this one. Our individual soul (*psychē*), ultimately derived from the One, yearns to rejoin the One. The natural world too, what we call the material world, is ultimately derived from the One; as the material universe shows forth the glory of God, so our bodies are revelations of our souls. And as our minds contemplate the Forms (*eidē*), they become united with the Mind (*nous*) of the Universe, in which those Forms have their being and reality. *See also GOD; HEN; NOUS; PHYSIS.*

PLURALITY. *See PLETHOS.*

PLUTARCH OF ATHENS (d. 432 CE). He seems to have studied with the successors of **Iamblichus** in Apamea (Syria); he reestablished the Platonic School in **Athens**. Plutarch was the teacher of **Hierocles** of **Alexandria**, **Syrianus**, and **Proclus**.

PLUTARCH OF CHAERONEA (c. 45–125 CE). A **Platonist**, born in Chaeronea, a town in Boeotia. He studied in **Athens** with a man named Ammonius, and he became a priest at Delphi. Plutarch is the author of many extant works: perhaps best known is his *Parallel Lives*, a literary-historical work pairing eminent Greek and Roman figures. Most of the remainder of his extant works are gathered under the general title of *Moralia*, and include over 70 dialogues and essays. In ethical matters, Plutarch tends to follow **Aristotle**, assuming that Plato and Aristotle have no conflicts in this area of investigation. Plutarch tends to be more dualist than many Platonists, influenced perhaps by Persian religion. His account of **Egyptian** religion, in *On Isis and Osiris*, is also strikingly dualistic.

PNEUMA. Literally, breath or wind; eventually, "spirit." Already in the Presocratic period the word was used with a range of meanings from a synonym for air to breathed air to the winds to soul (*psychē*). **Anaximenes** says, "As our soul being air holds us together, so air and breath encompass the whole universe" (f. 2). **Aristotle** says that the **Pythagoreans** believed that the universe breathes in empty space from the infinite (*apeiron*) "like taking a breath" (*Phys.* IV.6, 213b25). **Plato** was content to ridicule the idea that the soul is a material thing like breath, for example in the *Phaedo* (77e), "you seem to have this childish fear that the wind dissolve and scatter the soul as it leaves the body, especially if one happens to die on a windy day and not in calm weather." While Aristotle hardly mentions *pneuma* in the *De Anima*, in *Generation of Animals*, *Movement of Animals*, and some of the *Parva Naturalia* it is an important part of his biological explanations of life functions. In *GA* II, *pneuma* in semen carries the information about form from the male parent to the female contribution to generation, whether egg or menstrual fluid. In *Movement of Animals*, *pneuma* carries information from the sense organs to the central governing part, and back again to the parts involved in moving the animal from place to place. At the end of *GA* (V.8) Aristotle says, "It is reasonable that nature should perform most of her operations using *pneuma* as a tool, for as the hammer and anvil in the art of the smith, so *pneuma* in the things formed by nature."

In **Stoic** philosophy, *pneuma* is the material basis for the pervasive presence of the divine mind (*nous*). Physically, *pneuma* assures the coherence of individual bodies, not only of living things, but even of logs and rocks; because it is omnipresent in the world, it assures the **unity** and coherence of the entire **cosmos**. Since the Stoics were materialists it was crucial that they find an appropriately talented material that would assist them in carrying out their project.

Others, notably **Platonists** like Philo, seem to have dematerialized *pneuma*, a trend that we definitely see in the New Testament, where it is used of a presumably immaterial soul (especially in the Pauline epistles). The Christian Holy Spirit is, in Greek, the *Pneuma Hagion*. **Basil of Caesarea** wrote the definitive defense of the divinity of the *Pneuma Hagion*, in the fourth century. *See also AĒR; AITHĒR; PHYSIS*; WORLD SOUL.

POETRY. Before the time of **Thales** and **Anaximander**, we have little evidence of Greeks writing prose texts. **Homer** and **Hesiod**, Sappho,

Alcaeus, and Archilochus, and **Solon** composed whatever works are preserved in poetic meter and diction. Of the earliest philosophers, some wrote in established poetic styles: **Xenophanes** was primarily a poet, and a philosopher to the extent that some of his poems took up philosophical themes; **Parmenides** presented his revolutionary philosophical position in epic meter and diction, though some complain that the poem is not very poetical; **Empedocles** had a significant mastery of the poetic style while presenting a coherent philosophical position that included **cosmology**, physics, biology, psychology, and much else besides. At the same time, the philosophical tradition early demonstrates some ambivalence about poetry: **Heraclitus** says that Homer and Archilochus deserve to be whipped (f. 42); Hesiod, **Pythagoras**, **Xenophanes**, and **Hecataeus** (of Miletus) are grouped as ignorant polymaths (f. 40).

The normal education of ancient Greeks in the fifth century BCE included the memorization of a good bit of poetry—extensive passages of Homer, Hesiod, the lyric poets, Pindar, the dramatists such as Aeschylus, Sophocles and Euripides, for a start. Although only professionals like Ion (see Plato's *Ion*) were able to recite entire epics, many in their audience would have been able to sing along, more than can today sing "Un Bel Di" along with Butterfly or "Si, Mi Chiamo Mimi" along with Mimi. The **Sophists** reasonably took advantage of that shared education to further their own goals; we see **Gorgias** writing rhetorical defenses of Helen of Troy and of Palamedes, and **Protagoras**, as represented by Plato, not only recruiting the classical poets into the genealogy of the sophistic tradition, but challenging **Socrates** to outdo him in the interpretation of a morally charged poem by Simonides.

Socrates, **Plato**, and **Aristotle** all exhibited a somewhat ambivalent attitude toward the Greek poetical tradition as they knew it. Plato represents Socrates shredding the performance artist *Ion*, mainly because Ion appears to claim that if you know Homer's poems, you know everything worth knowing, because Homer knew everything worth knowing and put it in his poems. In the *Protagoras*, after amply demonstrating that he knows Simonides better and can interpret him better than Protagoras can, Socrates notoriously remarks (in the Lombardo-Bell translation), "Discussing poetry strikes me as no different from the second-rate drinking parties of the agora crowd. . . . (Our group) should require no extraneous voices, not even of poets" (347c). Still, Socrates, in both Plato and **Xenophon**, frequently quotes poets (especially Homer!) in support of his assertions.

Plato's attack on "the poets" in the *Republic* is justly famous not only for the energy put into it, but also for the level of detail, seeming to leave little that the poets of **Kallipolis** could write about. Nevertheless, in the *Republic* Socrates concludes "that education in music and poetry is most important . . . because rhythm and harmony permeate the inner part of the soul more than anything else" (401d). Again, in the *Phaedrus*, the great speech of Socrates on the nature of **Eros** is called a "palinode" after the manner of Stesichorus, and while it is not in poetic meter, is certainly "poetic."

Aristotle wrote a book, *Poetics*, that attempts to tell how to write a successful tragedy, after the manner of Aeschylus, Sophocles, and Euripides. Along the way he provides some comments on epic poetry as well. Throughout his works he occasionally quotes from various poets; sometimes he is amused by poets—for example at *EN* IX.7, 1168a2, he notes that poets are sometimes excessively fond of their poems, like parents of children.

In regard to the **Stoics,** we may note that **Cleanthes,** the second leader of the Stoic school, wrote a justly famous *Hymn to Zeus*, and that **Chrysippus** persistently supported his arguments with "proof texts" drawn from the poets.

Finally, **Lucretius,** the Roman **Epicurean,** presented the definitive account of that philosophy in the great poem, *De Rerum Natura*, returning to the tradition of **Empedocles** perhaps.

POIEIN, POIĒSIS, POIĒTIKĒ. *Poiein* means "to make or do"; *poiēsis* is the abstract noun built on this verb: "making, production"; *poiētikē* is the adjective based on the abstract noun: "productive." A *poiētēs* is a person who makes something; a *poiēma* is the object made. **Plato** talks about the *poiētēs* of a bed in *Republic* X, and of the **Demiourgos** as the *poiētēs* of the universe in *Timaeus* 28c, but generally *poiētēs* and *poiēma* refer to literary productions.

The verb *poiein* and some of the forms based on the verb are used in much more general senses philosophically, however. *Poiein* is contrasted with *paschein* to distinguish "active" and "passive"—these are two of Aristotle's **categories**, essentially the categories for verbs. But on the active side of that distinction there is a further division between *poiein* and *prattein*, between "making" and "doing"—as Aristotle sees it, *poiēsis* has as its goal a product, while in the case of *praxis* the activity itself is the goal.

Something or someone is *poiētikos* if it (he, she) is "productive" of something. Thus Aristotle uses this word to pick out (some cases of) the "cause" that he also calls "source of change."

POINT. *See STIGMĒ.*

POION. "Of what sort." *Poion* is used by **Aristotle** as the name of one of the **categories** (*Cat.* 8b-11a), the one we call "Quality" in English. "Quality" is really the Ciceronian translation of the abstract noun built on *poion*, i.e., *poiotēs*, possibly introduced by **Plato** in the *Theaetetus*, 182a. *See also KATĒGORIA.*

POIOTĒS. Quality.

POLEMON (c. 350–266/5 BCE). Scholarch of the **Academy** from 315/4. During the half-century that Polemon was Scholarch, the Academy moved away from the metaphysical speculations that had characterized the Academy of **Speusippos** and **Xenocrates**, and toward more emphasis on moral issues. Academic skepticism developed during this period, led by fellow Academics **Crantor** and **Crates**. **Zeno of Citium**, founder of the **Stoic** school, studied in the Academy during this period. *See also SKEPTIKOS.*

POLIS. City, state. In the Hellenic period (before the death of **Alexander of Macedon**), the Greek-speaking world was organized into many city-states. While the size of these *poleis* varied considerably, Attica, at a population of perhaps 200,000, would have to be counted among the largest. The political theories of both **Plato** (both *Republic* and *Laws*) and **Aristotle** assumed unquestioningly that political units of that size (or rather smaller) were good and right and natural. Yet they were well aware that the Greeks had fought off the Persians by uniting into a larger confederacy, that that confederacy was succeeded by the Delian League, ultimately dominated by the Athenians, and opposed by a confederacy led by the Spartans. They also knew the Empire of the Persians, of course, and the Macedonian kingdom, and Aristotle especially witnessed in the course of his lifetime the expansion of Macedonia to an empire greater than the world had ever seen.

Why did they cling to a model that could not survive? For Aristotle at least, the answer must be that the traditional *polis* offered the opportunity for a significant percentage of the citizens to have a direct participation in real political decision-making. While the Hellenistic kingdoms often left local affairs to the traditional local decision-making bodies, no one was fooled. Independence was gone.

But Hellenistic philosophers adjusted, one way or another. **Epicureans** simply avoided public life entirely, on the ground that it was more likely to be painful than pleasurable. **Stoics**, however, were willing to accept whatever responsibilities might come to them. From their perspective, the wise person is a "citizen of the universe," *kosmopolitēs* (SVF III.82).

POLITICS. *See POLITIKĒ.*

POLITIKĒ. Political theory and the "Art" of politics. In **Plato**, the art of justice; in the *Republic* (*Politeia* in Greek), **Socrates** expresses the hope that *politikē* and *philosophia* would coincide, become identical. In the *Statesman* (the *Politikos*, in Greek), *politikē* is characterized as the art of weaving together those who have courageous with those who have temperate natures for the happier life of all.

As **Aristotle** puts it, *politikē* aims at the highest goods achievable by action (*EN* I.2, 1095a15). For him, all praxis is subsumed under the "political art." His book, the *Politics*, brings together empirical investigation of existing states and a theory of the possible structure of civil society. For Aristotle, the basic unit of the *polis* is the family or household, not only because it is the locus for procreation and thus continuity, but also because, in Aristotle's world, the household was the primary location for the production of goods. Families are located in a complex web of social relationships, or "friendships" (*philiai*), which jointly form the community (*koinonia*) in which the family is located. For Aristotle, the human being is a *zoon politikon*, animal whose nature it is to live in a *polis*; human language has as its primary function making possible the social interactions that form the community and state.

In the time of Plato and Aristotle the philosophical schools seem to have had the production of political leaders as one of their major functions. This function continued to operate to some degree even in the Hellenistic period, as the structure of government became more imperial. For example, **Demetrius of Phaleron,** a student of Aristotle and Theophrastus, became the governor of **Athens** under the Macedonians for a period of time.

Eventually the **Stoic** philosophy was adopted by many Roman leaders—**Cicero, Seneca, Marcus Aurelius** for three especially notable examples—and became one of the cornerstones of Roman law and thus for Western political theory. *See also DIKĒ.*

POLYAENUS OF LAMPSACUS (d. 278/7 BCE). Co-founder of the **Epicurean** school. Having been a mathematician prior to his conversion to Epicureanism, he wrote, among other things, works critical of standard mathematics, though some members of the school seem to have thought, not critical enough.

PONOS. Hard work, toil, pain from working.

PORPHYRY OF TYRE (234–c. 305 CE). A **Neoplatonist**, educated by Longinus, he joined **Plotinus** in Rome; edited and published Plotinus' *Enneads*, and wrote a biography of Plotinus. Of his popular works, his *Life of Pythagoras, To Marcella* (his wife), *The Cave of the Nymphs* (about **Homer**), and *On Abstinence from Animal Food* survive. His introduction to **Aristotle**'s *Categories* had wide influence. His *Starting Points Leading to the Intelligibles* is intended to be an accessible introduction to some of the central issues in Neoplatonic thought. There are also fragments of his critique of **Christianity**, *Against the Christians*, and fragments of a commentary on the *Parmenides*.

A number of his writings were translated into Latin, and thus influenced the course of philosophy in the Latin west. Also, he seems to have taught in Rome or somewhere in Italy after the death of Plotinus, and his students established a Latin Platonist tradition, starting with **Marius Victorinus** and continuing with **Augustine**.

PŌS ECHEIN (PŌS ECHŌN), PŌS ECHEIN PROS TI (PŌS ECHŌN PROS TI). Two of the four **Stoic** categories, "how disposed," and "how disposed in relation to something." *See also ECHEIN, HEXIS.*

POSIDONIUS (*POSEIDONIOS*) OF APAMEA (c. 135–51 BCE). Posidonius was a **Stoic** philosopher from Syria. He studied with **Panaetius** in **Athens**, and traveled widely through the Roman world and beyond, before establishing a school in Rhodes. He was a prolific writer of scientific and literary works, surviving only in fragments today. His geographic and ethnographic writings gained him attention in the Roman world, and he attempted to improve the measurements of the size of the **earth**, moon, and sun, and the distances from earth to moon and sun. In addition, he extended the history written by Polybius to include the years 146–88 BCE. Philosophically, he is regarded as an eclectic Stoic, integrating Platonic and Aristotelian concepts into a fundamentally Stoic system.

POSITION. One of the "categories" (*katēgoriai*) or types of predicates; a paradigmatic example would be "So and so is *sitting.*" *See also KEISTHAI; THESIS.*

POSON. Literally, "how much," used by **Aristotle** as the name of one of the categories (*katēgoriai*) or predicates (*Cat.* 4a–6b), the one we call "quantity." Paradigmatic examples would include the height and **weight** of a person.

POSSESSION. An English name of one of **Aristotle**'s categories (*katēgoriai*) called *echein. Hexis* is the noun formed on this verb. A paradigmatic example of this category would be that a certain person is *wearing a hat.*

POTE. Literally, "when," used by **Aristotle** as the name of one of the 10 categories (*katēgoriai*), the one we call "time." His examples are "yesterday" and "next year."

POTENTIALITY. *See DYNAMIS.*

POU. Literally, "where," used by **Aristotle** as the name of one of the 10 categories (*katēgoriai*), the one called in English, "place." His examples at *Cat.* 2a1 are "in the **Lyceum**, in the agora." *See also TOPOS.*

POWER. *See DYNAMIS.*

PRAGMA. From the verb *prattein* (*prassein*), to do, *pragma* has as its primary sense "a thing done." Philosophically, the word gains the sense of "thing" as opposed to "word," for example in **Plato**'s *Craty-*

lus 391b; **Aristotle** claims (*de An.* III.8, 432a3) that there are no *pragmata* apart from "sensible spatial magnitudes." For the **Stoics**, *lekta* are intermediate between thoughts and *pragmata*.

PRAXIS, PRAKTIKĒ. Action, as opposed to production (which would be *poiēsis*), or as opposed to passivity (*pathos*). *Praktikē* is the adjective; in the feminine (as here), it is taken to be a "practical art" or "practical science" as opposed to productive on the one hand, or theoretical on the other. As **Aristotle** says, tragic drama is an imitation of *praxis* and life (*Poetics* 1450a16). Of course ethical and political studies examine specifically human *praxeis*. From that perspective, animals do not share in action (*EN* VI.2, 1139a20)—nor do the **Gods** (*EN* X.8, 1178b10), since *praxis* is unworthy of them; their life is totally involved with *theoria*.

Aristotle does use the word *praxis* in a wider sense as well, in which the activities of animals are called *praxeis* (*PA* II.1, 646b15), and the movements of the heavens (*ouranoi*) (which Aristotle thinks of as divine activities) are also *praxeis* (*Cael.* II.6, 288b30).

PRECONCEPTION. *See PROLĒPSIS.*

PREDICATE, PREDICATION. *See HYPARCHEIN; KATEGORIAI.*

PREFERABLES, PREFERRED. In **Stoic ethics**, since only virtue (*aretē*) is truly good (and vice truly bad), there are a number of things that other people may call good, but Stoics say are neither good nor bad; some Stoics say that some such things may be "preferred." Possible examples would be life, health, **beauty**, strength, pleasure, wealth, reputation, noble birth (DL 7.101). **Aristo of Chios** objected that those things too are indifferent. *See also ADIAPHORA; PROĒGMENA.*

PRESOCRATIC. Term commonly used to refer to philosophers who lived before **Socrates**. In several cases, it is used of people who were the contemporaries of Socrates. There is a sense that Socrates' attention to definition and moral issues was truly revolutionary, so that the word "Presocratic" picks out discernable philosophical characteristics. Many of the Presocratics were primarily concerned with developing an understanding of the material universe, often by some form of material reduction to a primary form of **matter**. Others, like the **Eleatics**, focused on the logical understanding of **being**. They also exhibit a rich variety of stances regarding religious issues, from the revolutionary doctrine of rebirth taught by the **Pythagoreans** and **Empedocles**, to the skeptical henotheism of **Xenophanes**, to the frank agnosticism of some of the **Sophists**.

Aristotle tends to group many of them together as *physiologoi*, those who talk about nature. This would appear to be especially true of the Milesians, including **Thales, Anaximander**, and **Anaximenes**; **Empedocles, Anaxagoras**, and **Diogenes of Apollonia**; and the Atomists, **Leucippus** and **Democritus**. It would be less true of **Pythagoras** and most of his followers, who were more concerned with a mathematical understanding of the world. Although **Heraclitus** does seem to make fire a fundamental material principle, that is surely not what his philosophy is "about."

If we count the earlier **Sophists** as Presocratics, it would be only in the sense that Socrates surpassed their relativism with a heightened attention to the possible foundations of value judgments.

PRIME MATTER. *PRŌTE HYLĒ. See HYLĒ.*

PRIME MOVER. *See PRŌTON KINOUN.*

PRINCIPLE. *See ARCHĒ; HYPOTHESIS.*

PRISCIAN OF LYDIA (5th to 6th centuries CE). One of the **Neoplatonists** exiled from Athens to Persia in 529 CE, part of his *Metaphrase* of **Theophrastus'** *On the Soul* survives.

PRIVATION. *See STERĒSIS.*

PROAIRESIS, PROHAIRESIS. Choice. Forms of this word appear in several places in **Plato** with an unproblematic meaning of "choice"— for example, at *Phaedrus* 245b4 **Socrates** talks about "choosing" as a friend someone who is in control of himself over someone who is disturbed. But serious focus on the word comes in **Aristotle**'s *Nicomachean Ethics*, where it is defined as "deliberative desire or desiderative deliberation" (***orexis** bouleutikē* or ***bouleusis** orektikē*)

(*EN* III). It is essential for Aristotle to get clear about *prohairesis* because "ethical virtue" is defined as "the habit of *choosing* the action that lies in a mean relative to us according to the right rule as determined by the person of practical wisdom." "Ethics" is *about* choices.

Epictetus also uses the term *prohairesis*, more nearly in the sense of the faculty of **assenting** or not assenting to one's perceptions (*aisthēseis*).

Outside the philosophical world, *prohairesis* eventually takes on the sense of "preference," so that it can mean a political party or a religious sect to which one belongs.

PROBLEM. *See APORIA.*

PROCESS. *See GENESIS.*

PROCLUS (412–485 CE). Born in Constantinople, Proclus studied rhetoric, law, and philosophy in **Alexandria** and in **Athens** with **Plutarch of Athens** and with **Syrianus**. Proclus succeeded Syrianus as **Scholarch** in Athens in 437. In a period of increasing Christian domination of Greek-language intellectual life, Proclus remained a "pagan" but wrote many works that strongly influenced theological writings both in Christendom and Islam during subsequent centuries. Most of his surviving works are formally commentaries on various dialogues of **Plato**, but these commentaries significantly expand upon and extend the Platonic philosophy in ways surely not envisioned by Plato himself. Proclus also wrote an important commentary on **Euclid**; it includes a very valuable account of the history of Greek mathematics (*mathematikē*) and influential comments on the mathematical character of **Plato**'s Forms (*eidē*).

His *Elements of Theology* presents a number of theses about **God** and other theological topics in the guise of geometrical proofs, in imitation of the Euclidian model. It was translated and adapted into Arabic; translated from Arabic into Latin under the title "Liber de Causis," it exerted an influence on the development of Scholastic theology.

His *Platonic Theology* was used extensively by (pseudo-) **Dionysius the Areopagite**, whose writings are in turn fundamental for Orthodox Christian theology. Perhaps the central feature of Proclus' thought is his unique synthesis of a profound understanding of classical mathematical reasoning with a **Neoplatonic** analysis of theological concepts. *See also* CHRISTIANITY.

PRODICUS OF CEOS (c. 460–after 399 BCE). Prodicus was a **Sophist** with a strong interest in language; his views were satirized in **Aristophanes** *Clouds*. **Socrates** seems to have had a certain respect for him (e.g., *Apol.* 19e); we get a flavor of his style at *Protagoras* 337. Perhaps his most famous composition was the *Choice of Heracles*, which represented Heracles at a crossroads with Virtue (*aretē*) down one road and Vice (*kakia*) down the other. We know of the contents of this work through a paraphrase by **Xenophon**. Prodicus had theories about the origins of the various deities worshipped by the Greeks and other peoples; although some concluded that he was an atheist, the evidence points rather to a theology somewhat similar to that of **Xenophanes**.

PRODUCTION. *See POIĒSIS.*

PROĒGMENA. In **Stoic** philosophy, "preferables," "things preferred." The Stoics distinguish things good, bad, and indifferent, but among indifferents, some things are "preferred" and others "dispreferred." When circumstances permit, one chooses health rather than disease, life rather than death, wealth instead of poverty. Not all Stoics accepted this concept; some thought that "preferred" and "dispreferred" things were still really indifferent, *adiaphora*.

PROĒGOUMENON AITION. Antecedent cause. For some **Stoics**, this was the term used to pick out what **Aristotle** calls the "source of movement." *See also AITION.*

PROLĒPSIS. Preconception. This is a central concept in post-Aristotelian epistemology, apparently introduced by **Epicurus**, who makes of it one of three criteria (*kritēria*) of truth (*alētheia*), the other two being sensations and feelings. For Epicurus, we put together a *prolēpsis* from repeated experiences of the same thing, either something external, or of ourselves. A *prolēpsis* is the starting point for any inquiry. For **Chrysippus**, a preconception is the "natural conception of universals" (DL 7.154). Skeptics, reasonably enough, thought that preconceptions (*prolēpseis*) were unreliable criteria of truth. *See also PHAINOMENON; SKEPTIKOS.*

PRONOIA. Providence, foresight, forethought. Human *pronoia* is intention, planning, even malice aforethought. Both **Plato** and **Aristotle** talk of the "forethought" of wise legislators. But especially in philosophic contexts this word seems increasingly applied to **God**. **Herodotus** 3.108: "Somehow the forethought of God (just as is reasonable) being wise has made all creatures prolific that are timid and edible, so that they do not become extinct through being eaten, whereas few young are born to hardy and vexatious creatures." Plato's **Demiourgos** is called *pronoia* at *Timaeus* 30C, for example, for bringing into existence the world "as a living creature, endowed with soul and intelligence."

For the Stoics, *Pronoia* is the most usual *name* of God. **Chrysippus**, for example, argued that God's providence was exercised especially for the benefit of humanity. **Neoplatonists** tended to be a good deal less anthropocentric; The One (**hen**) is surely beyond any form of forethought, but even lesser deities are concerned about their own tasks, and providence for human beings is the responsibility of human souls (**Plotinus** *Enn.* VI.8). The Neoplatonists were acutely aware of the tension between divine omnipotence and divine beneficence in a world where bad things happen (**Proclus** *Elem. Theol.* Prop. 122).

PROODOS. Procession. A **Neoplatonic** solution to the dialectic of **unity** and multiplicity going back to the **Eleatics** and **Plato**'s *Parmenides*: pluralities "proceed" from unities. **Proclus** bases his argument on an analogy between mathematical and ontological reasoning, in the *Elements of Theology*.

PROOF. *See APODEIXIS.*

PROPERTY. *See IDION.*

PROPORTION. *See ANALOGIA; LOGOS.*

PROS TI. Relation, one of **Aristotle**'s 10 categories (*katēgoriai*). Ancient thinkers returned repeatedly to the problem of understanding relational predicates. The **Sophists** loved to play tricks with relational predicates: in **Plato**'s *Euthydemus*, Dionysodorus asks Ctesippus if he has a dog, and if the dog had fathered puppies, and from two affirmative answers, Dionysodorus argues that the dog is Ctesippus' father, and that the puppies are his brothers (298d-e). Somewhat more seriously, in Plato's *Parmenides*, if equal things are equal in virtue of a share of equality itself, those shares must be less than equal, and if small things are small in virtue of a share of smallness itself, those shares must be smaller than smallness itself, and how could that be? How could anything be smaller than smallness itself? (*Parm.* 130d-3). Plato returns to relational issues very frequently—see, for example, *Theaetetus* 154b, and many other places.

In *Cat.* 7, **Aristotle** argues that relative terms imply a reciprocal relationship: "slave" and "master" are obviously reciprocal relative terms. In the context, Aristotle does some fancy footwork to support the thesis for terms like "wing" and "rudder." In **Metaphysics** V. 15, Aristotle distinguishes relative terms that are quantitative in character from those that are causative—that is, the relationship is a causal relationship; a third sort of relation is epistemological—the knower and the known, the hearer and the heard.

In their reduction of the categories to four, the **Stoics** highlight *pros ti* (*pōs echein pros ti*). The Pyrrhonian Skeptics found in relative predication ground for suspending judgment—if everything is relative, then nothing is reliable. *See also SKEPTIKOS.*

PROSĒGORIA. "Appelative." According to **Diogenes Laertius**, **Diogenes of Babylon** distinguished "name" (*onoma*) from *prosēgoria*, wanting to limit *onoma* to what we call in English "proper names," and applying *prosēgoria* to the other things called *onomata* in Greek, specifically common nouns and adjectives.

PROSLĒPSIS. Additional premise, in **Stoic** logic (DL 7.76). The Stoics tended to construe arguments as initially hypothetical ("If it is night, it is dark"); the "additional premise" here might be the assertion "It is night," which conjoined with the hypothetical yields, "It is dark." This term is sometimes translated "minor premise," but since the Stoic premises work differently than **Aristotelian** premises, a different translation seems appropriate. The easiest (possibly *too* easy) way to characterize the difference is to say that Aristotelian logic is a kind of predicate calculus, while Stoic logic is a kind of propositional calculus. *See also LOGIKĒ.*

PROTAGORAS OF ABDERA (c. 490–420). A **Sophist**, he lived and taught in **Athens** for many years, closely associated with Pericles and his family. Most of what we know about Protagoras we learn from the many representations and references to him in **Plato**'s dialogues, and the probably derivative references in **Aristotle**. The two most famous fragments of his writings are: "Human beings are the measure of all things: of the things that are, that they are, and of the things that are not, that they are not"; "Concerning the Gods I do not know whether they exist, nor if they exist what they are like, for the question is too difficult, and life is too short." The second may seem to us simply evasive, but in the context of the **Athens** that condemned Socrates for impiety, it must have seemed rather shocking. The first is the famous "homo mensura" doctrine, interpreted by Plato in the *Theaetetus* as holding that knowledge (***epistēmē***) and **being** are relative to each individual observer, but it is much more likely that the historical Protagoras believed that knowledge and reality are relative to various social groups, to communities of language-users. The *Protagoras* presents a vivid portrait of this leading Sophist.

PRŌTĒ PHILOSOPHIA. First Philosophy, one of **Aristotle**'s ways of referring to that study that we call "**Metaphysics**," *Metaph.* VI.1, 1026a16. It is "first" not by order of study, but because it examines the most fundamental realities.

PRŌTON KINOUN. First mover. **Aristotle**, *Phys.* VIII.5, 265aff: cause of all motion in the universe. One tends to assume that Aristotle is referring to an entity approximately equivalent to the Judeo-Christian (and Muslim) **God**, and that is surely how that tradition has understood *Physics* VIII and *Metaphysics* XII, where the "first mover" or "unmoved mover" (***akinēton kinoun***) is discussed most extensively. Still, especially in *Physics* VIII, the "first mover" appears more as a theoretical entity of **science** than as a potential object of worship.

PROVIDENCE. *See PRONOIA.*

PRUDENCE. *See PHRONESIS.*

(PSEUDO-) DIONYSIUS THE AREOPAGITE. *See* DIONYSIUS THE AREOPAGITE.

PSEUDOS. False. Considering **Aristotle**'s analysis at *Metaphysics* V.29, falsity is non-correspondence between a verbal formula and a state of affairs. In some cases one attributes the falsity to the object—a drawing that does not resemble, or a dream (*oneiros*)—and in some cases to the verbal formula, false of this object (though it might be true of another). A false *person* is one who is apt to try to get people to believe things that are not true.

PSYCHĒ. Soul. From the beginning of Greek literature, *psychē* signifies life or the principle of life. To what extent is it a principle of life that can in some sense be separated from the body? **Homer** speaks of souls of the dead as we would speak of "ghosts" in several places; thus there is a literary tradition of souls that are in a way "undying." At the end of the sixth century BCE several related things happened that changed the Greek view of *psychē* permanently. First, there was a growth of "mystery" religions that promised some form of life after death; the Orphic movement may be seen in this light. Second, **Pythagoras** seems to have introduced the idea of the transmigration of souls from some non-Greek source into the Greek world. There may have been some connection between Pythagoras and the Orphic movement—it is difficult to be sure from the evidence we have. Third, there was an increasing identification of the human personality with the "mind" and, at the same time, an identification of **God** as Mind (*nous*). Fourth, the universe, or parts of the universe, came to be thought of as alive, and thus endowed with a principle of life, a *psychē*. **Heraclitus**: "You will not find the limits of soul, no matter how far you go, so profound is its *logos*" (f. 45).

For some of the materialists among the **Presocratics**, it seemed obvious that soul would have to be some sort of material: perhaps **fire** for Heraclitus, **air** for **Anaximenes** and **Diogenes of Apollonia**, some special spherical atoms (*atoma*) for **Leucippus** and **Democritus**. Other Presocratics seemed to think soul distinct from spatial **matter**: **Anaxagoras**, in addition to the Pythagoreans and those influenced by the Pythagoreans, would be an example. Perhaps **Xenophanes**, too, would have to be committed to an immaterial "mind" (*nous*).

Plato seems to accept and to develop the Pythagorean theory of the soul: Pythagoras thought that he could remember his previous lives; Plato thought that one might also recollect experiences from the time *between* incarnate lives, that those recollections could be foundational for accurate knowledge. Plato depicts the human soul as having three different parts, or functions: the mind, the spirit, and the appetite. When in the body, those three parts are lodged in the head, heart, and organs below the diaphragm. But all three are represented in the image of the two-horse chariot in the *Phaedrus*, with the charioteer as mind, and the two horses as spirit and appetite.

In **Aristotle**'s treatise *On the Soul*, he represents earlier theories as beginning from two obvious phenomena ascribed to the soul: the capacity of living things to initiate movement; human consciousness. If one focuses on movement, it might be tempting to think of the soul as a particularly active material, such as fire or *pneuma*; that does not, however, help to understand the phenomenon of consciousness. We might see water by the water in us, but to see love and hate, we must have those in our composition as well.

Thus Aristotle argues that the soul is not some element of the body, not even an immaterial element (like a Platonic "self-moving number"), but is rather a consequence of the way the body is put together, a result of the form of the body. So he defines *psychē* as "the first level of **actuality** of a natural organic body." It is the "first" level because the soul is the capacity to do something, not necessarily the actual doing, and the body must be "organic" because it is the organs that have these capacities to do the various functions of living. The functions of the soul include, at the most basic, the capacity for nutrition and reproduction: those functions are shared by plants. Animals have, in addition, the ability to sense and react to their environment, and generally to move from place to place in pursuit of food or to avoid being eaten. Human beings are the only animals that possess the capacity to communicate, or at any rate have that capacity in the highest degree, and are the only ones to live in a *polis* and to engage in theoretical thought.

If we ask whether the Aristotelian *psychē* is separable from body, we get an ambiguous answer: there is just one capacity of the soul that must be thought of as logically (but not spatially) separable from the body, and that is the active power of the mind. The active power of the mind in a sense "supervenes" on the body; how that is possible in Aristotle's philosophy is rather mysterious, and puzzled even his closest disciple, **Theophrastus**.

Among post-Aristotelian philosophies, both the **Epicureans** and **Stoics** are resolutely materialist about *psychē*. However, there is an important difference in their materialism. Epicureans believe the soul to be composed of atoms that at death dissipate or disassociate and no longer have any of the functions they had when incorporated in a complex body. Stoics, however, believe the soul to be the effect of the presence of *pneuma*, particularly a special *pneuma* that constitutes the "governing faculty" of the body, and that *pneuma* is really ultimately a part of God.

Platonists in all periods held that the soul is a different kind of entity, separable from body and immortal. As Plato indicates in the *Timaeus*, human souls are formed from the leftovers of the soul of the universe, and thus are destined eventually to rejoin the **World Soul**.

PTOLEMY, CLAUDIUS (c. 90–c. 168 CE). Claudius Ptolemy was the author of several important scientific works: "The Great Treatise" (known by the Greco-Arabic name, *Almagest*), laying out the astronomical system we still call "Ptolemaic"; the *Geography*, presenting what was known about the physical world in his day; and the *Tetrabiblos* (four books), a work on **astrology**. He also wrote on music theory and optics. *See also* ASTRONOMY.

PTŌSIS. "Case." **Aristotle** notices (*Int*. 16a32) the differences in ontological commitment between nominative, genitive, dative, and accusative, the "cases" of Greek nouns, adjectives, and pronouns. The **Stoics** use the term *ptōsis* of inflected words, and include this concept under the idea of *lekta*, or "sayables."

PURIFICATION. *See KATHARSIS.*

PURPOSE. *See TELOS.*

PYR. Fire. **Heraclitus** f. 30: "This order, which is the same for all, none of Gods or men has made; but it was ever, is now and ever shall be an everliving Fire, fixed measures of it kindling and fixed measures going out." In **Plato**'s *Timaeus*, fire is the tetrahedron, the minimal regular solid. For **Aristotle**, fire is the natural element (*stoicheion*) with the natural place above the air (*aēr*). The **Stoics** describe **God** as *pyr technikon*, fire with the capacity of crafting things. When God has assimilated everything to himself, there is a universal conflagration (*ekpyrosis*), and everything starts over.

PYRRHO OF ELIS (c. 360–270 BCE). Founder of the Skeptical (*see SKEPTIKOS*) line of philosophy. Pyrrho was trained as a painter, and studied philosophy with the **Megarians** and **Democritus**; he traveled to **India** with **Alexander of Macedon**, where he met Hindu philosophers, called *gymnosophistai* by the Greeks. On his return to Greece, he acquired several disciples, notably **Timon of Phlius**. As reported by Timon, Pyrrho recommended not putting any trust in either perception (*aisthēsis*) or opinion (*doxa*); if one successfully avoids such commitments, the first result is aphasia, or speechlessness, then *ataraxia*, or freedom from disturbance, then happiness. **Sextus Empiricus** (second to third centuries CE), who gives Pyrrho a lot of credit for the development of skepticism in his *Outlines of Pyrrhonism*, nevertheless expresses some hesitation about the actual extent of Pyrrho's contribution to skepticism as he knew it 500 years later.

PYTHAGORAS OF SAMOS (c. 570–490 BCE). Pythagoras wrote nothing, but was well-known to his contemporaries and to the later Greek world as the person credited with bringing the idea of **metempsychosis** (transmigration of the soul) to Greece. It is clear that he established a community in Croton, in southern Italy, around 530 BCE, and fled with his followers to Metapontum in about 510, where he died in about 490. The evidence that Pythagoras traveled to **Egypt** as a young man is fairly strong; **Herodotus** strongly supports that idea, and **Isocrates**, in the early fourth century (*Busiris* 28), also indicates the Pythagoras brought religious ideas from Egypt to Greece. Later Greek authors claimed that he also went to Persia before returning to Samos and proceeding to Italy.

It is not clear how much of the mathematical knowledge and lore attributed to Pythagoras really stems from his teaching; his disciples tended to attribute to him their own discoveries. **Plato**'s *Timaeus* is the most complete and nuanced presentation of Pythagorean mathematics (*mathēmatikē*) from a time not too distant from that of Pythagoras himself, but it is in essence attributed to Timaeus himself, and not to Pythagoras. Similarly **Aristotle** generally speaks of the "people who call themselves **Pythagoreans**" as the source of the mathematical lore.

PYTHAGOREAN SCHOOL; PYTHAGOREANS. People who call themselves, or are called by others, "Pythagoreans" fall into two separate periods: the first are the immediate disciples of **Pythagoras**, and their successors in the first 200 years or so after his death; the second group appeared about 500 years after the death of Pythagoras and continued for at least 500 years. The second group are also known as **Neopythagoreans**; see that entry for them.

Pythagoras seems to have had two kinds of immediate followers, or to put that another way, his immediate followers had two distinct sorts of interest in his teaching. One group or sort of interest focused on the religious aspects, the promise of a better future life after this present life. This group is called by **Iamblichus**, who wrote an account of Pythagoras and his school, the *akousmatikoi*, or "enthusiastic audience." The other group or sort of interest seems to have focused on the scientific and mathematical aspects of his teaching, the *mathēmatikoi*, or "advanced students," as Iamblichus has it.

The teachings that are gathered under the title of *akousmata* tend to be a bit mysterious, with possibly moral or religious implications. We have more information about the "advanced" teaching, because **Aristotle** refers fairly frequently to Pythagorean scientific teachings.

According to the Pythagoreans, the world is fundamentally mathematical in character: geometrical principles describe the most real things about the world. Musical intervals are understood as whole-number ratios; **matter** ultimately divides into geometrically regular solids.

Of the more famous **Presocratics** who were influenced fairly directly by the teaching of Pythagoras and his school we may mention **Parmenides** (taught by Ameinias the Pythagorean); **Empedocles**, who refers to Pythagoras in a complimentary way; and **Alcmaeon**.

Diels-Kranz lists as "Older Pythagoreans" the following: Kerkops, Petron, Brontinos, Hippasos, Kallipon, Demokedes, and Parmeniskos. The next generations were led by **Philolaus of Croton** (c. 470–385) and his student Eurytos, and then **Archytas** (d.c. 350), of whom we know quite a lot, comparatively speaking. **Iamblichus** (*Vit. Pyth.* 267) lists dozens of early Pythagoreans, by their home *polis*. Included in Iamblichus' list are 16 women whom he counts as Pythagorean philosophers. Diels-Kranz name several who do not appear on Iamblichus' list, but are noted by other sources. It is clear that Pythagoreanism was in a position to have a pervasive influence during the fifth and fourth centuries BCE; at the very least this widespread movement accounts for the rapid acceptance of the word *philosophia* to describe the preoccupations typical of Pythagorean *mathēmatikoi*.

– Q –

QUALITY, QUALITATIVE CHANGE. *See ALLOIŌSIS; POION; POIOTĒS.*

QUANTITY. *See POSON.*

QUINTESSENCE. *See AITHĒR. Aithēr* is the "fifth" element (*stoicheion*), counting up from **earth**, **water**, **air**, and **fire**.

– R –

RATIO. *See LOGOS.*

REASON. *See LOGISTIKON; LOGOS; NOUS.*

RECEPTACLE. *See HYPODOCHĒ.*

RECOLLECTION. *See ANAMNĒSIS.*

REFUTATION. *See ELENCHUS.*

REINCARNATION. *See METEMPSYCHOSIS.*

RELATION. *See PROS TI.*

RELIGION. *See* GOD; *HOSIOTĒS; THEOS.*

RESPONSIBILITY. *See AITION.*

RHĒTORIKĒ. Rhetoric, the art of the *rhētōr*, or public speaker. In the latter part of the *Phaedrus*, there is a very interesting summary of the "Art of Rhetoric" as it was taught at the end of the fifth century BCE. **Socrates** mentions as teachers of Rhetoric, **Gorgias of Leontini** and his student Polus, **Thrasymachus**, **Theodorus** of Byzantium, Evenus of Paros, Tisias of Syracuse, **Prodicus** of Ceos, **Hippias** of Elis, Licymnius of Chios, **Protagoras**, and (prospectively) **Isocrates**. Some but not all of these people are counted as **Sophists**

as well. Protagoras and Hippias, for example, were quite proud of being Sophists, which meant for them that they were teaching *more* than just the skill of public speaking. As represented by **Plato**, Gorgias presented himself as a teacher of rhetoric as distinguished from a sophist in that he claimed to be teaching a skill and no particular content. Thus, the *Gorgias* might be understood as, in the first instance at least, a critique of content-free skill instruction. Similarly the latter part of the *Phaedrus* argues that a truly successful rhetoric would require knowledge of the subject, understanding of the beliefs of the audience and of psychology, and an understanding of what one was attempting to accomplish.

Aristotle wrote an extant book on *Rhetoric* that describes the art as that of persuasive speech, especially in political and juridical contexts. (There is also a work included in the **Corpus** called *Rhetoric to Alexander* that scholars tend now to attribute to a contemporary of Aristotle named Anaximenes.)

For some of the **Stoics**, the study of language divided into *rhētorikē* and *dialektikē*; since dialectic is essential for the discovery of truth (*alētheia*), it is the more important of the two divisions for the philosopher, but the Stoics did not totally ignore rhetoric.

Cicero, in *On the Orator*, makes philosophy the servant of *Rhetoric*, a view held even more strongly by Quintillian in the *Institutio Oratoria*. For Quintillian, the orator needs to know philosophy essentially for self-defense against those who might pose philosophical objections to positions defended by the orator.

RHOĒ. Flow, stream, flux. **Heraclitus** f. 12: "You cannot step twice into the same rivers; for fresh **waters** are flowing (*epirrei*) in upon you." According to **Aristotle, Plato** was persuaded by his teacher **Cratylus**, an enthusiast of Heraclitus, that the sensible world was always in radical change or flux. We see evidence of that especially in the *Cratylus* where many of the etymologies are based on *rhoē* and its relatives (e.g., 420a9, where *erōs* flows in through the eyes). In the *Theaetetus*, universal flux is a fundamental part of the argument (cf. e.g., 182d). In general, "flux" is part of the problematic of "**becoming**" or *genesis*.

RULE. *See ARCHĒ.*

– S –

SAGES. Before there was philosophy, there was "wisdom literature." In Greece, lists were made of the Wise Men (*sophoi*); some of the lists have seven members (so we hear of "Seven Sages"), but if we put the lists together, we get about 17. Some that are also counted as "philosophers" at one time or another include: **Thales**, **Solon**, and **Pherecydes**. **Diogenes Laertius** associates the names of the "sages" with various sayings, like "Nothing too much," "Know yourself," and so on. Later, in **Stoic** philosophy, the ideal or perfect human being is called the *Sophos*, or Sage. We would be hard put to find even one of those, let alone seven.

SCHĒMA. Form, shape, appearance. Used of the characteristic properties of something; for the **atomists**, the differences in shape of atoms were called *schēmata*. **Aristotle** uses the word for the different forms of **syllogism**; the word is also used for various grammatical constructions.

SCHESIS. State, condition, a temporary state of affairs in contrast to *hexis*, which tends to be permanent. **Stobaeus** notes that the **Stoics** distinguish between goods that are in *kinēsis*, and those that are in *schesis*. The latter appear to be more static. True virtues, according to the same passage, are *scheseis* that are in *tonos*, which appears to be another way of saying that they are *hexeis*.

SCHOLARCH. From the time of **Plato**'s founding of the **Academy**, the various ancient philosophical schools regularly had one person "in charge" of the school, and later histories, like that of **Diogenes Laertius**, tended to record the successions of these "Scholarchs." Elsewhere in this Dictionary, if a person is known to have held that position, it is noted in the entry.

SCIENCE. The word "science" derives from the Latin word *scientia*, meaning "knowledge"; *scientia* is the standard Latin translation of the Greek word *epistēmē*. In its most common usage, the English word "science" refers to a practice that to a large extent can be traced back to the early Greek philosophers. To be sure, much that those people did was anticipated in some way or other by earlier **Egyptians**, Babylonians, and others, but there is a combination of factors that seems particularly Hellenic.

- Early Greek philosophy focused on **matter**, hypothesizing that all phenomena are actualizations of potentialities present in the material substratum of the world.
- Early Greek philosophy developed a concept of nature, or *physis*, those material potentialities were understood as leading to or including processes of growth and development, with further consequences that could be studied empirically.
- The **Hippocratic** medical tradition took over from the Egyptians and further developed a habit of detailed investigation of (medically important) phenomena and keeping objective records of the observations. (*See IATROS.*)
- **Thales**, **Anaximander**, and **Pythagoras** introduced or at least strongly encouraged the idea that the world can best be understood in terms of mathematics (*mathēmatikē*), that explanations of natural phenomena are far more persuasive if they are expressed in terms of proportionality, geometry, or mathematical formulae.
- **Plato** developed the **Pythagorean** mathematical theory further by proposing the possibility of an intellectual discovery of the principles upon which all phenomena, of whatever sort, could be (must be) understood.
- **Aristotle** attempted to formulate an explanatory system, based on empirical observation, that would unify in a metaphysically and epistemologically satisfying way all existing knowledge in an interconnected and coherent manner.
- By the establishment of the **Academy** and **Lyceum**, Plato and Aristotle founded at least the ideal of cooperative investigation and formulation of explanatory systems, demonstrated in the early years of operation by the **Peripatetic** collection of writings known as the *Problemata*, and the establishment of the **Museum** of **Alexandria**, intended both to imitate and outdo the Athenian schools.

While it is easy to complain of ancient science that it did not advance further than it did, despite a number of advantages, it is worth noticing that in mathematics, **astronomy**, and medicine (*iatrikē*), for three, significant progress continued to occur in the Hellenistic and Roman periods. Certainly, the founders of modern science—people like Galileo Galilei, Nicolaus Copernicus, and William Harvey—were inspired by their studies of ancient science and were very conscious of building upon those foundations. *See also EPISTĒMĒ; HISTORIA.*

SELF-CONTROL. *See SŌPHROSYNĒ.*

SELF-EVIDENT. *See ENARGEIA*, an **Epicurean** term.

SELF-MOVING. *See AUTOKINĒTON.*

SELF-SUFFICIENCY. *See AUTARKEIA.*

SĒMAINEIN. To show by a sign, indicate; to mean something. In *Metaphysics* IV, **Aristotle** argues that those who deny the Law of Non-contradiction in a sense refute themselves as soon as they say something, and mean it, *sēmainei ti.* The **Stoics** too are very interested in sorting out the semantics of *lekta.*

SĒMEION. Sign, token, indication. **Aristotle** uses this word to pick out probable, not conclusive, arguments, in contrast to *tekmērion*, where he takes the conclusion as certain. For the **Stoics** and **Epicureans**, a *sēmeion* is a perceptible "sign" of something that is not observable or at least not currently observed. In many contexts *sēmeion* could well be translated "evidence" as that word is used in modern epistemology.

SENECA, LUCIUS ANNAEUS (c. 4 BCE–65 CE). Seneca was a **Stoic** philosopher, statesman, playwright, and tutor and advisor to the Emperor Nero. Seneca adapted the ethical and political thought of earlier Stoic thinkers to Roman Imperial circumstances. His *On Clemency*, addressed to Nero at the beginning of his reign, advised avoiding abuse of Imperial power; eventually Nero completely ignored that advice. His essays *On Anger* and *On Benefits* are interesting applications of Stoic concepts; *On the Happy Life* is a somewhat self-serving treatise arguing that it is all right for a philosopher to be wealthy. Several of his essays are "Consolations": to Marcia, to his mother, to Polybius. His essays *On the Shortness of Life* and *On Tranquility of Mind* are in the same direction.

The *Letters to Lucilius* are a rather popular collection, full of advice on a wide range of subjects. The *Natural Inquiries* deals primarily with **astronomy** and meteorology without much advancing the study.

There are also eight or more extant plays and a piece of comic writing called the *Apocolocyntosis Divi Claudii*, or the *Pumpkinification of the Divine Claudius*.

SENSATION. *See AISTHĒSIS.*

SENSORY RECOGNITION. *See EPAISTHĒSIS.*

SEPARATE. *See CHŌRISTON.*

SERIOUS. *See SPOUDAIOS.*

SEVENTH LETTER. Included in the collection of **Plato**'s writings are 13 letters ascribed to Plato. Most of these letters are clearly forgeries, but one or two might be genuine, or at least forged by someone with extremely good inside information about the events discussed. Perhaps the most important of those is the "seventh letter," a document with very detailed information about Plato's relationships with the Syracusan royal family and some significant pointers about how to read the dialogues.

SEXTUS EMPIRICUS (2nd to 3rd centuries CE). The writings of Sextus Empiricus are a major source of our understanding of philosophical skepticism during the Roman Imperial period. Indeed, his critiques of other philosophical positions are among our best sources for those philosophies as well. His extant works include *Outlines of Pyrrhonism*, *Against the Logicians*, *Against the Physicists*, *Against the Ethicists*, and *Against the Professors*; the latter four titles are sometimes taken together as one work, *Against the Mathematicians*. His entire opus is, in any case, directed at refuting all forms of dogmaticism and attaining a life of ***ataraxia***, or freedom from disturbance. We learn from his extant writings that he was, in addition, a practicing physician of the Empiricist school (thus the appellation "Empiricus"). *See also SKEPTIKOS.*

SHAPE. *See SCHĒMA.*

SIGN. *See SĒMEION.*

SIMILAR. *See HOMOIOS.*

SIMPLICIUS (c. 490–560 CE). Simplicius was from Cilicia, in what is now Turkey. He studied with **Ammonius** (d. after 538) in **Alexandria** and with **Damascius** in **Athens**. When Justinian closed the School of Athens in 529, Simplicius and others took refuge in Persia; a peace treaty between Justinian and the Persian king Chosroes allowed Simplicius to return to the Byzantine Empire. According to some scholars, he chose to live in Harran (in southeast Turkey, near the Syrian border) where he proceeded to write his commentaries. There are extant commentaries on **Epictetus'** *Encheiridion*, and **Aristotle's** *Cat.*, *Cael.*, *de An.*, and *Phys.* Others of his works are lost. Simplicius' commentaries are often a valuable source for information about the entire history of Greek philosophy since he generously quotes large chunks of material not available elsewhere. He is, for example, responsible for the preservation of most of the poem of **Parmenides**.

SKEPTIC, SKEPTICISM. *See SKEPTIKOS.*

SKEPTIKOS. Skeptic. Derived from the verb *skeptesthai*, "to consider carefully," the *skeptikos* is a person who reflects so thoroughly that he does not come to any conclusions. **Pyrrho of Elis** (c. 360–270 BCE) gets credit for establishing the skeptical manner of doing philosophy, although one might argue that a good many of his predecessors, not least **Socrates**, often seemed quite "skeptical" in the sense that we generally understand the term.

Plato's **Academy** became a center for skepticism beginning with the **Scholarch Arcesilaus** (c. 316–c. 241 BCE) and his successors, notably **Carneades** (214/213–129/128 BCE). It is not that difficult to conclude, from a reading of Plato's dialogues, that one should not make claims to knowledge (*epistēmē*); after all, many of the dialogues are purely aporetic, and Plato's Socrates repeatedly reduces those who do claim some form of knowledge to speechlessness. Arcesilaus, Carneades, and the others wielded the **dialectical** skills learned from close study of Socrates' techniques against the pretenses to knowledge emanating from the **Stoic** school.

Academic Skeptics typically argued on both sides of every issue, with the goal of demonstrating that one would be best off to suspend belief rather than commit to one side of the debate or the other.

Aenesidemus, a student of **Philo of Larissa**, broke with the Academy in the first century CE and established his own skeptical school in **Alexandria**, claiming Pyrrho of Elis as his spiritual inspiration. He formulated the Ten Modes of Skepticism, preserved by Sextus Empiricus and others:

- Why should we suppose that our way of perceiving the world is more accurate than the way other species of animals perceive the world? Think: dogs and rotten fish.
- Even people do not agree with each other: different philosophies make radically incompatible assertions.
- In fact you do not really agree with yourself—something that looks delicious can taste awful.
- Your emotional and physical state radically affects how you perceive things.
- How you are related to the object perceived (spatially etc.) makes a big difference in how it looks or sounds.
- Everything is experienced via a medium that has unknown influences on the result.
- Proportion makes a big difference in how you perceive things— a little hot sauce is delicious; a lot makes the food inedible.
- We always perceive things in relation to something else.
- How we perceive things often depends on our previous experience with things that we take as similar.
- People evaluate the same things in radically different ways: some think that gay marriage is normal, others that it is an abomination.

SKOPOS. Target. The **Stoics** use this word to refer to the goal or end of human life; i.e., *eudaimonia* or living in accordance with nature may be said to be the "target" of human life. **Panaetius** says that people achieve their "target" in different ways, just as there are different parts of the target aimed at by the archer.

SOCRATES OF ATHENS (469–399 BCE). His father was Sophroniscus, a sculptor, and his mother was Phaenarete, a midwife. He was married to Xanthippe and had three sons. Socrates fought as a hoplite at Potidaea (432–29), Delion (424), and Amphipolis (422), served as president of the Assembly, and presided at the trial of the generals defeated at Arginusae in 406. In 404–3, he refused the order of the oligarchy to participate in a posse arresting Leon of Salamis. On the restoration of the democracy in 399, he was accused of "corrupting the young" and of "impiety" by Meletus, Anytus, and Lycon, and was convicted and executed as outlined by **Plato** in the series of dialogues *Euthyphro, Apology, Crito,* and *Phaedo.* **Xenophon**'s *Apology* also recounts, in its fashion, the trial and death of Socrates.

Socrates appears as protagonist in most of Plato's dialogues and in Xenophon's *Memorabilia* and *Symposium.* It is rather difficult to disentangle a picture of the historical Socrates from those representations. A kind of evidence that might help is the fact that a character named "Socrates" appears in several comic plays, notably **Aristophanes**' *Clouds, Frogs,* and *Birds.* If one starts from the assumption that Aristophanes is depicting Socrates in his forties and Plato and Xenophon are depicting Socrates in his sixties, more or less, one might triangulate to arrive at one's own impression of the philosopher. Among **Aristotle**'s various comments on Socrates, two stand out for their usefulness in locating his historical importance: "In the time of Socrates, progress was made in defining the essence and entity, but investigation into nature went out of fashion, and philosophers turned to useful virtues and politics" (*PA* 642a29). "Socrates, disregarding the physical universe and confining his study to moral questions, sought here for the universal and was the first to concentrate upon definition; Plato followed him and assumed that the problem of definition is concerned not with any sensible thing but with entities of another kind" (***Metaphysics*** I.6, 987b1).

Some characteristics of Socrates that seem to have a reality beyond the fictions include:

- The *daimōnion*: Socrates claimed to have his own special **angel** that occasionally warned him not to do something or other. More than what we would call a "conscience," the *daimōnion* may have been what psychiatrists today would call an auditory hallucination.
- In the *Apology* he claims that the Delphic Oracle had responded to a question posed by Chaerephon that Socrates was the wisest man in Greece. Since he did not believe that he had any particular wisdom, he took it that the wisdom to which the Oracle referred was

that consciousness of ignorance. In the *Apology*, he says that that was the inspiration of his quizzing various people in **Athens**, demonstrating that they did not know what they thought they knew.

- In any case, Socrates is often depicted persuading his interlocutors to state their most fundamental beliefs and then demonstrating that those beliefs are incoherent or inconsistent with each other. Very frequently, the challenge that proves insurmountable is a demand that one define one's terms.

- Occasionally Socrates does claim to know something (after all); notably about Love (*erōs*). He does offer definitions of Love, both in the *Symposium* (a definition he says he got from **Diotima**) and in the *Phaedrus*.

- When he finds a sympathetic and cooperative interlocutor, he sometimes gets a fair number of accepted ideas from them; this process is called, in the *Theaetetus,* "midwifery," as if he were helping his interlocutors give birth to ideas just as his mother had helped women give birth to babies.

- The allegiance of Socrates to the Delphic Apollo extends to his enthusiastic acceptance of the motto of that deity, "Know Thyself" (*gnōthe seauton*). Socrates clearly aimed at helping people know themselves, first and foremost.

- Some supposedly paradoxical moral positions are attributed to Socrates on the basis of the dialogues: "Virtue (*aretē*) is Knowledge, Vice is Ignorance, Wrongdoing is (therefore) Involuntary."

- **Cicero** says of his work: *philosophia de caelo devocata*, philosophy was called down out of heaven.

SOCRATICS. This word is used of people known to have associated with **Socrates**, especially those who founded philosophical schools or wrote works influenced by the teaching of Socrates. Examples of followers of Socrates include **Plato, Xenophon, Antisthenes, Aristippus of Cyrene, Critias**, Cleombrotus, **Euclides of Megara**, Aeschines, **Phaedo**, Callias, **Hermogenes**, Critoboulos, Apollodorus, Epigenes, Menexenus, Crito, Chairephon, Charmides, Alcibiades, Simmias, Cebes, Phaedondes, Terpsion of Megara, Glaucon, and Nicias. To some extent, it is possible to reconstruct the thought of the historical Socrates, as distinguished from the Socrates of Plato's dialogues, by looking at the teachings of his other successors. When one does that, one is tempted to agree with Søren Kierkegaard (*Concept of Irony*), that Socrates was fortunate in having been misunderstood in so many different ways.

SOLON OF ATHENS (c. 635–558 BCE). Poet and political reformer. Solon replaced the Athenian law code attributed to Drako with a system that provided for a mix of democratic and oligarchic elements and reformed the economic system. Having provided the law code, Solon left in voluntary exile for some 10 years, during which time Peisistratus gained political ascendancy in **Athens**, while respecting, for the most part, the Solonic provisions. Solon figures in **Plato**'s *Timaeus* as the person who learned from the **Egyptian** priests the story of the destruction of Atlantis.

SOLUTION. *See LYSIS.*

SŌMA. Body. For the **Presocratics**, *sōma* is, for one thing, that which occupies **space**; typically also, the elements (***stoicheia***: **earth**, **air**, **fire**, **water**) or the atoms (***atoma***) of **Leucippus** and **Democritus** are thought of as *sōmata*.

For human beings one finds an analysis into body and soul, *sōma* and *psychē*. In the *Cratylus* (400b–c), **Socrates** suggests that some people thought that the *sōma* is the *sēma* of the soul, an ambiguous word that can mean either "tomb" or "sign." He goes on to attribute to the **Orphics** a derivation of *sōma* from the verb *sōzetai,* kept or saved, in that the soul is "kept" in the body until "the penalty is paid."

In the *Timaeus*, Plato derives the classical elemental "bodies" from triangles formed into regular solids (53ff). In general, however, he is more interested in human bodies, and their relationship to souls. In the *Phaedo*, for example, **Socrates**, about to die, assures his friends and associates that he will be well rid of his body, that the body is a kind of prison that distracts the mind. In the latter part of the *Timaeus*, for example, a more complex relationship of soul and body is presented, arguing that many "mental" illnesses can be attributed to bodily conditions (86bff).

In the *Sophist*, at 246ff, the **Eleatic** Stranger discusses with Theaetetus the history of theories about body in a passage called the Battle of the Gods and Giants: the Giants are those who believe that only bodily things are real, while the Gods believe in incorporeal forms and souls.

Aristotle has a great deal to say about all the senses of *sōma*, from the mathematical sense (three-dimensional object, *Metaph.* V.13), to the basic physical sense (you cannot have two bodies in the same place at the same time, *GC* I.8, 321a8), to the body of astronomical entities (*Cael.* I.3) and the four terrestrial elements, to the bodies of living animals. One might well say that Aristotle's philosophy is focused on bodily existence, not reductively, but in all aspects of the capacities of bodily entities to function in their environments. *See also ASŌMATON.*

SOPHISTĒS, SOPHISTAI; SOPHISTIKĒ TECHNE. Sophist, Sophists; the sophistic art: sophistry. A Sophist is a person who claims to teach *sophia* (*see SOPHOS*). Theoretically that would mean any instruction in any advanced skill, and some Sophists claimed to teach a significant range of different sorts of things—**Hippias of Elis**, for example, appeared at the Olympic Games decked out in resplendent clothing and jewelry of his own manufacture, and **Euthydemus** and Dionysodorus in the *Euthydemus* claim to teach fighting in armor. But in general, Sophists were teachers of verbal argumentation. Since they were teaching their students to defend their own positions (whatever they might be), they often did not try to support positive theses of their own.

We are acquainted with the older sophists primarily through **Plato**'s dialogues; **Socrates** is represented demonstrating defects in sophistic stands repeatedly. In the *Protagoras*, Socrates demonstrates to the young Hippocrates that Protagoras actually knows little about virtue (*aretē*), so it is pointless to study with him—although we know that Protagoras had many apparently satisfied customers. Although his fees were high, Protagoras told his students that if they were willing to go into a temple and swear that they had not learned anything from him, they would not have to pay him.

In the *Theaetetus*, Socrates examines and refutes the relativism implied by Protagoras' famous statement, "Human beings are the measure of all things: of the things that are, that they are, and of the things that are not, that they are not."

Socrates reveals the moral relativism consequent on the teaching of **Gorgias**, in the *Gorgias*; demonstrating the inherent contradictions in the positions of **Thrasymachus** gets the argument of the **Republic** going. Ultimately, if we judge the art of the sophists by what we read in Plato's dialogues, we might reach the conclusion that the sophists are hapless purveyors of invalid arguments. Still, many have been inspired to take the part of the sophists against Socrates. Plato himself, as an honest dramatist, is often more sympathetic to the sophists than one might suppose at first glance. Indeed, in his dialogue the *Sophist* there is a description of a person called "the sophist of noble lineage" that seems very like the Socrates of the **eristic** dialogues. Still, the conclusion of this dialogue is that the Sophist deals in appearance, rather than reality.

Aristotle follows this line of interpretation, for example in *Metaphysics* IV.2, where he says: "Dialectic is merely critical where philosophy claims to know, and sophistic is what appears to be philosophy but is not" (1004b25). His book, *Sophistical Refutations*, part of the *Organon* (or *Logical Works*), examines arguments that appear to be valid but are not. An example of one sort of argument he has in mind as "sophistical" is this: "If x belongs to y, then x is the property of y; human beings belong to the animal kingdom; therefore human beings are the property of the animal kingdom" (cf. *SE* 17, 176b).

Despite their bad press from Plato and Aristotle, the sophists remained in business as distinguished teachers of rhetoric (*rhetorikē*) and argumentation more or less throughout antiquity and into the Byzantine period. A period known as the Second Sophistic, stretching from the reign of Nero until the middle of the third century, included a number of illustrious literary people, including **Philostratus** and **Herodes Atticus**, for example. A valuable source for information about sophists (and others) in late antiquity is **Eunapius**, *Lives of the Sophists*. One might well argue that the sophistic art remains a large part of post-secondary education even today.

SOPHOS, SOPHOI, SOPHIA. A "*sophos*" is a wise or able person; "*sophoi*" is the plural form; "*sophia*" is the abstract noun, denominating wisdom or an admired ability. Before "philosophy" came into existence there were people noted for their wisdom and talents; lists were made of these "**sages**" and people memorized their pithy sayings. The practice of writing down collections of wise advice was widespread throughout the literate eastern Mediterranean region. The Biblical *Ecclesiastes* is an excellent example of the genre; among the several **Egyptian** examples we might note especially the *Instructions of Amenemope*. The Babylonians, too, had a wisdom literature of this kind. Some of the earliest people that make it onto our lists of ancient Greek philosophers were also on the list of "*sophoi*"; **Thales** is an excellent example.

Around 500 BCE, there was the beginning of a change in attitude about "wisdom" in the Greek world. **Pythagoras** refused the title "*sophos*," preferring to call himself *philosophos*, lover of wisdom, aware that he did not possess the wisdom to which he aspired. **Heraclitus** (f. 41) says that "wisdom is one thing, to know the thought that steers all things through all things." The wisdom of the Seven Sages and of the various Wisdom Literatures tended to be practical or at least applicable to one's life; the wisdom of Pythagoras and Heraclitus as well as other early philosophers was transcendent and was not necessarily focused on practical application. Perhaps the extreme case of theoretical "wisdom" (without, however, using any form of the word *sophia*) among the **Presocratics** is that of **Parmenides;** it is worth noticing that the immediate successors of the **Eleatics** took those conclusions very seriously.

Democritus says quite a lot about *sophia*: for example, "Medicine cures diseases of the body; wisdom rids the soul of **passion**s" (f. 31). Of course the **Sophists** also say a lot about *sophia*, since they claim to be able to teach "wisdom" to their students. In some respects the wisdom of the Sophists is a continuation of the ancient wisdom literature tradition in the respect that they believed that their teaching would enable their students to get along better in society and in positions of authority. But the Sophists are distinguished by their strong tendency to various sorts of relativism, whether social or individual, epistemological or moral.

Socrates in the *Apology* famously denies that anyone is wise, via the story that the Delphic Oracle, when asked whether Socrates was the wisest person in Greece, responded "yes"; Socrates took the oracle to mean that the only sort of wisdom available to mortal human beings would be the sort that he had, being quite sure that he was not wise. We note that in his attempt to find a wise person, he says in the *Apology* that he interviewed poets and craftsmen, two classes of individuals traditionally regarded to have *sophia* in a narrow sense, but even there he was disappointed, he says, because those people claimed to have knowledge that they clearly did not have, and that, from a Socratic point of view, immediately disqualified them from being "wise."

Of the many **Platonic** texts that focus on *sophia*, we refer here only to the most famous, the *Republic*, in which *sophia* is the cardinal virtue of the Mind (***nous***) and of the Philosopher Rulers, ensuring that each faculty of the soul and each class of participants in the ideal state does its proper job in harmony with the other elements of the soul and state, so as to bring about the just individual and the just state. We are led to understand that *sophia* is to be gained by coming into full cognition of the Forms (***eidē***), the intended outcome of the education of the future Philosopher Rulers outlined by Socrates in this text.

Aristotle, in *EN* VI.7, 1141a9, points out the distinction between *sophia* as skill in the arts and a more general intellectual virtue, "the most finished of the forms of knowledge," involving both knowledge of first principles and of what follows from those principles. In the context, he needs to distinguish **sophia** from **phronēsis**, since *phronēsis* is the intellectual basis of **praxis**. In the **Metaphysics**, he can focus entirely on the sorts of principles and derivations that one must know in order to be counted truly wise. "Such a knowledge **God** alone can have, or God above all others" (*Metaph.* I.2, 983a9). One may describe the work that we call the *Metaphysics* Aristotle's attempt to present whatever he can of that divine knowledge.

In **Stoic** philosophy, *sophia* and the *sophos* occupy an even more special role, if that is possible. **Seneca** (*Letters* 89.4) puts it this way: "Wisdom is the good of the human mind (***nous***) brought to perfection; philosophy is the love and pursuit of wisdom; it strives for the goal that wisdom has achieved." Stoicism presents the image of the *Sophos*, the Sage, the person who has achieved this intellectual and moral perfection, and then goes on to say that everyone else is seriously imperfect.

SŌPHROSYNĒ. Temperance, moderation, self-control, mental health. In the *Odyssey*, when Odysseus' old nurse first tells Penelope about the carnage Odysseus and Telemachus have wreaked among the suitors, Penelope responds: "Dear nurse, the Gods have made thee mad, they who can make foolish even one who is full wise, and set the simple-minded in the paths of understanding (*sōphrosynē*); it is they that have marred thy wits, though heretofore thou wast sound of mind." The word (in verb form) appears again in **Herodotus** 3.35, in a story about Cambyses. Cambyses asked his hit-man, Prexaspes, what the Persians thought of him; Prexaspes responded that some of them thought that he drank too much. Cambyses took it that the Persians were saying that he was out of his mind. "We will see about that," he responded, "you see your son there standing on the porch; if I can shoot him with my bow and hit him in the heart, the Persians are wrong; if I miss, they are right and I am not in my right mind (*mē sōphronein*)." Of course Cambyses hit his target, demonstrating that he was a good shot but definitely not *sōphrōn*.

Sōphrosynē is discussed in some detail in **Plato**'s *Charmides*, though inconclusively—perhaps we can take away the idea that it does involve some form of self-knowledge. In other Platonic dialogues, for example the *Republic*, it is taken to be the virtue (*aretē*) of the appetitive part of the soul (*psychē*), that is, moderation of the appetites. In the *Ethics*, **Aristotle** makes it very clear that he thinks of *sōphrosynē* as the mean between over-indulgence and under-indulgence in food, drink, and sex. It is the virtue of satisfying one's appetites to the right degree, at the right time, in the right manner.

We may note that in Plato's *Laws* (908a), one of the institutions of incarceration is called the *sōphronistērion*, or place for inculcating *sōphrosynē*. The modern linguistic equivalent is "Reformatory." *See also ARETĒ, EPITHYMIA.*

SOUL. *See PSYCHĒ.*

SOURCE. *See ARCHĒ.*

SOURCE OF MOVEMENT. *See ARCHĒ KINĒSEŌS.*

SPACE. *See CHORA; TOPOS.*

SPECIES. *See EIDOS.*

SPERMA. Seed. Primarily the seed of plants, but the word is often used metaphorically for the origin of something; **Anaxagoras** uses the word for one level of his analysis of the material structure of the world. The word is also used of male semen, although when a biologically aware individual like **Aristotle** is writing carefully, the word for semen is *gonē*.

SPERMATIKOS LOGOS. In **Stoic** philosophy, rational form present in **matter**, the cause of emergent properties of complex entities. *See also LOGOS.*

SPEUSIPPUS (c. 410–340 BCE). **Plato**'s nephew and heir, Speusippus became **Scholarch** of the **Academy** upon his uncle's death in 348. Although **Diogenes Laertius** provides a "life" of Speusippus, it is difficult to figure out from that account the extent to which Speusippus may have agreed or disagreed with Plato on various issues. *Aristotle* mentions Speusippus' name in connection with his views twice in the *Metaphysics*, VII.2, 1028b21 and XII.7, 1072b31. In the first of these passages he says that while Plato posited Forms (*eidē*), the objects of mathematics (*mathēmata*), and the entity of perceptible bodies, Speusippus "started from the One, making *archai* for each kind of entity, one for numbers, one for spatial magnitudes, and another for souls." From that we would at least figure that Speusippus did *not* believe in Platonic Forms, but that he was within the **Pythagorean** ambit in his ontology. That supposition is supported by the other *Metaphysics* passage, where Aristotle says that "the Pythagoreans and Speusippus" are wrong to claim that **beauty** and goodness are not present in the *archē* on the grounds that beauty and goodness develop as effects of the causative process.

At *Metaph.* XII.10, 1075b30, Aristotle says that "those who say that mathematical number is first and go on to generate one kind of entity after another and give different *archai* for each make the entity of the universe a series of episodes. . . ." Scholars reasonably suppose that this is directed against Speusippus, given the earlier characterization of his views. In the same vein, compare *Metaph.* XIII.9, 1085a31 and other places in the later books of the *Metaphysics* where Aristotle is critiquing the Pythagoreanism of the contemporary Academy.

In the *Nicomachean **Ethics*** (I.6, 1096b6), Aristotle says that Speusippus "seems to have followed" the Pythagoreans in "putting the One in the column of goods," rather that following the standard Platonic theory of Forms. In *EN* VII.13, 1153b5, we gather than Speusippus did not believe that pleasure is a good; putting this passage together with X.2, 1173a6, we conclude that Speusippus argued that just because pain is an evil does not show that pleasure is a good. Aristotle believes that that argument is unsuccessful. Others have concluded that Speusippus believed that both pain and pleasure are evils, and that the good is, as **Clement** reports, "unperturbedness" or *aochlēsia*.

SPHAERUS OF BOSPORUS (c. 285–after 222 BCE). Stoic, student of **Zeno of Citium** and **Cleanthes**, Sphaerus became the advisor of Cleomenes III, king of Sparta. In that position he wrote a treatise on the Spartan constitution, known only by repute. He seems to have been taken to **Alexandria** by Ptolemy Philopator in 222; **Diogenes Laertius** recounts that Ptolemy asked whether he would be guided by opinion; when Sphaerus said that he would not, Ptolemy offered him some wax pomegranates, and when Sphaerus was fooled by them, Ptolemy argued that he had believed a false proposition. Not at all, Sphaerus said; I believed the true proposition that they might be pomegranates.

SPIRIT. *See ANIMA; PNEUMA; THYMOS.*

SPONTANEOUS. *See AUTOMATON.*

SPOUDAIOS. Serious, eager, excellent. In *Republic* IV, 423d, when discussing the education of the future **Guardians, Socrates** says that they will look for a *spoudaios* offspring of the non-guardian classes. In the *Nicomachean Ethics*, Aristotle essentially makes the *spoudaios* person the standard of the ethical virtues (V.2, 1130b5, for example). Aristotle also says of laws and of states that they may be *spoudaioi*.

STARS. *See ASTRA.*

STATE. In the sense of "condition," *see HEXIS, PŌS ECHEIN, SCHESIS*; in the sense of "political structure," *see POLIS.*

STERĒSIS. Privation, negation, deprivation. **Aristotle** distinguishes several senses of *sterēsis* at *Metaphysics* V.22: a blind person, a mole, and a plant, are "deprived" of sight in three different ways— plants do not have vision at all; moles are blind as a species although the genus to which they belong is normally sighted; for a blind person, the blindness is an individual characteristic, contrary to the natural disposition of the human race. Aristotle claims that there are as many kinds of *sterēsis* as there are kinds of words that can be negated.

Chrysippus wrote a book about *sterēsis*.

STIGMĒ. Point. **Aristotle** attributes to the **Pythagoreans** the thesis that "the limits of body"—surface, line, and point—are *ousiai* (*Metaphysics* VII.2, 1028b16). If the Pythagoreans had committed themselves to the real existence of points before the time of **Zeno of Elea**, that would certainly help to explain why he argues as he does in some of his famous paradoxes.

STILPO (c. 360–280 BCE). According to **Diogenes Laertius**, Stilpo was the most eminent member of the **Megarian School** of philosophy. The rather slim evidence about his views seems to indicate that he propounded an ontological and linguistic theory that resembled **Eleatic** monism, defended with puzzles like those of **Zeno of Elea**; in ethical theory he pursued *ataraxia*, or freedom from disturbance, like his contemporaries the **Cynics** and his successors the **Stoics**. **Zeno of Citium** is said to have studied with him for a period of time.

STOA, STOIC SCHOOL. The Stoic School was founded in **Athens**, in the Stoa Poikile (or Painted Porch, a shopping mall) in about 300 BCE by **Zeno of Citium**. Zeno, a Phoenician by ancestry from Crete, had studied with **Crates the Cynic**, **Polemo** the Platonist, **Stilpo**, and others, before establishing his own philosophical school. The school seems to have attracted a significant number of members. In 261, Zeno was succeeded as **Scholarch** by **Cleanthes**, best known today as the author of the (extant) Hymn to Zeus. Cleanthes was succeeded as Scholarch by **Chrysippus**, a very prolific writer. Although we do not have any complete works by Chrysippus, we do have significant fragments, and it is apparent that a great deal of what we know about the earlier Stoics, those of the period from Zeno through Chrysippus, go back most precisely to Chrysippus.

Panaetius was Scholarch beginning in 129 BCE; he frequently traveled to Rome, where he strongly encouraged the tendency of Roman intellectuals to favor the Stoic philosophy. He seems to have brought a good deal of **Aristotelian** doctrine into the Stoic system. **Posidonius**, one of Panaetius' students, traveled widely in the Roman world before establishing his school in Rhodes. Posidonius tended to synthesize **Platonic** themes into the Stoic system. The teachings of Panaetius and Posidonius are reflected extensively in the writings of **Cicero.**

Stoics of the Roman period provide the only complete works that we have from the Stoic school; in addition to Cicero (who might better be described as "eclectic"), we should notice the works of **Seneca**, **Epictetus**, and **Marcus Aurelius**. There are also extensive accounts or quotations of Stoic philosophy in **Diogenes Laertius**, **Galen**, and **Stobaeus**. **Plutarch of Chaeronea** wrote two extant books critiquing the Stoic philosophy from a Platonic perspective; **Sextus Empiricus** wrote extensively critiquing the Stoics from a **Skeptical** angle; **Plotinus** has a number of critical comments, and several early Christian church fathers also attacked Stoicism, although we must recognize that all of those movements, including early **Christianity**, imitated or borrowed at the same time.

Stoicism is a seriously systematic philosophy, coordinating logic (philosophy of language), physics (philosophy of nature), and **ethics** (practical philosophy) into an integrated whole. It is a materialist philosophy in the sense that in principle anything that truly exists is a material thing. That definitely includes **God**, who is present everywhere in the material universe as creative fire and as immanent rationality. Since the physical universe is the visible manifestation of divine rationality, the Stoic believes in a rigid determinism.

There is, for the Stoic, no serious gap between physics and morality; both are expressions of God's thought. The goal for human beings is to conform one's life to that divine rationality; Stoicism is well known for its image of the person who achieves that goal perfectly, the **Sage**, and its assertion that all who fall short of that ideal are immoral and fools.

Stoicism was attractive to the Roman leadership—it is a philosophy that offers a way of understanding one's life experiences and encourages the acceptance of whatever tasks fate may bring. A Stoic soldier or administrator may readily see himself as an instrument bringing divine order to this particular corner of the universe. *See also LOGIKĒ; PHYSIS.*

STOBAEUS, JOHN (JOHN OF STOBI) (Early fifth century CE). Stobaeus put together a massive anthology for the sake of educating his son. As the most popular such work in the Middle Ages, a good deal of it survived. Many of our "fragments" of various writers stem from this anthology. Since he does not quote Christian authors, it is assumed that he was not a Christian. Stobaeus' works as a whole have not been edited since the late 19th century, and there is no translation into a modern language.

STOICHEION, STOICHEIA. Element, elements. The primary sense of this word is the minimal sound of speech, symbolized by a letter of the alphabet, thus also a letter of the alphabet itself.

Plato seems to have been the first to apply the term *stoicheia* to the minimal components of the material and/or sensory world, in the *Theaetetus*. Subsequently **Aristotle, Theophrastus,** and others used the term in their interpretation of the early philosophers from **Thales** onward to characterize what those people took to be the ultimate material of the physical universe. Thus, Thales is thought to have made **water** the "element," **Anaximander** the **indefinite, Anaximenes air, Heraclitus fire,** and **Empedocles earth,** water, air, and fire.

For Plato and Aristotle, at least, these so-called elements are hardly irreducible: Plato argues in the *Timaeus* that the four are not really "elements" on the ground that they can be divided into geometrical subunits; and Aristotle believed that they could be transformed into each other. Aristotle's widespread use of the four Empedoclean elements in his physical writings helped to establish them as part of "normal physics" until the early modern era.

The word *stoicheia* came to be applied to the "elements" of any field whatever, whether geometry, arithmetic, or theology. *See also* MATTER; *PHYSIS.*

STRABO (64 BCE–24 CE). Author of a sizable (largely extant) *Geography*, describing a great deal of the Roman Empire. Although he did a fair amount of traveling, many of his descriptions were based on literary sources, including **Homer,** for whom he had great respect. Modern scholars regard Strabo's work as generally reliable, as ancient sources go. There are indications that he was trained as a **Stoic.** Strabo also wrote a massive *History,* now lost.

STRATO OF LAMPSACUS (c. 340–268 BCE). Strato was a student of **Theophrastus**, and became the third **Scholarch** of the **Lyceum** after the death of his teacher. His major interest was physics; he asserted the existence of **void** within **matter** to account for differences in **weight** between objects of the same size; he also observed that falling bodies accelerate. *See also PHYSIS.*

STRIFE. *See ERIS; NEIKOS.*

SUBSIST. *See HYPHISTASTHAI.*

SUBSTANCE. *See OUSIA.*

SUBSTRATUM. *See HYPOKEIMENON.*

SUN. The sun was widely regarded as a deity in preclassical and classical Greece—Apollo, Zeus, or *Hēlios*. **Hecataeus** took the **Egyptians** as identifying the sun with Osiris and the moon with Isis (DL 1.10). The **Presocratic** philosophers speculated about the distance of the sun from the **earth**, its size, and its composition; that is, they took the sun as an object of scientific investigation, whether a deity or not. **Parmenides** knew that the moon was "wandering around the earth shining with borrowed light" (f. 14) "always straining her eyes toward the light of the sun" (f. 15).

We get some idea of the astronomical understanding of the Sun gained by the earlier natural philosophers from **Plato**'s description of the construction of the solar system at *Timaeus* 38C. At *Metaphysics* XII.8, 1073b18ff, **Aristotle** rapidly summarizes the findings of **Eudoxus**, an attempt to give a mechanical explanation of the phenomena of the sun, moon, and planets, based on the assumption of geocentrism. They were aware that some of the **Pythagoreans** had proposed a heliocentric theory, but that remained a minority opinion throughout antiquity.

SUN-LINE-CAVE. Plato's *Republic* VI.507–VII.518 presents an analogy between the sun and its relationship to the visible world, on the one hand, and the form of the Good (*to agathon*) and its relationship to the knowable world, on the other, followed by an allegory sketching the progress that one may make from guesswork on the basis of sensory images, through confidence in material objects, to true knowledge of transcendent realities. This passage is generally taken to be the epitome of Plato's metaphysical and epistemological theory. *See also DIANOIA; DOXA; EPISTĒMĒ; LOGOS; PISTIS.*

SUSPENSION (OF BELIEF). *See EPOCHĒ.*

SWERVE. The deviation from totally regular straight-line motion attributed to atoms (***atoma***) "falling" through space, in **Epicurean** physics. *See also PARENKLISIS; PHYSIS.*

SYLLOGISM. *See SYLLOGISMOS.*

SYLLOGISMOS. Literally, putting *logoi* together. In the *Theaetetus*, 186d, **Socrates** says that knowledge is "not in the experiences but in the *syllogismos* about them." **Aristotle** adopts the word as a technical term for formalized argument structures. A standard *syllogismos* has two premises and a conclusion that follows from the premises in virtue of a connection between the premises via a middle term. An actual example (from *Prior Analytics* II.23, 68b15): If all bileless animals are long-lived, and horses are bileless, then horses are long-lived. In a sense, the "syllogism" brings together *logoi* in the sense of definitions, and demonstrates relationships between those definitions.

SYMBEBĒKOS, SYMBEBĒKOTA. **Accident, attribute.** This is a participle formed on the verb *symbainein*, "to come together, to occur." For Aristotle, it is a technical term, defined as "that which attaches to something and can be truly asserted, but neither of necessity nor for the most part" *Metaph.* V. 30, 1025a14. *Ta symbebēkota* are non-essential attributes: that a particular musician has pale skin, for example. **Epicurus** seems to have adopted *ta symbebēkota* to refer to *essential* attributes, to refer to qualities inhering in bodies as bodies (size, shape, **weight**, motion), and applied the word *symptomata* to qualities arising through the perceptual process (color, sound, etc.) (*Letter to Herodotus*).

SYMBOLON, SYMBOLA. **Empedocles** hypothesizes that the male and female each contribute something "*hoion symbolon*," like a "symbol," to sexual generation. If you break a twig, each half will fit precisely only the other half, so this was used to guarantee the bona fides of a messenger. Empedocles suggests that the male and female parents contribute something that fit the other part thus precisely and give rise to the new individual in this way. **Aristotle** occasionally uses the word to refer to parts that naturally fit together, as for example "air" (*aēr*) is composed of "fluid" and "hot" "as from *symbola*" *Meteor.* II.4, 360a26.

The "identity token" sense was much extended to any method of guaranteeing the identity of the bearer, or in general, to guarantees of other sorts. As a "token," a *symbolon* may be a sign of something else, like a portent of the weather or a symptom of a disease.

In a different sense, the (somewhat mysterious) **Pythagorean** sayings, like "Do not stir the **fire** with a knife," and "Do not sit on a bushel basket," are collectively known as the *symbola*. Of course it is possible that those sayings are "tokens" of something else, some meaning that was understood by those who were initiated.

SYMPASCHEIN, SYMPATHEIA. Literally, "feeling together." The verb may be translated "interact" and the abstract noun not only "sympathy" but also "interaction." In the best ordered state of **Plato**'s *Republic*, if one citizen is injured, the whole state feels it, just as in an individual person, if a finger is injured, the whole person feels it (*Rep.* V.462d). **Poetry**, too, can arouse our sympathy (*Rep.* X, 605d). **Aristotle** tended to use the word in a directly physiological sense: if the outer surface of the brain is heated or cooled, there is an immediate response from the heart, "for it is most delicate in its sympathies" (*PA* II.7, 653b7). **Epicurus**, in *Letter to Herodotus* 50–53, also used *sympatheia* in a physical sense, that is, that perceptual movements are communicated among the atoms (*atoma*) in the body via *sympatheia*. **Chrysippus** used the "interaction" of soul (*psychē*) and body to demonstrate that the soul must be a body. The **Poseidonius** extended "*sympatheia*" to the cosmic scale, essentially on the grounds that the **cosmos** is one great living being. **Plotinus** also believed in cosmic sympathy, and used it to explain such things as divination, **astrology**, and **magic** (*Enn.* IV.4).

SYMPERASMA. Conclusion of a **syllogism** in **Aristotle**'s logic; the word is also used by the **Stoics**. *See also LOGIKĒ.*

SYNAGEIN; SYNAGŌGĒ; SYNAKTIKOS. To bring together, collect; a collection. *Synagōgē* is the title of a lost book by **Hippias of Elis** that seems to have summarized the opinions of earlier thinkers. **Plato** uses the word as something close to "induction," gathering together the examples before dividing them (*diairēsis*). This "method of collection and division" appears particularly in *Phaedrus* 265d and is applied at length in the *Sophist* and *Statesman*.

In **Stoic** usage, these words mean "deduce," "deduction," and "deductive." *Synaktikos* in that context thus means approximately "deductive."

More generally *Synagōgē* means a gathering of people, thus its application to Jewish temples.

SYNAITION. Joint cause. In **Stoic** physics, a *synaition* is roughly what we call a "necessary condition" where there is some set of conditions regarded as jointly sufficient. *See also PHYSIS.*

SYNARTĒSIS. Cohesion. In **Stoic** logic, a conditional is sound if the contradictory of the consequent conflicts with the antecedent; they call that "cohesion" (**Sextus Empiricus**, *Outlines of Pyrrhonism*, 2.112). *See also LOGIKĒ.*

SYNECHEIA. Continuity. **Aristotle** *Physics* IV.13, 222a10: "The 'now' is the *synecheia* of time." *HA* VIII.1, 588b5: "Nature proceeds little by little from soulless things to animals so that their distinctions escape notice because of their *synecheia*." The continuity of nature is a favorite theme of the **Stoics** as well. *See also CHRONOS; PHYSIS.*

SYNECHEIN. Sustain, hold together (*synektikē dynamis*). Sustaining power.

SYNEIMARMENON. Co-fated. **Chrysippus** criticized the so-called Lazy Argument that said that if everything is fated, you do not need to bother to make an effort to achieve anything. Chrysippus replied that your level of effort and your success and failure were BOTH predetermined. When a slave complained to his Stoic master that it was unjust to punish him because he was fated to steal from his master, the Stoic master replied, "And I was fated to beat you." *See also* *ANAGKĒ; HEIMARMENĒ; MOIRA.*

SYNEKTIKON AITION. Sustaining cause. According to the **Stoics**, *pneuma* provides the power or cause holding things together as unities.

SYNERGON (AITION). Auxiliary (cause). In **Stoic** theory of causation, something that contributes to the effect being produced. The modern term "synergy" was borrowed from this usage.

SYNKATATHESIS. In **Stoic** epistemology, "assent." Knowledge follows upon assent to correct perceptions (*aisthēseis*); false opinions follow upon assent to incorrect perceptions. The wise man withholds assent from incorrect perceptions. When Ptolemy Philopator (ruler of **Egypt**) presented the Stoic philosopher Sphaerus with wax pomegranates, and Sphaerus appeared to be fooled by them, Ptolemy gleefully pointed out that Sphaerus had assented to an incorrect perception. "Not at all," said Sphaerus, "I assented to the perception that it was reasonable to believe that they were pomegranates." (**Diogenes Laertius** 7.177)

SYNOLON. **Aristotle** uses this word for a "whole," especially the whole body (*PA* I.5, 645b16), and for the combination of **matter** and form (*eidos*) that makes up an *ousia* (***Metaphysics*** VII.11, 1037a30). *See also HOLON.*

SYNONYMOI. According to **Aristotle** in the *Categories*, if two entities share the same name and the **definition** is the same in both cases, then they are "synonymous." *See also HOMONYMOI; PARONYMOI.*

SYNTHESIS. For **Aristotle**, a *synthesis* is a combination of parts in which the parts actually change in nature as a consequence of the combination; this is distinguished from a *krasis* in which the component bits could, in principle, still be distinguished and separated. In **Epicurean** epistemology, notions can be derived from perceptions (*aisthēseis*) via *synthesis*, for example. Similarly in **Stoic** epistemology, *synthesis* is one of the activities of the faculty of imagination; an example of a result is the hippocentaur (DL 7.53). *See also MIGMA; MIXIS.*

SYNTHETON. Literally, put together. A "*syntheton*" is a compound, for example of elements. "The people become a monarch *syntheton* (compounded) of many," **Aristotle** *Pol.* IV.4, 1292a11.

SYRIANUS (d. c. 437 CE). A **Neoplatonist,** student of **Plutarch of Athens**, he became **Scholarch** of the **Athenian** school upon the death of Plutarch and was succeeded by **Proclus.** He was also the teacher of **Hermeias,** who moved to **Alexandria,** and was the father and teacher of **Ammonius,** who was in turn one of the teachers of **Damascius,** the last (official) head of a pagan philosophical school in the Christian Byzantine Empire. Syrianus' commentary on several books of **Aristotle**'s *Metaphysics* is extant, as well as his commentaries on rhetorical works by Hermogenes.

SYSTASIS. Composition or constitution; used both of the construction of an individual living body and of a political organization. **Plato** uses it of the organization of the state (*polis*), in *Republic* VIII, 546a, for example; **Aristotle** most frequently uses it for the arrangement or development of the parts of an animal. In **Stoic** philosophy, this is the standard word for the constitution of the body (*sōma*) and the relation of the soul (*psychē*) to the body.

SYSTĒMA. Literally, something that stands together, or a whole composed of parts. In *GA* II.4, 740a20, **Aristotle** argues that the embryo is a *systēma* as soon as the embryonic heart begins to serve as an *archē* for the development of the whole.

– T –

TABULA RASA. Literally, "blank (or smoothed) tablet" (in Latin). In the *Theaetetus*, **Plato** proposes, hypothetically, that memory is like a block of wax upon or in which experiences are written or impressed (191c ff). One kind of writing tablet in antiquity was a wooden board, painted black and then covered with a layer of bees wax; one could write or draw on it by scratching with a stylus and erase by smoothing out the wax again. "When a man is born, the Stoics say, he has the commanding part (*hegemonikon*) of his soul (*psychē*) like a sheet of paper ready for writing upon. On this, he inscribes each one of his conceptions" (**Aetius** 4.11.1–4). Web sources trace the phrase "tabula rasa" to John Locke or to Thomas Aquinas; the idea, if not definitely the phrase, is older.

TAXIS. Order, arrangement. In ordinary Greek, *taxis* is normally the arrangement of military forces. In the **Anaximander** fragment, things that come into being pay for their injustice "according to the *taxis* of time." The **Pythagoreans** apparently used the word to describe the "ordering" of the astronomical bodies (DK 1.452, 18, et al.). In **Plato**, *Timaeus* 30A, the ***Demiourgos*** imposes *taxis* on disorder (*ataxia*). **Aristotle** is interested in all forms of order, from the ordering of the elements in relation to each other (*Meteor* I.3, 339b5), to the ordering of the parts of animals (*HA* I.6, 491a17), to the arrangement of magistracies in the state (*Pol.* III.6, 1278b9), to the everlasting arrangement of the universe (*Cael.* II.14, 296a34, *Metaph.* XII.10, 1075a12).

TECHNĒ. Art, craft, skill. In **Homer**, examples of *technai* would be metal-working, ship-building, soothsaying, general trickiness; the Hippocratic texts hold that medicine (*iatrikē*) is a *technē*. There is a sense that *technē* is in some measure opposed to nature (*physis*); *see TECHNIKOS, PHYSIS*.

In classical society, there was a widespread belief that mastery of one or more arts was tantamount to *sophia*, or wisdom. In that context, the **Sophists** proposed to instruct in the "arts" of speaking, use of language, and especially governance (*politikē*)—**Protagoras**, **Gorgias**, and **Thrasymachus** are all reported to have used "*Technē*" in the title of an instructional book.

Socrates turned the tables on the Sophists by demanding that they demonstrate appropriate knowledge of the art. In the *Protagoras*, for example, Protagoras claims that he can teach virtue (*aretē*) as if it were an art, but Socrates demonstrates that Protagoras' verbalizable knowledge of virtue is rather limited. In *Republic* I, Thrasymachus readily agrees with Socrates that there is an "art" of governing, analogous to medicine and sheep-herding; Socrates turns that admission against Thrasymachus, arguing that the end of the art of medicine is the benefit of the patient, that of the art of sheep-herding the well-being of the sheep, thus the end of the art of governance is the well-being or benefit of the governed. This discussion sets up a major thread of the *Republic* as a whole—that there is an art of governing, and that it can be learned by the **Guardians** and the Philosopher-Rulers.

Plato takes the analogy of the arts a step further with the image of the *Demiourgos* in the *Timaeus*; the physical universe is a product of the *technē* of a creative deity.

For **Aristotle**, *technē* is contrasted with nature (*physis*), in that the source of change for a product of *technē* is external to that which is produced, but the source of change for a natural production is within the thing that changes. There is a bit of continuity in this contrast: nature is like a physician who cures herself; and *technē* partially imitates nature, partially completes what nature cannot finish. Aristotle also explores the epistemic requirements for *technē*: "experience" (*empeiria*) deals with individuals (*kath' hekasta*) but the "art" knows the universal (*katholou*) and can teach (*Metaphysics* I.1). But "art" is not the same as "knowledge" (*epistēmē*), because *epistēmē* is about "**being**" and art is about "becoming" (*genesis*).

Technē can be distinguished into *poiētikē* and *praktikē*, productive and practical.

It should be pointed out that there is no specific concept of "fine art" as that is understood in the modern world. The closest approach would be *mousikē*, but that is both partial and not understood in quite the same way as "fine art" is today. The visual and plastic arts especially were expected to have some function, whether religious, educational, political, or at least decorative.

TECHNIKOS. Skillful, but also often "artificial." In **Stoic** philosophy, *pyr technikon*, creative fire, is the material aspect of **God**.

TELOS, **TELEOLOGY. Alcmaeon**, f. 2, says: "Human beings perish because they are not able to join their beginning to their end." The *telos* is the end or goal of some activity. In fact the word is so widely used that it gains a range of senses, depending on context. It can mean "the end" as in death—"Call no man happy until you see his end," **Solon** said (*EN* I.11, 1100a10); or it can be the purpose—that for the sake of which something is done.

Thus *telos* is one of the standard names for that mode of **Aristotelian** explanation called "final causation" or "teleology." Of course teleological explanation did not begin with Aristotle; **Socrates** often appeals to teleology. For example, in *Phaedo* 97–98, he tells of hearing how **Anaxagoras** made Mind (*nous*) the cause of motion in the universe and how disappointed he was that Anaxagoras did not go on to explain how Mind arranged things as they are because it would be better thus.

However, Aristotle was convinced that no one had adequately presented a truly teleological system of explanation. Appeals to a cosmic force of Love (*erōs*) or even a providential Demiurge (*demiourgos*), would not ultimately succeed. No, we have to assume from the start that "**being** is better than non-being, life is better than death, having a soul is better than not having a soul, having a mind is better than not having a mind" (*GA* II.1). If we assume from the start that the continued existence of individual entities and of natural kinds is *good*, then one sort of investigation that we can carry out is toward understanding what processes contribute to the persistence of entities and kinds.

Thus, the organic parts of animals exist *for the sake of* the life of the animal and for reproduction; the nature of the individual and of the kind is *telos* and that on account of which it comes into being (*Phys.* II.2, 194a34).

For the human being, not only life but a happy (*eudaimōn*) life should be the goal—not the Solonic "end" of life but the fullness of life itself is the purpose. *See also ENERGEIA; ENTELECHEIA; EUDAIMONIA.*

TEMNEIN, TOMĒ. Cut—*temnein* is the verb, *tomē* is the noun. **Chrysippus** proposed dealing with a whole class of reductive arguments with a move called the "cut." Take, for example, **Zeno of Elea**'s dichotomy argument that you cannot go from A to B without going halfway first, and then repeating that indefinitely with the conclusion that you cannot get started because you cannot go any finite distance without taking an infinite number of steps first. The "cut" says that there is a (rough) minimum distance you can go and still call it a "step," so that is what you add up to go the distance from A to B.

TEMPERANCE. *See SŌPHROSYNĒ.*

TENOR. This word is used as a translation of the word *hexis* when it occurs in **Stoic** contexts. It refers then primarily to the capacity of *pneuma* to hold things together, or to non-moral dispositions of people, like the ability to play a musical instrument. *See also TONOS.*

TENSION. *See TONOS.*

TETRAKTYS.

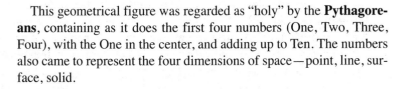

This geometrical figure was regarded as "holy" by the **Pythagoreans**, containing as it does the first four numbers (One, Two, Three, Four), with the One in the center, and adding up to Ten. The numbers also came to represent the four dimensions of space—point, line, surface, solid.

TETRAPHARMAKON. "Fourfold cure," the **Epicurean** way to a happy life. Keep the following in mind:

1. The Gods do not punish or reward.
2. Death is nothing to us.
3. The greatest pleasure is the elimination of pain.
4. Prolonged pain is tolerable, acute pain is short.

THALES OF MILETUS (c. 620–540 BCE?). Thales was traditionally named as the "first" Greek philosopher, partly because he was thought to have been the teacher of **Anaximander**. **Herodotus** tells us that Thales was of Phoenician descent, that he predicted (in some sense) a solar eclipse on the basis of Babylonian records (many figure that this would be the eclipse of 585 BCE). Herodotus also says that Thales attempted to organize the Ionian Greeks to defend against the Persians. He is credited with introducing some geometrical knowledge into the Greek world. A number of amusing stories are told about him; for example, **Aristotle** says that he expected a bumper crop of olives one year and managed to corner the local market on olive presses, establishing a profitable monopoly (*Politics,* 1259 a 6–23). Aristotle suggests that Thales thought that **water** was the fundamental material for all things, and Thales is credited with the idea that magnets and amber have a principle of soul (*psychē*).

THAUMASIA. Wonder. **Empedocles** f. 35, end:

> The multitudinous tribes of mortal things,
> Knit in all forms and wonderful (thauma) to see.

At the beginning of the *Phaedo* (58e), **Phaedo** tells Echecrates that the experience of being present at the death of **Socrates** was "amazing"; in the *Symposium* (220a), Alcibiades says that "amazingly" no one ever saw Socrates drunk. So **Aristotle**, at the beginning of the *Metaphysics* (I.2, 982b12) says that people began to philosophize "because of wonder." Aristotle points out that the experience of wonder implies a desire to know (*Rhetoric* I.11, 1371a32); the **Peripatetic** *Mechanica* (847a10) notes that our wonder is excited by natural events when we do not know the cause and by works of art (technology) for the benefit of humanity. He refers a few times to the "marvelous *automata*" which provide a model for the movements of living beings.

THEAETETUS (414–369 BCE?). In **Plato**'s *Theaetetus*, he is represented as a teenager discussing the meaning of the word *epistēmē* (knowledge) with **Socrates** shortly before the trial and execution of Socrates; the frame-dialogue indicates that this discussion is being recalled a significant number of years later, while Theaetetus lies dying of wounds received in battle. There is a tradition that Theaetetus became a member of Plato's **Academy** and contributed significantly to the development of mathematics (*mathēmatikē*). Others are skeptical, supposing that the battle in question may have occurred in 391 when Theaetetus would have been in his early twenties.

THEIOS, THEION. *See THEOS.*

THEMA. Literally, that which is placed or put down. It is the origin of the English word "theme," and the Greek word can mean the same as its English derivative. As a technical term in **Stoic** logic (*see logikē*), a *thema* is a rule for determining whether a given deduction is valid.

THEMISTIUS (c. 317–388 CE). Themistius was a **Peripatetic** commentator on **Aristotle** who also had a political career. He taught in Constantinople, a city that had recently been made a cultural center by the Emperor Constantine (306–363). The surviving speeches of Themistius fill three volumes; his surviving commentaries on Aristotle are in five volumes of the *Commentaria in Aristotelem Graeca*.

THEODORET OF CYRRHUS (393–466 CE). Christian apologist, interesting to historians of ancient philosophy for his work *Cure of the Greek Maladies or Knowledge of the Gospel Truth from the Greek Philosophy*, attempting to support Christian **dogma** from philosophical sources. Theodoret was also involved in the Nestorian controversy, parsing how human and how divine Christ may have been. Theodoret is the source for one of the comments that led to the reconstruction of the **doxographer Aetius**. *See also* CHRISTIANITY.

THEODORUS (Fifth to fourth centuries BCE). A visitor from Cyrene, Theodorus appears in **Plato**'s *Theaetetus* as the teacher of **Theaetetus**; we learn from the dialogue that he had studied with **Protagoras**, and that he had an interest in theoretical mathematics. **Diogenes Laertius** (3.6) says that Plato visited him in Cyrene after the death of **Socrates**.

THEOLOGIA, **THEOLOGY**. *See THEOS*.

THEOPHRASTUS OF ERESUS (371–c. 287 BCE). Theophrastus was a student of both **Plato** and **Aristotle** and was the successor of Aristotle as **Scholarch** of the **Lyceum**. After Plato died (347), Theophrastus appears to have accompanied Aristotle in his various travels, and probably helped him set up his school in Lesbos (345). Eresus is a town on the island of Lesbos.

Theophrastus wrote a great deal; surviving texts include two large works on plants, the *Historia Plantarum* (Investigation of Plants) and the *Causa Plantarum* (Explanation of Plants), that parallel Aristotle's works on animals; there is a short work on **metaphysics**, an important doxographical work on sense perception, several short treatises on various topics, and his well-known *Characters*, sketching various kinds of people, partially from a literary perspective.

THEŌRIA, THEŌREIN. *Theōrein* (the verb) means, in the first instance, to look at, to be a spectator, to observe. An old sense of the noun (*theōria*) is of an official delegation to the Olympic Games or other event. **Plato** and **Aristotle** adapted the word to mean the activity of the mind in relation to its proper objects. In the Cave passage in the *Republic* (517), *theōria* is the activity of those who have gotten out of the Cave; for Aristotle (*EN* X.7–9), the "*theoretikos bios*" or life of *theōria* is the most *eudaimōn* life for those who can achieve it. "Theoretical" knowledge is about *ousia*, nature (*physis*), and the causes (*aitia*), for their own sake (*Metaphysics* I.2, 982a29ff); mind (*nous*) can also be exercised for the sake of *praxis*: that is *phronēsis*, or for the sake of *poiēsis*: that is *technē*. **Plotinus** says that *everything* comes from *Theōria* and strives for *Theōria* (*Enn.* III.8). *See also* SUN-LINE-CAVE.

THEOS, THEIOS, THEOLOGIA. **God**, The Divine, Account of God and the Divine. **Homer** represents the Gods, most of the time, as superhuman but anthropomorphic beings that have many human characteristics. **Hesiod**'s Gods are more varied—some are anthropomorphic, some are conceptual, and many are hardly more than names handed down from one tradition or another. The philosophical tradition tends to be anti-anthropomorphic. **Heraclitus** f. 32. "The Wise is one only. It is willing and unwilling to be called by the name of Zeus." **Xenophanes** is well known for critiquing anthropomorphic deities and positing one supreme God. "God is one, supreme among Gods and men, and not like mortals in body or in mind." **Socrates** was charged with "not believing in the Gods of the state but introducing new and different divinities." It is remarkable that in his defense in **Plato**'s *Apology* he absolutely does *not* say "but of course I believe in Athena and Poseidon and all the other deities worshipped in **Athens**."

Aristotle sometimes characterizes the subject matter of his work that we know as the *Metaphysics* as *theologia*. For the most part, it would be difficult to think of that work as a discussion of deities in the ordinary sense, but it is clear that he thinks of the most fundamental realities as *theia*, divine, so that the study of "**being** qua being" (another characterization of the subject matter) is automatically and directly "theology."

This way of seeing things is taken up both by the **Stoics** and by the Platonic tradition; neither makes much of a distinction between what we call "metaphysics" and what we call "theology."

THEOURGIA. Theurgy. Literally, "divine work." In some cases, it means nothing more than performance of sacred rituals or sacraments. But in the **Neoplatonic** tradition there are texts that propose that one might persuade a deity to show up locally and even perhaps do what you want. **Iamblichus** *de Myst.* III.4–7, and a number of places in **Proclus**, are examples. *See also* CHALDEAN ORACLES; HERMES TRISMEGISTUS.

THĒRIOTĒS. Beastliness. In *EN* VII, with this word **Aristotle** describes individuals who pursue their appetites with no rational governance. In general, a *thērion* is a wild beast, either with the connotation of hostility to human beings, for example a poisonous snake or a lion, or with the connotation of a hunted animal, for example a deer.

Aristotle opposes beastliness to "godliness." Neither the beastly nor the godly make choices about what they will do—the godly naturally do good things, the beastly naturally do bad things or have become beastly as a result of disease or bad habituation. Aristotle's examples of *thēriotēs* are telling: several of them are of cannibalism, but he also includes the habit of pulling out one's hair or chewing one's fingernails, as well as pederasty. Aristotle eventually admits that some individuals are borderline cases, since they might, like the wicked Phalaris, have *chosen* to eat babies, in which case they are extreme examples of ***akolasia***; or Phalaris might have sometimes restrained the desire to eat a baby and sometimes failed to restrain the desire so that his action perhaps now seems due to ***akrateia*** (*EN* VII.5, 1149a).

THESIS. Noun formed from the verb *tithēmi*, "put." The word is used in both a physical and a metaphorical sense. Physically, the word means approximately "position," as in **Aristotle** *Cat.* 4b21: some quantities have parts that have *thesis* in relation to each other. So, for example, the parts of the body have their *thesis* (e.g., *PA* III.4, 666a27). Metaphorically, a *thesis* is a proposition posited for discussion and possible defense (e.g., *Prior Analytics* II.17, 65b26). Thus the modern word "thesis."

THINKING. *See DIANOIA; LOGISMOS; NOĒSIS; THEŌRIA.*

THRASYLLUS (d. 36 CE). Personal astrologer to the Emperor Tiberius, he seems to have been responsible for the arrangement of the works of Plato and Democritus into tetralogies.

THRASYMACHUS OF CHALCEDON (Late fifth century BCE). **Sophist.** Although he is easily most famous for his appearance in Book I of **Plato**'s *Republic*, where he defends the thesis that "Justice is the will of the stronger," he is also known as a teacher and writer on the art of rhetoric (Plato, *Phaedrus* 261ff; **Aristotle**, *Rhetoric* III. 1, 1404a14; III.8, 1409a2; III.11, 1413a8). *See also RHETORIKĒ.*

THUCYDIDES OF ATHENS (Fifth century BCE). Thucydides was the author of the *History of the Peloponnesian War* (431–411); he is said to have died before he could complete the work. The work includes a time-line narrative, speeches by various leading figures, and analysis. The speeches appear to be something of a mixture of what they may actually have said and what Thucydides believes that the person would or should have said. **Sophistic** influences show in many of the speeches. The Melian dialogue (5.89) is taken to be a paradigmatic example of Sophistic reasoning. But Thucydides himself was no Sophist; he believed firmly in the rule of law; his own firmly held beliefs seem to come across in the Periclean Funeral Oration (2.34–46).

THYMOS. The first (surviving) line of **Parmenides'** poem says that the horses took him—*hoson t'epi thymos*—as far as he wanted to go. **Heraclitus** f. 85: "It is hard to fight with *thymos*; whatever it wishes to get, it purchases at the cost of soul." A common **Homeric** word for "desire," it also often has the sense of "mind" or "spirit" in epic poetry. In classical philosophical texts, it comes to mean "anger" or the ability to become angry or at least "passionate." **Aristotle** *EN* 1149a24: "***Akrasia*** with respect to *thymos* is less disgraceful than *akrasia* with respect to **epithymia**," because *thymos* "listens to reason to some extent."

TI ESTI. "What is . . . ?" One of **Socrates'** standard questions: What is courage? What is friendship? **Aristotle** supposes that the answer to the question—in Greek, *to ti esti*—should be a definition of the term, and that what corresponds to that definition is the "**essence**." Thus, *to ti esti* is one of the designations for what we call essence.

TIME. *See CHRONOS.*

TIMĒ. Honor. **Empedocles** f. 119: "From what great honor (*timē*) and prosperity have I fallen to take a turn with mortals." In the Hellenic tradition, there are three possible lifestyles: the pursuit of pleasure, the pursuit of honor, and the pursuit of understanding. In the *Republic*, **Plato** uses this idea to distinguish three classes of people in the ideal state (*polis*); those who pursue honor in particular would be designated as the "**Guardians**" (military) of the state; their special virtue (*aretē*) would be courage (*andreia*), for which they would receive the honors due them from the state.

    Aristotle also uses this idea but as a motivation for the pursuit of all the "ethical" virtues (*EN* I.5), though he makes sure that it is understood that one wants to be truly deserving of the honors, whether or not one actually receives them.

TIMON OF PHLIUS (c. 325–235 BCE). Student of **Pyrrho,** author of satirical verses, surviving in fragments. His *Silloi* satirize various philosophers and philosophical positions, representing **Xenophanes** in a positive light, doubtless because of his critical stand toward religious dogmatism. As a student of Pyrrho, the founder of the skeptical mode of philosophy, one may count Timon as in some fashion a skeptic, although it is hard to determine exactly how from the remaining fragments. *See also SKEPTIKOS.*

TO AUTOMATON. See AUTOMATON.

TO TI EN EINAI. See ESSENCE.

TODE TI. Literally, "this something." **Aristotle** uses this phase to indicate individual entities: this **particular** person (Coriscus), this particular horse (Dobbin), *Cat.* 2a, *Metaph.* III.6, 1003a5–15. *Tode ti* is contrasted with *kathōlou*, and is regarded as paradigmatic of *ousia.*

TONOS. Tension. In non-philosophical usage, *tonos* typically refers to the tension on a bow-string, for example, but by extension, the stress given certain notes in music or certain syllables in speaking. The **Stoic** philosophers appropriated this word to refer to the physical activity of *pneuma* in sustaining the integrity of bodily entities.

TOPOS. Place. One of the puzzles that interested Greek philosophers was the existence of space and place. **Zeno of Elea** argued (A24) that if the universe is in a place, that place itself is in a place, and thus there is an infinite progression of places. Indeed, the paradoxes of motion are as much paradoxes about place and places. **Plato** in the *Timaeus* (52) was more concerned with "space" (*chora*) as the matrix within which **becoming** occurs. **Aristotle** wanted to give an adequate account of movement; he addressed the question of place in *Physics* IV, taking up a solution of Zeno's paradoxes.

Aristotle also asserts that the each of the four **elements, earth, water, air**, and **fire**, has its natural place—earth in the center, water around it, air around that, and then fire. These places determine the natural directions of up and down: each element tends to proceed to its natural place, and once in its natural place, tends to circulate. *See also* MATTER; *PHYSIS*; *STOICHEION*.

TOUCH. *See HAPHĒ.*

TRANSCENDENCE. *See HYPEROUSIA.*

TRANSMIGRATION (OF THE SOUL). *See METEMPSYCHOSIS.*

TRIAS. Triad. The **Platonic** tradition inherited from the **Pythagoreans** a bit of a tendency to look for trinities. For all that **Philo** is a dedicated Jewish monotheist, he still distinguishes **God** as creator, the *Logos*, and the **World Soul**. In **Plotinus**, that triad becomes The **One, Mind**, and the World Soul. But **Proclus** finds triads everywhere, because he has "cause," "effect," and "mean term" (*meson*) on every ontological level.

TRIPARTITE SOUL. Plato distinguishes the functions of the soul (*psychē*) into Mind (*nous*), Spirit (*thymos*), and Appetite (*epithymia*), in the *Republic*; in the *Timaeus*, he locates the mind in the head, the spirit in the heart, and the appetites below the diaphragm; somewhat similarly, in the *Phaedrus* the disembodied soul is represented as a two-horse **chariot**, with the charioteer representing the mind and the two horses presumably spirit and appetite.

While **Aristotle** repeatedly insists on the **unity** of the soul, he also sometimes talks of "rational" versus "irrational" soul, and most similarly to Plato he distinguishes mind, sensory-locomotive soul, and nutritive-generative soul.

In later Greek thought, particularly with the **Stoics** and **Galen**, tripartition stages a kind of comeback with the assertion that *pneuma*, the material basis of psychic activity, comes in three different grades: *physikon*, *zotikon*, and *psychikon*, corresponding to the nutritional, sensory-motor, and intellectual functions.

TROPOS. Trope, mode. In Pyrrhonian Skepticism as developed by **Aenesidemus**, there are 10 ways of arguing to skeptical conclusions; these are called the "tropes." The most complete account is given by **Sextus Empiricus** in *Outlines of Pyrrhonism*. *Tropos* is also used by the **Stoics** to refer to the "modes" of arguments, for example different syllogistic forms. *See also SKEPTIKOS.*

TRUTH. *See ALĒTHEIA.*

TYCHĒ. Luck (especially good luck), Chance. In *Physics* II, **Aristotle** accuses earlier philosophers of relying on "good luck" to explain the existence of the universe rather than providing a teleological explanation. He argues that the claim that some event is lucky *presupposes* a similarity with events that could be explained teleologically—for example, if you run into a friend who owes you money, you can ascribe that to luck, because you would have gone to meet him intentionally had you known. But the existence of the universe is a unique event; therefore it cannot be lucky and must be explained teleologically. *See also AITION, TELOS.*

TYPOS, TYPŌSIS. Delineation, Imprinting, Impression. **Theophrastus** uses this term in discussing perception (*Sens.* 53); both **Epicureans** and **Stoics** also use this term in accounting for perception. In

Stoic thought, ***phantasia***, or the faculty of having an appearance, "imprints" on the soul (***psychē***). *See also AISTHĒSIS.*

– U –

UNDERSTANDING. *See DIANOIA.*

UNIT. *See HEN, MONAS.*

UNITY. How do the parts of something make up a "whole" unity? In brief, for **Aristotle**, the answer is "form" (***eidos***); for the **Stoics**, "tension" (***tonos***). For **Plato**, it seems that unity is in the Forms, not in the phenomena.

Is the universe a unity? For the **Eleatics**, the answer is obvious: **Being** is absolutely One. From that perspective, **atomism**, for example, would seem to be a denial of the unity of the universe. **Platonists** came to assert that The One is the principle and source of everything, "beyond" being. *See also COSMOS; HENAS; HOLON; MONAS; PHAINOMENA.*

UNIVERSAL. *See KATHOLOU.*

UNIVERSE. *See COSMOS.*

UNKNOWABLE. *See AGNŌSTOS.*

UNLIMITED. *See APEIRON.*

UNMOVED, UNMOVED MOVER. *See AKINĒTON; AKINĒTON KINOUN; PROTON KINOUN.*

UNPROVEN. *See ANAPODEIKTON.*

UNWRITTEN LAW. *Agraphos Nomos. See NOMOS.*

UNWRITTEN TEACHINGS. Thales, Pythagoras, Socrates, and several other well-known ancient philosophers seem not to have written anything; our knowledge of their teachings comes from reports from other people. In the case of Pythagoras, there was a large and active group of followers who tended to give credit to the Founder not only for his teachings but for their own discoveries as well.

Socrates had a significant number of followers also, and two of them, **Plato** and **Xenophon**, have left extensive written characterizations of Socratic teaching. We have plenty of written text from Plato, but we also have some reports that in person he taught some things that are not in the dialogues. One good example: **Aristoxenus'** report of Plato's lecture on the Good, *Elementa Harmonica* ii. 1 (tr. Myles Burnyeat, 78): "Everyone came expecting they would acquire one of the sorts of things people normally regard as good, on a par with wealth, good health, or strength. In sum, they came looking for some wonderful kind of happiness. But when the discussion turned out to be about mathematics, about numbers and geometry, and **astronomy**, and then, to cap it all, he claimed that Good is One, it seemed to them, I imagine, something utterly paradoxical. The result was that some of them sneered at the lecture, and others were full of reproaches."

Aristotle uses the phrase *exoterikoi logoi* in a somewhat mysterious way. It means "external accounts," but it is not obvious what or whose accounts he means. The phrase does suggest a contrasting group of *logoi* that would be "esoteric" teachings. We understand that distinction as one between teachings available to those outside a particular philosophical school and teachings limited to those within the school. While that distinction does not precisely track the distinction between "written" and "unwritten" teachings, since oral teaching could be public and some writings could be jealously guarded, there is obviously considerable overlap, so that "esoteric" is almost a synonym for "unwritten" in this context. In late antiquity, "esoteric" teachings were much in vogue.

We have reports of many post-Platonic philosophers who were influential teachers without writing anything; **Pyrrho** the Skeptic and **Diogenes of Sinope**, the Cynic, are two. Another well-known philosopher who did not write anything himself but whose teachings are preserved to a considerable extent is **Epictetus. Arrian** wrote down as much as he could of the otherwise unwritten teaching of this **Stoic** master. *See also EXŌTERIKOI LOGOI; MATHĒMA.*

– V –

VACUUM. *See KENON.*

VICTORINUS, MARIUS (280–365 CE). Rhetorician and commentator on **Aristotle**'s *Categories* and *Interpretation*, Victorinus was a **Neoplatonist** who converted to **Christianity**. After his conversion, he became a passionate defender of Trinitarian doctrine against the Arians; he wrote several commentaries on New Testament books. He was an important influence on **Augustine**.

VIRTUE. *See ARETĒ.*

VOID. *See KENON.*

VORTEX. *See DINĒ.*

– W –

WATER. Thales, the traditional "first" ancient Greek philosopher, is credited with the opinion that the world "rests on" water, or alternatively, that everything is made of water. He very well might have thought that water is the principle of life, and in that sense would be the "source" (***archē***) of everything.

   Empedocles makes water one of the four fundamental elements, along with **earth**, **air**, and **fire**. *See also STOICHEION.*

WEIGHT. How do things have weight? As far as we can tell, the **Presocratic** philosophers, as a group, did not think much about this question. **Anaxagoras** is reported (by a much later author) to have included "weight" among the primary qualities distributed everywhere; several Presocratics, starting with **Anaximenes**, put some stress on the importance of density and rarity of material things, thus massiveness. But there is a very telling line from **Aetius**, that **Democritus** made size and shape the primary qualities of atoms (***atoma***), and that **Epicurus** added weight. The atoms of Democritus move in an unoriented space, freely in all directions, and only change directions by collision with each other. The atoms of Epicurus, in contrast, are "falling" through space, that is, they would all continue forever on parallel tracks were there not the "**swerve**."

Aristotle specifically addresses the problem of weight, and "solves" it with a theory that is simple, satisfying, and wrong. He says that the center of the universe is occupied by **earth**, and it is the nature of earthy things to tend to go toward the center unless somehow prevented. On top of the earth is **water**, which also tends toward the center but not as strongly as earth. On top of the water is **air**, which goes up in water but otherwise down until it meets water. Above the air is the natural place of **fire**, which goes up through air until it gets to its natural sphere. Once water, air, and fire get to their natural location, they tend to circulate within that sphere (ocean and wind currents, and the movement of the fiery astronomical entities).

The standard story is that there was no progress on this part of physics until Galileo came along. *See also PHYSIS.*

WHEN. *See POTE.*

WHERE. *See POU.*

WHOLE. *See HOLON.*

WISDOM. *See PHRONĒSIS; SOPHIA.*

WISH. *See BOULĒSIS.*

WOMEN IN ANCIENT PHILOSOPHY. Although ancient philosophy has a deserved reputation for being primarily a male endeavor, there are some noteworthy instances both of participation in the philosophical tradition, and of serious contributions by and from women.

Ancient Greek societies differed significantly in terms of the participation of women in public and intellectual life: in many places, including Athens in the classical period, most women spent most of their adult lives working very hard to contribute to the household economy. The few female members of wealthy families who might have had the leisure to engage in intellectual pursuits were largely limited in their social contacts with other women and were not, on the whole, provided with a level of education that would have made it possible for them to interest themselves in philosophical issues. Most ancient Greek philosophers seem to have shared the general social assumption of their time that the role of women is inside the home, and the role of men is outside the home; philosophy is generally seen as one of the outside activities.

Some of the Ionian states seem to have had a more open and liberal attitude about the role of women. In the pre-philosophical period, Sappho won recognition for her poetry; **Plato** was to call her the "tenth muse."

Pythagoras established a philosophical community that according to reports readily accepted women as full members: **Iamblichus** lists some 16 women who were early members of the school, and there are fragmentary writings attributed to several of them, included in Diels and Kranz.

We know that Plato also accepted at least a few women as members of the Academy, and he recommends in the *Republic* that women of the Guardian class receive the same education as men and have the same positions of responsibility open to them. That recommendation is part of a critique of a radical social and political structure of contemporary Athens; to end tyranny, you must end tyranny in the family.

Although the active participants in Plato's dialogues are all male, at least two women are cited in the dialogues as sources of important ideas. In Plato's *Menexenus*, **Aspasia**, an immigrant from Ionia and the mistress of Pericles, is credited with having written the famous funeral oration delivered by Pericles and recorded in Thucydides' *History*. Socrates, in the *Menexenus*, delivers an alternative speech that he also says he learned from Aspasia. In the *Symposium*, Socrates credits the priestess **Diotima** with teaching him the theory of love that he presents. While some may doubt that the ideas in question really came from Aspasia or Diotima, these instances do, at the very least, indicate that Plato believed, and expected his audience to believe, that some women could contribute importantly to philosophical discourse.

Aristotle's views on the role of women were more nearly in line with those of contemporary society. Contrary to Plato, he believed that the family, not the individual person, is the basic building block of a functional and happy *polis*, and that does seem to him to imply that there are significantly different roles for women and men within the family structure. It is within that context that he comments (*Pol.* I.13, 1260a12) that the slave has "no deliberative faculty," that the woman has the deliberative faculty but it is "*akuron,*" or "without authority," and the child has but it is immature. One may wonder whether Aristotle believed that lack of authority to be the result of immutable natural differences or the consequence of the particular society with which he was most familiar.

Aristotle's comments about women in Sparta, in *Pol.* II.9, have considerable social interest, at least, since he essentially argues that the failure of Sparta to give an appropriate education to the women of the state led to its downfall. At 1269b30, he points out that in Sparta's period of greatness, "many things were managed by their women," but more recently, at the time of the Theban invasion, "unlike the women of other cities, they were utterly useless and caused more confusion than the enemy" (1269b37).

During Aristotle's lifetime, the **Cyrenaic** school of philosophy was directed by Arete, the daughter of **Aristippus**, so he had at least one example of a contemporary female philosopher, had he cared to cite it. Closer to home but a little later (within a few years of Aristotle's death), **Hipparchia** of Maroneia was in her very public marriage with **Crates** the Cynic. A few years after that, **Epicurus** set up his school in Athens with several women as full members of the group.

Once Stoicism had established a foothold in Rome, quite a few upper-class women gained the reputation of followers of the Stoic philosophy; **Musonius Rufus**, a leading Roman Stoic, composed an essay defending the teaching of philosophy to women.

Finally, toward the end of the history of ancient philosophy, **Hypatia** of Alexandria, a highly respected teacher of philosophy and mathematics, died a martyr at the hands of a fanatical mob. *See also MUSIKĒ.*

WONDER. *See THAUMASIA.*

WORLD SOUL. *Psychē tou pantos.* The idea that the Universe as a whole is alive is a persistent idea in Greek philosophy. **Anaximenes**, for example, appears to think of the sphere of the fixed stars as a giant membrane containing life-sustaining air; **Aristotle** attributes to the

Pythagoreans the idea that the universe "inhales vacuum" from outside (*Phys*. IV.6, 213b23). He attributes to **Xenophanes** the idea that **God** is the mind of the universe, or conversely that the physical universe is the body of God (***Metaphysics*** I.5, 986 b20–25).

In **Plato**'s *Timaeus* (36), the ***Demiourgos*** creates Circles of the Same and Different and sets them spinning in the heavens as the soul (*psychē*) of the universe; other souls are ultimately created from the leftovers of that primal soul-creation. Somewhat less poetically, Aristotle in *Metaphysics* XII describes a First Mover outside the universe, but the celestial Moved Movers, the direct causes of movement of astronomical entities, are deities.

In the **Stoic** philosophy, God as *pyr technikon* is the World Soul, permeating and organizing everything until everything is consumed in it. In the **middle Platonists**, such as **Philo** and **Plutarch**, the World Soul is clearly not identical to the supreme deity but is a somewhat distinct actualization of divinity: there is a triad or trinity of **One**, the *Logos*, and the World Soul. From then on, at least, some form of World Soul is a standard part of Platonistic philosophy, whether in **Alcinous**, **Numenius**, or **Plotinus**. *See also* COSMOS; *OURANOS*.

– X –

XENOCRATES OF CHALCEDON (396/5–314/3 BCE). Third **Scholarch** of the **Academy**. No actual pieces of his writing survive; most of what we know of the philosophy of Xenocrates is derived from **Aristotle**'s criticisms in the ***Metaphysics***, supplemented by comments by **Sextus Empiricus** and **Simplicius** among others.

Xenocrates appears to have made a serious attempt to systematize the metaphysical theories presented in **Plato**'s dialogues while remaining a faithful **Pythagorean**. Aristotle's criticisms, in *Metaphysics* XIII and XIV, focus on how the Forms (*eidē*) and mathematics (*mathēmatikē*) are related. Plato, in Aristotle's account, had asserted that the Forms are Numbers, but those numbers are not the same as the mathematical numbers that we use in normal arithmetic operations. Aristotle represents Xenocrates as breaking down this distinction, doubtless for the sake of metaphysical coherence, but unfortunately, as Aristotle sees it, to the detriment of mathematics.

Taking the *tetraktys* as inspiration, Xenophanes appears to have asserted that the One is also the point, Two is the line, Three is the surface, and Four is the solid. He took that to imply that there are actual spatial minima of each of those geometrical kinds, an idea for which he could find support in Plato's *Timaeus*.

Xenocrates probably anticipated and inspired the Pythagoreanizing **Platonists** of the Roman Imperial period. He may be the source of the triadic relationship between One or Mind (*nous*), Indefinite Dyad or **Matter**, and **World Soul**.

XENOPHANES OF COLOPHON (570–478 BCE). Xenophanes was a traveling poet with serious interest in philosophic questions. He dates himself by telling us (in fragment 8) that he left Colophon at the age of 25 when it was taken by the Persians (546/5), so he was born in 570 or close to it; he goes on to say that he had been bouncing around the Greek world for 67 years since that time, so he was 92 when he wrote the poem in question, and thus in 478 or so. Xenophanes is critical of traditional anthropomorphic religion, tending to satirize it.

> Ethiopians say that their Gods are snub-nosed and black;
> Thracians that theirs are blue-eyed and red-haired. (B16)

He also suggests that if horses or oxen could make statues, they would make their Gods look like horses and oxen—and of course there were plenty of "horse" and "oxen" Gods around the Mediterranean in those days. His positive concept of God includes the statement that there is:

> One God greatest among Gods and men,
> not at all like mortals in body or in thought. (B23)

This deity perceives as a whole (not with organs) and always stays in the same place, "moving all things with the thought of his mind (*nous*)" (B25).

Xenophanes is also famous for comments critical of the possibility of human knowledge.

> . . . and of course the clear and certain truth no man has seen nor will there
> be anyone who knows about the Gods and what I say about all things.
> For even if, in the best case, one happened to speak just of what has
> been brought to pass, still he himself would not know. But opinion is
> allotted to all. (B34, Lesher translation)

Some have seen Xenophanes as a precursor of **Parmenides** (because of the emphasis on **unity**) and others have seen him as a pantheist, possibly influenced by the characterizations of his thought offered by **Plato** (*Sophist* 242c–d) and **Aristotle**: "he contemplates the whole heaven and says the One is God" (*Metaphysics* I, 986b18–27). Nevertheless, his impact on the development of classical epistemology might be his greatest legacy.

XENOPHON OF ATHENS (c. 430–after 355 BCE). Student of **Socrates**, author of many extant works. In 401, he decided to join the army, along with many Spartans, being raised by Cyrus against Artaxerxes. Cyrus was killed in battle, and the Greek forces found themselves in the middle of what is now Iraq. Xenophon took charge and got them back to Greece, as recounted in his *Anabasis*. He continued his association with Sparta and was rewarded with a home near Olympia, where he wrote many of his works. For example, he continued the history and aftermath of the Peloponnesian Wars from where **Thucydides** left off; he wrote about Cyrus, horses, and dogs.

From a philosophical perspective, his most important works are those concerned with **Socrates**, including an *Apology* directed at attacks made on Socrates after 399, four volumes of *Memorabilia of Socrates*, and a *Symposium*. Xenophon's Socrates is less speculative, more practical, than **Plato**'s.

– Z –

ZENO OF CITIUM (c. 334–261/2 BCE). Founder of the **Stoic** school. Citium (or Kition) is a city on the southern coast of Cyprus, the Biblical Kittim and modern Larnaca; its inhabitants at the time of Zeno were primarily Phoenician in origin. Zeno is said to have come to **Athens** as a young man, perhaps on business; he apparently studied with **Crates** the **Cynic, Polemo** the **Scholarch** of the **Academy, Stilpo**, and others. After several years in Athens, he started teaching publicly in the Stoa Poikile, or Painted Porch (a shopping mall). He attracted a significant number of students and wrote several treatises, none of which survive except in scattered fragments. We do have a detailed account of Stoic doctrine included in the biography by **Dio-**

genes Laertius, and to a considerable degree it is possible to distinguish the teachings of Zeno from those of his successors.

Zeno divided philosophy into logic (*logikē*), physics (*physikē*), and **ethics** (*ethikē*). What we call "metaphysical" and "epistemological" issues were included in logic, as indeed were all inquiries concerning language. "Physics" includes all investigation of nature; "ethics" includes political theory.

Many of the attested Stoic advances in logic, at least in the narrow sense, seem to have been the work of Zeno's successors; his originality seems to have been primarily in physics and ethics. If we start from the physics end, we note that Zeno is resolutely materialist, believing that everything that is, is a material thing. Soul (*psychē*) is *pneuma*, **God** is creative fire. At the same time, God's rationality is omnipresent, so that natural law, properly understood, is also divine law, and indeed the best guide to morality. But since the universe is totally governed by rational mind (*nous*), every event is totally determined ("fated"). Indeed, the standard Stoic view, probably going back to Zeno, is that the universe goes through great cosmic cycles, from birth to conflagration (*ekpyrosis*); each cycle is precisely the same as the previous ones.

The hallmark of Stoic ethics, clearly a centerpiece of Zeno's philosophy, is the figure of the **Sage**, or the perfectly and completely wise and moral individual. This person is one who totally follows the divine/natural law and in a sense cannot be mistaken about anything.

Of Zeno's writings, perhaps the one we know most about is his *Republic*, a work that revealed his Cynical roots to an extent somewhat embarrassing to some of his Stoic successors. Assuming a community of sages, Zeno asserted that they would need no human legislation to govern their activity, no temples, no law courts, and no money. Like all Stoics, he believed in equality of the sexes; for him, that implied that everyone, men and women, should wear the same clothing, that clothing should not totally cover any part of the body, and citizens should freely choose with whom to have sexual relations, somewhat as the **Guardians** in **Plato**'s *Republic*.

Of the many charming stories about Zeno preserved in Diogenes Laertius, one stands out: at the age of 98, on his way to a temple, he stubbed his toe on a rock; looking down at the ground, he said, "Oh Great Mother, I hear your call," and held his breath until he died. *See also HEIMARMENĒ.*

ZENO OF ELEA (c. 490–c. 425 BCE). We learn from **Plato**'s *Parmenides* that Zeno was about 40 in about 450 BCE, that he was the associate of **Parmenides,** and that they had been lovers in Zeno's youth. Zeno had written a treatise that seems to have been a collection of arguments—**Proclus**, in his commentary on the *Parmenides*, says that there were 40 such arguments—supporting, indirectly, the thesis proposed by Parmenides, that **Being** is One. **Aristotle** paraphrases several of the arguments (*Physics* I.3, 187a3; IV.1, 209a23, 3, 210b22; VI.9, 233a21; VII.5, 250a20, and some other places), and **Simplicius** in his commentary on some of these passages in the *Physics* also presents some of the arguments, possibly closer to the original text. Zeno's "paradoxes" have tended to attract mathematical commentary.

ZENO OF TARSUS (or SIDON) (Late third–early second BCE). Successor of **Chrysippus** as **Scholarch** of the **Stoa**.

***ZŌĒ, ZŌON,* ZOOLOGY.** *Zōē* is one of two generally used words in Greek translated "life," the other is *bios*. *Zōē* tends to mean animal life, while *bios* tends to mean a way of life, or the general web of life. Thus a *zōon* is an animal, although the word is also used to denote a statue or picture, not necessarily that of an animal. In the *Timaeus*, **Plato** described the whole visible universe, endowed by the **world soul**, as a *zōon*, imitating the form (*eidos*) of the universe, which is said to be a "knowable animal" or *zōon noēton*.

Aristotle wrote three large and several smaller works focusing on animals: the *History* (or Investigation) *of Animals*, the *Parts of Animals*, the *Generation of Animals*, the *Progression of Animals*, the *Movement of Animals*, and some of the treatises included in the *Parva Naturalia*. No doubt, Aristotle believed that this study was valuable for its own sake, but he also seems to have believed that if he sorted out an explanation of the being of animals, his metaphysical theory about primary *ousia* would be better supported, since animals are paradigm cases of entities in his ontological theory.

ZOROASTRIANISM. Zoroastrianism is the modern name applied to the ancient religion of Persia—a major traditional prophet of that religion was named Zarathustra or Zoroaster. It is a monotheistic religion; the deity is typically known as Ahura Mazda, so one of the older names of the religion is Mazdaism. **Heraclitus** was very likely influenced by the Zoroastrian religion, and we know that ancient **Judaism**, during the Babylonian Captivity (which ended in 537 BCE), was also influenced by the religion of the Persians. The priests of the religion were known as Magi.

Plato mentions the Zoroastrian instruction received by the future kings of Persia in the *First Alcibiades* (122a); **Aristotle**, in defending his teleological principle of explanation, says that the Magi make the "The Best" the originating principle of everything (*Metaph.* XIV.4, 1091b10). **Diogenes Laertius** says that Aristotle believed that the religion of the Magi was older even than the religion of the **Egyptians** (DL I.8), that "Zoroaster" means "star worshipper," and that there is in addition to the good deity (Ahura Mazda) an evil deity, Ahriman. Aristotle says in *Metaphysics* XII that the worship of the **stars** is the oldest religion; he may well have had Zoroastrianism in mind when writing that passage.

The dualism of Zoroastrianism becomes evident in two of its manifestations during Hellenistic and Roman periods, Mithraism and **Manichaeanism**. Mithras is represented as a mediator between human beings and Ahura Mazda; the cult of Mithras became very popular in the Greek and Latin-speaking worlds during the second and first centuries BCE and remained a serious competitor with **Christianity** during the first few centuries of the common era. Some **Neoplatonists** were pleased to assimilate the image of Mithras into their **allegorical** accounts of the universe.

In the third century CE, Mani initiated (in Baghdad) a syncretistic religion, very strongly dualist, and asserting a "good" deity with limited rather than infinite power. While his religion, known as Manichaeanism, was regarded as heretical by the Zoroastrians of the day, it is more Zoroastrian than anything else. In any case, the religion rapidly made many converts, including **Augustine**, who subsequently repented the error of his ways.

Glossary

This Glossary lists all of the terms discussed in this Dictionary, minus the proper names. Greek, English, and a few Latin terms are included, in (English) alphabetical order; the major entries are listed in **BOLD**. In most cases, the major entries are under the Greek term; the English equivalents or translations are provided here to make it easier to find those entries. In some cases, there are relatively extensive entries under both the Greek and English terms, particularly when it is necessary to disambiguate when there are several terms in one language and only one in the other. In that case, both the English and Greek terms are in **BOLD**. Greek and Latin terms are in *italics*, whether bold or not.

– A –

ABSTRACTION. *Aphairesis.*
ACCIDENT, ACCIDENTAL. *SYMBEBĒKOS, KATA SYMBE-BĒKOS. See also TYCHĒ, AUTOMATON, SYMPTOMATA.*
ACCOUNT. *LOGOS.*
ACTUALITY. *ENERGEIA, ENTELECHEIA.*
ADĒLON. Unclear, non-evident.
ADIAPHORA. Indifferents.
ADDITIONAL PREMISE. *See PROSLĒPSIS.*
ADIKIA. Injustice.
AĒR. Air.
AFFECTION. *See PATHOS.*
AFFINITY. *See OIKEIŌSIS.*
AGATHON. Good.
AGENT INTELLECT. *Nous poiētikos. See also NOUS.*
AGNŌSTOS. Unknowable.

283

AGRAPHOS NOMOS. Unwritten law. *See* **NOMOS.**

AGREEMENT. *See* **HOMOLOGIA.**

AIDIOS. Everlasting.

AIŌN. Individual lifespan, "age"; timeless eternity.

AISTHĒSIS. Perception, sensation.

AITHĒR. "Ether."

AITION, AITIA. Responsibility, cause.

AKATALĒPTON. Non-cognitive, as applied to sensory impressions.

AKINĒTON. Unmoved, immovable.

AKOLASIA, AKOLASTOS. Licentiousness, intemperance, the vice opposed to *sōphrosynē*. The *akolastos* is the person who has the vice.

AKOLOUTHEIN, AKOLUTHEIA. To follow; consequentiality.

AKOUSMATA; AKOUSMATIKOI. Literally, things heard; eager hearers. Applied to Pythagorean teachings and their audience.

AKRASIA, AKRATEIA; AKRATĒS. *Akrasia* and *akrateia* are alternate spellings of the word meaning "lack of power, debility, lack of self-control." The *akratēs* is the person who exhibits a lack of control.

AKRON, AKRA. Extremity.

ALĒTHEIA. Truth.

ALGOS. Pain of body or mind.

ALIENATION. *Allotriōsis*, the opposite of **OIKEIŌSIS.**

ALLĒGORIA. Speaking in such a way as to be interpreted other than literally; interpretation of speech or text other than literally.

ALLOIŌSIS. Qualitative change.

ALTERATION. *ALLOIŌSIS, HETEROIŌSIS, KINĒSIS, METABOLĒ.*

AMBIGUITY. **AMPHIBOLIA.**

AMPHIBOLIA. Ambiguity.

ANAGKĒ, ANANKĒ. Necessity. *See also* **HEIMARMENĒ.**

ANALOGIA. Proportion, Analogy.

ANAMNĒSIS. Recollection.

ANAPODEIKTON. Unproven, indemonstrable, inconclusive.

ANDREIA. Courage, literally "manliness."

ANEPIKRITOS. Undecidable, in a fundamental sense.

ANGEL. *Angelos* in classical Greek is simply a "messenger."

ANIMA. Latin translation of **PSYCHĒ**, "soul."

ANIMAL. **ZOŌN.**

ANOMIA. Lawlessness.

ANTECEDENT CAUSE. *PROĒGOUMENON AITION.*
ANTHRŌPOS. Human being.
ANTIKOPĒ. Collision.
AOCHLĒSIA. Unperturbedness, *see also ATARAXIA.*
AORISTON. Indefinite.
APATHEIA. Condition of being unaffected.
APAXIA. Stoic term for "disvalue."
APEIRON. Literally, "without limit" or "without definition."
APODEIXIS. Exposition, demonstration, proof.
APOKATASTASIS. Restoration.
APORIA. "No path"; puzzle.
APPELATIVE. *PROSĒGORIA.*
APPETITE. *EPITHYMIA.*
APPROPRIATE. *KATHĒKON, OIKEION.*
APOGEGENĒMENON. Development, emergent property.
APOPROĒGMENA. Things dispreferred. *See also ADIAPHROA.*
APOTELESMA. Completion; effect of causes.
ARCHĒ. Origin, beginning, source, rule. *See also AITION.*
ARCHĒ KINĒSEŌS. Beginning of movement.
ARETĒ. Virtue, Excellence.
ARGUMENT. *LOGOS.*
ARITHMOS. Number.
ART. *POIEIN, TECHNĒ.*
ASŌMATON. Without body, disembodied, incorporeal.
ASSENT. *SYNKATATHESIS.*
ASTRA. Stars.
ASTROLOGIA. **Astronomy,** astrology.
ASTRONOMY. *ASTROLOGIA.*
ATARAXIA. Freedom from disturbance, tranquility of the soul.
ATAXIA. Disorder.
ATHANATOS. Immortal, Deathless.
ATOMON. Atom, the uncutable smallest bit of matter.
ATTENTION. *EPIBOLĒ.*
ATTEST. *EPIMARTYREIN.*
AUXILIARY (CAUSE). *SYNERGON.*
ATTRIBUTE. In the sense of "predicate," this is one of the ways that
   SYMBEBĒKOS is translated into English.
AULOS. An ancient musical instrument with a single or double reed.

AUTARKEIA. Self-sufficiency.
AUTOMATON. Self-moved.
AXIA. Worth, value.

– B –

BEAUTY. *TO KALON.*
BECOMING. *GENESIS.*
BEGINNING. *ARCHĒ.*
BEING. *ESTI, HYPARCHEIN, ON, ONTA, OUSIA.*
BELIEF. *DOXA, PISTIS.*
BELONG. *HYPARCHEIN, OIKEION,* **PREDICATE.**
BENEFIT. *ŌPHELĒMA.*
BIOS. Life.
BLEND. *KRAMA, KRASIS, MIGMA, MIXIS, SYNTHESIS.*
BODY. *SŌMA.*
BOULĒSIS. Wish.
BOULEUSIS. Deliberation.
BREATH. *PNEUMA.*

– C –

CANON. *KANŌN.*
CATEGORIES. *KATEGORIAI.*
CATHARSIS. *KATHARSIS.*
CAUSE, CAUSATION. *AITION, APOTELESMA.*
CHANCE. *KATA SYMBEBĒKOS, TYCHĒ.*
CHANGE. *ALLOIŌSIS, GENESIS, KINĒSIS, METABOLĒ.*
CHARA. Joy.
CHARIOT, CHARIOTEER. *OCHĒMA.*
CHARISMA. Grace.
CHARACTER. *ETHOS.*
CHOICE. *HAIRETON, PROAIRESIS.*
CHŌRA. Place, Space.
CHŌRIS, CHŌRISTON. Separate, separable.
CHRONOS. Time.

COGNITION. *DIANOIA, KATALĒPSIS, NOĒSIS, NOUS.*
COHESION (logical). *SYNARTĒSIS.*
COLLECTION. *SYNAGOGĒ.*
COLLISION. *ANTIKOPĒ.*
COMMANDING FACULTY. *HĒGEMONIKON.*
COMMON SENSE. *AISTHĒSIS KOINĒ: See AISTHĒSIS.*
COMPLETE CAUSE. *AITION AUTOTELĒS.*
COMPOSITE. *SYNTHETON.*
CONCEPT. *ENNOIA, ENNOĒMA.*
CONCOMITANCE, CONCOMITANT. *PARAKOLOUTHĒSIS, PAR-*
  AKOLOUTHOUN.
CONCLUSION. *EPIPHORA.*
CONTEMPLATION. *THEŌRIA.*
CONTINUITY. *SYNECHEIA.*
CONVINCING. *PITHANOS.*
COSMOS, COSMOLOGY. *KOSMOS.*
COURAGE. *ANDREIA, ARETĒ.*
CRITERION OF TRUTH. *ALĒTHEIA, KRITĒRION.*
CUT. *TEMNEIN, TOMĒ.*

– D –

DAIMŌN, DAIMŌNION. Lesser divinity.
DEDUCE. *SYNAGEIN.*
DEDUCTION. *SYNAGŌGĒ.*
DEDUCTIVE. *SYNAKTIKOS.*
DEFINE. *HORIZEIN.*
DEFINITION, *HORISMOS; LOGOS.*
DIEZEUGMENON. Disjunctive proposition.
DEIXIS. Indication, demonstration, demonstrative reference.
DELIBERATION. *BOULEUSIS.*
DELINEATION. *TYPOS.*
DEMIOURGOS. Literally, someone who works for the city; the Deity
  responsible for putting the **cosmos** in order.
DEMOCRACY. *DEMOKRATIA.*
DEMOKRATIA. Rule by the people.
DEMONSTRATION. *APODEIXIS, DEIXIS.*

DESIRE. *EPITHYMIA*, *ERŌS*, *HORMĒ*, *OREXIS*, *THYMOS*.
DEVELOPMENT. *APOGEGENĒMENON*.
DIAIRĒSIS. Division, distinction.
DIALECTIC. *DIALEKTIKĒ*.
DIANOIA. Reasoning.
DIAPHORA. Difference.
DIARTĒSIS. Disconnection.
DIASTĒMA. Interval, Dimension, Distance.
DIATHESIS. Disposition, character, state.
DIATRIBĒ. Literally, "pastime"; philosophical discourse.
DIKĒ. Justice personified; proper procedure.
DIKAIOS. Just person.
DIKAIOSYNĒ. Abstract concept of justice.
DINĒ. Vortex.
DISCONNECTION. *DIARTĒSIS*.
DISCOURSE. *LOGOS*.
DISJUNCTIVE PROPOSITION. **DIEZEUGMENON.**
DISORDER. *ATAXIA*.
DISPOSED. *PŌS ECHŌN* (one of the Stoic categories).
DISVALUE. *APAXIA*.
DIVINATION. *MANTIKĒ*.
DIVINE. *DEMIOURGOS, GOD, THEOS*.
DIVISION. *DIAIRĒSIS*.
DOCTRINE. *DOGMA*.
DOGMA. Teaching, opinion, doctrine.
DOGMATIKOS. Doctrinaire, opinionated.
DOXA. Opinion, expectation.
DOXOGRAPHY. Collection of opinions.
DREAM. *ONEIROS*.
DYAS. Dyad.
DYNAMIS, DYNAMEIS. Power, potentiality, capacity.

– E –

EARTH. *GĒ*.
ECHEIN. To have, to be in some condition.
EDUCATION. *PAIDEIA*.

EFFICIENT CAUSE. *AITION POIĒTIKON, ARCHĒ KINĒSEŌS.*

EIDŌLON. Insubstantial image, illusion; in Epicurean philosophy, substantial image.

EIDOS. Form, shape, kind, species.

EIKASIA. Conjecture, guesswork.

EIKŌN. Image.

EKPYROSIS. Conflagration.

EKSTASIS. Displacement, excitement, amazement.

ELEMENTS. *STOICHEIA.*

ELENCHUS. Examination.

ELEUTHERIA. Freedom, as opposed to slavery.

ELEUTHERIŌTĒS. Liberality, generosity: the virtue of acting like a free person as opposed to slavishly.

ENANTIA. Opposites.

ENARGEIA. The self-evidence of perceived facts.

END. *TELOS.*

ENDOXA. Accepted opinions.

ENERGEIA. Activity, actuality.

ENKRATEIA. Self-control.

ENKRATĒS. Self-controlled person.

ENNOĒMA. Concept.

ENNOIA. Concept or idea; literally, something in the mind.

ENTELECHEIA. Actuality.

EPAGŌGĒ. A method of persuasion; induction.

EPAISTHĒSIS. Sensory recognition.

EPH' HĒMIN. Up to us, in our power.

EPIBOLĒ. Focus of attention on the perceptual given.

EPIEIKEIA. Reasonableness, equity.

EPIMARTYREIN. Attest.

EPIPHORA. Term used by **Chrysippus** to denominate the conclusion of a syllogism.

EPISTĒMĒ. Knowledge, particularly knowledge of necessary truths,

EPITHYMIA. Appetite, desire.

EPOCHĒ. Suspension of judgment.

EQUITY. *EPIEIKEIA.*

ERGON. Work, function.

ERIS. Strife.

ERISTIC. Verbal competition aimed at victory, not necessarily truth.

ERŌS. Love or desire—especially sexual; personified as the God of love.

ESOTERIKOI LOGOI. Literally, "interior accounts." In late antiquity this phrase comes to mean something like "secret doctrine."

ESSENCE. *To ti ēn einai,* ***EIDOS, OUSIA, TI ESTI.***

ESTI. IS.

ETERNITY. ***AIŌN.***

ETHER. ***AITHĒR.***

ĒTHIKE ARETĒ. Moral virtue.

ĒTHOS. Character.

EUDAIMONIA. Happiness; literally, the condition of having a good **angel**, widely regarded as the ultimate goal of human existence.

EULOGOS. Reasonable, sensible, probable.

EUPATHEIA. The state of having positive feelings about something; the condition of having innocent emotions.

EVERLASTING. ***AIDIOS.***

EVIL. ***KAKON.***

EXISTENCE. ***HYPARCHEIN, OUSIA.***

EXŌTERIKOI LOGOI. Literally, "exterior accounts." Public teachings.

EXPERIENCE. ***AISTHĒSIS.***

EXPERTISE. ***TECHNĒ.***

EXPLANATION. ***AITION.***

EXPRESSION (LINGUISTIC). ***LEXIS.***

EXTENSION. ***DIASTĒMA.***

EXTREMITY. ***AKRA, AKRON.***

– F –

FACULTY (OF THE SOUL). ***DYNAMIS.***

FALSE. ***PSEUDOS.***

FAMILIAR. ***OIKEION, PAR' HĒMIN.***

FATE. ***ANAGKĒ, HEIMARMENĒ.***

FEELING. ***PATHOS.***

FIGMENT (OF IMAGINATION). ***PHANTASMA.***

FINAL CAUSE. ***TELOS.***

FIRE. ***PYR.***

FIRST MOVER. *ARCHĒ KINĒSEŌS, PRŌTON KINOUN.*
FIRST PHILOSOPHY. *PRŌTĒ PHILOSOPHIA.*
FORM. *EIDOS, MORPHĒ, IDEA.*
FORMAL CAUSE. *EIDOS, GENOS, OUSIA.*
FREEDOM. *ELEUTHERIOTĒS.*
FREEDOM FROM DISTURBANCE. *ATARAXIA.*
FRIENDSHIP. *PHILIA.*
FUNCTION. *DYNAMIS, ENERGEIA, ERGON.*

– G –

GĒ. EARTH.
GENESIS. **BECOMING.**
GENOS. Offspring, descent, hereditary group; larger classificatory group.
GNŌMĒ. The faculty by which one knows or opines; thought, judgment, opinion.
GNŌRIMON. Well-known; intelligible.
GNŌRIMŌTERON. Better known.
GNŌRIMŌTATON. Best known.
GNŌSIS. Knowledge by acquaintance; cognition.
GNŌSTIKOS. Cognitive.
GOD, GODS. *THEOS.*
GOOD. *AGATHON, KALON.*
GRAMMATIKĒ (TECHNĒ). Writing; the art of writing.
GUARDIANS. *PHYLAKES.*
GYMNASION. Gymnasium, extended to mean a school for young people in their late teens and early twenties.
GYMNOSOPHISTAI. The Greek name for the Hindu wise men; the word literally means "naked sophists."

– H –

HABIT. *HEXIS.*
HAIRETON. Choiceworthy.
HAMARTĒMA. Error, failure, fault.

HAPHĒ. Touch, the sense of touch, the point of contact between bodies.

HAPPINESS. *EUDAIMONIA.*

HARMONIA. HARMONY.

HEART. *KARDIA.*

HĒDONĒ, HĒDYN. Pleasure, the pleasurable.

HĒGEMONIKON. The directive aspect or power of the soul. A *hēgemōn* is a leader.

HEIMARMENĒ. Fate.

HEN. One.

HENAS, HENADOS. HENAD, Unity.

HETERON. The Other, otherness, difference.

HEXIS. A having, a disposition to act.

HISTORIA. Investigation, inquiry.

HOLON. Whole, organic unity, universe.

HOMOIOS. Similar, like.

HOMOIŌSIS. A process of making similar.

HOMOLOGIA, HOMOLOGOUMENOS. Agreement, agreeing.

HOMONYMOI. Two or more things with the same name but different whose definitions.

HONOR. *TIMĒ.*

HONORABLE. *KALOS.*

HORISMOS. Definition.

HORIZEIN. To delimit, to define.

HORMĒ. Innate drive or instinct.

HOSIOTĒS. Piety, holiness.

HOU HENEKA. "On account of what," a locution indicating a final cause.

HYLĒ. MATTER.

HYPARCHEIN. BE, BELONG.

HYPEROUSIA. Transcendence.

HYPHISTASTHAI. Subsist.

HYPODOCHĒ. Receptacle.

HYPOKEIMENON. Substratum.

HYPOLAMBANEIN. Suppose.

HYPOLĒPSIS. Supposition.

HYPOSTASIS. Substance.

HYPOTHESIS. Literally, something that is "put under"; proposal.

– I –

IATROS. Physician.
IATRIKĒ. The art of medicine.
IDEA. Visible form; form in general.
IDIŌMA. Peculiarity, specific property, unique feature.
IDION. That which belongs to the individual, private.
IMAGE. **EIDŌLON, EIKŌN, PHANTASMA.**
IMAGINATION. **PHANTASIA.**
IMITATION. **MIMĒSIS.**
IMMORTAL. **ATHANATOS.**
IMPASSIVITY. **APATHEIA.**
IMPRESSION. **AISTHĒSIS, TYPŌSIS.**
IMPULSE. **HORMĒ.**
INDEFINITE, INFINITE. **AORISTO, NAPEIRON.**
INDEMONSTRABLE. **ANAPODEIKTON.**
INDIFFERENT. **ADIAPHORAN.**
INDIVIDUAL. **KATH' HEKASTON, TODE TI.**
INDUCTION. **EPAGŌGĒ, SYNAGŌGĒ.**
INSTINCT. **HORMĒ.**
INTELLECT. **NOĒSIS, NOUS, PHRONĒSIS.**
INTELLIGIBLE. **GNŌRIMON.**
INTUITION. **NOUS.**
ISONOMIA. Equality of political rights.

– J –

JUDGMENT. **DOXA.**
JUSTICE. **DIKAIOSYNĒ, DIKĒ.**

– K –

KAKIA. Vice, badness.
KAKOS, KAKON. Bad, ugly, lowborn, cowardly, unskilled; evil.
KALOGATHIA. The condition of having all the social virtues.

KALON. Beautiful, noble, good.

KANŌN. Canon, standard, measure.

KARDIA. Heart.

KATALAMBANEIN. To grasp, to cognize.

KATALĒPSIS. The act of grasping an impression; cognition.

KATĒGORIAI. Categories; accusations.

KATH' HEKASTON. Individual.

KATHARSIS. Purification.

KATHĒKONTA. Appropriate actions or proper functions, i.e., moral duties.

KATHODOS. Descent.

KATHOLOU. As an adverb, "in general"; **TO KATHOLOU:** the universal.

KATORTHŌMA. That which is straight, correct; morally correct action.

KEISTHAI. To lie, be placed; the category of position.

KENON. Empty, void, vacuum.

KINĒSIS. Movement.

KINOUN, TO. Participle of the verb "to move"; *to kinoun* means "that which causes motion."

KOINŌNIA. Community.

KNOWLEDGE. **EPISTĒMĒ, GNŌSIS, NOĒSIS.**

KOSMOS. COSMOS.

KRAMA, KRASIS. Blending mixture.

KRITĒRION. Criterion, basis of judging.

– L –

LANGUAGE, THEORY OF. **LEXIS, LOGOS, ONOMA.**

LAW. **NOMOS.**

LEKTON. Something said, or sayable.

LEXIS. Speech, style of speech, diction, word, expression, text.

LIFE. **BIOS, ZOĒ.**

LIMIT. **PERAS.**

LOCOMOTION. **PHORA.**

LOGIKĒ. Logic.

LOGISMOS. Calculation, reasoning.

LOGISTIKON. Skilled in calculation; the rational part of the soul.

LOGOS. Word, account, ratio, definition, proposition, discourse, language.

LOVE. *ERŌS, PHILIA.*

LYPĒ. Bodily pain, opposed to bodily pleasure.

LYSIS. Solution, seeing free, deliverance.

– M –

MANIA. Madness.

MAGIC. *Mageia,* the theory and practice of the "Mages" or Persian; *manganeia,* "trickery."

MAGNITUDE. *DIASTĒMA, MEGETHOS.*

MANTIKĒ. Divination, prophecy.

MATHĒMA. Something that can be learned.

MATHĒMATA, TA. Mathematical knowledge: arithmetic, geometry, astronomy, harmonics.

MATHĒMATIKA, TA. Mathematical entities such as odd and even, point, line, and surface considered separately from bodies, and so on.

MATHĒMATIKOI. Serious students in the early Pythagorean School.

MATTER. *HYLĒ.*

MEAN. *MESON.*

MEDICINE. *IATRIKĒ.*

MEDIUM OF PERCEPTION. *MESON, METAXY.*

MEGALOPREPEIA. Magnificence, as a personal quality.

MEGALOPSYCHIA. "Great-souled-ness" or pride, as a personal quality.

MEGETHOS. Size, magnitude.

MEIGMA. Mixture, compound. Alternate spelling for *MIGMA.*

MĒ ON. Non-being.

MESON, MESOTĒS. Mean, middle, medium.

METABASIS. Transition, "going across"; the change of the elements into each other; the continuity of living kinds; regress.

METABOLĒ. Change.

METAXY. Between.

METEMPSYCHOSIS. Transmigration of souls.

METHEXIS. Participation.

MIGMA. Mixture, compound.

MIMĒSIS. Imitation.
MIXIS. Mixture, blending, sexual intercourse.
MIXTURE. **KRASIS, MIGMA, MIXIS, SYNTHESIS.**
MODERATION. **SŌPHROSYNĒ.**
MOIRA. Allotment, portion, fate.
MONAS. One, unit.
MORPHĒ. Shape, form.
MODE. **TROPOS.**
MODERATION. **SŌPHROSYNĒ.**
MOTION. **KINĒSIS, PHORA.**
MOVER. **KINOUN.**
MOUSIKĒ. The arts of the Muses.
MYTHOS. Any verbal performance, whether in speech or writing; fiction.

– N –

NAME. **ONOMA.**
NATURAL LAW. **NOMOS, PHYSIS.**
NATURAL PHILOSOPHER. **PHYSIKOS.**
NATURE. **PHYSIS.**
NECESSITY. **ANAGKĒ (ANANKĒ).**
NEIKOS. Strife.
NEMESIS. Retribution; righteous indignation.
NON-BEING. **MĒ ON.**
NOĒSIS. Thinking, especially thinking about Being.
NOĒMA. Thought.
NOĒTON. Object of thought, something that is thinkable.
NOMOS. Law; convention.
NOUS (NOOS). Mind.
NUMBER. **ARITHMOS.**
NUTRITIVE SOUL. **PSYCHĒ THREPTIKĒ.**

– O –

OCHĒMA. Carriage or vehicle, especially the vehicle of the soul.
OIKEION. That which is one's own; proper to oneself.

OIKEIŌSIS. Appropriation; the process of making something one's own.
ON, ONTA. **BEING, BEINGS.**
ONE. *HEN.*
ONEIROS. Dream.
ONOMA. Name, noun.
ŌPHELEIN. To owe a debt.
ŌPHELĒMA. A debt, obligation.
OPINION. *DOXA.*
OPPOSITES. *ENANTIA.*
ORDER. **COSMOS,** *TAXIS.*
OREXIS. The capacity of initiating movement shared by all animals.
ORGANON. Tool; logic.
ORIGIN. *ARCHĒ.*
OU MALLON. No more, used in Skeptical arguments with the connotation "no more this than that."
OURANOS. Sky, heaven.
OURANIA. Heavenly.
OUSIA. Reality, something real; substance.

– P –

PAIDEIA. Education: reading, writing, and the arts.
PAIN. *ALGOS, LYPĒ, PONOS.*
PALINGENESIS. Regeneration, rebirth, resurrection.
PAR' HĒMIN. Familiar, "by us."
PARABOLĒ. Comparison, illustration, parable, parody.
PARADEIGMA. Example, standard.
PARAKOLOUTHĒSIS. Concomitance.
PARAKOLOUTHOUN. Concomitant.
PARENKLISIS. Swerve.
PARONYMOI. Something is a paronym if a word or name applied to it is derived secondarily from something that has that appellation in a primary sense. Apples are "healthy" in a paronymous sense because people who eat them are "healthy" in a primary sense.
PARTICIPATION. *METHEXIS.*
PARTICULAR. *HENAD, KATH' HEKASTON, TODE TI.*
PASCHEINALGOS. To be affected, to suffer.

PASSION. *PATHOS.*

PASSIVE INTELLECT. *NOUS PATHĒTIKOS.*

PATHOS, PATHĒ. That which happens to a person (or anything else); experience, either good or bad. Emotion.

PERAS. Limit, end (in the sense of limit).

PERFECTION. *ENTELECHEIA, TELOS.*

PHAINOMENON. That which appears, a phenomenon, an appearance.

PHANTASIA. Any appearance; the faculty of imagination; *false* appearance. Sometimes *phantasia* is the faculty, sometimes the activity of the faculty, and sometimes it is the content or object of the faculty.

PHANTASMA. Figment of the imagination.

PHAULOS. Small, insignificant, worthless, bad.

PHENOMENON. *PHAINOMENON.*

PHILIA. Friendship, love.

PHILOSOPHIA, PHILOSOPHOS. Philosophy, philosopher.

PHŌNĒ. Sound.

PHORA. The act of carrying or that which is carried; used as a very general term for local movement.

PHRONĒSIS. Thought, understanding, prudence.

PHTHORA. Destruction.

PHYLAKES. **GUARDIANS.**

PHYSICIAN. *IATROS.*

PHYSIKOI, PHYSIOLOGOI. Philosophers of nature; scientists.

PHYSIS, HISTORIA PERI PHYSEŌS. Nature; the study of Nature.

PIETY. *ARETĒ, HOSIOTĒS.*

PISTIS. Belief.

PITHANOS. Convincing, inspiring *pistis*.

PLACE. *TOPOS.*

PLEASURE. *HĒDONĒ.*

PLEONEXIA. Getting more than one's fair share.

PLĒTHOS. Plurality, large number, quantity, magnitude.

PLURALITY. *PLETHOS.*

PNEUMA. Breath, wind, spirit.

POIEIN. To make or do.

POIĒMA. An object that is made.

POIĒSIS. Making, production.

POIĒTĒS. A person who makes something.

POIĒTIKĒ. Productive.

POINT. *STIGMĒ.*

POION. Of what sort, quality.

POIOTĒS. Quality.

POLIS. City, State.

POLITIKĒ. Political theory and the art of politics.

PONOS. Hard work, toil, pain from working.

PŌS ECHEIN (PŌS ECHŌN), PŌS ECHEIN PROS TI (PŌS ECHŌN PROS TI). Two of the four Stoic categories, "how disposed," and "how disposed in relation to something."

POSITION. *KEISTHAI, THESIS.*

POSON. How much, Quantity.

POSSESSION. *ECHEIN, HEXIS.*

POTE. When, time.

POTENTIALITY. *DYNAMIS.*

POU. Where; place.

POWER. *DYNAMIS.*

PRAGMA. A thing done; "thing" as opposed to "word."

PRAXIS. Action, as opposed to production.

PRAKTIKĒ. Practical art or practical science as opposed to productive on the one hand, or theoretical on the other.

PRECONCEPTION. *PROLĒPSIS.*

PREDICATE, PREDICATION. *HYPARCHEIN, KATEGORIAI.*

PREFERABLES, PREFERRED. PROĒGMENA.

PRIME MATTER. *PRŌTE HYLĒ. See HYLĒ.*

PRIME MOVER. *PRŌTON KINOUN.*

PRINCIPLE. *ARCHĒ, HYPOTHESIS.*

PRIVATION. *STERĒSIS.*

PROAIRESIS. Choice.

PROBLEM. *APORIA.*

PROCESS. *GENESIS.*

PRODUCTION. *See POIĒSIS.*

PROĒGMENA. Things preferred.

PROĒGOUMENON AITION. Antecedent cause.

PROLĒPSIS. Preconception.

PRONOIA. Providence, foresight, forethought.

PROODOS. Procession.

PROOF. *APODEIXIS.*
PROPERTY. **IDION.**
PROPORTION. **ANALOGIA, LOGOS.**
PROS TI. Relation.
PROSĒGORIA. "Appelative."
PROSLĒPSIS. Additional premise.
PRŌTĒ PHILOSOPHIA. First Philosophy.
PRŌTON KINOUN. First Mover.
PROVIDENCE. *PRONOIA.*
PRUDENCE. *PHRONESIS.*
PSEUDOS. False.
PSYCHĒ. Soul.
PTŌSIS. "Case," as in the declension of Greek nouns and adjectives.
PURIFICATION. *KATHARSIS.*
PURPOSE. *TELOS.*
PYR. Fire.

– Q –

QUALITY, QUALITATIVE CHANGE. *ALLOIŌSIS, POION, POIO-
TĒS.*
QUANTITY. *POSON.*
QUINTESSENCE. *AITHĒR.*

– R –

RATIO. *LOGOS.*
REASON. *LOGISTIKON, LOGOS, NOUS.*
RECEPTACLE. *HYPODOCHĒ.*
RECOLLECTION. *ANAMNĒSIS.*
REFUTATION. *ELENCHUS.*
REINCARNATION. *METEMPSYCHOSIS, PALINGENESIS.*
RELATION. *PROS TI.*
RESPONSIBILITY. *AITION.*
RHĒTORIKĒ. Rhetoric, the art of the *rhētōr*, or public speaker.

RHOĒ. Flow, stream, flux.

RULE. *ARCHĒ.*

– S –

SAGES. *SOPHOI.*

SCHĒMA. Form, shape, appearance.

SCHESIS. State, condition, a temporary state of affairs in contrast to *hexis*, which tends to be permanent.

SCIENCE. EPISTĒMĒ.

SELF-CONTROL. *ENKRATEIA, SŌPHROSYNĒ.*

SELF-EVIDENCE. *ENARGEIA.*

SELF-MOVING. *AUTOKINĒTON.*

SELF-SUFFICIENCY. *AUTARKEIA.*

SĒMAINEIN. To show by a sign, indicate; to mean something.

SĒMEION. Sign, token, indication.

SENSATION. *AISTHĒSIS.*

SENSORY RECOGNITION. *EPAISTHĒSIS.*

SEPARATE. *CHŌRISTON.*

SERIOUS. *SPOUDAIOS.*

SHAPE. *MORPHĒ, SCHĒMA.*

SIGN. *SĒMEION.*

SIMILAR. *HOMOIOS.*

SKEPTIKOS. A person who reflects so thoroughly that he does not come to any conclusions.

SKOPOS. Target.

SOLUTION. *LYSIS.*

SŌMA. Body.

SOPHOS, SOPHOI, SOPHIA. A "*sophos*" is a wise or able person; "*sophoi*" is the plural form; "*sophia*" is the abstract noun, denominating wisdom or an admired ability.

SOPHISTĒS, SOPHISTAI; SOPHISTIKĒ TECHNE. Sophist, Sophists; the sophistic art: sophistry.

SŌPHROSYNĒ. Temperance, moderation, self-control, mental health.

SOUL. *PSYCHĒ.*

SOURCE. *ARCHĒ.*

SOURCE OF MOVEMENT. *ARCHĒ KINĒSEŌS.*

SPACE. *CHORA, TOPOS.*

SPECIES. *EIDOS.*

SPERMA. Seed.

SPERMATIKOS LOGOS. Rational form present in matter, the cause of emergent properties of complex entities.

SPIRIT. *PNEUMA, THYMOS.*

SPONTANEOUS. *AUTOMATON.*

SPOUDAIOS. Serious, eager, excellent.

STARS. *ASTRA.*

STATE. In the sense of "condition," *HEXIS, PŌS ECHEIN, SCHESIS*; in the sense of "political structure," *POLIS.*

STERĒSIS. Privation, negation, deprivation.

STIGMĒ. Point.

STOICHEION, STOICHEIA. **ELEMENTS**, phoneme, letter of the alphabet; basic information about a subject.

STRIFE. *ERIS, NEIKOS.*

SUBSTANCE. *OUSIA.*

SUBSIST. *HYPHISTASTHAI.*

SUBSTRATUM. *HYPOKEIMENON.*

SUSPENSION (OF BELIEF). *EPOCHĒ.*

SWERVE. *PARENKLISIS.*

SYLLOGISMOS. Literally, putting *logoi* together; technical term for certain formalized argument structures.

SYMBEBĒKOS, SYMBEBĒKOTA. Accident, attribute.

SYMBOLON, SYMBOLA. Identity token; object or phrase meaningful to the initiated.

SYMPASCHEIN. To "feel together," interact, co-experience.

SYMPATHEIA. Physical, emotional, or social interaction of feelings.

SYMPERASMA. Conclusion of a syllogism.

SYNAGEIN. To bring together, collect; deduce.

SYNAGŌGĒ. Collection, induction; deduce; congregation.

SYNAKTIKOS. Deductive.

SYNAITION. Joint cause.

SYNARTĒSIS. Cohesion.

SYNECHEIA. Continuity.

SYNECHEIN. Sustain, hold together.

SYNEIMARMENON. Co-fated.

SYNKATATHESIS. Assent.

SYNEKTIKĒ DYNAMIS. Sustaining power.

SYNEKTIKON AITION. Sustaining cause.

SYNERGON (AITION). Auxiliary (cause).

SYNOLON. Whole, especially the combination of matter and form that results in an entity.

SYNONYMOI. If two entities share the same name and the definition is the same in both cases, they are "synonymous."

SYNTHESIS. A *synthesis* is a combination of parts in which the parts change in nature as a consequence of the combination; the intellectual process of constructing ideas from perceptions.

SYNTHETON. Put together; is a compound.

SYSTASIS. Composition or constitution; used both of the construction of an individual living body and of a political organization.

SYSTĒMA. A whole composed of parts.

– T –

TABULA RASA. Blank (or smoothed) tablet (in Latin).

TAXIS. Order, arrangement.

TECHNĒ. Art, craft, skill.

TECHNIKOS. Skillful, but also often "artificial."

TELOS. End, goal, purpose.

TEMNEIN. To cut.

TENOR. HEXIS, in Stoic contexts.

TENSION. **TONOS.**

TETRAKTYS. The geometrical form best illustrated by the arrangement of the pins in bowling, taken as importantly symbolic by the Pythagoreans.

TETRAPHARMAKON. Fourfold cure, the Epicurean way to a happy life.

THAUMASIA. Wonder.

THEIOS. The divine.

THEMA. Literally, that which is placed or put down; a rule for determining whether a given deduction is valid.

THEOLOGIA. Account of God and the divine.

THEŌRIA, THEŌREIN. *Theōrein* (the verb) means, in the first instance, to look at, be a spectator, observe. *Theoria* may be translated contemplation.

THEOS. GOD.

THEOURGIA. Theurgy; divine work. Performance of sacred rituals or sacraments; persuading a deity to do what you want.

THĒRIOTĒS. Beastliness.

THESIS. Noun formed from the verb meaning "to put." The word is used in both a physical and a metaphorical sense. Physically, the word means approximately "position"; metaphorically, a *thesis* is a proposition posited for discussion and possible defense."

THINKING. *DIANOIA, LOGISMOS, NOĒSIS, THEŌRIA.*

THYMOS. Desire, mind, spirit; anger.

TI ESTI. "What is . . . ?" *to ti esti* is one of the designations for what we call essence.

TIME. *CHRONOS.*

TIMĒ. Honor.

TO TI EN EINAI. **ESSENCE.**

TODE TI. This something; individual entity.

TOMĒ. A cut.

TONOS. Tension.

TOPOS. Place.

TOUCH. *HAPHĒ.*

TRANSCENDENCE. **HYPEROUSIA.**

TRANSMIGRATION (OF THE SOUL). *METEMPSYCHOSIS.*

TRIAS. Triad.

TROPOS. Trope, mode.

TRUTH. *ALĒTHEIA.*

TYCHĒ. Luck.

TYPOS, TYPŌSIS. Delineation, Imprinting, Impression.

– U –

UNDERSTANDING. *DIANOIA.*

UNIT. *HEN, MONAS.*

UNITY. *HEN, HOLON, MONAS.*

UNIVERSAL. *KATHOLOU.*

UNIVERSE. **COSMOS.**

UNKNOWABLE. *AGNŌSTOS.*

UNLIMITED. *APEIRON.*

UNMOVED, UNMOVED MOVER. *AKINĒTON, AKINĒTON KI-NOUN.*

UNPROVEN. *ANAPODEIKTON.*
UNWRITTEN LAW. *AGRAPHOS NOMOS. See NOMOS.*

– V –

VACUUM. *KENON.*
VIRTUE. *ARETĒ.*
VOID. *KENON.*
VORTEX. *DINĒ.*

– W –

WHEN. *POTE.*
WHERE. *POU.*
WHOLE. *HOLON.*
WISDOM. *PHRONĒSIS, SOPHIA.*
WISH. *BOULĒSIS.*
WONDER. *THAUMASIA.*
WORLD SOUL. *PSYCHE (TOU PANTOS).*

– Z –

ZŌĒ. Life.
ZŌON. Animal.

Bibliography

Constructing a general bibliography for ancient philosophy is a complex task. Fortunately there are ongoing bibliographic resources to which the student may turn for assistance. The most important of these is *L'Année Philologique*, including well over 400,000 bibliographic records since 1969, with over 12,000 added each year. The published volumes of *L'Année Philologique* go back to the 1920s; currently new materials are added online. As a rule, scholarly libraries subscribe. The major drawback is that they are usually two or three years behind in updating the system. For more information, here's the site: http://www.annee-philologique.com/.

The *Philosopher's Index* began publication in 1967. While it is not as complete as *L'Année Philologique*, it tends to be more nearly up-to-date. Their home page is http://www.philinfo.org/. A very good general index is Periodicals Index Online (formerly known as Periodicals Content Index). The home page is http://pio.chadwyck.co.uk/marketing.do. Many libraries subscribe to one or both of these services.

The major journals specializing in ancient philosophy and publishing articles in English are *Phronesis*, *Ancient Philosophy*, and *Apeiron*. Many of the general philosophy or classics journals also publish a significant number of articles in ancient philosophy—the *Review of Metaphysics*, *Philosophical Review*, *Mind*, *Journal of the History of Philosophy*, *Archiv für Geschichte der Philosophie*, *American Journal of Philology*, and *Classical Quarterly* are a few examples of journals that often publish high quality articles in ancient philosophy.

The print resources consulted frequently for constructing the present work include, most importantly, Liddell, Scott & Jones, *Greek-English Lexicon*, 9th ed., and F. E. Peters, *Greek Philosophical Terms*, New York University Press, 1967, for the Greek words, and Donald J. Zeyl, ed., *Encyclopedia of Classical Philosophy*, Greenwood, 1997, for philosophers. Our entries are, on the whole, not as detailed as those of either Peters or Zeyl, but are more inclusive, with more Greek terms than Peters and more philosophers than Zeyl.

We also used several online resources, most notably the *Stanford Encyclopedia of Philosophy*, http://plato.stanford.edu/, and the *Internet Encyclopedia of Philosophy*. http://www.iep.utm.edu/. These two sites feature signed articles, often (not always) by one of the ranking authorities in the world on the topic discussed. If one of these sites has an article on an ancient philosopher or topic, it is very possibly the most complete, most reliable, and most up-to-date reference resource available.

Brill's New Pauly is the only print source that can compete. One noticeable difference between the Stanford and the IEP is that if Stanford doesn't have a *good* article on a topic, it doesn't have one at all; IEP includes "stubs" or material cribbed from out-of-copyright sites elsewhere on the web, often better than nothing, but not necessarily better than a good print source.

Wikipedia (http://en.wikipedia.org/wiki/Main_Page) is, we may say, controversial as a scholarly resource. For topics in ancient Greek philosophy many or most of the articles are ultimately based on the 11th ed. of the *Encyclopedia Britannica*, published in 1911, and then made available to anyone who wishes to edit them, essentially. The result is that it is extremely likely that there will be *some* information on almost any ancient philosopher, and on many philosophical topics that can be formulated clearly enough to be searched. Sometimes Wikipedia articles are every bit as good as the competing articles on Stanford or IEB, but given the fluidity of the Wiki process, there is always a question about reliability. For most (not all) topics in ancient philosophy, there is little motivation for people to do wholesale flim-flam on a Wikipedia page, but there is always a possibility that you are reading an article edited most recently by a high school student with a sense of humor. One article I checked recently, on a minor Hellenistic philosopher, ended with the sentence: "And in addition, he loved bacon double cheeseburgers." Two days later, the sentence was gone; the Wikipedia managers can be pretty efficient. Given the fluid nature of the Wikipedia articles, we have decided not to include them in the bibliography; at the same time, recognize that Wikipedia *might* be the most convenient place to find out significantly more on a topic discussed in this dictionary, and could have information not otherwise readily available.

The Perseus Project, based at Tufts University (www.perseus.tufts.edu/), mainly concentrates on digitizing classical texts, but there are some encyclopedia-like features present on the site. There is a fairly steep learning curve to achieve the ability to use this site effectively.

The Catholic Encyclopedia of Philosophy (http://www.newadvent.org/cathen/) is mainly useful for short biographical essays on some of the lesser figures, especially in late antiquity. It resembles Wikipedia in being based on a work originally published in 1911, but it has been much less (if at all) updated since that original publication.

Philosophy Pages (http://www.philosophypages.com/) includes a general dictionary of philosophy, including a number of Greek terms. It can be useful, but it is clearly incomplete, and is not kept up-to-date.

J. J. O'Connor and E. F. Robertson posted on the St. Andrews University website in and around 1999 a fairly large number of biographies of mathematicians and people of interest to mathematicians, including quite a few ancient figures. In many cases these are the best online resources for the people that they discuss. The URL is http://www-gap.dcs.st-and.ac.uk/~history/.

In terms of texts and translations of ancient authors, this bibliography emphasizes print versions. It should be recognized, however, that there are significant online resources for both original text and for translations into English of many ancient authors. Easily the most complete is the Thesaurus Linguae Graecae (TLG), http://www.tlg.uci.edu/. The Perseus Project is an accessible alternative, using transliterated Greek text. For classic English translations of major authors, the Internet Classics Archive, http://classics.mit.edu/, is perhaps the best bet. Unlike TLG, it includes Latin authors, such as Cicero and Seneca.

The online sources are not very good for philosophers that we have only in fragmentary form. Perhaps the most convenient online source for the philosophers included is http://philoctetes.free.fr/index2.htm, a French site with Greek, French, and English versions of Thales, Anaximander, Heraclitus, Parmenides, Zeno, and Empedocles fragments. For other Presocratics the online environment is not good: for example, the most likely site that one would find for Democritus is http://evans-experientialism.freewebspace.com/democritus.htm, and it has only 44 of the fragments, out of 298 included in Diels and Kranz.

If anything, the situation is worse for most post-Aristotle philosophers. The C. D. Yonge translation of Diogenes Laertius is available online at http://classic persuasion.org/pw/diogenes/, and there is a good index of Epicurean texts at http://www.epicurus.info/etexts.html; one can find similar sites for the Stoics, for example http://www.btinternet.com/~k.h.s/stoic-foundation.htm. There is not, however, any online collection that can begin to compete with the Long and Sedley *Hellenistic Philosophers*.

Ultimately, students need to acquire hard copy collections of the fragments of the Presocratics and of post-Aristotelian philosophers.

For philosophical works in late antiquity, the online availability of translations, especially, is spotty at best. Indeed, many of the most interesting philosophical works from late antiquity have only recently been translated, and it will be many years before those translations are out of copyright. Some useful online versions that do exist include Plutarch's *Moralia* at http://oll.libertyfund.org/Home3/Set.php?recordID=0062 and Plotinus' *Enneads* at http://classics.mit.edu/.

This bibliography is arranged historically and topically: the major sections correspond with the major periods distinguished in the historical survey of ancient philosophy; within each section the divisions are between major philosophers and schools. At the end of the bibliography, there is a section for studies that span more than one period of ancient philosophy.

STRUCTURE OF THIS BIBLIOGRAPHY

Dictionaries, Encyclopedias, and Concordances   311
Historical Periods and Major Authors   312
     Before Thales   312
     Homer   312

Presocratics, General Works   312
   Milesians   313
   Heraclitus   313
   Xenophanes   313
   Pythagoras and Early Pythagoreans   313
   Eleatics: Parmenides, Zeno, Melissus   314
   Empedocles   314
   Anaxagoras   314
   Early Atomism   315
Fifth Century BCE Literature, Science, Medicine, Etc.   315
   Herodotus   315
   Hippocrates   315
   Thucydides   315
Sophists of the fifth Century BCE   315
   Gorgias   316
   Hippias   316
   Prodicus   316
   Protagoras   316
   Thrasymachus   317
Classical Philosophy: Comparative Studies   317
   Socrates   317
   Students of Socrates and Their Schools   318
   Plato   318
   Early Academy   320
   Aristotle   320
   Lyceum; Early Peripatetic School   324
   Other Fourth-Century BCE Philosophers and Scientists 325
Hellenistic Philosophy   325
   Epicurus and Epicureanism   326
   Cynics   327
   Hellenistic Stoicism   327
   Skepticism   327
   Other Hellenistic Persons of Interest   328
   Antiochus and the First Century BCE Academy   329
   Cicero, Marcus Tullius   329
Roman Imperial Philosophy   329
   Stoicism in the Roman Period   329
   Epicureanism in the Roman Imperial Period   330
   Aristotelianism in the Roman Imperial Period   330
   Cynicism in the Roman Period   331
   Skepticism in the Roman Period   331
   The Second Sophistic   331
   Ptolemy   332

Medicine in the Roman Period	332
Doxography	333
Middle Platonism	333
Neopythagoreanism	334
Neoplatonism	334
Plotinus	334
Porphyry	335
Victorinus, Marius	335
Augustine	335
Iamblichus	336
Proclus	336
Neoplatonist Commentators	336
Other Neoplatonists of the Roman Imperial Period	339
Aristotelians of the Roman Period	339
Christian Church Fathers	340
Gnosticism, Hermeticism, Chaldean Oracles, Dreams	341
Other Imperial Period Texts	341
Modern Studies of Cross-Period Topics	341
Natural Philosophy	342
Mathematics	342
Astronomy	342
Metaphysics	342
Ethics	342
Art and Music	342
Women in Ancient Philosophy	343
The Transmission of Ancient Philosophy, 7th to 15th Centuries	343

DICTIONARIES, ENCYCLOPEDIAS, AND CONCORDANCES

Abbott-Smith, George. *A Manual Lexicon of the Greek New Testament*. Edinburgh: T. and T. Clark, 1936.

Bonitz, Herman. *Index Aristotelicus*. Graz: W. de Gruyter, 1955.

Brandwood, Leonard. *A Word Index to Plato*. Leeds: W. S. Maney, 1976.

Cancik, Hubert, and Helmut Schneider, eds. *Brill's New Pauly: Encyclopedia of the Ancient World*, 20 vols. Leiden: Brill, 2002.

Liddell, Henry George, and Robert Scott, et al. *A Greek-English Lexicon*. Oxford: Oxford University Press, 1968.

Peters, F. E. *Greek Philosophical Terms: A Historical Lexicon*. New York: New York University Press, 1967.

Zeyl, Donald J., ed. *Encyclopedia of Classical Philosophy*. Westport, Conn.: Greenwood, 1997.

HISTORICAL PERIODS AND MAJOR AUTHORS

Before Thales

Bernal, Martin. *Black Athena*. 2 vols. New Brunswick, N. J.: Rutgers University Press, 1987, 1991.
Evangeliou, Christos. *When Greece Met Africa: The Genesis of Hellenic Philosophy*. Binghamton, N.Y.: Institute of Global Cultural Studies, 1994.
Guthrie, William K. C. *Orpheus and Greek Religion: A Study of the Orphic Movement*. Princeton: Princeton University Press, 1993.
Hine, Daryl, tr. *Works of Hesiod and the Homeric Hymns*. Chicago: University of Chicago Press, 2005.

Homer

Homer: The Odyssey with an English Translation. Augustus T. Murray, tr. Cambridge, Mass.: Harvard University Press, 1919. (Loeb).
Iliad. Augustus T. Murray, tr. Cambridge, Mass.: Harvard University Press, 1999. (Loeb).
Lefkowitz, Mary. *Black Athena Revisited*. Chapel Hill: University of North Carolina Press, 1996.
Schibli, Hermann S. *Pherecydes of Syros*. Oxford: Oxford University Press, 1990.
Solōnos Nomoi: die Fragmente des Solonischen Gesetzeswerkes. E. Ruschenbusch, ed. Wiesbaden: Steiner, 1966.

Presocratics, General Works

Text
Diels, Hermann, and Walter Kranz, eds. *Die Fragmente der Vorsokratiker*, 3 vols. Berlin: Weidmann, 1952. Text and German translation.

Translation
Barnes, Jonathan, *Early Greek Philosophy,* Hammonsworth, UK: Penguin, 1987.
Freeman, Kathleen. *Ancilla to the Pre-Socratic Philosophers*. Cambridge, Mass.: Harvard University Press, 1948.
Kirk, Geoffrey S., John E. Raven, and Malcolm Schofield. *The Presocratic Philosophers*. Cambridge: Cambridge University Press, 1983.
McKirahan, Richard D. *Philosophy Before Socrates*. Indianapolis, Ind.: Hackett, 1994.
Waterfield, Robin. The First Philosophers. Oxford: Oxford University Press, 2000.

Secondary Sources
Barnes, Jonathan. *The Presocratic Philosophers*. Boston: Routledge, 1982.
Caston, Victor, and Daniel Graham, eds. *Presocratic Philosophy*. Aldershot, UK: Ashgate, 2002.
Navia, Luis E. *The Presocratic Philosophers: An Annotated Bibliography*. New York: Garland, 1993.

Preus, Anthony. *Essays in Ancient Greek Philosophy*. Vol. VI, *Before Plato*. Albany: State University of New York Press, 2001.

Milesians

Thales
O'Grady, Patricia. *Thales of Miletus*. Aldershot, England: Ashgate, 2002.

Anaximander
Couprie, D. L., Robert Hahn, and Gerard Naddaf. *Anaximander in Context*. Albany: State University of New York Press, 2002.

Hahn, Robert. *Anaximander and the Architects*. Albany: State University of New York Press, 2001.

Kahn, Charles H. *Anaximander and the Origins of Greek Cosmology*. New York: Columbia University Press, 1960; 1994.

Heraclitus

Text and Translation
Kahn, Charles H. *The Art and Thought of Heraclitus*. Cambridge: Cambridge University Press, 1979.

Kirk, G. S. *Heraclitus: The Cosmic Fragments*. Cambridge: Cambridge University Press, 1954.

Marcovich, Miroslav. *Heraclitus: Greek Text with a Short Commentary*. Merida, Venezuela: University of the Andes Press, 1967.

Robinson, T. M. *Heraclitus: Fragments*. Toronto: University of Toronto Press, 1987.

Secondary Sources
Graham, Daniel. "Heraclitus," *Internet Encyclopedia of Philosophy*. 2005. http://www.utm.edu/research/iep/h/heraclit.htm.

The Monist 74.4 (October, 1991), special issue devoted to the philosophy of Heraclitus.

Xenophanes

Finkelberg, Aryeh. "Studies in Xenophanes." *Harvard Studies in Classical Philology* 93 (1990) 103–168.

Lesher, James H. *Xenophanes Fragments*. Toronto: University of Toronto Press, 1992.

Pythagoras and Early Pythagoreans

Huffman, Carl. *Archytas of Tarentum: Pythagorean, Philosopher and Mathematician King*. 2005.

———. "Alcmaeon." *Stanford Encyclopedia of Philosophy*. 2003: http://plato.stanford.edu/entries/alcmaeon/.

——. "Philolaus." *Stanford Encyclopedia of Philosophy*. 2003: http://plato.stanford .edu/entries/philolaus/.

——. "Pythagoras." *Stanford Encyclopedia of Philosophy*. 2005: http://plato.stanford .edu/entries/pythagoras/.

Kahn, Charles H. *Pythagoras and the Pythagoreans: A Brief History*. Indianapolis, Ind.: Hackett, 2001.

Kingsley, Peter. *Ancient Philosophy, Mystery and Magic: Empedocles and Pythagorean Tradition*. Oxford: Oxford University Press, 1995.

Navia, Luis E. *Pythagoras: An Annotated Bibliography*. New York: Garland, 1990.

Riedweg, Christoph. *Pythagoras: His Life, Teaching, and Influence*. Ithaca, N.Y.: Cornell University Press, 2005.

Eleatics: Parmenides, Zeno, Melissus

Curd, Patricia. *The Legacy of Parmenides*. Princeton: Princeton University Press, 1998.

Faris, John A. *The Paradoxes of Zeno*. Aldershot, UK: Avebury, 1996.

Gallop, David. *Parmenides, Fragments: Text and Translation*. Toronto: University of Toronto Press, 1984.

Henn, Martin J. *Parmenides of Elea*. London: Praeger, 2003.

Mourelatos, Alexander P. D. *The Route of Parmenides*. New Haven, Conn.: Yale University Press, 1970.

——. "Parmenides." *Encyclopedia of Classical Philosophy*. Edited by Donald J. Zeyl. Westport, Conn.: Greenwood, 1997, pp. 363–69.

O'Connor, John J., and Edmund F. Robertson. "Zeno of Elea." 1999: http://www .groups.dcs.st-and.ac.uk/~history/Mathematicians/Zeno_of_Elea.html.

Reale, Giovanni. *Melissus: Testimonianze e Frammenti*. Firenze: La Nuova Italia, 1970.

Empedocles

Campbell, Gordon. "Empedocles (of Acragas)." *Internet Encyclopedia of Philosophy*. 2006: http://www.iep.utm.edu/e/empedocl.htm.

Inwood, Brad, editor and translator. *The Poem of Empedocles*. Toronto: University of Toronto Press, 1992.

Kingsley, Peter. *Ancient Philosophy, Mystery, and Magic: Empedocles and the Pythagorean Tradition*. Oxford: Oxford University Press, 1995.

Trépanier, Simon. *Empedocles: An Interpretation*. New York: Routledge, 2004.

Wright, M. R., ed. *Empedocles: The Extant Fragments*. New Haven, Conn.: Yale University Press, 1981.

Anaxagoras

Laks, Andre. "Mind's Crisis. On Anaxagoras' Νοῦς." *Southern Journal of Philosophy* 31 (1993): supplement 19.

Sider, David, editor. *The Fragments of Anaxagoras*. Meisenheim am Glan: Hain, 1981.

Early Atomism

Cole, Thomas. *Democritus and the Sources of Greek Anthropology.* Cleveland, Ohio: Western Reserve University Press, 1967.

Procopé, J. F. "Democritus on Politics and Care of the Soul." *Classical Quarterly* NS 39.2 (1989): 137ff.

Taylor, Christopher C. W., ed. *The Atomists, Leucippus and Democritus: Fragments.* Toronto: University of Toronto Press, 1999.

Fifth Century BCE Literature, Science, Medicine, Etc.

Aristophanes. *The Complete Plays*, tr. P. Roche. New York: New American Library, 2005.

Corpus Medicorum Graecorum. 21 vols., various editors. Berlin: Akademie Verlag, 1956–.

Herodotus

The Histories. Robin Waterfield, tr. Oxford: Oxford University Press, 1998.

Spalding, Tim. "Herodotus." http://www.isidore-of-seville.com/herodotus/.

Hippocrates

Hippocrate, Oeuvres Compléte. Emile Littré, tr. 10 vols. (1839–1861). Reprinted Amsterdam: Hackert, 1967–1978. This is the only complete modern edition; it includes a French translation, the only complete translation into any modern language.

Hippocrates. W. H. S. Jones et al., ed. and tr. 7 vols. Cambridge, Mass.: Harvard University Press, 1957–. (Loeb).

Old Oligarch. The text and translation are available in Vol. VII of the Loeb Xenophon. E. C. Marchant, ed. and tr. Cambridge, Mass.: Harvard University Press, 1958.

Thucydides

A History of the Peloponnesian War. Stephen Lattimore, tr. Indianapolis, Ind.: Hackett, 1998.

Hornblower, Simon. *Thucydides.* London: Duckworth, 1987.

Orwin, Clifford. *The Humanity of Thucydides.* Princeton: Princeton University Press, 1994.

Sophists of the Fifth Century BCE

Kerferd, George B. *The Sophistic Movement.* Cambridge: Cambridge University Press, 1981.

Sprague, R. Kent, ed. *The Older Sophists*. Columbia: University of South Carolina Press, 1972; 1990.

Antiphon

Gagarin, Michael. *Antiphon the Athenian*. Austin: University of Texas Press, 2002.

O'Connor, John J., and Edmund F. Robertson. "Antiphon." 1999: http://www-groups.dcs.st-and.ac.uk/~history/Mathematicians/Antiphon.html.

Pendrick, Gerard J., ed. and tr. *Antiphon the Sophist, The Fragments*. Cambridge: Cambridge University Press, 2002.

Rihll, T. E. "Antiphon." 2004: http://www.swan.ac.uk/classics/staff/ter/grst/Antiphon.htm.

Callicles

Barney, Rachel. "Callicles and Thrasymachus." *Stanford Encyclopedia of Philosophy*. 2004: http://plato.stanford.edu/entries/callicles-thrasymachus/.

Critias

Dissoi Logoi. Alexander Becker and Peter Scholtz, ed. and (German) tr. Berlin: Akademie Verlag, 2004.

Morison, William. "Critias." *Internet Encyclopedia of Philosophy*. 2005: http://www.iep.utm.edu/c/critias.htm.

Gorgias

"Encomium of Helen," tr. B. Donovan. 1999: http://classicpersuasion.org/pw/gorgias/helendonovan.htm.

"On the Non-Existent," relevant text from Sextus Empiricus. *Against the Schoolmasters*, vii 65–87: http://www.wfu.edu/%7Ezulick/300/gorgias/negative.html.

Hippias

O'Connor, John J., and Edmund F. Robertson. "Hippias of Elis." 1999: http://www.groups.dcs.st-and.ac.uk/~history/Mathematicians/Hippias.html.

Prodicus

Suzanne, Bernard. "Prodicus." 1998: http//plato-dialogues.org/tools/char/prodicus.htm.

Protagoras

Schiappa, Edward. *Protagoras and Logos: A Study in Greek Philosophy and Rhetoric*. Columbia: University of South Carolina Press, 1991.

Thrasymachus

Rauhut, Nils. "Thrasymachus." *Internet Encyclopedia of Philosophy*. 2006: http://www.iep.utm.edu/t/thrasymachus.htm.

Classical Philosophy: Comparative Studies

Anton, John, George Kustas, and Anthony Preus, eds. *Essays in Ancient Greek Philosophy*. 6 vols. Albany: State University of New York Press, 1971–2001.

Fine, Gail. *On Ideas. Aristotle's Criticism of Plato's Theory of Forms*. Oxford: Oxford University Press, 1995.

Konstan, David. *The Emotions of the Ancient Greeks*. Toronto: University of Toronto Press, 2006.

Lee, Mi-Kyoung. *Epistemology after Protagoras*. Oxford: Oxford University Press, 2005.

Nightingale, Andrea W. *Spectacles of Truth in Classical Greek Philosophy: Theoria in Its Cultural Context*. Cambridge: Cambridge University Press, 2004.

North, Helen. *Sophrosyne: Self-Knowledge and Self-Restraint in Greek Literature*. Ithaca, N.Y.: Cornell University Press, 1966.

Price, A. W. *Love and Friendship in Plato and Aristotle*. Oxford: Oxford University Press, 1990.

Smith, Robin. "Dialectic." *Encyclopedia of Classical Philosophy*. Edited by Donald J. Zeyl. Westport, Conn.: Greenwood, 1997, 174–77.

Snell, Bruno. *The Discovery of the Mind*. Cambridge, Mass.: Harvard University Press, 1953.

Sorabji, Richard. *Time, Creation and the Continuum*. Ithaca, N.Y.: Cornell University Press, 1983.

Vuillemin, Jules. *Necessity or Contingency: The Master Argument*. Stanford, Calif.: Stanford University Press, 1996.

White, Nicholas. *Individual and Conflict in Greek Ethics*. Oxford: Oxford University Press, 2002.

Socrates

Ahbel-Rappe, Sara, and Rachana Kamtekar, eds. *A Companion to Socrates*. Oxford: Blackwell, 2006.

Benson, Hugh H., ed. *Essays on the Philosophy of Socrates*. Oxford: Oxford University Press, 1992.

Brickhouse, Thomas C., and Nicholas D. Smith. *Plato's Socrates*. Oxford: Oxford University Press, 1994.

Brickhouse, Thomas C., and Nicholas D. Smith. *The Philosophy of Socrates*. Boulder, Colo.: Westview, 2000.

Nails, Debra. "Socrates." *The Stanford Encyclopedia of Philosophy*. 2005: http://plato.stanford.edu/entries/socrates/.

Navia, Luis E. *Socrates, the Man and His Philosophy.* Lanham, Md.: University Press of America, 1989.

Strauss, Leo. *Xenophon's Socrates.* Ithaca, N.Y.: Cornell University Press, 1972.

Students of Socrates and Their Schools (Except Plato and the Academy)

Antisthenes

Antisthenes, Fragmenta. F. Decleva Caizzi, ed. Milan: Varese, 1966.

Luz, Menahem. "Antisthenes' Concept of *Paideia.*" 1998: http://www.bu.edu/wcp/Papers/Anci/AnciLuz.htm.

Navia, Luis E. *Antisthenes of Athens: Setting the World Aright.* Westport, Conn.: Greenwood, 2001.

Aristippus and the Cyrenaic School

O'Keefe, Tim. "Aristippus." *Internet Encyclopedia of Philosophy.* 2005: http://www.iep.utm.edu/a/aristip.htm#h1.

O'Keefe, Tim. "Cyrenaics." *Internet Encyclopedia of Philosophy.* 2005: http://www.iep.utm.edu/c/cyren.htm.

Tsouna, Voula. *The Epistemology of the Cyrenaic School.* Cambridge: Cambridge University Press, 1999.

Megarian and Dialectical Schools

Bobzien, Suzanne. "Dialectical School." *Stanford Encyclopedia of Philosophy.* 2004: http://plato.stanford.edu/entries/dialectical-school/.

Dancy, Russell M. "Megarian School." *Encyclopedia of Classical Philosophy.* Edited by Donald J. Zeyl. Westport, Conn.: Greenwood, 1997, pp. 328–30.

Mendell, Henry. "Theaetetus." *Encyclopedia of Classical Philosophy.* Edited by Donald J. Zeyl. Westport, Conn.: Greenwood, 1997, pp. 542–43.

Tsouna-McKirahan, Voula. "Socratic Circle." *Encyclopedia of Classical Philosophy.* Edited by Donald J. Zeyl. Westport, Conn.: Greenwood, 1997, pp. 513–15.

White, Michael J. "Diodorus Cronus." *Encyclopedia of Classical Philosophy.* Edited by Donald J. Zeyl. Westport, Conn.: Greenwood, 1997, pp. 185–87.

Xenophon

Xenophon. C. L. Brownson et al., ed. and tr. 7 vols. Cambridge, Mass: Harvard University Press, 1947–1953. (Loeb).

The Xenophon Page, alternate access to online materials: http://www.accd.edu/sac/english/bailey/xenophon.htm.

Plato

Plato, The Collected Dialogues. Edith Hamilton and Huntington Cairns, eds. Princeton: Princeton University Press, 1961.

Plato, Complete Works. John M. Cooper, ed. Indianapolis, Ind.: Hackett, 1997.

Platonis Opera. E. A. Duke et al., eds. Oxford: Oxford University Press, 1995.

Translations of Individual Dialogues

Alcibiades. Nicholas Denyer, tr. Cambridge: Cambridge University Press, 2001.

Apology. Michael Stokes, tr. Warminster, UK: Aris and Phillips, 1997.

Charmides. Thomas West and Grace Starry West, trs. Indianapolis, Ind.: Hackett, 1986.

Cratylus. C. D. C. Reeve, tr. Indianapolis, Ind.: Hackett, 1998.

Euthydemus. Rosamond Kent Sprague, tr. Indianapolis, Ind.: Hackett, 1993.

Gorgias. James Nichols, tr. Ithaca, N.Y.: Cornell University Press, 1998.

Ion and *Hippias Major: Two Comic Dialogues of Plato*. Paul Woodruff, tr. Indianapolis, Ind.: Hackett, 1983.

Laches and Charmides. Rosamond Kent Sprague, tr. Indianapolis, Ind.: Hackett, 1992.

Laws: The Laws of Plato. Thomas L. Pangle, tr. New York: Basic Books, 1980.

Meno. Dominic Scott, ed. Cambridge: Cambridge University Press, 2006.

Parmenides

Parmenides' Lesson. Kenneth M. Sayre, tr. Notre Dame, Ind.: Notre Dame University Press, 1996.

Parmenides. Samuel Scolnicov, tr. Berkeley: University of California Press, 2003.

Phaedo. David Gallop, tr. Oxford: Oxford University Press, 1999.

Phaedrus. Alexander Nehamas and Paul Woodruff, trs. Indianapolis, Ind.: Hackett, 1995.

Philebus. Dorothea Frede, tr. Indianapolis, Ind.: Hackett, 1993.

Protagoras. Adam Beresford, tr. New York: Penguin Books, 2006.

Republic. C. D. C. Reeve, tr. Indianapolis, Ind.: Hackett, 2004.

Sophist: Plato's Sophist, Or the Professor of Wisdom. Eva Brann et al., eds. Newburyport, Mass.: Focus Publishing, 1996.

Statesman. Robin Waterfield, tr. Cambridge: Cambridge University Press, 1995.

Symposium. Christopher Gill and Desmond Lee, trs. New York: Penguin Books, 2006.

Theaetetus. Myles Burnyeat, tr. Indianapolis, Ind.: Hackett, 1990.

Timaeus. Donald J. Zeyl, tr. Indianapolis, Ind.: Hackett, 2000.

Studies of Plato

Bobonich, Christopher. *Plato's Utopia Recast*. Oxford: Oxford University Press, 2002.

Brandwood, Leonard. *The Chronology of Plato's Dialogues*. Cambridge: Cambridge University Press, 1990.

Brisson, Luc. "Bibliography of Plato 1958–1975." *Lustrum*. 1977.

Dancy, Russell M. *Plato's Introduction of Forms*. Cambridge: Cambridge University Press, 2004.

Ferrari, G. R. F. *City and Soul in Plato's Republic*. Chicago: University of Chicago Press, 2005.

Kraut, Richard, ed. *The Cambridge Companion to Plato*. Cambridge: Cambridge University Press, 1992.

Lafrance, Ivon. *Pour Interpreter Platon*. Paris: Belles Lettres, 1986.

Ledger, Gerard R. *Re-Counting Plato: Computer Analysis of Plato's Style*. Oxford, 1989.

Lutoslawski, Wincenti. *The Origin and Growth of Plato's Logic*. London: Longman's, 1897; reprinted 1966.

Nails, Debra. *The People of Plato*. Indianapolis, Ind.: Hackett, 2002.

Osborne, Catherine. *Eros Unveiled, Plato and the God of Love*. Oxford: Oxford University Press, 1994.

Santas, Gerasimos, ed. *The Blackwell Guide to Plato's Republic*. Oxford: Blackwell, 2006.

Shorey, Paul. *The Unity of Plato's Thought*. Chicago: University of Chicago Press, 1903 (reprinted Archon Press, 1968).

Thesleff, Holger. *Studies in Platonic Chronology*. Helsinki: Societas Scientiarum Fennica, 1982.

Turnbull, Robert G. *The Parmenides and Plato's Late Philosophy*. Toronto: University of Toronto Press, 1998.

Young, Charles M. "Plato and Computer Dating." *Oxford Studies in Ancient Philosophy* 12 (1994): 227–50.

The Plato bibliography is vast; fortunately it is kept up-to-date by the International Plato Society at: http://www.platosociety.org/bibliografia/pdfeng.htm.

Bernard Suzanne maintains a page with links to the online versions of the dialogues: http://plato-dialogues.org/links.htm.

Early Academy

Dancy, Russell M. *Two Studies in the Early Academy*. Albany: State University of New York Press, 1991.

———. "Speusippus." *Stanford Encyclopedia of Philosophy*. 2003:http://plato.stanford.edu/entries/speusippus/.

Dillon, John. *The Heirs of Plato: A Study of the Old Academy (347–274 BC)*. Oxford: Oxford University Press, 2003.

Eudoxus of Cnidos. *Die Fragmente*. François Lasserre, ed. and tr. (German). Berlin: De Gruyter, 1966.

Speusippus. Frammenti. Margherita Isnardi Parente, ed. and tr. (Italian). Naples: Bibliopolis, 1980.

Xenocrates: *Frammenti/Senocrate, Ermodoro*. Margherita Isnardi Parente, ed. and tr. Naples: Bibliopolis, 1982.

Aristotle

Text or Translation of Works

Aristotelis Opera. Immanuel Bekker, ed. Berlin 1837; reprint Berlin: W. de Gruyter, 1960.

Aristotle: The Complete Works. Jonathan Barnes, ed. Princeton: Princeton University Press, 1984.

Aristotle. Loeb Classical Library, 25 vols., various editors and translators. Cambridge, Mass.: Harvard University Press, 1950–2006.

General Works on Aristotle

Barnes, Jonathan, ed. *The Cambridge Companion to Aristotle.* Cambridge: Cambridge University Press, 1995.

Barnes, Jonathan, Richard Sorabji, and Malcolm Schofield. *Aristotle: A Selective Bibliography.* Oxford: Oxford University Press, 1977.

Düring, Ingemar. *Aristotle in the Ancient Biographical Tradition.* Göteborg: Almqvist and Wiksell, 1957.

Long, Christopher. *The Ethics of Ontology.* Albany: State University of New York Press, 2004.

Natali, Carlo. *The Wisdom of Aristotle.* Albany: State University of New York Press, 2001.

Rist, John M. *The Mind of Aristotle: A Study in Philosophical Growth.* Toronto: University of Toronto Press, 1989.

Wedin, Michael. *Mind and Imagination in Aristotle.* New Haven, Conn.: Yale University Press, 1988.

Wians, William. *Aristotle's Philosophical Development.* Lanham, Md.: Roman and Littlefield, 1996.

Organon

Bäck, Allan. *Aristotle's Theory of Predication.* Leiden: Brill, 2000.

Lear, Jonathan. *Aristotle and Logical Theory.* Cambridge: Cambridge University Press, 1980.

Patterson, Richard. *Aristotle's Modal Logic.* Cambridge: Cambridge University Press, 1995.

Categories

Evangeliou, Christos. *Aristotle's Categories and Porphyry.* Leiden: Brill, 1988.

Wedin, Michael. *Aristotle's Theory of Substance: The Categories and Metaphysics Zeta.* Oxford: Oxford University Press, 2000.

Prior and Posterior Analytics

Aristotle. *Posterior Analytics.* Jonathan Barnes, tr. Oxford: Oxford University Press, 1994.

Byrne, Patrick. *Analysis and Science in Aristotle.* Albany: State University of New York Press, 1997.

Goldin, Owen. *Explaining an Eclipse: Aristotle's Posterior Analytics 2.1–10.* Ann Arbor, Mich.: University of Michigan Press, 1996.

McKirahan, Richard. *Aristotle's Theory of Demonstrative Science.* Princeton: Princeton University Press, 1992.

Sophistical Refutations

Schreiber, Scott. *Aristotle on False Reasoning.* Albany: State University of New York Press, 2003.

Natural Philosophy
Physics
Bolotin, David. *An Approach to Aristotle's Physics*. Albany: State University of New York Press, 1998.

Broadie, Sarah. *Nature Change and Agency in Aristotle's Physics*. Oxford: Oxford University Press, 1982.

Morison, Benjamin. *On Location. Aristotle's Concept of Place*. Oxford: Oxford University Press, 2002.

Sachs, Joe. "Aristotle: Motion and Its Place in Nature." *Internet Encyclopedia of Philosophy*. 2005: http://www.iep.utm.edu/a/aris-mot.htm.

On Generation and Corruption
Symposium Aristotelicum. *Aristotle: On Generation and Corruption Book I*. Frans de Hass and Jaap Mansfeld, eds. Oxford: Oxford University Press, 2004.

De Anima and Parva Naturalia
Translations
Aristotle. *On Sleep and Dreams*. David Gallop, tr. Warminster, England: Aris & Phillips, 1996.

Aristotle. *On the Soul*. Joe Sachs, tr. Santa Fe, N.M.: Green Lion Press, 2001.

Secondary Sources
Granger, Herbert. *Aristotle's Idea of the Soul*. Dordrecht: Kluwer, 1996.

Nussbaum, Martha Craven, and Amelie O. Rorty, eds. *Essays on Aristotle's De Anima*. Oxford: Oxford University Press, 1992, 1995.

Biological Works
Gotthelf, Allan, and James Lennox, eds. *Philosophical Issues in Aristotle's Biology*. Cambridge: Cambridge University Press, 1987.

Lennox, James. *Aristotle's Philosophy of Biology*. Cambridge: Cambridge University Press, 2001.

Nussbaum, Martha Craven. *Aristotle's De Motu Animalium*. Princeton: Princeton University Press, 1986.

Pellegrin, Pierre. *Aristotle's Classification of Animals*. Anthony Preus tr. Berkeley: University of California Press, 1986.

Preus, Anthony. *Science and Philosophy in Aristotle's Biological Works*. Hildesheim: Olms, 1975.

Preus, Anthony. *Aristotle and Michael of Ephesus on the Movement and Progression of Animals*. Hildesheim: Olms, 1981.

Metaphysics
Aristotle. *Metaphysics Book 3*. Arthur Madigan, tr. Oxford: Clarendon Press, 1999.

Blair, George A. *Energeia and Entelecheia: Act in Aristotle*. Ottawa: University of Ottawa Press, 1992.

Bodeus, Richard. *Aristotle and the Theology of Living Immortals*. Albany: State University of New York Press, 2000.

Cohen, S. Mark. "Aristotle Metaphysics." *Stanford Encyclopedia of Philosophy.* 2003: http://plato.stanford.edu/entries/aristotle-metaphysics/#SandE.

Katayama, Errol. *Aristotle on Artifacts: A Metaphysical Puzzle.* Albany: State University of New York Press, 1999.

Owens, Joseph. *The Doctrine of Being in the Aristotelian Metaphysics.* Toronto: University of Toronto Press, 1978.

Witt, Charlotte. *Ways of Being: Potentiality and Actuality in Aristotle's Metaphysics.* Ithaca, N.Y.: Cornell University Press, 2003.

Yu, Jiyuan. *The Structure of Being in Aristotle's Metaphysics.* Dordrecht: Kluwer, 2003.

Ethics

Translations

Aristotle. *Nicomachean Ethics.* Roger Crisp, tr. Cambridge: Cambridge University Press, 2000.

Secondary Sources

Achtenberg, Deborah. *Cognition of Value in Aristotle's Ethics.* Albany: State University of New York Press, 2002.

Anagnostopoulos, Georgios. *Aristotle on the Goals and Exactness of Ethics.* Berkeley: University of California Press, 1994.

Bartlett, Robert C., and Susan D. Collins, eds. *Action and Contemplation: Studies in the Moral and Political Thought of Aristotle.* Albany: State University of New York Press, 1999.

Bodeus, Richard. *The Political Dimensions of Aristotle's Ethics.* Albany: State University of New York Press, 1993.

Fortenbaugh, William W. *Aristotle on Emotion*, 2nd ed. London: Duckworth, 2002.

Kraut, Richard, ed. *The Blackwell Guide to Aristotle's Nicomachean Ethics.* Oxford, England: Blackwell, 2006.

Natali, Carlo. *The Wisdom of Aristotle.* Albany: State University of New York Press, 2001.

Pangle, Lorraine Smith. *Aristotle's Philosophy of Friendship.* Cambridge: Cambridge University Press, 2003.

Schollmeier, Paul. *Other Selves.* Albany: State University of New York Press, 1994.

Sparshott, Francis E. *Taking Life Seriously.* Toronto: University of Toronto Press, 1994.

Stern-Gillet, Suzanne. *Aristotle's Philosophy of Friendship.* Albany: State University of New York Press, 1995.

Politics

Translations

Aristotle. *Politics.* Peter Simpson, tr. Chapel Hill: University of North Carolina Press, 1997.

Aristotle. *Politics.* C. D. C. Reeve, tr. Indianapolis, Ind.: Hackett, 1998.

Aristotle. *Politics V and VI.* David Keyt, tr. Oxford: Oxford University Press, 1999.

Secondary Sources

Kraut, Richard. *Aristotle: Political Philosophy*. Oxford: Oxford University Press, 2002.

Kraut, Richard, and Steven Skultety, eds. *Aristotle's Politics: Critical Essays*. New York: Roman and Littlefield, 2005.

Miller, Fred. *Nature, Justice, and Rights in Aristotle's Politics*. Oxford: Oxford University Press, 1995.

———. "Aristotle's Political Theory." *Stanford Encyclopedia of Philosophy*. 2002: http://plato.stanford.edu/entries/aristotle-politics/.

Nagle, D. Brendan. *The Household as the Foundation of Aristotle's Polis*. Cambridge: Cambridge University Press, 2006.

Rosler, Andrés. *Political Authority and Obligation in Aristotle*. Oxford: Oxford University Press, 2005.

Yack, Bernard. *The Problems of a Political Animal*. Berkeley: University of California Press, 1993.

Poetics

Aristotle. *On Poetics*. Seth Benardete and Michael Davis, trs. South Bend, Ind.: St. Augustine's Press, 2002.

Aristotle. *Poetics*. George Whalley, tr. Montreal: McGill University Press, 1997.

Husain, Martha. *Ontology and the Art of Tragedy*. Albany: State University of New York Press, 2002.

Aristotle Bibliographies

Barnes, Jonathan, Richard Sorabji, and Malcolm Schofield. *Aristotle: A Selective Bibliography*. Oxford: Oxford University Press, 1977.

Ingardia, Richard. *Aristotle Bibliography*: http://www.aristotlebibliography.com/jsp/index.jsp.

Johnson, Monte. http://www.chass.utoronto.ca/~mojohnso/aristbib.htm.

Lyceum; Early Peripatetic School

Huby, Pamela. "Peripatetic School." *Encyclopedia of Classical Philosophy*. Edited by Donald J. Zeyl. Westport, Conn.: Greenwood, 1997, pp. 369–73.

Lynch, John Patrick. *Aristotle's School*. Berkeley: University of California Press, 1972.

Morison, William. "Lyceum." *Internet Encyclopedia of Philosophy*. 2005: http://www.iep.utm.edu/l/lyceum.htm.

Rihll, T. E. "Lyceum." 2003: http://www.swan.ac.uk/classics/staff/ter/grst/What's %20what%20Things/lyceum.htm.

Wehrli, Fritz, ed. and comm. *Die Schule des Aristoteles*. 10 vols. Basel 1967–1969.

Individual Early Peripatetics

Aristoxenus

The Harmonics of Aristoxenus (Elementa Harmonica), tr. H. S. Makran. 1902; reprint Hildesheim: Olms, 1974.

Elementa Harmonica, ed. R. da Rios. Rome: Typis Publicae Officinae Polygraphi- cae, 1954.

Elementa Rhythmica. Lionel Pearson, ed. and tr. Oxford: Oxford University Press, 1990.

Eudemus

Bodnar, Istvan, and William W. Fortenbaugh, eds. *Eudemus of Rhodes*: New Brunswick, N.J.: Transaction Books, 2002.

Dancy, Russell M. "Eudemus." *Encyclopedia of Classical Philosophy*. Edited by Donald J. Zeyl. Westport, Conn.: Greenwood, 1997, pp. 234–35.

Lyco of Troas and Hieronymus of Rhodes. William W. Fortenbaugh and Stephen White, trs. New Brunswick, N.J.: Transaction Books, 2004.

Strato of Lampsacus

Huby, Pamela. "Strato of Lampsacus." *Encyclopedia of Classical Philosophy*. Edited by Donald J. Zeyl. Westport, Conn.: Greenwood, 1997, pp. 537–39.

Theophrastus

Characters. James Dingle, tr. Cambridge: Cambridge University Press, 2004.

De Causis Plantarum. Benedict Einarson and George K. K. Link, ed. and tr. 3 vols. Cambridge, Mass: Harvard University Press, 1976. (Loeb).

Historia Plantarum. Arthur Hort, ed. and tr. 2 vols. Cambridge, Mass: Harvard Uni- versity Press, 1948–1949. (Loeb).

Metaphysics. Marlein van Raalte, tr. Leiden: Brill, 1993.

Theophrastus of Eresus. William W. Fortenbaugh, ed. and tr. 5 vols. Leiden: Brill, 1992.

Other Fourth-Century BCE Philosophers and Scientists

Gottschalk, Hans B. *Heraclides of Pontus*. Oxford: Oxford University Press, 1980.

Knoepfler, Denis. "Menedemos, Philosopher and Statesman." *Swiss School of Ar- chaeology in Greece*. 1999: http://www.unil.ch/esag/page26159.html.

Isocrates

Gagarin, Michael. "Isocrates." *Isocrates Home Page*. http://www.isocrates.com/. Accessed July 19, 2006.

Isocrates. G. Norlin and L. Van Hook, ed. and tr. 3 vols. Cambridge, Mass.: Har- vard University Press, 1928–1945. (Loeb).

Works. David Mirhady and Y. L. Too. Austin: University of Texas Press, 2000.

Hellenistic Philosophy

Annas, Julia. *Hellenistic Philosophy of Mind*. Berkeley: University of California Press, 1994.

Barnes, Jonathan, and Miriam Griffin, eds. *Philosophia Togata II: Plato and Aris- totle at Rome*. Oxford: Oxford University Press, 1997.

Brunschwig, Jacques, and Martha Craven Nussbaum, eds. *Passions and Perceptions: Studies in Hellenistic Philosophy of Mind*. Cambridge: Cambridge University Press, 1993.

Dancy, Russell M. "Academy." *Encyclopedia of Classical Philosophy*. Edited by Donald J. Zeyl. Westport, Conn.: Greenwood, 1997, pp. 1–5.

Inwood, Brad, and Lloyd P. Gerson, eds. *Hellenistic Philosophy: Introductory Readings*. Indianapolis, Ind.: Hackett, 1998.

Long, Anthony A. *Hellenistic Philosophy: Stoics, Epicureans, Sceptics*. Berkeley: University of California Press, 1986.

Long, Anthony A, and David N. Sedley. *The Hellenistic Philosophers*. 2 vols. Cambridge: Cambridge University Press, 1987.

Nussbaum, Martha Craven. *The Fragility of Goodness, Luck and Ethics in Greek Tragedy and Philosophy*. Cambridge: Cambridge University Press, 1986.

———. *The Therapy of Desire*. Princeton: Princeton University Press, 1996.

Schofield, Malcolm, et al., eds. *Doubt and Dogmatism: Studies in Hellenistic Epistemology*. Oxford: Oxford University Press, 1979.

Schofield, Malcolm, and Gisela Striker, eds. *The Norms of Nature: Studies in Hellenistic Ethics*. Cambridge: Cambridge University Press, 1986.

Sharples, Robert W. *Stoics, Epicureans and Skeptics: An Introduction to Hellenistic Philosophy*. New York: Routledge, 1996.

Striker, Gisela, ed. *Essays on Hellenistic Epistemology and Ethics*. Cambridge: Cambridge University Press, 1995.

Epicurus and Epicureanism

Epicurus

Figulus, P. Nigidius. *Operum Reliquiae*. A. Edited by Swoboda, Wien, 1889, reprint Amsterdam: A. M. Hackert, 1964.

Konstan, David. "Epicurus." *Stanford Encyclopedia of Philosophy*. 2005: http://plato.stanford.edu/entries/epicurus/.

Letters, Principal Doctrines, and Vatican Sayings. Russel Geer, tr. Indianapolis, Ind.: Hackett, 1964.

Morison, William. "The Garden of Epicurus." *Internet Encyclopedia of Philosophy*. 2005: http://www.iep.utm.edu/g/garden.htm.

Rist, John M. *Epicurus, An Introduction*. Cambridge: Cambridge University Press, 1972.

Lucretius

Lucretius. John Godwin, ed. London: Bristol Classical, 2004.

On the Nature of Things. tr. M. F. Smith, tr. Indianapolis, Ind.: Hackett, 2001.

Sedley, David. "Lucretius." *Stanford Encyclopedia of Philosophy*. 2004: http://plato.stanford.edu/entries/lucretius/.

Simpson, David. "Lucretius." *Internet Encyclopedia of Philosophy*. 2005: http://www.iep.utm.edu/l/lucretiu.htm.

Metrodorus

Sedley, David. "Metrodorus of Lampsacus." *Encyclopedia of Classical Philosophy.* Edited by Donald J. Zeyl. Westport, Conn.: Greenwood, 1997, pp. 342–43.

Cynics

Branham, Bracht, and Marie-Odile Goulet-Cazé, eds. *The Cynics: The Cynic Movement in Antiquity and Its Legacy.* Berkeley: University of California Press, 1996.

Dudley, Donald Reynolds. *A History of Cynicism from Diogenes to the 6th Century AD.* London, 1937; reprinted Hildesheim: Olms, 1967.

Malherbe, Abraham J., ed. and tr. *The Cynic Epistles.* Missoula, Mont.: Scholar's Press for the Study of Biblical Literature, 1977.

Oenomaus. *Die Orakelkritik des Kynikers Oenomaus.* Jürgen Hammerstaedt, tr. Frankfurt: Athenaeum, 1988.

Paquet, Léonce. *Les Cyniques grecs. Fragment et témoinages.*[2] Ottawa: University of Ottawa Press, 1988.

Relihan, J. C. *Ancient Menippean Satire.* Baltimore, Md: The Johns Hopkins University Press, 1993.

Hellenistic Stoicism

Asmis, Elizabeth. "Panaetius." *Encyclopedia of Classical Philosophy.* Edited by Donald J. Zeyl. Westport, Conn.: Greenwood, 1997, pp. 361–63.

Bobzien, Suzanne. *Determinism and Freedom in Stoic Philosophy.* Oxford: Oxford University Press, 1998.

Edelstein, Ludwig, and Ian G. Kidd, ed. and tr. *Posidonius* (3 vols.). Cambridge: Cambridge University Press, 1988–1989.

Gould, Josiah B. *The Philosophy of Chrysippus.* Leiden: Brill, 1970.

Panaetius of Rhodes. *Fragmenta.* Modestus van Straaten, ed. Amsterdam: Brill, 1946.

Rist, John M. *The Stoics.* Berkeley: University of California Press, 1978.

Rubarth, Scott. "Stoic Philosophy of Mind." *Internet Encyclopedia of Philosophy.* 2006: http://www.iep.utm.edu/s/stoicmind.htm.

Stoicorum Veterum Fragmenta. Hans Friedrich von Arnim, ed. 4 vols. Stuttgart: Teubner, 1903–1924; Reprint Stuttgart, 1964.

Tieleman, Teun. *Galen and Chrysippus on the Soul.* Leiden: Brill, 1996.

Tieleman, Teun. *Chrysippus on Affections.* Leiden: Brill, 2003.

Skepticism

Burnyeat, Myles, ed. *The Skeptical Tradition.* Berkeley: University of California Press, 1983.

Groarke, Leo. "Ancient Skepticism." *Stanford Encyclopedia of Philosophy*. 2003: http://plato.stanford.edu/entries/skepticism-ancient/.

Klein, Peter. "Skepticism." *Stanford Encyclopedia of Philosophy*. 2005: http://plato.stanford.edu/entries/skepticism/.

Academic Skepticism

Allen, James. "Carneades." *Stanford Encyclopedia of Philosophy*. 2004: http://plato.stanford.edu/entries/carneades/#1.

Pyrrhonian Skepticism

Annas, Julia, and Jonathan Barnes. *The Modes of Scepticism: Ancient Texts and Modern Interpretations*. Cambridge: Cambridge University Press, 1985.

Bett, Richard. *Pyrrho, His Antecedents and His Legacy*. Oxford: Oxford University Press, 2000.

Timon of Phlius. *Timone di Fliunte: Silli*. Massimo di Marco, ed. and tr. Rome: Ateneo, 1989.

Other Hellenistic Persons of Interest

Apollonius of Rhodes

Argonautica, P. Green, tr. Berkeley: University of California Press, 1997.

Archimedes

O'Connor, John J., and Edmund F. Robertson. "Archimedes." 1999: http://www.groups.dcs.st-and.ac.uk/~history/Mathematicians/Archimedes.html.

Aristarchus

Heath, Thomas. *Aristarchus of Samos*. Oxford: Clarendon Press, 1913; reprinted Mineola, N.Y.: Dover, 1981.

O'Connor, John J., and Edmund F. Robertson. "Aristarchus." 1999: http://www.groups.dcs.st-and.ac.uk/~history/Mathematicians/Aristarchus.html.

Erasistratus

von Staden, Heinrich. "Erasistratus." *Encyclopedia of Classical Philosophy*. Edited by Donald J. Zeyl. Westport, Conn.: Greenwood, 1997, pp. 219–20.

Eratosthenes

O'Connor, John J., and Edmund F. Robertson. "Eratosthenes." 1999: http://www.groups.dcs.st-and.ac.uk/~history/Mathematicians/Eratosthenes.html.

Euclid

Euclid. *Elements*. Thomas Heath, tr. New York: Dover, 1956.

Mueller, Ian. "Euclid." *Encyclopedia of Classical Philosophy*. Edited by Donald J. Zeyl. Westport, Conn.: Greenwood, 1997, pp. 229–31.

O'Connor, John J., and Edmund F. Robertson. "Euclid of Alexandria." 1999: http://www.groups.dcs.st-and.ac.uk/~history/Biographies/Euclid.html.

Herophilus

von Staden, Heinrich, ed. and tr. *Herophilus: The Art of Medicine in Early Alexandria*. Cambridge, Cambridge University Press, 1989.

Strabo

Geography. Horace Jones, ed. and tr. 8 vols. Cambridge, Mass: Harvard University Press, 1982–1989. (Loeb).

Nagy, Blaise. "Strabo." *Perseus Encyclopedia:* http://www.perseus.tufts.edu/cgi-bin/ptext?doc=Perseus%3Atext%3A1999.04.0004%3Aid%3Dstrabo.

Antiochus and the First Century BCE Academy

Glucker, John. *Antiochus and the Late Academy.* Göttingen: Vandenhoeck und Ruprecht, 1978.

Tarrant, Harold. "Antiochus of Ascalon." *Encyclopedia of Classical Philosophy.* Edited by Donald J. Zeyl. Westport, Conn.: Greenwood, 1997, pp. 36–38.

Cicero, Marcus Tullius

Translations

Cicero. *On Duties.* Miriam T. Griffen and E. Margaret Atkins, trs. Cambridge: Cambridge University Press, 1991.

——. *On Ends.* R. Rackham, tr. Cambridge, Mass.: Harvard University Press, 1914. (Loeb).

——. *On the Nature of the Gods. Academics.* H. Rackham, tr. Cambridge, Mass.: Harvard University Press, 1933. (Loeb).

——. *On Old Age. On Friendship. On Divination.* W. A. Falconer, tr. Cambridge, Mass.: Harvard University Press, 1923. (Loeb).

——. *On the Republic, On the Laws.* Clinton W. Keyes, tr. Cambridge, Mass.: Harvard University Press, 1928. (Loeb).

——. *Tusculan Disputations.* J. E. King, tr. Cambridge, Mass.: Harvard University Press, 1927. (Loeb).

Studies

Clayton, Edward. "Cicero." *Internet Encyclopedia of Philosophy.* 2005: http://www.iep.utm.edu/c/cicero.htm.

DeFilippo, Joseph. "Cicero." *Encyclopedia of Classical Philosophy.* Edited by Donald J. Zeyl. Westport, Conn.: Greenwood, 1997, p. 139.

Fortenbaugh, William W., ed. *Cicero's Knowledge of the Peripatos.* New Brunswick, N.J.: Transaction Books, 1989.

See also: the Cicero Homepage. http://www.utexas.edu/depts/classics/documents/Cic.html. Accessed July 17, 2006.

Roman Imperial Philosophy

Stoicism in the Roman Period

Arius Didymus. *Epitome of Stoic Ethics.* A. J. Pomeroy, tr. Atlanta: Society of Biblical Literature, 1999.

Aurelius, Marcus Aurelius Antoninus

The Meditations of the Emperor Marcus Antoninus. A. S. L. Farquharson, ed. and tr., comm., 2 vols. Oxford: Clarendon Press, 1944.

Rutherford, R. B. *The Meditations of M. Aurelius: A Study.* Oxford: Oxford University Press, 1989.

Epictetus

The Discourses of Epictetus. Robin Hard, tr. London: Everyman, 1995.

Long, Anthony A. "Hierocles." *Encyclopedia of Classical Philosophy.* Edited by Donald J. Zeyl. Westport, Conn.: Greenwood, 1997, pp. 269–70.

Seddon, Keith. "Epictetus." *Internet Encyclopedia of Philosophy.* 2005: http://www.iep.utm.edu/e/epictetu.htm.

Musonius Rufus

Deux prédicateurs de l'antiquité: Télès et Musonius. André Jean Festugiére, tr. Paris: Vrin, 1978.

Moles, John L. "Musonius Rufus." *Encyclopedia of Classical Philosophy.* Edited by Donald J. Zeyl. Westport, Conn.: Greenwood, 1997, pp. 350–51.

Musonius Rufus. *Entretiens et Fragments.* Amand Jagu, tr. Hildesheim: Olms, 1979.

"A Roman Philosopher Advocates Women's Education." Mary Lefkowitz and Miriam Fant, eds. *Women's Life in Greece and Rome.* Baltimore: The Johns Hopkins University Press, 2005.

Seneca, Lucius Annaeus

Four Dialogues. Charles D. N. Costa, ed. and tr. Warminster, UK: Aris and Phillips, 1994.

Moral and Political Essays. John M. Cooper and J. F. Procopé, ed. and tr. Cambridge: Cambridge University Press, 1995.

Seneca. Thomas H. Corcoran et al., ed. and tr. 10 vols. Cambridge, Mass.: Harvard University Press, 1953–2002. (Loeb).

Seventeen Letters. Charles D. N. Costa, ed. and tr. Warminster, UK: Aris and Phillips, 1988.

Epicureanism in the Roman Imperial Period

Diogenes of Oenoanda. *The Epicurean Inscription.* Martin Ferguson Smith, ed. and tr. Naples: Bibliopolis, 1993.

Aristotelianism in the Roman Imperial Period

Fortenbaugh, William W., ed. *On Stoic and Peripatetic Ethics: The Work of Arius Didymus.* New Brunswick, N. J.: Transaction Books, 1983.

Fortenbaugh, William W., and E. Schutrumpf, eds. *Dicaearchus of Messana. Text, Translation, and Discussion* (Rutgers University Studies in Classical Humanities, V. 10), 2001.

Hahm, David. "Arius Didymus." *Encyclopedia of Classical Philosophy*. Edited by Donald J. Zeyl. Westport, Conn.: Greenwood, 1997, pp. 97–98.
Wehrli, Fritz. *Die Schule des Aristoteles* (10 volumes). Basel: Schwabe, 1966–1969.

Cynicism in the Roman Period

Hammerstaedt, Jürgen. *Orakelkritik des Kynikers Oenomaus*. Frankfurt am Main: Athenäum, 1988.
———. "Oenomaus." *Encyclopedia of Classical Philosophy*. Edited by Donald J. Zeyl. Westport, Conn.: Greenwood, 1997, pp. 356–57.

Skepticism in the Roman Period

Sextus Empiricus
Text and Translation
Against the Ethicists. Richard Bett, tr. Oxford: Oxford University Press, 1997.
Against the Grammarians. David Blank, tr. Oxford: Oxford University Press, 1998.
Against the Logicians. Richard Bett, tr. Cambridge: Cambridge University Press, 2005.
Outlines of Skepticism. Jonathan Barnes and Julia Annas, trs. Cambridge: Cambridge University Press, 1994.
Sextus Empiricus. R. G. Bury, ed. and tr. 4 vols. Cambridge, Mass.: Harvard University Press, 1939–1949. (Loeb).
The Skeptic Way: Outlines of Pyrrhonism. Benson Mates, tr. Oxford: Oxford University Press, 1996.

Studies
Allen, James. "Sextus Empiricus." *Encyclopedia of Classical Philosophy*. Edited by Donald J. Zeyl. Westport, Conn.: Greenwood, 1997, pp. 488–90.
Kardimas, Dimitrios. *Sextus Empiricus against Aelius Aristides: The Conflict between Philosophy and Rhetoric in the Second Century A.D.* Lund, Sweden: Lund University Press, 1996.

The Second Sophistic

Dio Chrysostom. *Discourses*, 5 vols. J. W. Cohoon and H. D. Crosby, trs. Cambridge, Mass.: Harvard University Press, 1932–1951. (Loeb).
Jones, Christopher P. *The Roman World of Dio Chrysostom*. Cambridge, Mass.: Harvard University Press, 1978.

Lucian of Samosata
Philostratos. *Life of Apollonius of Tyana*. Christopher P. Jones, ed. and tr. Cambridge, Mass.: Harvard University Press, 2005. (Loeb).
Philostratus and Eunapius. *The Lives of the Sophists*. Wilmer Cave Wright, ed. and tr. Cambridge, Mass.: Harvard University Press, 1925. (Loeb).

Selected Dialogues. Desmond Costa, tr. Oxford: Oxford University Press, 2005.
Vitarum Auctio, Piscator. Joel B. Itzkowitz, ed. Leipzig: Teubner, 1992.

Ptolemy

Barker, Andrew. *Scientific Method in Ptolemy's Harmonics.* Cambridge: Cambridge University Press, 2000.
Ptolemy, Claudius. *Ptolemy's Almagest.* G. J. Toomer, tr. and notes. Princeton: Princeton University Press, 1998.

Medicine in the Roman Period

Aelius Aristides. *The Complete Works.* 2 vols. Charles A. Behr, tr. Leiden: Brill, 1981, 1986.

Celsus, Aulus Cornelius (Medical Writer)
De Medicina. Walter G. Spencer, tr. 3 vols. Cambridge, Mass.: Harvard University Press, 1953. (Loeb).
von Staden, Heinrich. "Celsus." *Encyclopedia of Classical Philosophy.* Edited by Donald J. Zeyl. Westport, Conn.: Greenwood, 1997, pp. 123–25.

Galen
Text and Translation
Galen on Antecedent Causes. R. J. Hankinson, tr. Cambridge: Cambridge University Press, 1998.
Galen on the Passions and Errors of the Soul. P. W. Harkins, tr. Columbus: Ohio State University Press, 1963.
Galen on the Therapeutic Method Books I and II. R. J. Hankinson, tr. Oxford: Oxford University Press, 1991.
Galen on the Usefulness of the Parts of the Body. Margaret T. May, tr. Ithaca, N.Y.: Cornell University Press, 1968.
Galeni Opera Omnia. C. G. Kuhn, ed. (Leipzig: 1821–1833, reprint Hildesheim: Olms, 1965. This is the standard Greek text, slowly being replaced by individual works in *Corpus Medicorum Graecorum.*
Galien Traités philosophiques et logiques. Pierre Pellegrin, tr. (French). Paris: Flammarion, 1998.
Oeuvres anatomiques physiologiques et medicales de Galien. Charles Daremberg, tr. Paris: J. B. Ballière, 1856. The most nearly complete translation of Galen's works.
On the Doctrines of Hippocrates and Plato. Phillip DeLacy, ed., tr. Berlin: Akademie Verlag, 1978, 1980.
On the Natural Faculties. A. J. Brock, tr. Cambridge, Mass.: Harvard University Press, 1952. (Loeb).

Three Treatises on the Nature of Science. Michael Frede, ed. Indianapolis, Ind.: Hackett, 1985.

Secondary Sources on Galen

Boylan, Michael. "Galen." *Internet Encyclopedia of Philosophy.* 2006: http://www.iep.utm.edu/g/galen.htm.

Temkin, Owsei. *Galenism: The Rise and Decline of a Medical Philosophy.* Ithaca, N.Y.: Cornell University Press, 1973.

Doxography

Clement of Alexandria

Diels, Hermann. *Doxographi Graeci* (1879). Reprinted Berlin: De Gruyter, 1965.

Protrepticus. Miroslav Marcovich, ed. Leiden: Brill, 1995.

Stromateis. John Ferguson. Washington, D.C.: Catholic University of American Press, 1991.

Diogenes Laertius

Lives of Eminent Philosophers. R. D. Hicks, ed., tr. 2 vols. Cambridge, Mass.: Harvard University Press, 1925, 1959. (Loeb).

Mejer, Jørgen. *Diogenes Laertius and His Hellenistic Background.* Wiesbaden: Steiner, 1978.

Hippolytus

Mansfeld, Jaap. "Doxography of Ancient Philosophy." *Stanford Encyclopedia of Philosophy.* 2004: http://plato.stanford.edu/entries/doxography-ancient/.

Nemesius. *De Natura Hominis.* Moreno Morani, ed. Leipzig: Teubner, 1987.

Osborne, Catherine. *Rethinking Early Greek Philosophy: Hippolytus of Rome and the Presocratics.* London: Duckworth, 1987.

Refutation of All Heresies. Miroslav Marcovich, ed. Berlin: De Gruyter, 1986.

Stobaeus, John. *Anthologium.* Curtius Wachsmuth and Otto Hense, eds. Berlin: Weidmann, 1884–1912.

Middle Platonism

Apuleius. *Rhetorical Works.* Stephen Harrison et al., tr. Oxford: Oxford University Press, 2001.

——. *Alcinous, the Handbook of Platonism.* Oxford: Oxford University Press, 1993.

Dillon, John. *The Middle Platonists.* Ithaca, N.Y.: Cornell University Press, 1977.

Philo of Alexandria

Text and Translation

Philo of Alexandria, Works. F. H. Colson and G. H. Whitaker, eds. and trs. 10 vols. Cambridge, Mass.: Harvard University Press, 1991–1994. (Loeb).

Studies

Hillar, Marion. "Philo." *Internet Encyclopedia of Philosophy*. 2006: http://www.iep .utm.edu/p/philo.htm.

Runia, David T. *International Philo Bibliography Project*. http://www.nd.edu/~ philojud/37.htm.

Seland, Torrey. *Philo Online Resource Page*. http://www.torreys.org/bible/philopag .html.

Wolfson, Harry Austryn. *Philo*. Cambridge, Mass.: Harvard University Press, 1948, 1962.

Plutarch of Chaeronea

Moralia. F. C. Babbitt, ed. 14 vols. Cambridge, Mass.: Harvard University Press, 1949–. (Loeb).

The International Plutarch Society maintains a bibliographic site: http://www.usu.edu/ history/ploutarchos/plutbib.htm.

Neopythagoreanism

Navon, Robert, ed. *The Pythagorean Writings*. K. Guthrie and T. Taylor, trs. Kew Gardens, N.Y.: Selene Books, 1986.

Nicomachus of Gerasa. *Introduction to Arithmetic*. D'Ooge, tr. New York: Macmillan, 1926; Johnson Reprint, 1972.

O'Connor, John J., and Edmund F. Robertson. "Nicomachus of Gerasa." 1999: http://www-groups.dcs.st-and.ac.uk/~history/Biographies/Nicomachus.html.

O'Meara, Patrick J. *Pythagoras Revived*. Oxford: Oxford University Press, 1989.

Neoplatonism

Moore, Edward. "Neoplatonism." *Internet Encyclopedia of Philosophy*. 2006: http:// www.iep.utm.edu/n/neoplato.htm#H1.

Watts, Edward. "Where to Live the Philosophic Life in the Sixth Century? Damascius, Simplicius, and the Return from Persia." *Greek, Roman, and Byzantine Studies* 45 (2005): 285–315.

Plotinus

Emilsson, Eyjólfur Kjalar. *Plotinus on Sense Perception*. Cambridge: Cambridge University Press, 1988.

Enneads. Arthur Hilary Armstrong, ed. and tr. 8 vols. Cambridge, Mass: Harvard University Press, 1989. (Loeb).

The Enneads. Stephen MacKenna, tr. Burdett, N.Y.: Larson Publications, 1992.

Rist, John M. *Plotinus, The Road to Reality*. Cambridge: Cambridge University Press, 1967.

Porphyry

Text and Translation

(*Eisagoge*) *Porphyry's Introduction*. Jonathan Barnes, ed. and tr. Oxford: Oxford University Press, 2003.

The Homeric Questions. Robin R. Schlunk, ed. and tr. New York: P. Lang, 1993.

Porphyry. On Aristotle's Categories. Stephen Strange, tr. Ithaca, N.Y.: Cornell University Press, 1992.

Porphyry Against the Christians: The Literary Remains. R. Joseph Hoffmann, tr. Oxford: Oxford University Press, 1994.

Porphyry on the Cave of the Nymphs. Robert Lamberton, ed. and tr. Barrytown, N.Y.: Station Hill Press, 1983.

Porphyry's Letter to His Wife Marcella Concerning the Life of Philosophy and the Ascent to the Gods. Alice Zimmern, tr. Grand Rapids, Mich.: Phanes Press, 1986.

Select Works of Porphyry. Thomas Taylor, tr. Sturminster Newton: The Prometheus Trust, 1994. Contains *Abstinence from Eating Animal Food*, the *Sententiae*, and the *Cave of the Nymphs*.

(Sentential) Launching-Points to the Realm of Mind. Kenneth S. Guthrie, tr. Grand Rapids, Mich.: Phanes Press, 1988.

Study

Emilsson, Eyjólfur Kjalar. "Porphyry." *Stanford Encyclopedia of Philosophy*. 2005: http://plato.stanford.edu/entries/porphyry/.

Victorinus, Marius

Opera. P. Henry and P. Hadot, eds. 2 vols. Vienna: Hoelder-Pichler-Tempsky, 1971–1986.

Theological Treatises on the Trinity. Mary T. Clark. Washington, D.C.: Catholic University Press, 1981.

Augustine

Augustine, Bishop of Hippo. *The City of God Against the Pagans*. Robert W. Dyson, tr. Cambridge: Cambridge University Press, 1998.

Celsus (Neoplatonist). *On the True Doctrine: A Discourse Against the Christians*. R. J. Hoffman, tr. Oxford: Oxford University Press, 1987.

Mendelson, Michael. "Augustine." *Stanford Encyclopedia of Philosophy*. 2000: http://plato.stanford.edu/entries/augustine/.

O'Donnell, James. *Augustine, Selected Bibliography*. http://ccat.sas.upenn.edu/jod/twayne/twaynebib.html.

Rist, John M. *Augustine: Ancient Thought Baptized*. Cambridge: Cambridge University Press, 1994.

Iamblichus

Exhortation to Philosophy [Protrepticus]. Thomas M. Johnson, tr. Grand Rapids, Mich.: Phanes Press, 1988.

Finamore, John. *Iamblichus and the Theory of the Vehicle of the Soul*. Chico, Calif.: Scholars Press, 1985.

On the Mysteries. Stephen Ronan, ed., Thomas Taylor and A. Wilder, trs. Hastings, UK: Chthonios, 1989.

On the Pythagorean Way of Life. John Dillon and Jackson Hershbell, trs. Atlanta, Ga.: Scholars Press, 1991.

Shaw, Gregory. *Theurgy and the Soul: The Neoplatonism of Iamblichus*. University Park, Penn.: Pennsylvania State University Press, 1971.

The Theology of Arithmetic. Robin Waterfield, tr. Grand Rapids, Mich.: Phanes Press, 1988.

Proclus

Bibliography of available texts: http://www.hiw.kuleuven.ac. be/dwmc/plato/proclus/proeditions.htm.

A Commentary on the First Book of Euclid's Elements. Glenn R. Morrow, tr. Princeton: Princeton University Press, 1970.

The Elements of Theology. Eric R. Dodds, ed. and tr. Oxford: Oxford University Press, 1992.

On the Eternity of the World. Helen S. Lang and Anthony D. Macro trs. Berkeley: University of California Press, 2001.

On the Existence of Evils. Jan Opsomer and Carlos Steel trs. London: Duckworth, 2003.

Proclus: Alcibiades I. William O'Neill, tr. The Hague: Nijhoff, 1965.

Proclus' Commentary on Plato's Parmenides. Glenn R. Morrow and John Dillon, trs. Princeton: Princeton University Press, 1987.

Neoplatonist Commentators

General Comments

Blumenthal, Henry J. *Aristotle and Neoplatonism in Late Antiquity: Interpretations of the De Anima*. Ithaca, N.Y.: Cornell University Press, 1996.

Sorabji, Richard, ed. *Ancient Commentators on Aristotle*. Ithaca, N.Y.: Cornell University Press, 1987.

Sorabji, Richard. *Aristotle Transformed: The Ancient Commentators and their Influence*. London: Duckworth, 1990.

Westerink, L. G. *The Greek Commentaries on Plato's Phaedo*. 2 vols. Amsterdam: North Holland, 1976, 1977.

Individual Commentators

Ammonius Hermiae

Blank, David. "Ammonius." *Stanford Encyclopedia of Philosophy*. 2005: http://plato
.stanford.edu/entries/ammonius/.

On Aristotle's Categories. S. Marc Cohen and Gareth Matthews, trs. Ithaca, N.Y.:
Cornell University Press, 1991.

On Interpretation. David Blank, tr. 2 vols. Ithaca, N.Y.: Cornell University Press,
1996, 1998.

Asclepius of Tralles

Asclepii in Aristotelis Metaphysicorum Libros A–Z Commentaria. Michael Hay-
duck, ed. Berlin: Reimer, 1888.

Commentary on Nicomachus Introduction to Arithmetic. Leonardo Taran. Philadel-
phia: American Philosophical Society, 1969.

Calcidius

Timaeus a Calcidio translatus commentarioque instructus. Jan Hendrick Waszink.
Leiden: Brill, 1975.

Waszink, Jan Hendrick. *Studien zum Timaioskommentar des Calcidius*. Leiden:
Brill, 1964.

Damascius

Bibliography of available texts: http://www.hiw.kuleuven.ac.be/dwmc/plato/
damascius/dameditions.htm.

O'Meara, Dominic J. "Damascius." *Encyclopedia of Classical Philosophy*. Edited
by Donald J. Zeyl. Westport, Conn.: Greenwood, 1997, pp. 166–67.

The Philosophical History. Polymnia Athanassiadi, ed. and tr. Athens: Apamea Cultural Association, 1999.

David

Wildberg, Christian. "David." *Stanford Encyclopedia of Philosophy*. 2003: http://
plato.stanford.edu/entries/david/.

Dexippus

Dillon, John. *Dexippus on Aristotle's Categories*. Ithaca, N.Y.: Cornell University
Press, 1990.

Elias

Wildberg, Christian. "Elias." *Stanford Encyclopedia of Philosophy*. 2003: http://plato
.stanford.edu/entries/elias/.

Hermeias

In Platonis Phaedrum Scholia. P. Couvreur, ed. Paris, 1810; reprinted Hildesheim:
Olms, 1971.

Olympiodorus
Commentary on Plato's Gorgias. R. Jackson et al., trs. London: Brill, 1998.
Commentary on the First Alcibiades of Plato. L. Westerinck, ed. Amsterdam: North-Holland, 1956.
In Platonis Phaedonem Commentaria. W. Norvin, ed. Leipzig: Teubner, 1913; 1968.

Philoponus, John
Against Proclus' "On the Eternity of the World" 1–5. Michael Share, tr. Ithaca, N.Y.: Cornell University Press, 2005.
Commentaria in Aristotelem Graeca, vols. 13–17. Berlin: Reimer, 1882–1909.
On Aristotle's "On the Soul 3.1–8." William Charlton, tr. Ithaca, N.Y.: Cornell University Press, 2000.
On Aristotle's "On the Soul 3.9–13." William Charlton, tr. Ithaca, N.Y.: Cornell University Press, 2000.
On Aristotle's Coming-to-Be and Perishing 2.5–11. Inna Kupreeva, tr. Ithaca, N.Y.: Cornell University Press, 2005.
On Aristotle's "On the Soul 2.7–12." William Charlton, tr. Ithaca, N.Y.: Cornell University Press, 2005.
On Aristotle's "On the Soul 2.1–6." William Charlton, tr. Ithaca, N.Y.: Cornell University Press, 2005.
On Aristotle's Physics I.1–3. Catherine Osborne, tr. Ithaca, N.Y.: Cornell University Press, 2006.
Sorabji, Richard, ed. *Philoponus and the Rejection of Aristotelian Science.* Ithaca, N.Y.: Cornell University Press, 1987.
Wildberg, Christian. "Philoponus." *Stanford Encyclopedia of Philosophy.* 2003: http://plato.stanford.edu/entries/philoponus/.

Simplicius
Text and Translation
The Greek text of the Aristotle commentaries is in the *Commentaria in Aristotelem Graeca*, vols. 7, 8, 9, 10, 11.
Commentaire sur le manuel d'Epictète. Ilsetraut Hadot, ed. and tr. Paris: Belles Lettres, 2001.
On Aristotle's Categories. 4 vols. Richard Gaskin, Michael Chase, Frans A. J. de Haas, B. Fleet, trs. Ithaca, N.Y.: Cornell University Press, 2000–2003.
On Aristotle's De Anima 1.1–2.4. J. O. Urmson, tr. Ithaca, N.Y.: Cornell University Press, 1995.
On Aristotle's De Anima 3.1–5. H. J. Blumenthal, tr. Ithaca, N.Y.: Cornell University Press, 2000.
On Aristotle's On the Heavens I.10–12. R. J. Hankinson, tr. Ithaca, N.Y.: Cornell University Press, 2006.
On Aristotle's Physics 2. Barrie Fleet, tr. Ithaca, N.Y.: Cornell University Press, 1997.
On Aristotle's Physics 3. J. O. Urmson, tr. Ithaca, N.Y.: Cornell University Press, 2002.

On Aristotle's Physics 7. Charles Hagen, tr. London: Duckworth, 1994.
On Epictetus' Handbook. 2 vols. Charles Brittain and Tad Brennan, trs. Ithaca, N.Y.: Cornell University Press, 2002.

Secondary Study

Hadot, Ilsetraut. "Simplicius." *Encyclopedia of Classical Philosophy.* Edited by Donald J. Zeyl. Westport, Conn.: Greenwood, 1997, pp. 490–91.
Syrianus. In Aristotelis metaphysica commentaria. Berlin: Reimer, 1902.

Themistius

Commentaria in Aristotelem Graeca, (CAG) 5.1, 5.2, 5.4, 5.5, 5.8.
Themistii Orationes quae Supersunt. H. Schenkl et al., eds. Leipzig: Teubner, 1965, 1971, 1974.

Other Neoplatonists of the Roman Imperial Period

(Pseudo) Dionysius the Areopagite

Corrigan, Kathleen Anne, and L. Michael Harrington. "Pseudo-Dionysius the Areopagite." 2004: http://plato.stanford.edu/entries/pseudo-dionysius-areopagite/.
Hierocles of Alexandria. Hermann S. Schibli, tr. Oxford: Oxford University Press, 2002.*Oeuvres complètes du Pseudo-Denys L'Aréopagite,* tr. M. de Gandillac. Paris: Aubier, 1943.
Pseudo–Dionysius: The Complete Works, tr. C. Luibheid and P. Rorem. London: Society for the Promotion of Christian Knowledge, 1987.

Macrobius, Ambrosius Aurelius Theodosius

Commentary on the Dream of Scipio. W. H. Stahl, tr. New York: Columbia University Press, 1952.
Marinus. *Life of Proclus.* Kenneth R. Guthrie. Grand Rapids, Michigan: Phanes Press, 1986.
Numenius of Apamea. *The Neoplatonic Writings of Numenius.* Kenneth Guthrie. Lawrence, Kan.: Selene, 1987.
The Saturnalia. Percival V. Davies, tr. New York: Columbia University Press, 1969.

Origen (Pagan)

Moore, Edward. "Origen of Alexandria." *Internet Encyclopedia of Philosophy.* 2006: http://www.iep.utm.edu/o/origen.htm.

Aristotelians of the Roman Period

Alexander of Aprodisias, Text and Translation

Arius Didymus. *Epitome of Stoic Ethics.* A. J. Pomeroy, tr. Atlanta: Society of Biblical Literature, 1999.
Commentary on Aristotle's Metaphysics. Dooley and Madigan, tr. 4 vols. Ithaca, N.Y.: Cornell University Press, 1989.

Commentary on Topics I. J. van Ophuijsen, tr. Ithaca, N.Y.: Cornell University Press, 2001.

On Aristotle's Coming-to-Be and Perishing. 2.2–5. E. Gannagé, tr. Ithaca, N.Y.: Cornell University Press, 2005.

On Aristotle's On Sense Perception. A. Towey, tr. Ithaca, N.Y.: Cornell University Press, 2000.

On Aristotle's Prior Analytics. I. Mueller, tr. Ithaca, N.Y.: Cornell University Press, 1999.

On the Cosmos (Arabic and English). Charles Genequand, ed. and tr. Leiden: Brill, 2001.

Supplement to On the Soul. Robert W. Sharples, tr. Ithaca, N.Y.: Cornell University Press, 2004.

Andronicus of Rhodes

Falcon, Andrea. "Andronicus of Rhodes." *Stanford Encyclopedia of Philosophy.* 2005: http://plato.stanford.edu/entries/aristotle-commentators/supplement.html.

Boethius

The Consolation of Philosophy. Victor Watts, tr. London: Penguin, 1999.

The Fundamentals of Music. Calvin M. Bower, tr. New York: Yale University Press, 1989.

Marebon, John. *Boethius.* Oxford: Oxford University Press, 2003.

Christian Church Fathers

Text

Early Church Fathers: 38 volumes, available online at *Early Church Fathers*, http://www.ccel.org/fathers2/. Accessed July 17, 2006.

General Studies

Brown, Stephen F., and Juan Carlos Flores. *Historical Dictionary of Medieval Philosophy and Theology.* Lanham, Md.: Scarecrow Press, 2007.

Chrysostom, John. Bibliography available at: http://www.cecs.acu.edu.au/chrysostom bibliography.htm. Accessed July 17, 2006.

Eusebius. *Ecclesiastical History.* Christian F. Cruse, tr. Peabody, Mass.: Hendrickson, 1998.

Gregory Nazianzus: see The Gregory Nazianzus Homepage. http://nazianzos.fltr.ucl .ac.be/002Contents.htm.

Gregory of Nyssa: see The Gregory of Nyssa Homepage. http://www.bhsu.edu/arts sciences/asfaculty/dsalomon/nyssa/.

Prokurat, Michael, Michael D. Peterson, and Alexander Golitzin. *Historical Dictionary of the Orthodox Church.* Lanham, Md.: Scarecrow Press, 2006.

Origen (Christian)

Contra Celsum. H. Chadwick, tr. Cambridge: Cambridge University Press, 1953.

Origen Bibliography: *Patristics Bibliography #3.* William Harmless. http://moses .creighton.edu/harmless/bibliographies_for_theology/Patristics_3.htm.

Prat, F. "Origen and Origenism." *The Catholic Encyclopedia* 1911. 2003: http://www.newadvent.org/cathen/11306b.htm.

Theodoret of Cyrrhus
On Divine Providence. Thomas Halton, tr. New York: Newman Press, 1988.
Thérapeutique des maladies helléniques. Pierre Canivet, ed. and tr. 2 vols. Paris: Cerf, 2000–2001.

Gnosticism, Hermeticism, Chaldean Oracles, Interpretation of Dreams

Artemidorus. *The Interpretation of Dreams.* and comm. R. J. White, tr. and comm. Sheffield, UK: Noyes Press, 1975.

Hermes Trismegistus
Copenhaver, Brian P. *Hermetica: The Greek Corpus Hermeticum and Latin Asclepius in New English Translation.* Cambridge: Cambridge University Press, 1992.
Festugière, André Jean. *La révélation d'Hermès Trismégiste.* 4 vols. Paris: Lecoffre, 1949–1954.
Jonas, Hans. *Gnosis und spätantiker Geist.* Göttingen: Vandenhoeck und Ruprecht, 1934; 1988.
———. *The Gnostic Religion: The Message of the Alien God and the Beginnings of Christianity.* Boston: Beacon Press, 1958, 2001.
Julian the Theurgist. *The Chaldaean Oracles.* Gillette, N.J.: Heptangle Books, 1978.
Majercik, Ruth. *The Chaldean Oracles.* Leiden: Brill, 1989.
Miller, Patricia Cox. *Dreams in Late Antiquity.* Princeton: Princeton University Press, 1997.
Moore, Edward. "Gnosticism." *Internet Encyclopedia of Philosophy.* 2006: http://www.iep.utm.edu/g/gnostic.htm.
Preus, Anthony. "Hermetica." *Encyclopedia of Classical Philosophy.* Edited by Donald J. Zeyl. Westport, Conn.: Greenwood, 1997, pp. 263–65.
Spalding, Tim. "Ancient Divination and Astrology on the Web." http://www.isidore-of-seville.com/astdiv/index.html.

Other Imperial Period Texts
Martianus Capella. J. Willis, ed. Leipzig: Teubner, 1983.

MODERN STUDIES OF CROSS-PERIOD TOPICS

Frede, Michael. *Essays in Ancient Philosophy.* Minneapolis: University of Minnesota Press, 1987.
Gerson, L. P. *God and Greek Philosophy.* London: Routledge. 1990.
Guthrie, William Keith Chambers. *A History of Greek Philosophy.* 6 vols. Cambridge: Cambridge University Press, 1962.

Irwin, Terence. *Classical Thought: A History of Western Philosophy 1*. Oxford: Oxford University Press, 1989.
Jaeger, Werner. *Paideia*. Oxford: Oxford University Press, 1939, reprinted 1998.

Natural Philosophy

Hankinson, R. J. *Cause and Explanation in Ancient Greek Thought*. Oxford: Oxford University Press, 2001.
Naddaf, Gerard. *The Greek Concept of Nature*. Albany: State University of New York Press, 2005.

Mathematics

Heath, Thomas Little. *A History of Greek Mathematics*. Oxford: Clarendon Press, 1960.

Astronomy

Heath, Thomas Little. *Greek Astronomy*. New York: AMS, 1969 (reprint of the 1932 edition).

Metaphysics

Kretzmann, N., ed. *Infinity and Continuity in Ancient and Medieval Thought*. Ithaca, N.Y.: Cornell University Press, 1982.

Ethics

Cooper, John. *Reason and Emotion: Essays on Ancient Moral Psychology and Ethical Theory*. Princeton: Princeton University Press, 1999.

Art and Music

Anonymous. "The Ancient Greek Aulos": http://www.archaeonia.com/arts/music/aulos.htm.
Barker, Andrew. *Greek Musical Writings*. 2 vols. Cambridge: Cambridge University Press, 1984, 1989.

Women in Ancient Philosophy

Grams, Laura. "Hipparchia." *Internet Encyclopedia of Philosophy*. 2005: http://www.iep.utm.edu/h/hipparch.htm.
Hypatia: http://cosmopolis.com/people/hypatia.html (includes links to ancient sources about her).
Levin, Saul. "Diotima's Visit and Service to Athens." *Grazer Beiträge* 3, 1975.
Mayhew, Robert. *The Female in Aristotle's Biology*. Chicago: University of Chicago Press, 2004.
Waithe, Mary Ellen, ed. *Ancient Women Philosophers 600 BC–500 AD*. Boston: Martinus Nijhoff, 1987.

The Transmission of Ancient Philosophy, 7th to 15th Centuries

Gutas, Dmitri. *Greek Thought, Arab Culture: The Greco-Arabic Translation Movement in Baghdad and Early Abbasid Society*. New York: Routledge, 1998.
Ierodiakonou, Katerina, ed. *Byzantine Philosophy and Its Ancient Sources*. Oxford: Oxford University Press, 2002.
Lemerle, Paul. *Byzantine Humanism: The First Phase*. Translated by H. Lindsay and A. Moffatt. Canberra: Australian Association for Byzantine Studies, 1986.
Moran, Dermot. "John Scottus Eriugena." *Stanford Encyclopedia of Philosophy*. 2004: http://plato.stanford.edu/entries/scottus-eriugena/. Accessed 8/28/2006.
Spade, Paul V. "Medieval Philosophy." *Stanford Encyclopedia of Philosophy*. 2004: http://plato.stanford.edu/entries/medieval-philosophy/. Accessed 8/29/2006.
Tatakis, Basil. *Byzantine Philosophy*. Translated by Nicholas Moutafakis. Indianapolis, Ind.: Hackett, 2003.

About the Author

Anthony Preus is professor of philosophy at Binghamton University where he has taught since 1964. A graduate of Luther College in Decorah, Iowa, he was a Rhodes Scholar at Trinity College, Oxford, where he earned an M.A. in Literae Humaniores and a Woodrow Wilson and Fels Fellow at The Johns Hopkins University, where he earned his Ph.D. in 1968. He is the author of *Science and Philosophy in Aristotle's Biological Works* and *Aristotle and Michael of Ephesus on the Movement and Progression of Animals,* both published by Olms, Hildesheim. He is co-editor or editor of *Essays in Ancient Greek Philosophy*, volumes 2–6, published by the State University of New York Press. He has also written many articles and reviews, mainly on ancient philosophy, biology, and medicine. He is faculty master of College-in-the-Woods at Binghamton University and has written several guidebooks to the Finger Lakes Trail. He and his wife have three children.

345